fated
attraction

your relationship
horoscope guide

sarah bartlett

Thorsons

Thorsons
An Imprint of HarperCollins*Publishers*
77–85 Fulham Palace Road
Hammersmith, London W6 8JB

The Thorsons website address is:
www.thorsons.com

Published by Thorsons 2001

1 3 5 7 9 10 8 6 4 2

© Sarah Bartlett 2001

Sarah Bartlett asserts the moral right to
be identified as the author of this work

A catalogue record for this book
is available from the British Library

ISBN 0 00 710665 3

Printed and bound in Great Britain by
Creative Print and Design Wales, Ebbw Vale

to

Jess

contents

Acknowledgements

Thanks to Colin Miles at Astrocalc for all his techno support. To my teachers and fellow students of astrology at the CPA; particularly Liz, Darby, Melanie, Juan, Rani, and the late Charles Harvey. And, mostly, my thanks to my friends, family, and all the other stars in the sky.

Introduction

Fated Attraction is an astrological guide to your relationships with men. Now you can find out how and why you click with certain men and not with others. Using this book you can give yourself the kind of revealing and accurate compatibility reading that is usually only available from a professional astrologer.

'It's the chemistry between us' has become a familiar phrase for the physical and emotional magnetism that draws two people together. This book reveals how and why you attract certain men to you, which men will be drawn to you, which men you fall for, which to avoid and which will provide the perfect match. It describes how you express yourself outwardly in your relationship life and how others see you, and reveals your emotional needs and what it is you are really looking for in a relationship. Are you always drawn to the same type of man or same patterns in relationships? If so, this book explains why and what you can do about it.

It also reveals the secret world of men – everything you want to know for complete harmony, from what he thinks about his own

body to what he wants from a relationship and, most
importantly, what he really feels about you.

Likewise, your man can also discover everything he needs to
know about you and you can both learn how you can make your
relationship work.

astrology and psychology

Your birthchart carries the blueprint of your personality, your
needs, wants, desires and sexual style. Each planet in the chart
will show something of this. That's why it's important to know
what all the planets are doing in your chart, not just the Sun.
The Sun sign, or star sign as most people know it, is our core, the
centre of our universe. But it's often unlived and unnoticed,
because it's not the be-all and end-all of our existence. The other
planetary influences express all the extraordinary energies of our
life force.

For example, your instinctive feelings towards someone are the
Moon's territory, how you go about getting what you want is
Mars' territory, how you go about falling in love is Venus's
territory, how you get defensive and build boundaries is Saturn's
world, as is how you can become civilized in your relationships,
while Jupiter's world is where you are most persuasive and
where you deal with your imagination and your beliefs. If you
truly believe you will fall in love with an eccentric guru from
Rajastan, for example, you probably have Jupiter in
unconventional Aquarius, along with strong Jupiterian
dynamics in the chart.

Remember, the chart is you. And it does not lie. You only deceive
yourself. That's human psychology.

Your chart can also tell you how your good and not so good traits come to life in any relationship. The word 'relate' comes from an ancient Greek word meaning 'to bear' and we have to learn to bear other people, just as we have to bear being in the world and bear ourselves, otherwise we could not exist. This isn't always easy. So we lie to ourselves, cheat a bit and often pretend to be something we aren't. This is because along the way we've been conditioned by the expectations of society, family and life.

We are also often unconscious of our emotions, unaware that we suppress certain joys and deny certain emotions, desires and feelings of love. And we're rarely able to contemplate what it is in ourselves that is unlived. But an awareness of who you are can enrich all your relationships.

This book gives you an easy way of finding more about yourself and how you relate. Then you can begin to live out your life as you are and enjoy your relationships, rather than think of them merely as traps of further pain. Yes, sometimes love hurts. But with every relationship you enter into, you are learning more about yourself. If, in the process, you keep repeating patterns of pain and rejection, then this book will certainly give you reason to change your style of loving and, most importantly, begin to know yourself better.

So, what does this book include? There are easy-to-use tables and simple instructions so you can discover:

✳ your complete relationship horoscope
  how, why and with whom your personal chemistry resonates
  your outer image
  who is drawn to you
  the way you fall in love
  the kind of relationship you are looking for

what you need from another person
your ideal man
how to stay in synch once you've made the connection
how to avoid repeating unsuccessful or fatal relationships
the secret dynamics of your relationship nature

✳ his complete relationship horoscope
how, why and with whom his personal chemistry resonates
what he is really looking for in a relationship
his ideal woman
his beliefs, ideals, strengths, values, defences and what he
thinks about his body
what he thinks and feels about you and your relationship
his needs, lovestyle and lifestyle

✳ how well you mirror each other
an in-depth horoscope chart for you to create, showing where
you hit it off, where there could be tension, where there
could be issues around power, whether it's purely physical
or whether there's room for love, and where the relationship
is going
generation gaps – why someone much older or younger than
you could be a disaster match or a perfect hit

Whether you're already in love or still looking for the man of
your dreams, this book will help you discover what your inner
desires are and what type of man is for you!

part i

you

attraction
factor

Sometimes we are attracted to people without knowing why or attract other people without knowing why. And what you see isn't always what you get.

The part of us that others first see when we walk into a room is called the Rising sign, or Ascendant. It's a bit like a doorway to the rest of the personality. What goes on behind the door, well, that's for the planets and other dynamics in the birthchart to reveal. But the Rising sign describes both the way you are seen by others and the outer image you want others to see. Often we don't realize what it is we are expressing outwardly or know enough about ourselves to realize what we want others to see anyway! We may know we prefer certain fashions, like certain types of people or are drawn to certain kinds of love affairs. But we are often blind to what we are actually displaying to the world. This may, of course, lead to problems!

discovering your rising sign

Your Rising sign is the sign of the zodiac that was rising in the
sky east of where you were born at the time of your birth. So
sometimes it's difficult to know exactly what your Rising sign is,
simply because often the time of birth isn't recorded. Asking
parents is always one option, but mothers are, quite frankly,
notorious for remembering only vague times like 'around
midnight' or 'just before tea-time'.

The method I have given at the end of the book is very simple,
but it can be difficult to know exactly which Rising sign you are
because there all sorts of complications like time changes and
local daylight-saving times. So read the sign just before and just
after the sign given if you're not sure whether you are one sign or
another, especially if you're on the cusp.

If you have access to the Internet, then there are many good
websites where you can find out your Rising sign and the exact
position of your planets free of charge, as long as you know your
birth time. But the quick method I have included in this book
will give you a pretty good idea of your Rising sign.

so what does it mean?

Your Rising sign is the way you look out at the rest of the world,
as well as the way others see you. Whatever Sun sign you are, the
Rising sign colours or shades it with a different quality (unless,
of course, Sun sign and Rising sign are the same).

In relationships, your Rising sign is the first thing that will
attract certain people to you. It can also tell you how you express
yourself, often unknowingly, towards the opposite sex and also

the kind of magnetic pull you have on certain people, how
seductive you are and which men you will fall for.

Often we fall in love with men who are apparently very different
from ourselves. But it might just be someone's Rising sign that
you're drawn to. His sexual values and his way of loving may not
be the same as his Rising-sign 'come hither' approach. His inner
world is still locked behind that door and you're faced with the
qualities he projects onto the world, rather than the qualities
which are equally valid, but hidden from view.

If we are attracted to the opposite sign to our Rising sign, which
is quite common, it is because we are projecting that part of
ourselves onto others. So we like what we see in them and don't
realize it's part of ourselves too. Often we don't even know we're
projecting this image onto other people and just find ourselves
infatuated with Sun-sign men who echo our Rising-sign style.

To take an example, on the zodiac wheel on page 10, Sagittarius
is rising. If this were your chart, you might come across as wildly
enthusiastic about life, seductive, persuasive, freedom-loving
and prone to exaggerate all kinds of stories. On the other hand,
you might not be aware you had these qualities, especially if you
were heavily influenced by other planetary dynamics in your
chart. If you were a security-conscious Sun-sign Taurus, for
example, you might find it difficult to combine these two very
different qualities in your life. The most important thing about
the Rising sign is that it's the way you want others to see you. But
you don't go around saying, 'I'm going to be very Sagittarius
rising today. I want the world to see me this way!' More likely
you're not even aware you're doing it.

In this chart, you can see that the sign opposite Sagittarius is
Gemini. Frequently it's the sign opposite our Rising sign which

we find most physically, or initially, attractive in the opposite sex. So if you have Sagittarius rising you'll often be attracted to Gemini types, or if you've Cancer rising, you'll often be attracted to Capricorn men. This doesn't mean they are necessarily a Sun-sign Capricorn or Gemini, but the quality that they exude will somehow resonate with Gemini or Capricorn.

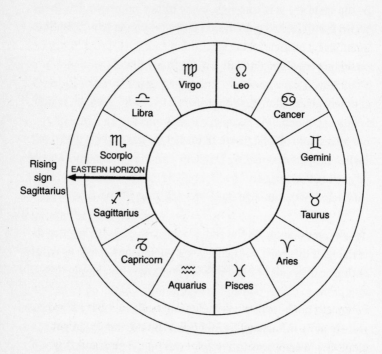

sun signs aren't always obvious

The Sun sign is the core of our being, but sometimes you have to really know someone for quite a long time before you see how their Sun sign is operating. It is often surrounded by smokescreens about what we should or shouldn't be. Social and family pressures may not be in line with our Sun-sign destiny.

Quite simply, though, the Sun represents your urge to be yourself, while the Rising sign shows how you unconsciously want others to see you and what in fact they see. That's why it's important to look at the Sun sign and the Rising sign in tandem. The Rising sign is how you express yourself and the Sun is your very essence.

There is often a strong attraction between people who have the same Rising sign and Sun sign. So, if you are a Gemini Sun, you could be very attracted to Rising-sign Geminis. If you're a Sagittarius rising, you could find your greatest freedom lies with people who are Sun-sign Saggies too.

Let's look at each Rising sign in turn.

ARIES RISING

you appear

feisty ★ aggressive ★ driven

Feisty, aggressive, driven. Dare-devil at best, impulsive at worst, you are usually reckoned to be fiery, outgoing and impatient. Men can't keep up with your demonstrative nature and they certainly can't keep up with your spirited approach towards any new relationship, especially when you're out and about. That's when you're at your most positive and exciting. You thrive in social environments. If there's food on the table, you'll be the first to eat it. If there's a man standing alone in a corner, you'll be the first to make a move in his direction – whether he's got a date or not! You appear eager to form relationships, but you also want to be number one, or alone. At all the best restaurants or parties you're the first to leap in and defend your friends and lovers, often without thinking, and often with plates flying, or, at the very least, a few well-aimed glasses of wine over your rival's designer bag.

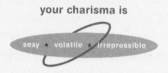

your charisma is

sexy ★ volatile ★ irrepressible

Sexy, volatile, irrepressible. Formidable, courageous and daring. You can't wait to be noticed. You'll screech to a halt at traffic lights and expect every man to notice your new hairdo or your latest investment in techno-mania. You have to be first – first to impress, to start a new fashion, to find new romance. You seem to be sexy, radiant and permanently on red-alert. Depending on the other planetary influences in your chart and your level of awareness about yourself, what you project either gels with your inner needs or forces you into difficult scenarios.

Action-packed and spicy, you demand that others are aware of your motivated and sexual energy. Vital, passionate, potent, there's an aura of impatient passion about you as you storm into a room or out of the door. You move fast and bristle with self-confidence and *joie de vivre*. Men just can't resist your fast-paced lifestyle. If you stop for breakfast, his luck's in. If you stop for lunch as well, you're infatuated. You have an air of self-interest and self-centredness. You smell of success and bravery, sexual determination and sexual hunger. But you're not easily led astray, except by your own appetite.

you fall for

romantic ★ beautiful ★ idealistic

Romantic, beautiful, idealistic, peace-loving men. A man who conveys those qualities might not be your life-long soul-mate, but he's certainly going to make you desire whatever it is that he seems to possess in abundance and you don't. There's always something inevitably attractive about the opposite sign from your Rising sign. This is usually a magnetic pull, for good or ill, depending on the other factors in your chart. Your opposite sign is Libra, so you might hate a Libran for being so unselfish and run a mile, or you might fall in love with him for being so compromising, so apparently unlike yourself. This is a man who wants to perfect the world, to finish it off with love and peace. How different is this from the image you project onto the world? You storm through creating havoc. He follows behind picking up the pieces. Physically, this is a fated attraction. You have the energy, the passion and the imagination, he has the harmony, the ideals and the mind to seduce. You love to play the game of seduction and he loves to think about it. This particular relationship can be long term if the planets form good links and there are good contacts elsewhere in your chart. Your problem is that you look on life in terms of 'me', while he looks on it in terms of 'we'.

you attract

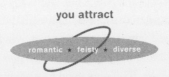

romantic ★ feisty ★ diverse

With such a dynamic outer persona, you'll attract anyone from romantic Librans to equally feisty Sun Aries men. The latter will

probably put up with your self-absorbed and extrovert
appearance, the former might be fascinated for a while, but may
not be able to take the pace, unless they have a very Arian side to
their nature too (i.e. planets in Aries, Aries rising or Mars in a
Fire sign).

your seductive technique is

Impulsive, immediate and wanting it all *now*.

TAURUS RISING

you appear

Sensual, realistic, utterly feminine. You convey an air of self-
satisfaction, as if whatever anyone else does, you can tolerate it.
Reliable and yet serene, people find your presence comforting and
stabilizing. You appear to live for the moment and your patience is
always noted. You may be waiting for your date to turn up and he's
late, but who cares, you'll wait and wait and enjoy the good wine
or look around the restaurant for the most beautiful man. You wear
the most exquisite perfumes and clothes, and as you enter a room
your beauty draws men like flies. Men find you subtly sexual and
completely sensual. Money seems to mean a lot to you. That's
either because you dedicate yourself to acquiring it or you hang
out with those who seem capable enough with their own.
Investing in a glass of wine is a profoundly moving experience for
you and you appear to indulge yourself in the most luxurious of
foods, clothes and men. If he's not good looking in your eyes, you
won't offer him a lift in your cab, let alone an invitation for coffee.
Appearances really do seem to matter.

your charisma is

natural ★ loyal ★ artistic ★ rich

Natural, loyal, artistic, rich. Placid and gentle, you want men to
take their time to get to know you. You adore the seduction game.
And a man must think you're the most beautiful thing on this
planet. If someone eyes you up in the supermarket, you'll plot a
way to let him know your number. But you'll make sure it's *next
time* you bump into him. Sensually dressed, you'll walk
gracefully through an airport lounge, hoping the glamorous man
in the corner will think you an heiress or a famous or wealthy
sculptor. Depending on the other planetary influences in your
chart and your level of awareness about yourself, what you
project either gels with your inner needs or forces you to become
defensive.

You're a natural professional and demand that men see you as a
self-contained yet sensually aware woman in your own right.
Earthy, seductive and voluptuous, you convey an aura of pure
feminine sexuality which is enough to turn any man on. But
you're choosy. When you enter a room most men will notice your
perfume first, your eyes second and your sultry intentions last.
You move slowly, carefully, with your feet firmly on the ground
and your mind grounded and together. You have an air of grace
and a willingness to sit and listen all night if you have to. If he's
beautiful enough, you might even suggest a walk in the
moonlight or a kiss beneath the stars.

you fall for

hypnotic ★ beautiful ★ powerful

Hypnotic, beautiful, powerful, intense men. A man who conveys those qualities might not be your life-long soul-mate, but he's certainly going to make you desire whatever it is that he seems to possess in abundance and you don't. There's always something inevitably attractive about the opposite sign from your Rising sign, which in this case is Scorpio. There is a magnetic pull, for good or ill, depending on the other factors in your chart. You might well fall in love with a Scorpionic type because he's simply beautiful. Yet what lurks beneath the surface may be an emotional, moody and sexually intense involvement with his feelings. How very different from the image of earthy realism you project. You love the Earth, nature and music, he wants to change your musical tastes, cut down the trees and suppress your natural instincts. You're hunting financial security and tranquillity, he's aiming to totally plunder any stability. If he has Scorpio rising or a very Scorpio-based chart, i.e. Sun in Scorpio or Venus in Scorpio, then remember, this is a part of your own inner world too. What we are attracted to is what we also carry deep within ourselves. This particular relationship can be long term if the planets form good links and there are good contacts elsewhere in your chart. Your main problem with a Scorpio type is that you want life to be secure and he doesn't.

you attract

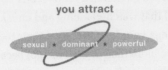

sexual ★ dominant ★ powerful

Men who love sensual women, rather than merely glamorous ones. Sexually dominating, powerful men who pick up on your need for security. Often men with Taurus planets who resonate to your essence of earthiness and respond well to your desire for beauty. They'll also be fascinated by your need to hunt out the pleasures of life. Men with Scorpio planets or Taurean types will play a big part in your relationship life. The only problem with Scorpio types is that the best things in life aren't necessarily what they're after. Power is. On the other hand, Sun or Moon Taurus men could prove long-term partners, depending on other links and dynamics between your charts.

your seductive technique is

passive ★ smoochy ★ controlled

Passive, smoochy and always carefully controlled.

GEMINI RISING

you appear

fascinating ★ restless ★ sparkling

Fascinating, restless, sparkling. Inquisitive at best, downright nosy at worst, you're usually reckoned to be mentally alert, extrovert and always on the look-out for freedom of speech and movement. You hate to be tied to a rendezvous or date for longer than necessary. All that watch-glancing and checking your mobile for calls keeps your boyfriends on their toes. And admit it, you usually have more than one on the go, because that means you won't be tied down or fixed to one area of town. If there's the chance of a conversation with a man on the train, plane or bus, you'll have it. You seem to adore instant friendships, but they can be instantly over if you get bored. When you enter a restaurant you seem ready to eat, drink and pay the bill even before you've sat down. A first date is magical, the second exciting, by the third you're either totally hooked or fidgeting with boredom. But you'll never refuse an invite to anything, just in case it turns out to be as fascinating as you are.

your charisma is

intelligent ★ friendly ★ romantic

Intelligent, friendly, romantic. Witty, elusive and remarkably observant, you want men to think you're an encyclopaedia of knowledge, both intellectual and physical. You'll observe every leaf on the tree just as he's about to pass out with desire, then the next minute you'll be chatting about how love is such an overrated word. You have to show you have more friends than he has hairs on his chest. And if you don't make an impression with your wit and cunning, he's certainly out to lunch. You want to show you're romantic but sensible, seductive but reasonable. Depending on the other planetary influences in your chart, what you project either gels with your inner needs or forces you into making compromises.

Sparkling and curious, you demand that men see you as the most fascinating woman in the cosmos. Vibrant, energetic and unpredictable fun just exudes out of every pore. As you zoom about the place at the speed of lightning, men just can't resist your unpredictable nature. One minute you're oozing charm, the next running off to check your e-mails and abandoning your date at the restaurant table. If he invites you to a fast-food place you're happy, if it's that trendy restaurant that takes four hours over gourmet delights, forget it. You have an air of sexual vibrancy, laced with an interest in everything. And you seem more interested in his words than his physical proportions.

you fall for

travellers ★ gurus ★ independence

Travellers, freedom lovers, gurus and incredibly independent men. A man who conveys these qualities may not be your life-long soul-mate, but he's certainly going to make you either drool or hate him, simply because he seems to represent those qualities you don't have. There's always something incredibly magnetic about the opposite sign from your Rising sign and for you that's Sagittarius. You might hate a Sagittarian type for being so visionary about the future and not interested in the present, or you might fall for him because of his huge smile and huge love of life. This is a man who wants to find a bigger purpose to life. He's concerned with the meaning behind everything, while you're concerned with scattering your ideas. That's spicy, but often leads to verbal fireworks. He might resent your sharp wit when the novelty's worn off and he's looking for something 'bigger'. Philosophical lessons in bed might not be your idea of fun, but he's a hoot when he's pontificating on life. This relationship can be long term if the planets form good links and there are good contacts elsewhere in your chart. Your problem is that you rationalize everything from sex to genetics and he would rather simply imagine it.

you attract

humorous ★ diverse

Because you're so extrovert and friendly, you'll meet many men who will simply adore the witty, humorous person they see before them. Your light approach to life, or at least what passes on the surface, will always attract men to you like proverbial moths. But Sagittarians and Geminis will often play a key role in your relationship life, the former fascinated by your apparent differences, the latter because you resemble their long-lost twin. A Sun Sagittarius will prefer even more freedom than you, but if he's a Sun or Moon Gemini, this could be a long-lasting relationship.

your seductive technique is

quick ★ unpredictable ★ romantic

Quick, unpredictable and utterly romantic.

CANCER RISING

you appear

caring ★ sensitive ★ unpredictable

Caring, sensitive, unpredictable. Genuine at best, prickly and defensive at worst, you are seen as being gentle, serene and sensitive. Men adore your secretive allure. In fact it makes them want to get to know you inside-out, sure that behind that compassionate façade there lies a shrewd and resourceful woman. Socially, you prefer to keep in the background. In fact, the kitchen at the party is probably your favourite haunt. Men will have to find their way to the oven before they get anywhere near you. *And* pass a few cookery tests. Can he scramble eggs and is he generous enough to take you to the best restaurant, when you're in the mood? Yes, you can seem moody, because you're unpredictable when it suits you. But men are fascinated by your independent spirit and your subtle yet sensual antics across the bar, like running your finger around the rim of your wine glass as if it's your lover's knee. When actually you're just in a state of sheer nervous panic because someone might be attracted to you.

your charisma is

ambitious ★ shrewd ★ capable

Ambitious, shrewd, capable, sensual. Secretive and yet fickle, you put on an air of calm authority, as if you know what is going to happen next or you are sure you can help others out. You're always cautious about whom you choose as friends or confidantes. It's hard for you to let anyone get close to you. You want to be seen as sensual, a real woman, one who knows how serious life is. Depending on the other planetary influences, especially where the Moon is in your chart, and your level of self-awareness, what you project either gels with your inner needs or makes you more defensive.

Shrewd and spontaneous, you know the difference between a man who is serious about commitment and one who's just after a fling. Charming, ultra-feminine and sultry, there's an aura of quietness and serenity as you walk into a room. You have a calming effect on most men, but also a very sensually aware influence too. Men can't resist your ultra-feminine wiles. You're more likely to cook him a meal than go to a restaurant, because you're convinced the way to his heart is through his stomach. At home you feel most relaxed and ooze all that sensual mystery. But if he doesn't compliment you on your cooking, then he won't see the evening through.

you fall for

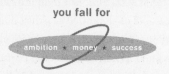

ambition ★ money ★ success

Earthy, ambitious whizz kids, celebs and business magnets. Basically, men with money! A man like this is one you you'll either adore or hate – probably the former, but it always depends on other factors in your chart. There is something inevitably attractive about the opposite sign to your Rising sign and for you this means that Capricorns are generally going to play some part in your relationship life. You might loathe a Capricorn type for being self-motivated and fanatical about money or you might fall in love with his successful image, his self-control and predictability. How different this is from your own image of unpredictable and spontaneous restlessness. Physically, this is often a fated attraction. But you have the compassion and the shrewdness to sense that his need for stability relies solely on his own power. This relationship could be long term if other planets form good links and there are good contacts elsewhere in your chart. Your only problem is that you want closeness and emotional unpredictability, while he wants money to buy him love.

you attract

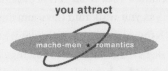

Because you're so feminine and sensual, you attract many macho types who want to appear in control. But you'll also attract romantic, poetic types who hunger for your apparent warmth and need for emotional closeness. It's highly likely, though, that men with Cancerian or Capricorn planets will play a key role in your relationships, the former responding to your highly sensitive nature, the latter seduced by your femininity. If you are a Sun Cancer person, you'll know you're sensitive, but if you're Cancer rising, you don't often realize how easily touched you are. This liaison could awaken you to the fact. Nicely, of course. If he has Cancerian planets, you could find this a long-term relationship.

your seductive technique is

Passive, slinky, wanting to delay the moment for as long as possible.

LEO RISING

you appear

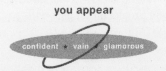

Confident, vain, glamorous. Dramatic and extrovert at best, egocentric at worst, you are usually seen as fiery, theatrical and

showy. Men either adore your flashy style or hate it. You appear
to be totally at ease as you walk into the room and whatever is
happening beneath the surface, you never let it show. You appear
to play roles, one day exaggerating your feelings like an actress,
the next being dizzy and delightfully feminine. You thrive in
social places and you need to be adored by men. Depending on
your Sun sign, what's going on behind this stage show will either
be a hindrance or a help. You ooze so much confidence men just
can't resist forming relationships with you. At parties you have
to be the centre of attention or (preferably and) surrounded by a
group of doting males. Exclusive, special and glamorous, you
just want to be seen! It doesn't matter who notices you, as long as
someone does. Particularly if it's the male variety. And then
you'll devote your exclusive attention to any new predator and
turn the hunt into your game.

your charisma is

luscious ★ demanding

Luscious, demanding and glamorous. If you aren't dressed to
kill, then you'll be dressed to hunt. Either way you usually look
physically stunning and if you decide it's time to put on a
different show, you'll just change roles and outfits. You want
men to see how fiery and passionate you are about life, and they
have little choice but to respond the same way. Depending on
other planetary influences in your chart and your level of
awareness, what you project either gels with your inner needs or
makes you appear self-interested.

Passionate, wild, spicy, there is an air of flamboyancy about you,
even though you may not notice it yourself. You move like
nobility and you exude sexual desire and sensual longing, as if

you are truly aware of your feminine needs. Men can't resist your stylish and bold approach to life.

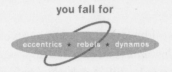

you fall for

eccentrics ⋆ rebels ⋆ dynamos

Eccentrics, rebels with causes, strong, independent, dynamic men with taste. There is always something compelling about the opposite sign to your Rising sign, so for you Aquarian men can be a magnetic pull for good or ill. You might loathe an Aquarian type who's different, glamorous and intellectual or you might fall in love with his independence and eccentricity, his idealism and his love of humanity. This is a man who wants to save the world and who prefers the company of many friends to a one-to-one relationship. You may be drawn physically to him, fated to meet him and yet loathe him and love him at the same time. You project an egotistic air, he projects an altruistic one. You appear to prefer the best restaurants, he prefers the most bizarre, unusual or exotic eating haunt. He's usually a vegetarian and proud of it, you're usually unconcerned. You dance through life lightening up those around you. He follows, clearing up your rubbish and recycling your cosmetic empties. This relationship could be long term if there are good contacts elsewhere in your charts. Your main problem is that you believe life revolves around you and he believes life just evolves.

you attract

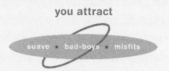

suave ★ bad-boys ★ misfits

Men with taste, wealthy, well-dressed business baddies who drool over your glamorous and extrovert appearance or misfits and dissidents, just to be different. It's highly likely that Aquarians and Leos will play a key role in your relationship world. An Aquarian type might want to save the whales, but he'll find your self-confident stalk down the corridor alarmingly attractive. Sun Leo men or men with many Leo qualities will be fascinated by your air of superiority, your regal, self-made woman look. Drawn by your sexual vibrancy, they'll find it hard to resist your charismatic nature. They know they want to be special too.

your seductive technique is

outrageous ★ flamboyant

Outrageous, flamboyant, pushy, wanting it all when you say so.

VIRGO RISING

you appear

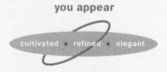

cultivated ★ refined ★ elegant

Cultivated, refined, elegant. Polished and immaculate, you sweep through a social gathering with discretion. At your best, you're discriminating, charming and ordered, at your worst, obsessive. Men view you as capable and wise. Your intellectual virtuosity gets you noticed and so does your simmering sensuality. Cool, aloof and utterly feminine, you can seduce with your words and persuade with your looks. You can seem formidably intelligent, which can make some men hold back. Others will simply realize you need great minds to think alike, rather than just sexual innuendoes. Your cupboards will be full of your favourite things and your mind, likewise, is full to brimming. If your first date isn't planned down to the last detail, you'll flip. You're seen as a perfectionist, but it's not so much a perfect world you want as one that is ordered. If a man reminds you you're being too critical of his suit, or his taste in underwear, what he's seeing is your need for attunement in all things. Twist a few knobs, get the levels down and the music will be just right.

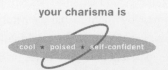

your charisma is

cool ★ poised ★ self-confident

Cool, poised, self-confident, intelligent. When you walk into a party or restaurant, there's a serene tidiness and a cool self-possessed air about you, as if you're sure which food you're going to eat and you didn't ever get into a state about which dress to wear. You always use perfume that stands out from the crowd in the most sensual and feminine of ways. You're calm, discreet and never raise your voice, but you won't let anyone provoke you either. You seduce quietly with a few clever words of wisdom as your back-up. There's never anything uncomfortable about you and because you appear to be so realistic and down to earth on the surface, men feel at ease in your company. Refined, discriminating and critically astute, you'll rarely let a man make a pass at you without weighing up all the pros and cons involved. Timing the moment to perfection,

you'll make him feel either welcome or a waste of space.
Whichever it is, your sparkling wit and amazing humour will
often startle the most street-wise of men into realizing you're not
just a pretty face.

you fall for

romantics ★ dreamers ★ musicians

Romantics, dreamers and musicians. Poetic types with wit, style
and cool passion. There is always something compelling about
the opposite sign to your Rising sign and for you Piscean men
can be a magnetic pull, for good or ill. In fact they may seem to
possess an abundance of qualities that you don't realize are also
within you. So it's likely that Piscean types will play a key role
in your relationships. You might loathe their indecision and their
elusive, inconsistent behaviour, or you might fall totally in love
with their romantic passionate sensitivity. A Piscean man is a
dreamboat, but he needs changing wildernesses, unreality and to
be alone, while you prefer things to be civilized, reliable and
above all real. This relationship could be long term if there are
good contacts elsewhere in your charts. But the main problem is
that you want a relationship which works and is based on reality,
while he wants to dream about it instead.

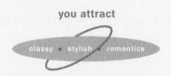

you attract

classy ★ stylish ★ romantics

Cool-headed, materialistic types, men with class and style or
hopeless romantics and dreamers. It's highly likely that Piscean
men or Virgo types will play a key role in your relationship

patterns. They don't necessarily have to be Sun-sign Virgos – if a man has the Moon, Sun or Venus in Virgo, this could a long-term relationship, depending on other contacts between your charts. Virgo men will feel comfortable with your discreet charm and realistic attitude towards life. A Pisces man will probably just fall head over heels with your poise and your ability to help him when he feels like being emotionally rescued.

LIBRA RISING

you appear

considerate ★ harmonious

Considerate, harmonious, romantic. Idealistic at best, compliant at worst, you are seen as being co-operative, mindful and disturbingly calm. In fact men find you not only utterly feminine, but also dangerously seductive, as you naturally radiate a kind of charm that many would die for. You have moments of indecisiveness, but only because you regard the world as so full of possibilities that it would be a shame to waste all the options. Even when you're choosing what to pick from the menu, or whether to drink white or red wine, your date or partner may find it all frighteningly rational. You appear eager to form relationships and if you're not in one, then you seem to find your way into someone's heart with the greatest of ease. But what's more important to you is to have company and good conversation. And because you're a skilled diplomat, you always choose your words with care, changing the conversation to anything that you think will fascinate your chosen partner. Strangely, men either instantly adore you or instantly step back – the latter only because you appear to be such an idealist that some men unconsciously feel they can't live up to your expectations.

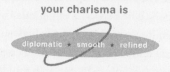

your charisma is

diplomatic ★ smooth ★ refined

Diplomatic, smooth, refined. To say you appear tranquil would
be an understatement. You radiate an aura of complete serenity,
because you have made an art of being the perfect diplomat. Men
just can't help but admire your taste in beauty, fashion and
design. You walk into a room and the whole party lightens up.
There's always a smile on your face and an eagerness to be
socially acceptable. Peaceful conversations or romantic dinners
for two keep you sane, but loud mouths, noisy parties and
know-it-alls bore you. There's an air of poise and purpose about
you which men find fascinating and other women find
threatening. Depending on other planetary activity in your chart
and your own level of awareness about yourself, what you
project either gels with your inner needs and values or forces you
into petty arguments – the kind where you just can't resist
disagreeing with everything someone says. This is just a minor
compensation for usually agreeing with everything that is said!
Often these become the kind of discussions where you keep
shifting sides. You take a different point of view from your
partner simply because you're trying to find the midpoint
between both views and create a balance.

you fall for

assertive ★ passionate

Assertive, passionate, independent tearaways, whizz kids with
time and money to devote to you, sporty types with class and
fiery, sexy men with a dare factor. A man who conveys these

qualities may not be your life-long soul-mate. It's often those qualities that he seems to possess in abundance and you don't think you have that make you desire him even more. There's often something utterly compelling about the opposite sign from your Rising sign and for you that's Aries. An Arian type can be a magnetic pull, for good or ill. Of course, you might hate him for being so self-centred and unable to compromise, or you might adore him because he's so unlike you, so demanding, so passionate, impatient and aggressive. He's very macho, you're very feminine. This is a man who wants to take on the world single-handed. He has no time for compliancy or co-operation, whereas you do. See how different his image is from the one you project on the world? You walk around creating harmony and sweeping all his chaotic thoughts under the table.

Physically, an Aries liaison is often a fated attraction for a person with Libra rising. You have the seduction techniques, the romance and the feminine charm, while he has the passion and the imagination to rise to it. This relationship can certainly be long term if there are other good links in your charts, the only problem being that you look on life in terms of 'we' and his terms are 'me'.

If you're not aware of your Libran tendencies, then you might also find yourself very attracted to Sun or Moon Librans, who will give you the chance to express these qualities.

you attract

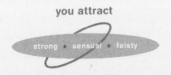

strong ★ sensual ★ feisty

Because you appear so mentally alert and physically alluring, you'll attract many men, from strong sensual Taureans who long

to protect you to feisty Arians who long to sexually devour you.
Men with the Sun in Libra will also be drawn towards you and
this could be an excellent relationship if your other planets form
strong links. A Sun-sign Aries might need to have some Libran
planets to calm him down enough to tolerate your balanced
approach to life, but if a man has Aries rising, the Moon in Libra or
Venus in Gemini, there could be an instant attraction between you.

your seductive technique is

charming ★ bewitching ★ eager

Charming, bewitching and willing to please.

SCORPIO RISING

you appear

mysterious ★ enigmatic

Mysterious, enigmatic, controlling. Compassionate at best,
ruthless at worst, you seem suspicious, mistrustful and stubborn,
yet formidable and intensely sexual. Men find you a compelling
force and they are either terrified by your powerful eye contact or
fascinated by your passionate and profound self-expression.
You're definitely a force to be reckoned with. Depending on
other planetary influences in your chart, on the surface you
might appear to be a very private person. That means that getting
close to you is initially difficult. Your defensive tactics are your
strong point and you rarely let any man get within a few yards
unless you're sure you can trust him. If he does get past the first
test – and yes, you are always testing, either through probing his

mind or probing his sexual vices and virtues – then he'll feel as though he's been thrown in a bubbling cauldron with you. Deep down inside, you sense there's an animal at the heart of every person and that's why you appear very sensual and alert to your own sexuality. Men also find you irresistible because you seem so secretive. In fact, if someone gets past the first date, he still won't know where he stands with you, simply because you must maintain an air of mystery around yourself. So it's usually up to you to invite him back – but only on your terms.

your charisma is

hypnotic ★ sexual ★ powerful

Hypnotic, sexual, powerful. You literally crackle with atmosphere and drench others with your powerful sensual vibrations. Sexy, passionate and intense, people will stop in awe in the presence of your powerful aura, even though you may not be aware of it yourself. Depending on your own self-awareness and the other planetary influences in your chart, this force is one that can either be used for good or ill. Men will find your will-power and your inner strength fascinating. You exude an air of exclusivity and also express your dislike of superficiality. The more men flirt with you, the more likely you are to try and take control. Intensely challenging, you prefer subtle gestures and permeate any party or restaurant with a highly-charged sexual energy flow. Love and sex are serious business to you, and if a man takes it all too lightly, he'll be the first to feel daggers in his back as he mooches out of the door. And he'll probably go on feeling them for years afterwards, as your image remains locked in his psyche. Once met, you're never forgotten. What you project either gels with your inner needs or forces you into difficult and dangerous liaisons, depending on how well your outer expression connects with your inner values and needs.

you fall for

practical ★ sensual ★ artistic

Practical, sensual, artistic types, interior designers, men with pockets or wallets loaded with cash, rock stars and seriously rich rogues, men with planets in Taurus or Scorpio. A man like this might not be your life-long soul-mate, but he's certainly going to make you leap out of your car seat when he crosses the road. There's something inevitably attractive about the opposite sign from your Rising sign, whether you like it or not, so for you there is something fated about a Taurus man. Of course, you're less likely to tolerate his more obsessive side. He's usually fanatical about money and what it represents. Money can buy him love and you'll either loathe him for a lack of integrity or fall in love with him because he's so chillingly honest about his motives. This is a man who wants the world to be a beautiful place, to listen to good music, to be natural, wealthy and wise. So, how different is this from the image you project onto the world? He trusts too easily, you trust rarely. He makes you feel like a woman, and physical beauty and simplicity are important to him. What you project onto the world is a more surrealistic vision. But physically, this is a fated attraction. He'll seem like one of the sexiest men in the zodiac, simply because he loves what he values most: women. This relationship can be long term if other planets in the chart have good contacts. Your only problem is that you feel your way through emotional undercurrents, while he prefers to avoid them altogether.

you attract

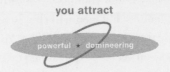

powerful ★ domineering

With such a mysterious and powerful aura, you attract men who
want to have power, from vain Taureans to menacing Scorpios.
The latter will understand your very secretive outer persona and
a man with a Sun Scorpio could form a very long-term and
beneficial relationship with you. But if you have conflicting
planets, like a Gemini or Sagittarius Sun, when they get to know
you well, they could be in for a surprise. Men with Taurus
planets are naturally reliable and steadfast, but if you play the
slightest underhand game, they'll never forgive you.

your seductive technique is

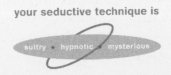

sultry ★ hypnotic ★ mysterious

Sultry, hypnotic, covertly sexual.

SAGITTARIUS RISING

you appear

restless ★ rampant ★ exhilarating

Restless, rampant, exhilarating. Enthusiastic at best,
unpredictable at worst, you are usually seen as being extrovert,
idealistic and everyone's friend. Men adore your direct approach
and it takes a strong man to put up with your restless and
idealistic view of love and life. When you sail into a party or

restaurant, women may resent your *joie de vivre* or flirtatious up-front *double entendres*, but men will simply be drawn to you as if you're the only woman left on terra firma. You thrive in social surroundings and get bored quickly if you're not being amused or amusing yourself. You adore playing romantic games and pushing your luck. You seem to get away with all kinds of tricks and tactics, and if you actually promise you'll meet him at eight, either you've fallen for him in a big way or you've forgotten how unlikely it is you'll get there in time. Freedom is essential and you hate to be thought simply part of the furniture. You're more likely to ask him for a date than he is to ask you, and if you find someone to believe in, you'll believe you've met the man of your dreams – that is, until you need to find another one to dream about. You're like a tap, turning off and on the charm to suit yourself. Excitement always beckons and routine sex bores you senseless. You're a romantic on the surface, so be proud of it.

your charisma is

infectious ★ free and easy

Infectious, free and easy, eternally optimistic. If you're not asking questions, then you're philosophizing about everything. You exude an air of self-confidence and extraordinary humour. Men just can't resist your inspiring words and your independent self-motivated self-assurance. You're a conversational animal. Without words you're off on a crusade or travelling for new experiences, with them you're instantly in love with whatever or whoever has come across your path. You're more likely to bump into romance in foreign places or by meeting strangers on trains, buses and tubes than any other Rising sign, simply because you exude such an optimistic aura that men feel immediately at ease in your company. Depending on the other planetary influences in your chart and your level of self-awareness, what you project either gels with your inner values and the urge to be yourself or forces you into exaggerated romantic scenarios. You're intuitively in the right place at the right time, just to make sure you meet the next Mr Right.

you fall for

witty ★ enigmatic ★ foreign

Funny, witty fast-talkers, youthful fascinating writers, media men, philosophers and travellers, strangers, foreigners and younger men. Because you're such a romantic it's not hard for you to fall in love more often than any other Rising sign, perhaps apart from Libra. Whatever else, you're instantly attracted to younger or just youthful, fun-loving, sharp-tongued and incredibly intelligent men. A man who conveys these qualities might not be exactly your long-term soul-mate, but he's certainly going to make you feel as if he is. There's always something very magnetic about the sign opposite your Rising sign, so you'll often fall for Gemini types. Men with planets in Gemini are notoriously impulsive and restless and you might loathe your Gemini type for being so superficial and light-fingered, but you'll fall hopelessly in love with him because he's so hilarious and sexy with it. This is a man who wants to enjoy life, flirt with it and flirt with women as much as possible. He's irresistible because he can't wait for tomorrow. He's dangerous because he won't notice you if he catches sight of a pretty face in his car mirror. He's a genie and a genius with words. Loathe him because he's so fickle and mischievous, but love his cheeky, *debonair* and know-it-all sexuality. You project an air of enthusiasm and the need for adventure in the world, he runs around like a headless chicken organizing your next trip.

Physically magical, mentally unnerving, you won't have time to think, let alone think about time. This is often a fated attraction and can be a long-term gold-mine of fun, especially if he has a Sagittarius Sun or Moon and if other planets form good links between you. Your main problem is that you need to explore life and give it some kind of meaning, but he doesn't have time to think about it, never mind wonder what it all really means.

you attract

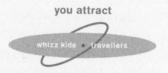

whizz kids ★ travellers

With such a dynamic, flirtatious outer persona, you'll attract bright whizz kids, travelling rogues and opportunists. Foreigners will find your thirst for cultural knowledge fascinating. Don't you still keep all those letters from the Juans, the Dominiques and the Romeos of the world? Independent Sagittarians and inquisitive Geminis will be queuing up at your door. The latter will adore your fast mind and your free spirit, the former will understand your impatience and the way you brush your teeth with anything. But Geminis could become evasive and elusive if you start spouting off about how cross-cultures are more interesting than sex.

your seductive technique is

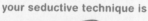

direct ★ hilarious ★ fun

Direct, loaded with innuendoes, usually hilarious.

CAPRICORN RISING

you appear

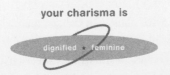

controlling ★ subtle ★ cool

Controlling, subtle, cool and classy. Ambitious at best, cynical at worst, you're seen as being powerful, serene and yet cautious in forming relationships. Men can't resist trying to probe behind that aloof and often distant aura. But you rarely let them anywhere near you, unless you have something to gain or they've got something worth giving. When you sweep into a party, all the 'animals' come out to check whether you're as sophisticated as you make out. You're seen as controlled and calculating, with nerves of steel. Serious ambition and security seem important to you, whether it's your own shrewd financial judgement or your urge to attract a man with money. Accomplishment is everything you represent and you seem able to organize, flirt, play the unseen power behind the throne and still have time to polish your nails quietly in a corner. Socially, you're impeccable and men adore your manners, your style and your icy gaze. And that's one special look that melts many hearts without defrosting your own. Serious on the surface, you project an air of incredible invulnerability. But, of course, as any wise Capricorn rising knows, what you see is not always what you get.

your charisma is

dignified ★ feminine

Dignified, feminine, ultra-experienced. Practical and down to earth, you convey an aura of quiet efficiency and steamy sensuality beneath your fey persona. What you exude is real womanly wisdom – not just sexuality, but also knowledge and emotional strength. Men just want to drink your beauty and civilized spirit like a mature claret. There's an air of dignity and success as you walk in a room. If you make a man breakfast in bed, it will be with grace and charm and will be tactically correct – in other words, eggs and sex timed to perfection. Depending on the other planetary influences in your chart and your level of awareness about yourself, what you project either gels with your inner needs or forces you into being obsessively cautious about whom you attract. Feminine and delightful, you can seduce anyone from the chairman of the board to the window cleaner. You adore the financial power-tripping influence of the former and the humour of the latter.

you fall for

talented ★ artists ★ musicians

Emotionally expressive men with taste, artists and musicians, ambitious and wealthy men who exude talent and skill. A man who conveys some of these qualities might not be your life-long soul-mate, but he will certainly paint a very attractive picture, one you'd like to hang on your wall and in your heart.

There's always something compelling and inevitably fated about the sign opposite your Rising sign in your chart. That means you often fall for men with planets in Cancer, men whose life purpose is compatible with your own expression and outlook on life. You could, of course, loathe your Cancerian type for his overt sensitivity and crabby nit-picking, his lack of structure and his acute restlessness. Alternatively, you might fall in love with him for being so in tune with the cosmos, with his feelings and

his very different sentimental streak. Physically, there's often
a very strong magnetic pull, for good or ill. You're looking for
emotional safety, for someone to organize and restore like an
antique or a priceless painting. He's looking for home and a
woman who represents power, prestige and a sense of mothering.
You project an image of exactly that. He's running after
emotional comfort, you're running scared of feeling. This
particular relationship can be long term if you have good links
between other planets in your charts or if you have a Cancer
Sun or Moon. His wealth will also have a lot to say about your
compatibility. Is he in the money because of his talent and skills
or successful because he's greedy for power? Your main problem
together is that he wants to find a power behind the throne,
while you would rather sit on it yourself.

you attract

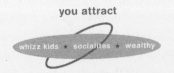

whizz kids ⋆ socialites ⋆ wealthy

With such a high-profile, classy and sophisticated aura, you'll
attract rich whizz kids, ambitious social climbers and
conventional city slickers. Capricorns and Cancers will drool
over your uptown, quality image. They'll find your cool,
detached charisma as compelling as making money on the stock
market. If he has a Sun or Moon Capricorn this could be a very
long-lived relationship, depending on the other planetary links
in your charts. Cancerians will adore your need to be in control,
then at least they can avoid making all the decisions. But they
may freak out when you start getting hungry for more than just a
quiet night in watching the satellite channels and would rather
own one yourself.

your seductive technique is

cautious ★ passive ★ penetrating

Cautious, passive, but unnervingly penetrating. Like a salamander.

AQUARIUS RISING

you appear

idealistic ★ analytical ★ proud

Idealistic, analytical, proud, independent. Free and easy at best, hypocritical at worst, you're seen as being controlled, rational and unique. Men find your independence either alarming or safe – alarming because they can't control you, safe because it means they don't have to commit themselves. In any discussion you're the first to point out that equality is fine for humanity. But you sometimes forget it's essential for you too. Emotionally, you prefer to keep the shutters down and that means some men will instantly feel at ease with you while others will be shocked by your lack of feeling. You thrive in social settings. The bigger the occasion, the more you rely on your idealistic vision of the greatness of human nature to get you out of any embarrassing scenes with rivals, or women who bleat and groan about how unattractive they are. The way you analyse every subject under the sun can make men nervous. Push a few psychological buttons and you've found a man's weakness before he's got past the peanuts and aperitifs. You'll be quietly planning how radically reforming him could make him actually quite perfect. Your aloof, glamorous image gives people much to wonder about.

That 'don't tie me down' attitude doesn't always last long if
you've got planets in more emotional signs, though. Shock
tactics are usually your best defence, and that's always a bonus
when you're feeling petulant and sexy.

your charisma is

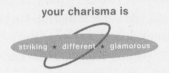

striking ★ different ★ glamorous

Striking, different, glamorous. There's an aura of the unusual, the
weird and mostly the wonderful when you breeze into a room.
Socially, you're in demand and there is an air of success and the
cool seductress about you. Men are drawn to your striking
appearance and unusual wit and unpredictable words. The latest
fashion and the greatest hi-tech gadgets are what you rave about.
And that gets you more attention from those independent men
who won't tie you down. Anything new goes. You're the first to
set a new trend or revolutionize hairstyles and as soon as the
latest fad hits the high streets you've found another one, or
totally reverted to a different style or anything which makes you
stand out from the crowd. Your unconventional approach to
lonely men makes other women seethe with envy. You ooze
friendliness and are adored because of your unconventional
tactics and experimental attitude to relationships. For you, the
more unusual, the better.

you fall for

stylish ★ confident ★ sophisticated

Stylish, confident, sophisticated, classy men, clever actors,
political dreamboats and drama-kings. A man who conveys these

qualities might not be your life-long soul-mate, but he's certainly
going to be a big physical and mental attraction. Men who have
class and style are bound to be attractive because they represent
qualities which you may not be consciously expressing. There's
always something magnetically attractive about the opposite sign
to your Rising sign, so for you, Leo types are usually going to
steal the show. You might either loathe this kind of man when
you first meet him or fall head over heels. But he'll be attractive,
whether you admit it or not. You might hate him for being so
proud and conceited and want to put him down with one of your
more sarcastic comments, or you might fall in love with his air of
superiority or his sophisticated smile or because he's a fashion-
conscious show-off. He's rugged and can be ruthless, but he's
also above the garbage of the world. Spirited, absorbed in every
aspect of his life, he's looking for success and an audience of one.
You're looking for the highest ideals in someone, or a way to
restyle his behaviour, or radically change his image. But you'll
do it with the wider audience in mind, not just yourself. He'll
expect you to hike across the Himalayas tying up his shoelaces,
but you'll want to paint the landscape, reform the locals and
make him walk bare-footed. Who needs hiking boots when
you've got the world to revolutionize? Physically, this is a fated
attraction. You have an unconventional approach, while he's a
conformist, so you'll adore redesigning his flat or his business
card. Your only problem is that you see life as a cosmopolitan
and cosmic experience, while he sees it as a personal battle,
never mind the universe and everyone in it!

you attract

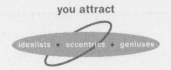

idealists ★ eccentrics ★ geniuses

Because you appear so independent and intellectual, you'll attract men who are idealists, eccentrics, wise guys, mad geniuses, rebels or sophisticated business types with an eye for glamour. Men with Aquarius Sun, Venus or Moon will adore your clever mind and free spirit. This could be a successful long-term relationship if he has the Sun or Moon in Aquarius, depending on other planetary links in your charts. Leo men will be drawn to your glamorous nature, but they may want more attention than you're prepared to give. After all, they need an audience, while you like to maintain your distance and observe the drama from the wings.

your seductive technique is

intelligent ★ bizarre

Intelligent, bizarre, different for the sake of being different.

PISCES RISING

you appear

romantic ★ dreamy ★ imaginative

Romantic, dreamy, imaginative, elusive. Sensitive at best, deceptive at worst, you're usually seen as utterly romantic and utterly wrapped up in a world of your own. Men can't resist your

feminine charm, yet they're confused by your rather evasive
tactics when they try to seduce you. But that's just your own
passive way of seducing *them*. You're an authority on escaping
from awkward candlelit dinners, but you're also fascinated by
the lure of any romantic interlude. Reality bugs you, fantasy
charms you and men find you mysterious. The more excuses
you make up to avoid another date, the more they'll phone you.
When you walk in a room women are often spooked by your
psychic powers. Not that you always know you're intuitive, but
it oozes out of every pore. When you meet stray men at parties
you'll either feed them with kindness or seduce them because
they're lonely. Waifs and poets can't resist your ultra-cool
composure. You're never dazed by glamour or charm, but you'll
probably go off into dreamland when others make too many
demands on you. Then you'll just escape through the bathroom
window or drown yourself in a bottle of champagne rather than
hurt anyone face to face. Walking round with a pained
expression on your face also brings you lots of gallant types who
want to go on a rescue mission. Sensitive men are attractive, but
then that's because you want to rescue them too. Getting caught
up in victim–saviour relationships is all very well, but it means
you're always choosing a role to fit with your man's psychology,
rather than being yourself.

your charisma is

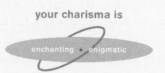

enchanting · enigmatic

Enchanting, enigmatic, spellbinding, awesome. You convey a
sense of mystery, one that makes men immediately want to find
out more. Compliments make your knees turn to jelly and
surprise parties or romantic dalliances make you come alive.
When you breeze into a restaurant for a candlelit dinner, your

aura is like a velvet glove. What you do with it depends on the
rest of your chart, but your man will just want to wear it himself.
Because you're so feminine, men with very masculine natures
find you adorable. Offer your date a drink or a coffee after the
meal – if you dare, that is, because you know how easily you are
led astray. Meantime, he'll notice you have a habit of running
your fingers over things, like the rim of wine glasses and the
forks on the table, and when you move out of range it's as though
a hole has been made in his head. Disappearing tricks are your
favourite pastime and escaping from real confrontations the only
way to get back to your own kind of reality – imagination. The
fantasy world you appear to live in is envied. And compelling.

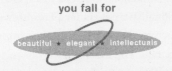

you fall for

beautiful ★ elegant ★ intellectuals

Body-conscious, physically beautiful men, elegant rogues,
philosophical types, curious intellectuals, perfectionists. A man
who conveys these qualities might not be your life-long soul-
mate, but he'll certainly have a powerful effect on you, for good
or ill. There's always a magnetic attraction about the opposite
sign from your Rising sign, so watch out for those Virgo types.
You might loathe such a man for being more interested in the
tablecloth than your ear-rings or you might fall instantly in love
because he's so physically perfect. This is a man who wants to
find out the details of your past love life and knows every detail
of his own. He wants exact information and ritual romance. You
probably can't remember your first love's second name, let alone
the colour of his socks. But physically this is often a fated
attraction. You have the gentleness, the sensitivity and the
dreams to keep a Virgo man romantically sane, while he has
the sense to stay grounded and keep you from running scared.

His communication style is elegant, laced with wit and words
like 'research', 'define', 'describe' and 'exactly' – the latter being
used when you give the right answer. On the other hand, his nit-
picking could make you escape to the sauna to chill out. Still, his
timing is always spot on, whether it's picking you up at the office
or making love in front of a log fire. Your main problem is that he
needs to rely on love, while you love to lie a bit.

you attract

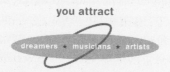

dreamers ★ musicians ★ artists

Anyone from poetic dreamers, musicians and artists to film buffs
and addictive personality types. In fact, because you appear so
feminine and seductive, you'll attract anyone from elegant Virgos
to visionary Pisces men. The latter will be hooked by your
imagination and gentleness, the former by your apparent need
to be saved from the dregs of the Earth. If he has the Sun, Moon
or Venus in Pisces, this could be a successful long-term
relationship, depending on other planetary links in your charts.
Virgos will adore the fact you'd never neglect them. But they
could start shuffling bits of paper obsessively when you dream
all day, rather than checking your bank statement.

your seductive technique is

passive ★ deceptive ★ teasing

Passive, deceptive, low pressure, wanting to prolong the
anticipation.

SUN/RISING SIGN COMBINATIONS

Your Rising-sign and Sun-sign combination describes what you need to develop in yourself or learn through your relationships to give yourself personal meaning. For example, if you're always falling into the same patterns of behaviour in your relationships, or falling for the same kinds of men, it might be because you aren't aware of these two sides of your nature. Your Rising sign might be locking horns with your Sun and often we don't access our Sun-sign qualities until we've been to hell and back a few times, or read enough astrology books to begin to recognize what we need to develop in ourselves.

Use this simple reference to discover what you need to learn, so that your Sun really shines with your Rising sign.

aries rising

sun in aries, leo or sagittarius

Learn ... to be less self-centred. You have strength, guts and drive, so choose men who can honour that feisty 'me now' image.

sun in gemini, libra or aquarius

Learn ... to think first, act afterwards. Fall for those who are more interested in mind than body.

sun in taurus, virgo or capricorn

Learn ... to keep track of your sensual side. Emotional closeness
is essential, however much you'd rather be competing.

sun in cancer, scorpio or pisces

Learn ... to cook. Make up recipes for love and then follow them
to the letter, however much you'd rather improvise.

taurus rising

sun in aries, leo or sagittarius

Learn ... to be wiser. Keep your bag packed and look for a man as
travelled and informed as you are.

sun in gemini, libra or aquarius

Learn ... to be adaptable. Show him you can read in the bath *and*
scrub his back.

sun in taurus, virgo or capricorn

Learn ... to be less possessive. Give him leeway and space. Your
sexual desire is fantastic, but your controlling streak can sting.

sun in cancer, scorpio or pisces

Learn ... to be more unpredictable. Your beauty, grace and
practical sense are envied. But relationships thrive on change,
too.

gemini rising

sun in aries, leo or sagittarius

Learn ... to act like a VIP. Dropping into relationships as if they were snack-bars doesn't help your need for recognition.

sun in gemini, libra or aquarius

Learn ... to communicate. You have the power of intellect and reason, so let it really flow with understanding.

sun in taurus, virgo or capricorn

Learn ... to be charming. Multiply your feelings and let them ooze all over him.

sun in cancer, scorpio or pisces

Learn ... to be sensitive. Ask him how he feels and really show you care.

cancer rising

sun in aries, leo or sagittarius

Learn ... to compromise. Fall for men who won't wind you up. Feeling you always have to resist means you just get defensive.

sun in gemini, libra or aquarius

Learn ... to be shocking. Imagine how your spirited independence can knock men off their bar stools – and then you'll have a captive audience!

sun in taurus, virgo or capricorn

Learn ... to be patient. Smooth operating in love relies on careful planning. Wine him and dine him with grace and charm.

sun in cancer, scorpio or pisces

Learn ... to be secretive. Reveal bits about yourself slowly ... and with feeling.

leo rising

sun in aries, leo or sagittarius

Learn ... to be dignified. Ask him for his phone number *only* after he's asked for yours.

sun in gemini, libra or aquarius

Learn ... to be direct. Tell him your ambitious streak comes first. But he's a close contender.

sun in taurus, virgo or capricorn

Learn ... to appreciate beauty. Tell him he's gorgeous and mean it.

sun in cancer, scorpio or pisces

Learn ... to trust your instinct. Challenging relationships are stimulating, but remember you need privacy too.

virgo rising

sun in aries, leo or sagittarius

Learn ... to be courageous. Seduce him before you have time to organize it first.

sun in gemini, libra or aquarius

Learn ... to laugh. Laughing about the world makes love and life so much more liveable.

sun in taurus, virgo or capricorn

Learn ... to be aware of your body. The more you exercise those limbs, the more he'll desire you.

sun in cancer, scorpio or pisces

Learn ... to relax. Make sure you give yourself enough free time for your love life. And for him.

libra rising

sun in aries, leo or sagittarius

Learn ... to be fearless. Be assertive and turn disputes into passion.

sun in gemini, libra or aquarius

Learn ... to experiment. Tell him you want to try out something far more challenging than Tantric sex.

sun in taurus, virgo or capricorn

Learn ... not to be swayed by beauty alone. Physical desire is wonderful, but love has other moods and tangents too.

sun in cancer, scorpio or pisces

Learn ... to be modest. Show off your IQ in small doses and let your feelings show sometimes.

scorpio rising

sun in aries, leo or sagittarius

Learn ... to develop your own philosophy and your spirit. Tell him you need space to do both.

sun in gemini, libra or aquarius

Learn ... to negotiate. Make those phone calls and be seductive. Love is about articulating your desire as well as feeling it.

sun in taurus, virgo or capricorn

Learn ... to double-check his history. Assuming you can change his ways only makes it an anti-climax when you can't.

sun in cancer, scorpio or pisces

Learn ... to be passionate. Tell him how powerful your sex drive really is.

sagittarius rising

sun in aries, leo or sagittarius

Learn ... to be creative. Paint him nude, or just paint each other.

sun in gemini, libra or aquarius

Learn ... to be eccentric. Try making your latest food fad and serve it to him under the table, or between the sheets.

sun in taurus, virgo or capricorn

Learn ... to be realistic. Taking control of your feelings means you can seduce sensibly, rather than riskily.

sun in cancer, scorpio or pisces

Learn ... to use your imagination. Romance isn't just about scoring a few points over a candlelit dinner, it's also about being cool and elusive.

capricorn rising

sun in aries, leo or sagittarius

Learn ... to enjoy your freedom. Relationships improve if you both have your own space and independence.

sun in gemini, libra or aquarius

Learn ... to chill out now and then. Love requires passion and laughter, as well as hard work.

sun in taurus, virgo or capricorn

Learn ... to develop your integrity. Show him your priceless antiques only when you're sure he's not after your money.

sun in cancer, scorpio or pisces

Learn ... to be charming. Be seductive and sensual, rather than ambitious and cool.

aquarius rising

sun in aries, leo or sagittarius

Learn ... to be less defiant. You need to feel special, but you won't love with complete confidence unless you give way a bit.

sun in gemini, libra or aquarius

Learn ... to respect equality. Let him choose the wine – and the way home.

sun in taurus, virgo or capricorn

Learn ... to be less controlling. Free yourself from all those judgements you make about every man you meet.

sun in cancer, scorpio or pisces

Learn ... to laugh more. Your serious side is valuable, but if you lighten up, men will find your two-tone moods strangely desirable.

pisces rising

sun in aries, leo or sagittarius

Learn ... to give healing. Wrap him in your arms and tell him he's the most desirable man in the world.

sun in gemini, libra or aquarius

Learn ... to be witty and crazy. He'll love you for being so unpredictable.

sun in taurus, virgo or capricorn

Learn ... to love music. He won't resist your voice, or your choice.

sun in cancer, scorpio or pisces

Learn ... to respect your own sensitivity. You have megabytes of charm, but you also have deep, deep feelings.

getting
personal

Apart from the Sun, Moon and Venus (you can read about Venus and the Moon in more depth in the next chapter), four other planets describe the way you express yourself in your relationships:

Mercury describes how you communicate.

Mars describes what makes you angry and how you go about getting what you want.

Jupiter describes your natural talent in love and the kind of lover you imagine yourself to be.

Saturn describes how you put up barriers and boundaries, and how you can deal with your vulnerable side so you're less defensive.

Look up your planets in the tables at the end of the book. If you find you have Mars or Jupiter in the same sign as your Sun, it will boost the qualities of that sign. For example, if you have both Jupiter and the Sun in Aries you could come across as very assertive and self-motivated. On the other hand, Saturn in the same sign as the Sun can often be in conflict with it. So if Saturn and the Sun were both in Aries, you might accuse others of being pushy, impulsive and demanding and deny that you were like that yourself, because you fear the assertive side of your character.

Don't forget that you may not be living out all these 'love bytes' of your personality and that some of your planets might need bringing alive.

ARIES PLANETS

Planets in Aries are basic, instinctual and assertive, what are usually known as masculine qualities. Women with planets in Aries often have trouble with this side of their personality. That's because we've been conditioned over thousands of years to think we have to behave in a certain way. But if you have Aries planets you'd rather be hunting men than playing with them or sprouting another pair of legs rather than an offspring. This is warrior energy and it needs expressing. If you're not in touch with this side of your nature and you're living out other bytes of your personality or pretending you're a sweet passive romanticist, you could become fearful rather than fearless and angry rather than assertive.

mars in aries

how you go about getting what you want

Usually with as much panache and impulsiveness as you can. You've hardly put down the phone, made arrangements for a date, whizzed through the bathroom and liberally doused

yourself with sporty perfume than you're off meeting your man.
You can be ultra-aggressive and when you want to make love,
you usually just steam ahead. Competitive men put you into gear
like a dynamo and of course you're ready to win any challenge.
Spot the gorgeous guy at the party and you'll move in fast. Spot
the bottle of best champagne left on the table and it's in your
hand on the way to chat him up. You won't take 'no' for an
answer. And yet you'd rather he were honest than two-faced.
Any kind of directness suits you, impresses you and woos you,
but evasion definitely makes your blood run cold.

who makes you angry

Men who accuse you of being too direct, potent and selfish. Wise
guys who slow you down or hold you up at the traffic lights.

your ideal male image

Aggressive, masculine, fast to react to your sexual style. He's got
to have guts, spirit and above all drive. Passion and red roses are
fine, as long as he'll pull the thorns off with his teeth and drive
you to the coast at a moment's notice. He has to have sport on his
mind and sport in his loins. The greater his libido, the more
you'll rise to the challenge. You want to be first in bed and first
out of it. If he fights you all the way, with pillows, so much the
better.

mercury in aries

how you communicate

Quickly. You talk fast and you listen to men who can fascinate
you with what they're going to do next week, rather than what
they did five minutes ago. Forget men who pontificate on past

love-life stories. You loathe ditherers, men who can't make up their minds or string a sentence together. You're fast-forwarding every conversation, always looking for a new subject or a new tactic. Quick wits impress you and you're impulsive enough to enjoy short to-the-point conversations on the phone. If he says, 'Meet me at eight and be there on time,' that means business. If it's 'Maybe see you at six, but I might not make it til seven, then again, you know what the traffic's like...', he's not on your wavelength.

how you ask for sex

Directly, honestly, with passion, fire and brimstone. Often on impulse. You'd ask him for sex in gale-force winds down the motorway or across the restaurant table to his face.

jupiter in aries

your natural talent when you're in love

Taking the lead and being number one. You've got to be first to suggest sex, the first to play, the first to score a tactical point. Competitive and feisty, it's easy for you to flirt, gamble with his heart and know he'll be back for more. Your self-assurance gets you noticed and your tendency toward egotism means you usually attract men who want self-motivated women. Depending on your other planets, you might exaggerate your single-mindedness or deny it. Look at where Saturn is to see whether you balance this side of your personality with a more serious, cautious side.

what and whom you adore

Sexual sport, hunting men, catching men, catching his eye,
flirting, sexual bravado, excitement and passion. Buccaneers,
self-starters, dynamic heroes.

saturn in aries

barriers and boundaries

You are incredibly self-contained and fear men who try to get
close to you. If they keep an emotional distance, you're laughing;
if they home in on your vulnerable side, you're an emotional
wreck, but the performance will be impeccable. Learn to balance
your independent spirit with your desire for passion. Civilize
your bottom-line 'me only' instinct and become an expert on
courageous relationships, those where you take the lead. Don't
fear your own aggressive nature. It's volatile, but attractive.

TAURUS PLANETS

Taurus planets are sense-oriented. They're feminine and ultra-
practical. If you have Taurus planets you should be able to
identify with them, unless most of your other planets are in Fire
or Air signs (Aries, Libra, Gemini, Leo, Sagittarius or Aquarius).
Taurus makes you aware of your sensual side, whether it's the
sound of a beautiful voice on the phone or the sun setting across
the sea. You'll be in tune with your body, and you'll need to take
something in and really know it before you let rip, whether it's
information or your sexual needs. If you don't identify with this

side of your nature, you might feel emotionally brittle or accuse men of being too possessive.

mars in taurus

how you go about getting what you want

Slowly, but forcibly. Will-power is your weapon. You develop an astute awareness of how to negotiate without causing trouble. The solid hunk on the bar stool might be playing hard to get, but you can play it even harder. You're after meat, not gristle. Move in close and he'll have little option but to be bulldozed into action. It's not that you're pushy, more that you can move mountains – or stubborn men. But you'll do it sensually, and probably touch his arm, tweek your nose and make all kinds of suggestive messages with your tongue and lips. Tactile sexiness oozes out of you like a boa constrictor, but with class. Money talks, and so does beauty. You've so much patience you'll wait all night on the bar stool until he notices you. Passive seduction is an art you take a long time to perfect.

who makes you angry

Men who oppose your will. Egotists or laid-back types who always ask you to lend them cash. Men with bulging wallets but no soul. Men who reject nature for hi-tech living.

your ideal male image

Somewhere between the good, the bad and the lovely. Men who are physically hunky and have taste, class and a love of nature. Sensualists with commitment on their mind. Sexually, he has to have style and not be offended if you choose the time and the place. He's got to be a whizz at massage or battle with you for which side of the bed he's going to sleep. A man who does the washing up is a bonus, so is one who opens the champagne bottle without it hitting the ceiling. You'd actually rather he was hitting the sack with you.

mercury in taurus
how you communicate

Seriously. Every word must make sense to you before you open your mouth. When you do, it's like liquid gold. You are likely to have a beautiful voice, be a great singer and seducer, and ooze sensuality through your lips. Men drink your beauty with their ears. Don't waste it, develop it. Use it. You want answers, so you're good at asking questions, but you can be difficult when you don't want him to know your secrets. Pathetic innuendoes and glib or superficial small-talk bore you. After all, you want to know the depths of his soul, the profound things that he feels or senses in the world, not how he missed the bus or why he was held up at the office.

how you ask for sex

You just have to smile and he knows. Words are unnecessary. You'd ask him deep in the night or early in the morning. Kiss his back, his neck, push the words across his skin with your lips and he'll understand.

jupiter in taurus
your natural talent when you're in love

Indulging in all the pleasure you can. Sexually and emotionally you're generous, but you can be excessive. You actually look

more beautiful when you're infatuated and when you're in love
you act more seductively, laugh a lot and do all kinds of crazy
things. That's when your shyness flies out the window and
persuasiveness flies in. Sensually, you flow and your energy is
elegantly dignified, like the best wine poured into a crystal glass.
Romance makes you ooze confidence and you'll stun him with
all kinds of useful ideas. Music inspires you and you inspire
music in his soul. You attract men who want to indulge in
pleasures of the flesh as well as those of the mind. Check out
your Saturn sign to see whether you exaggerate these qualities or
suppress them. Balance is needed because this is such an
excessive place for Jupiter.

what and whom you adore

Beautiful men with music, rhythm and a taste for beauty or an
eye for quality. Long grass, long gazes, beautiful sunsets and sex
beneath the full moon.

saturn in taurus

barriers and defences

You are very defensive. You'll rise to the bait, but you won't be
pushed into corners. If he accuses you of being possessive, you'll
go into a huff. You feel responsible for everyone and everything
around you. Nothing can be taken for granted in a relationship.
It has to be worked, weeded, ploughed and watered. If your man
is talented, you'll support him. But sometimes you forget about
your own needs and lose yourself momentarily. So it's important
to realize you have your own talents too. Civilize your frustration
by becoming an expert in creative loving. Don't fear your own
possessiveness and don't always feel you have to control him to
keep him.

GEMINI PLANETS

Gemini planets are like flocks of birds. Wings, feathers and flight-times seem to whirr in your head or your heart. Thoughts circulate quickly, they fly in and out of your mind alarmingly fast. Any kind of information is always fascinating. And the more you absorb, the more you give out. Light conversation makes you curious and witty, profound discussion makes you less shallow. So remember you need to develop some gravitas to feel comfortable with all those ideas that whirl around. Your curiosity keeps you addicted to strangers, men with wit and charm. But sometimes your quick reactions give you headaches as well as beautiful ideas. You're best in relationship, worst when alone. If you don't identify with your Gemini planets you'll miss out on messages which tell you how you really feel and how you really love.

mars in gemini
how you go about getting what you want

Quickly. You're fast on the draw and drawn by fast men. You play mind games. If he can't keep up with your thoughts, he's out to lunch. If he can keep you guessing, keep you battling to win, you'll be asking him out to lunch. Witty duels and conversations that sparkle are your best tactics. You'll plan the night ahead, desire his body and mind, and head for the nearest restaurant for fast food. Work out all the possible scenarios and conversations in your head before the party and you'll walk through the door with the best chat-up lines ever. You're endlessly quotable and your tongue is like a satirist – sharp, humorous and to the point.

Cunning though you are, you'll wait for him to be more fiendish than you. Then you'll use that wicked humour to get your way. But don't forget to listen occasionally, because inarticulate men bore you senseless.

who makes you angry

Know-it-alls, time-wasters, men who can't think for themselves. Men who hunt in packs. Dopey types and dreamers. Men who leave the phone off the hook or whose mobiles are permanently switched off.

your ideal male image

Young, sparkling and humorous. If he writes, scribbles, talks non-stop and looks like a dreamboat, so much the better. Talented conversationalists turn you on, so does pillow-talk and pillow fights. Teasing is fine. If he lies a bit, wriggles out of where he was last night when he should have been with you, you're challenged, and usually hooked. The more flirtatious he is, the more you adore him. Men who never frown and men who never moan about women keep you fascinated. But more importantly, he must be available on the phone at any time of day. And of course at night he should be with you.

mercury in gemini

how you communicate

Like the dodgems. You want to be smart, tease, jest and win mental battles. Your ideas are all over the place and you get lost in all the different corridors of thoughts swirling around your head. Professional talking suits you, but you don't brag about it. Gossiping to everyone at the party and chatting up a man at the same time is what you're horribly good at. You prefer phones to e-mails, but you'll use either to make a date, or just to fall in love. If your man wants you to be reliable, you'll change the subject quickly. If he wants you to be stable in your thoughts, you'll swerve purposefully off at another tangent. Conversationally you're stunning, but you don't always listen to what's being said, because your mind is already two steps ahead.

how you ask for sex

Clearly. Whether it's two in the morning or eight at night, you'll be deliciously forward – unless you are a Scorpio rising, in which case you'll be torn between speaking your mind and guarding your tongue.

jupiter in gemini

your natural talent when you're in love

Enthusiasm. You're bubbling, hilarious and intelligent. He won't have time to make plans – you'll make them for him. You'll be the nerve-centre of the relationship. Forward and deliberately persuasive, you must talk about everything under the sun and he must want to listen. You'll have sex while carrying out a wicked conversation, or you'll make him a spaghetti and read him an erotic novel at the same time. Educating him to your sexual needs is easy, seducing him to your place a doddle. You love to show your fascination for everything around you. So when you're walking down the road you'll notice the colour of everyone's eyes – and of course you'll remember his forever.

what and whom you adore

Gangster types, passionate talkers, thinkers, philosophical
rogues. Younger men. Pretty pin-up types. Thinking about sex,
wicked phone calls, flirting.

saturn in gemini

barriers and defences

When he appears to think he knows best, you'll be immediately
suspicious and nervous. Your reaction is to overreact. So you get
clever, curious, demanding, and then he begins to misunderstand
you. You go too far. You might even resort to being the fount of
all knowledge instead, so that you always feel one up on him.
That way you cover up your fear of seeming less intelligent.
Instead of being defensive, learn the rules of conversation. Don't
fear them. Civilize your scattered mind and liberate yourself in
love by learning to think for yourself, rather than depending on
what others say. Think about which are your true thoughts and
which have flown in during the coffee break. Become an expert
in conversation and learn not to be cynical and fearful of your
own or another's words.

CANCER PLANETS

Watery and moody, Cancer planets shift with the cycles and
rhythms of life. They are easier for women to handle than men,
because the expectations society places on men to be rational,
logical and sensible means they can't easily express their

feelings. But that also means that your partner has to get used to you sometimes needing to be close to him to feel safe and other times wanting to be alone. Basically, if you have Cancer planets, you feel most secure when you let your feelings flow towards him and still allow yourself space when you really feel like it. If you don't identify with your Cancer planets and aren't living out some kind of rhythmical movement in your relationships, then you'll feel rejected and lonely. Enjoy the mood swings, because they tell you what's going on close to your heart.

mars in cancer

how you go about getting what you want

By being evasive. The more you retreat, disappear to the ladies' room or don't turn up for dates, the more you'll seduce him. But then the slightest threat to your security hurts you. So you leap quickly from mood to mood, and if you're not feeling optimistic and light-hearted when you meet him for a date, you can become very defensive. You sometimes feel as if you're fighting men, not loving them, but that's because you're only struggling against all those shadows and nuances of feelings within yourself. You want to be held, but then you want to keep your distance. When you swing from escaping the room to seeking him out, you can drive him crazy. Just as when you send endless messages and little flirtatious phone calls, then don't answer the phone when he rings back. Enjoy the seductive art of hide and seek, but don't let it make you run away when you discover he really does have feelings for you.

who makes you angry

Men who don't have feelings, hardliners and chauvinists who wind you up, staunch anti-feminists or anyone who makes you cry. Men who oppose your independence. Opportunists and one-night standers.

your ideal male image

Caring, devoted, clannish or homely types. Men who love their mothers, as long as you're a lover, not a mother substitute. He must know what it's like to feel and also to be held close with affection and tenderness. The more nesting his instincts, the better. You're incredibly home-loving, but that doesn't mean he has to be a couch potato. Actually, your very ambitious and independent side demands a man who has a career and a passport and who still returns to the peace and quiet of a cosy kitchen. If he's a good cook, so much the better. Stylish and yet emotionally understanding, he has to be in your arms most nights. The more he wines, dines and delights you with his warmth, the more you'll respond.

mercury in cancer

how you communicate

Gently and cautiously. You've got a photographic memory, so his face is more important than his name. Conversationally, you wait for information that tells you he's hooked before you ever admit you are yourself. Because you depend on your feelings to give you cues for conversation, you react to the atmosphere and to what is being said to you, rather than put your own point across. You prefer deep, profound dialogue to superficial gossip. You speak gently and softly, and you're hardly likely to spend long at a bar with a loudmouth or know-it-all. Your voice is usually kind and you adore talking about exes, as if the men in your past are still standing in the room right next to you.

how you ask for sex

Carefully. You fear rejection, so you'll make sure it's exactly at the right moment. When you do so it will be in a roundabout way, as in 'Don't you think we should go back to my place for coffee?' or 'Are you tired? I could give you a fabulous massage or teach you some yoga.'

jupiter in cancer

your natural talent when you're in love

Really caring. In fact you believe that caring so much for others means life and love will take care of you. You're like a pitcher of mulled wine which you pour into your relationships to give them depth and soul. You can create a feast for any man, whether it's sexual pleasure or a ready-meal in the microwave. Romance is your secret talent. It's like a magician's hat, out of which you pull all kinds of luscious delights to woo and seduce him. You can remember every detail of every date you ever had, from the name of the restaurant where you first met to the name of the barman in the place where you last shared a kir.

what and whom you adore

Knights in shining armour, men who like feeding the birds, artists. Emotional or weepy films. Sentimental types who know your favourite hotel, recipe and the back of your hand as if it were their own.

saturn in cancer

barriers and defences

You often feel trapped by the things which make you feel most
secure. Relationships are imperative, but once you're involved
and feel contained and needed, you also feel trapped, like a bird
in a cage. Because you have such vulnerable feelings when you
aren't feeling secure, you look for your sense of security in a
relationship. But you create barriers around your need for
intimacy and become defensive when you're judged. Civilize
your sensitive nature by realizing that the massive dose of
security you're looking for in a relationship won't hurt you.
Become an expert in knowing that your emotional and material
security doesn't just rely on another person, but on yourself.
Take the responsibility of finding some kind of balance.

LEO PLANETS

These are great planets when you need to be classy, brave and
compete for that man down the corridor. If you have planets in
Leo, you're usually contagious to men. You're like the lioness
with her pride of lions, simply because you can show off a part of
yourself that many women don't have a chance to express. Leo
planets give you that 'oomph' when you swing through the party
door, brazenly follow a man down to the shopping mall to check
out his taste in clothes or simply want to get him into bed.
Planets in Leo give you creative ideas, romantic dreams and
outrageous feminine wiles.

mars in leo

How you go about getting what you want

Confidently. Theatrically outrageous and known to be a bit of a
drama queen, you often push rivals aside to get to the front of the
queue – especially when a man is concerned. There's nothing
like a spot of fire and brimstone to make you create all kinds of
ways and means to be noticed. If you're not dressed to impress,
then you'll be talking your way through a barrage of hopefuls.
And getting there first. But of course you do it with dignity, class
and style. He's got to be a five-star type of man, but you'll give a
five-star performance in return. Intimidating other pretenders to
your relationship throne gives you a thrill a minute. You have a
haughty air about you as soon as you're challenged by a possible
competitor. Just like a lioness, you're fiercely territorial. That
means that as soon as you set eyes on him, he's basically yours or
nothing – and it's all or nothing.

who makes you angry

Wimps, men with sunglasses who don't reflect your beauty in
their eyes. Snails – men who can't keep up with your need for
action. Men who don't realize you're brilliant at everything you
do. Flea-brains and guys with warped ideology.

your ideal male image

He's got to have class, act as if he's famous and treat you as if
you're famous, all within the first 15 minutes of meeting. He
must make you feel the most special woman on Earth and offer to
buy the moon for you. Compliments are welcome and romance
essential. Proud and civilized, he'll have a gleaming car and a
bed draped in lavish linens, glamorous fake furs or silks. If he's a
leader, an aristocrat or exclusively yours, then you've met your

match. Tremendously warm-hearted, he must cherish your
independence but adore your need to have your back scratched
every night, or at least buy you a gold-plated backscratcher for
bath-time.

mercury in leo

how you communicate

Passionately and personally. When you speak it comes from the
heart. You know what you want to say and you'll say it. Even if
he's not ready to hear your stylish and creative words, he'll have
little option but to listen. You speak as if your voicebox and
tongue are made of velvet, and you think like a queen bee.
Whatever you say must be taken seriously, or you can take it
personally. You're too proud to admit to being wrong, so if he
argues, you'd rather find another subject to get passionate about.
In love, you're witty and brilliant at saying the right thing at the
right time. But he must have his eyes on you when you're
chatting and listen as if you're the next Madonna, or at least
elevated to the rank of goddess.

how you ask for sex

Ruthlessly. It's almost a kind of threat – 'If you don't make me
feel that I'm the best, then I'll leave.' Anytime, any place, you're
the first to ask and the last to give in.

jupiter in leo

your natural talent when you're in love

Being generous and loyal. You'll defy all kinds of obstacles to
meet him at eight when you're supposed to be working to a

deadline. You're effusive with your passion, effective at impressing him. The more you make him feel special, the more you feel it yourself. You want him to be delighted by your creative ideas, your style and your panache. You want to be the best lover, so you'll act the best, even if other planets make you more vulnerable sexually.

what and whom you adore

Passionate lovers, glamorous men, mirrors and make up, golden hair, famous film-stars, Don Juans and simply the best of the best.

saturn in leo

barriers and boundaries

Personal achievement in relationship is great, but you desperately want to be the creative force between you, not a supplement to his needs. But when you get haughty, he backs off. Then you realize you have to come down off that high horse and just be yourself. Shining doesn't come easily if you have Saturn in Leo and you may feel as though you're a woman in an iron mask, not a velvet glove. Don't get defensive just because he doesn't remind you daily that you're the best thing since sliced bread. You probably are, but feel it, don't assume he'll know it. Civilize your egotistic drive, but don't fear your wild instinctive streak. Become an expert in passion. Learn to balance personal performance with spontaneous reactions.

VIRGO PLANETS

It's all very well having Virgo planets if you can ground all that
exhausting need to intellectualize everything in your
relationships. You think like a university don, but you need to be
as practical as, dare I say it, a housewife. Virgo planets make you
physically aware and sometimes physically obsessed. Your body
must be efficient, your relationships equally so. The tiniest
details in a relationship either irk you or delight you. Men find
your company stimulating and your behind-the-scenes pruning
of the environment admirable – or utterly intolerable. But you
work at civilized relationships; you make them organic, useful,
readable. There must be something to talk about, even if you
don't have Mercury in Virgo. You thrive on relationships where
you know where you stand. Even if you're listening to why he
prefers your best friend to you, then at least you have knowledge
on your side. The more, the better.

mars in virgo

how you go about getting what you want

You work out an exact plan of action. Whether this means
shrewdly noticing his weak points or criticizing his ex-
girlfriends to his face, the risk factor means you get excited
enough to carry your scheme through to its conclusion. You can
plot tactics for months, if in the end it means a productive
relationship. When you spot the flaws in his character, you'll
play on them. Either you'll gamble and blatantly point out what
you admire and dislike about him, or you'll silently score points
and feel over the moon. You intellectualize, digest and sieve

77

information. At parties you watch the competition, at work you suss out his rank. Then you'll passionately cultivate his talents alongside your own and ensure he's as well-informed and as physically healthy as you are.

who makes you angry

Men with no rules, time-wasters, physically inactive and mentally neurotic fly-by-nights. Confused victim types, men who leave a line of curry round their plate or drop litter.

your ideal male image

Squeaky-clean body-conscious men who are smart enough to know the difference between a zebra and an okapi. Men who enjoy talking through the night, wear white shirts and have a passion for being massaged. Your man must have tact and elegance, be tactile and love the tiniest details of your skin. Handsome, refined and intellectually alert, he must adore cultivating a dream, then actually getting down to earth and making it a reality. He has to share your love of ergonomics, health foods, diets, work and who's got the biggest muscles. Then you're prepared to sort out his pens or his sock drawer. Sexually, he's got to be physically beautiful, unchaotic, the perfect gentleman and remember to discreetly place his underwear out of view of the bed or bath.

mercury in virgo

how you communicate

Informatively, with wit and style. You're best when you're in conversations on a one-to-one basis. You're fascinated by his expertise in bed and equally fascinating because you know all about sexual economics and alternative contraceptives. You'll pick up the phone anytime to speak to him, if you're feeling nervous, edgy and things aren't sorted out between you. Your voice is earthy and cultivated, and your words razor sharp and often critical. Smart and canny, you loathe men who can't hold their own in a discussion or debate, and adore men who give you the chance to come up with significant observations.

how you ask for sex

Directly, cleanly, discreetly, as if you've a feather duster in your hand. Usually only in privacy. The words are inevitably chosen with taste and style, often delivered with poetic panache and always well-timed. (If you have the Sun in Leo you'll be more demonstrative.)

jupiter in virgo

your natural talent when you're in love

Cultivating the day-to-day organization of your relationship – whose turn is it to make the phone call, who's going to cook dinner, who's going to pay for the restaurant? Making the relationship work is 100 per cent what you do best. You mentally arouse your lover and physically seduce him, because you make an effort with your body, your perfume, your hair. Crisp white sheets and a bottle of champagne before bedtime are always on your mind. And so is how to make this relationship the most perfect set-up. You will manage it, as long as you improve, inspire and organize the two of you fairly.

what and whom you adore

Cool men with style. Information and intelligentsia types.
Physically beautiful men with brains. White linen, white birds,
clean sheets and perfumed pillows.

saturn in virgo

barriers and defences

Usually you become highly critical when defending your
vulnerable side, but you're also your own worst critic. You work
to improve your body or your mind, possibly through obsessive
or routine acts like going to the gym ten times a week or always
eating your breakfast in the same chair. In relationships, you find
it difficult to balance your need for quality and organization with
your fear of criticism. Accepting your fertile emotional needs can
bring you the peace you're seeking. You often nit-pick when he
makes an effort to dust the hi-fi, because you fear that when you
dust it yourself you won't live up to your own standards. Then
you can go to the other extreme and never pick up a duster!
Learn to balance your critical overload with discrimination.
Become an expert in organizing your feelings, too, and turn your
obsession for love into the art of love.

LIBRA PLANETS

Libran planets are negotiable. If you have planets in Libra, you're
romantically designed for harmony and pleasure. Any planets in
Libra demand you find your peace and happiness through

relationships. But it doesn't always come easy. The problem with Libran planets is that the desire to find such a balance in your life means you often come out the loser, simply because you work so hard at trying to please others that you fail to please yourself.

Yet relationships can also become your area of expertise. You can become anything from an authority on love to a lover of authority – neither of which will compromise your need for popularity. Aiming to please brings with it a few mega problems, though, simply because you need to be in partnership. It's a kind of life-or-death scenario when you're not – and similarly when you are. But if you have planets in Sagittarius, Aries or Aquarius, you may find it difficult to reconcile this twosome double-act thing with your need for more solo-style living.

mars in libra

how you go about getting what you want

You are utterly feminine and wily. You'll fight to snare him with all the charm of a cobra. The principle behind your desire far outweighs whether you'll succeed or not. That's the last thing you'll think about. Your most potent weapon is your ability to appear so charming and eager to be exactly what he wants you to be. You'll look good and graceful and rally round your best friends for moral support. If there's a set of rules to hand, you'll follow them. Say you're in a club and dancing is the only rule in the place, you'll dance. If you're at an intellectual soirée and the only rule is to make polite noises about the best literature, art or stock market falls, you'll do so. Just to win his heart.

who makes you angry

Highly principled men with chips on their shoulders and aggressively patronizing snob values. Macho, contentious types. Six-pack arm-wrestlers in pubs.

your ideal male image

Peace-loving, well-dressed artists, writers, intellectuals and poets. Hopeless romantics and hopefully equally fantastic lovers. Your ideal man must have class, style and be able to talk about everything under the sun, but with reason and wit, not just mumble about what's on the TV or in the papers. Above all, he has to prefer harmony to constant bickering, peaceful discussions to conflicting viewpoints. Beauty must attract him and so must your mind as well as your body. He may be willing to please himself, but he must also be willing to please you.

mercury in libra

how you communicate

Diplomatically. You always start off a conversation quietly, simply because you're checking out whether he's worth getting to know. You have to weigh up all the alternatives before you'll move any further than the bar stool. With grace and charm you'll find out more about him than he cares to divulge. But you won't give much away yourself. And there's no way you want a dispute. Your voice is like honey and your words always gentle and beautiful. You are willing to listen to both sides of the argument. You're reasonable, rather than risqué, but you're evaluating every snippet of information you manage to suss out.

how you ask for sex

Beautifully. You use romantic words, poetry, subtle gestures and innuendoes to make it a moving experience. You negotiate a place, time and atmosphere, once you've thought it through for yourself. Smoothly and serenely, you'll speak up just when you know the moment is right.

jupiter in libra

your natural talent when you're in love

Being romantic. But order, balance and harmony are where you find most pleasure and through which you give most pleasure. You have to find the perfect relationship and you're so idealistic that every close encounter appears to be the romance to end all romances. You can be so graceful and just, so true and finely tuned to his desires that you really believe you're in love the moment you set eyes on him. You give with pleasure and you want to please. Seduction becomes your greatest art and you know all the best ways to keep him begging for more, of anything. Depending on your other planets you might exaggerate your seductive skills or deny you have them. Check out where Saturn is to see whether it balances these qualities.

what and whom you adore

Beautiful men, artists, musicians, hopeless romantics, idealists. Poetry, dream clothes, the perfect relationship. Men who care.

saturn in libra

defences and barriers

You want to find the perfect relationship, but it requires hard work. That means you often start getting defensive about who's right and who's wrong. You believe your ideals are the only ones. And they must be right. Justice becomes interwoven with personal happiness, so you stick by your ideals and refuse to budge. You have such a strong desire to be loved that often you don't learn how to love. And there's a subtle difference. Longings get in the way of the reality of love. Let your ideas change and grow with your man's own visions. Become an expert at creating an arena in which love can develop and grow. You fear not being in a relationship. So learn that when you're deprived of love you start yearning for it, because you can't live without it. You fall in love with the idea of love and then long for romance to never end. But longing for it is not the same as living it.

SCORPIO PLANETS

Torrid, wilful and passionate, if you've got planets in Scorpio you're a force to be reckoned with. You have deep emotions and an intensely single-minded approach to life. Anyone who gets in your way might feel as if they've just been boiled alive or shoved into a bubbling cauldron. There is a very covert dark side to Scorpio planets. Whether you live out this kind of menacing side or not depends on the rest of your chart, but if you're not aware of those powerful undercurrents of passion and darkness, you might attract them to you through your relationships. You may wake up with someone you thought was all sweetness and light, only to find he's had the grimmest past love affairs, or has glimpsed hell, or at the very least eats bitter chocolate and drinks Guinness. Even if you feel quite un-Scorpionic, you'll have events and experiences in your relationships which will have a Scorpio feel about them. Tragic torrid affairs, men who are never available, intense discussions into the middle of the night... Whatever you do, love your intensity, make conscious your passion and channel your power.

mars in scorpio

how you go about getting what you want

Like a secret agent. You don't want anyone to know how passionate you are, let alone yourself, so you'll use other bytes of your personality, depending on other bits of your chart, to appear alluring, kind, gentle or simply fascinating. You plot and manipulate all kinds of scenes and events. And because you're so shrewd, you can spot a man's weakness a mile off or spot his strength from the other side of the planet. Penetrating and formidable, you go all the way, play all the games and get pretty obsessive when you're on the hunt. A few bone-chilling ploys, a flash of your hypnotic eyes and you're in for the kill quicker than anyone else. It's more than a game to you, it's a matter of life and death. And if you don't get what you want, you'll let go as fast as a snake that's bitten a poisonous frog. Mystery lures you on and anything taboo compels you to act – passionately and always undercover.

who makes you angry

Superficial know-it-alls, men who think they're sexually 'it', lightweights and men who aren't serious about emotions, life, love and the darkness.

your ideal male image

A cross between a tragic hero and a power-tripper. He must have depth of feeling and be as passionate as you are when it comes to sex, power and money. Above all, you must be able to trust him with your secrets, your soul and your intimacy. Feelings must be as important to him as gold dust. If he has access to his own gold-mine you'll feel so much the richer in pocket and in emotion. Money, power and love must be equally shared. Ideally he must know how to cook an egg on the bonnet of his Ferrari, or at least be ruthless and spine-tinglingly *risqué* enough to do it on someone else's car. Hypnotic and dangerous, he has to be an all-or-nothing man and sexually crave you every night. For you, a few wicked vices are far more compelling than a bouquet of roses.

mercury in scorpio

how you communicate

Secretively. Probing him subtly for all kinds of info is one thing, but you hate to reveal much about yourself. You can sense all the undercurrents of what's not being said and yet nothing is easy for you to say, because everything said is so serious. That's why you must find the simplest way to communicate the most profound and complex ideas. Your voice is sexy, your manner compelling and you talk about the most taboo subjects under the sun, from sexual perversity to racism and bigotry. If he doesn't have an opinion, then you're out of the door before he's had time to scratch his head. You're moved by intense conversation, driven by the urge to transform your relationship through your words.

how you ask for sex

All-consumingly. Seriously magical words just utter forth from your mouth. You're like a magician or a witch and he won't be able to resist you, because you time the moment to perfection.

jupiter in scorpio

your natural talent when you're in love

Depth of understanding. You know instinctively what it's like to feel so deeply and you also know that it's not as scary as others might imagine. You can handle all kinds of the murkiest situations with ease. Sex doesn't throw you and you're always ready to take a plunge into a scandalous relationship if it means you can transform your life. Half-measures of sexuality aren't enough. You give all and demand all from him. Beautifully dangerous or dangerously beautiful, you just ooze the kind of dark compelling quality that he would die for. Check where Saturn is to see if you're suppressing or living out these qualities.

what and whom you adore

Black lingerie, unusually profound thinkers, serious money, men who are emotionally intense, erotic films, midnight.

saturn in scorpio

barriers and defences

There's a side of you that you keep well hidden. This means men can find you difficult to get close to. If they're serious enough to make a commitment then you might reveal some of your feelings. But your boundaries are very watertight. You're surrounded by watery emotional intensity, but like a submarine you keep the hatch well and truly closed. Money, sex and magic you take seriously, and if he doesn't then you'll breed resentment and breathe venom. Learn to contain your feelings, but channel this energy into investing in your own needs in a relationship. Become an expert in feelings. You don't have to give them away, just let them find their own level. Don't fear your own intensity – the darkness is just as valid as the light.

SAGITTARIUS PLANETS

If you have planets in Sagittarius you're blessed with a good sense of humour verging on the hilarious. If you're not living out this side of your character, it's certainly worth dragging it out into the light of day, especially if you have a very serious streak which prevents you from accessing your wild side. Adventure, knowledge and imagination are your best qualities, while at worst you can be tactless, restless and nomadic. For some women, Sagittarian planets can be a problem. Independence and freedom clash with the need for relationship. If you've got more than one planet in Sagittarius, there's a likelihood that your personal freedom becomes an issue in close relationships. Most importantly, you need to roam, whether in your head, your heart or just the world. If you live out your Saggy planets you'll find that amusing others, amusing yourself and getting globally on the road will all appeal to you and make you aware of the innumerable possibilities in the future. Looking ahead becomes more important than looking back. Planets in Cancer, Scorpio or Taurus could conflict with this propelling motivation.

mars in sagittarius

how you go about getting what you want

By crusading. It's a kind of all-or-nothing desire to get there
quickly on a matter of principle. You won't be stopped, you *will*
win and you will turn a few heads in the process. But what the
heck. If you're after him at a party, you'll push in front of any
rivals, then tell him you want to take him back to your place,
offer to drive him to the coast, however far away it is, and spend
the night out under the stars. You talk your way into his heart
with your knowledge, wit and wisdom, and if that doesn't work,
you just play a few jokes, laugh a lot and act like a mad genius all
at the same time. It's a sport, not a game of chess. There are no
wrong and right moves, only a challenge to win him. You always
feel it's your destiny to get what you want. Adventure propels
you into action and taking risks means you're in touch with your
imagination and your fire.

who makes you angry

Men who don't have a sense of humour, men with chips on their
shoulder about their size, evangelical types, lazybones and couch
potatoes.

your ideal male image

Feisty, adventurous, fun-loving. Big. He must have bags of energy
and no bags under his eyes. Sporty and assertive, he's got to
know how to rock-climb or sky-dive first, make passionate love
second. Globe-trotting types get extra brownie points and if he's
been somewhere more exotic than Maplethorpe, then you'll
expect him to take you there. If he's happy to pay the bill you
won't mind, as long as he lets you choose your own food and the
wine. He's got to be a pioneer and a joker all rolled into one. The

more he makes you laugh, the more he'll raise your adrenalin
level. He's got to adore casinos, horses and wild sex in equal
ratios. The crazier his schemes and the more outrageous his
dreams, the better.

mercury in sagittarius

how you communicate

Like a chatterbox with a megaphone. You have to be heard and
no one's going to stop you. Ideas tumble from your lips, words
are always on the tip of your tongue. But you often think they're
more important than they really are. Meaning has to be found in
every conversation. If he doesn't make sense, you'll make sense
for him. But you can be tactless and rash. Thinking doesn't
happen until after you've spoken, so be careful you say what you
really intend. Desire and enthusiasm are in every word and your
voice can be your vice, but it's always bubbling, laughing and
refreshing.

how you ask for sex

Honestly. There's no way you'll be discreet. If you feel like
making love you'll just go right out and say it, with as much
passion and exuberance as the mood takes you.

jupiter in sagittarius

your natural talent when you're in love

Believing passionately in travelling together. You'll gamble on
romance and know that even if it all ends tomorrow, a few mad
adventures and your guardian angel will get you through any bad
patches. You fire him with enthusiasm for new experiences, both

sexually and physically. Whether it's a chance idea to go to
Paris for the weekend or a new opportunity for both of you to
expand your mind intellectually, you always have beliefs,
philosophies and crazy ideas surging through your head. Your
hilarious antics and sense of humour keep romance alive,
dazzling and daring.

what and whom you adore

Pirates, scoundrels, gurus. Men with guts and spirit. Keeping a
bag packed under your bed. Sex in the great outdoors.

saturn in sagittarius

barriers and defences

You want to get everything right and that means you take your
beliefs and the law seriously. In relationships you promote your
ideas with authority, but you find it hard to accept others' wider-
ranging thoughts. You take yourself so seriously that sometimes
you forget to laugh. Develop your sense of adventure and don't
be afraid of moving out of that intellectual circle you create to
defend your beliefs. The more experiences you have in love, the
more you'll be able to develop your own personal philosophy of
life. Become an expert in why love matters.

CAPRICORN PLANETS

Self-discipline, work and ambition are all associated with
Capricorn planets. Living them is easier if you're a career type

with a head for how serious life really is. If you've got planets in something more lightweight, romantic or sensitive, like Gemini, Pisces or Libra, you might find a dilemma between your love of play and your desire for work. In relationships, Capricorn planets mean that everything is about status, achievement and solidity. These love bytes could be organizing your thoughts, tidying up your image or just being downright determined to have it your way. Even if you're not living out these bytes, you might experience Capricorn-type people in your life or draw very serious people into your space. You might always be falling in love with the boss, or older men, or sugar-daddies. Your need for constancy and 'the love business' means you need to feel secure before you'll leap into romance as others might do. Controlling relationships means you don't get caught up in your vulnerable side. In fact, underneath that careful shrewd-operator image, there's a part of you which is fiercely defensive.

mars in capricorn

how you go about getting what you want

With massive calculation, care and class. You're determined to have everything your way. But you'll do it shrewdly and cautiously, weighing up all the odds first. Is he worthy of your attention? What are his motives for being attracted to you? Will you make a fool of yourself or should you just hold back until he approaches? Your timing is always immaculate and you're classically frosty and cool enough to sweat it out beneath all that glamorous sophistication. If he makes you feel as though you're about to achieve your personal best, then you can strike when the moment is right. If he walks into a party with another woman, you work out exactly who she is in relation to him. If she's a wife, you'll probably wait a few years until they're divorced; if she's a lover, you'll probably charm him by the end

of the financial year; if she's a platonic friend, you'll have his
phone number in your mobile by the end of the evening.

who makes you angry

Classless, tasteless nobodys. Men who flash stupid sexy looks
your way and men who flash their wallets, wear cheap watches
and have designer labels sticking out of their shirts. Lager louts
and men munching pizzas on public transport.

your ideal male image

Sophisticated, cool, sexually experienced and businesslike.
Witty, ironic, dry and laconic. His car must be discreetly
expensive and his taste must reflect his status – the more worldly
and classy, the better. At the very least his style should represent
what he's serious about. Even if he's an expert on the world's
rarest ant, if he's serious about his career, profession or
motivation in life, then he's worthy of your interest. He must be
impeccably mannered, dignified and want love to be a life-long
achievement in togetherness. If he's willing to work his guts out
to achieve some kind of status, you'll help him do it. Traditional
values are *de rigueur* and so is his passion for loving only one
woman. You.

mercury in capricorn

how you communicate

Wryly and carefully. You want to find out the rules and the
regulations that inspire his words. So you take your time and ask
carefully contrived questions. The answers which confirm your
opinions will be taken in and absorbed as if you're a saucepan of
rice. The answers which don't make sense will be rejected.

Rational ability is your strength, judgement is your weakness. Your dry humour gets you noticed quickly, but it hides a very serious need to talk about things which matter. Your voice is sexy, classy and often has a notable accent or ring to it which oozes wisdom about life and love. Sexy and sensible, you have the patience to wait to say the right thing at exactly the right time, especially when you're in a persuasive mood.

how you ask for sex

Wisely. At the precise moment when you know he'll respond the way you want. The words you use are to the point or often tinged with dry, wry humour. You work at it, carefully. With precision you sculpt the suggestion out of a situation as if it were a piece of marble or stone.

jupiter in capricorn

your natural talent when you're in love

Working at it. You know how to craft your relationship into the best work of art. Organized and structured, you turn every twist in the tale into special moments that become a tradition in love. The value you place on your relationship makes you unique. You're down the line, frank, honest and committed. If he's worried, troubled and down, you'll find a practical solution to his problems. A pillar of strength may be a little bit of a cliché, but you're certainly a towering inferno of passion.

what and whom you adore

The biggest bouquet of the best roses, his promises (when he keeps them), successful, wise, cultivated, goal-oriented, slick yet discreet men. With taste.

saturn in capricorn

barriers and boundaries

Ignoring the rules of the game can make you decidedly difficult in close relationships. You need to balance serious loving with the love of mastering love. Accomplishment in relationship is like building a stone wall. It's lengthy, but can be achieved if you allow yourself the time and space to do so. You have to live by the law, anything less will make you defensive and stony. Learn the rules of relationship or you will have to pay heavy penalties. When you're unaware of this side of your nature, you might well admit to ignorance. He says, 'Look, I only wanted to find out why you didn't call.' Defensively, you reply, 'I didn't know there were any rules here!' But there *are* rules in relationships and even if you break them or change them, don't ignore them. Become an expert in the rules of the game or learn to change them and be aware of what you've changed.

AQUARIUS PLANETS

If you have planets in Aquarius then you're enthralled by your own identity and your own uniqueness. This is the sign of shocks, surprises, electricity, big ideals and ideas. Independence is the key to finding out how you relate in intimacy. The times in which you live and the people with whom you live and love will play a big part in your lifestyle. And all the time you have to navigate between group ideals and your own personal ones. Unconventionality is crucial to you, though ironically even your rebellion can become conventional. Relationships often start for you with a sense of breaking out. Someone is unexpected, different, unusual, but if you start to feel contained and normal, you break up. Aquarian planets need space and personal freedom. Your thoughts are always under pressure, waiting to find a different avenue or a different idea to update and recondition. You might find you're drawn to very Aquarian types in your relationships – the eccentric artist, the rebel without a cause, the freedom fighter, bungee jumper or man who's never married. But these are all a reflection of your own maverick streak. So look within and find your own mission, and your own human needs and desires.

mars in aquarius

How you go about getting what you want

Stubbornly or shockingly. When you find yourself in the presence of a possible male target you act in exactly the way he *won't* expect you to act. You'll work out what it is he anticipates and become perverse and different. You'll march into the restaurant and stand on your head if it's the last thing on Earth he'd expect. Or, of course, you might turn all seductive and glamorous, roll into the party with lightning flashing over your shoulder or just a couple of angel wings. You'll never conform. Making up your own rules as you go along gets you results. You can be awkward for the sake of awkwardness, not to mention downright difficult and eccentric. But you lure him by being utterly individual and experimental, and with your amazing capacity to think up all kinds of ruses, you'll outwit and outshock any potential rivals. In fact rivals just don't exist in your head and if they do crawl out of the woodwork, you'll invent some way of making them jump straight back in.

who makes you angry

All those men who hang around in groups or gangs. Men who get sentimental and soppy. Lonely-heart advertisers and men with chips on their shoulder about their sexuality. Macho types with gold chains and jewellery.

your ideal male image

Freedom-loving, independent rogues with missions. Talkers, writers, thinkers and radically different adventurers. If he talks, listens and gives you space to be yourself, you're in seventh heaven. He's got to know about the cosmos, read about the Earth and want to save something. Even if it's his cat. Materialism isn't his 'in' word and 'in' isn't either. Unconventionality gives him class, and traditional values – well, if you can change them, he's a possible grape on your vine. If you can't, then you'll lull him into a false sense of security and then do something really weird to get out of the room. The more bizarre his behaviour, the more you're hooked.

mercury in aquarius

how you communicate

Originally and often with sudden flashes of insight. You ask for things you want in a roundabout way. Sometimes even you can be shocked by your own tact – or lack of it. That's because you're an original thinker and whatever you say must be different and unmistakably you. The more you stand out as radical, the more you feel secure. But you must have conversation and filter all the information others give you so that you can treat it with your own individual style of conversation. Wit and brains are your passport to many intellectual discussions. Unique though your

voice and ideas are, you won't go with the flow of opinion
readily, just because you like to change it, or make irritatingly
difficult statements just to wind people up.

how you ask for sex

Madly. You'll choose moments when he's not expecting it or
situations that are bizarre or not normally the time or the place to
ask – the middle of a stuffy dinner party, in front of the other
guests, or in the street, or across the boardroom table – anything
which gets you noticed as being utterly different, difficult and
unique.

jupiter in aquarius

your natural talent when you're in love

Dreaming up all kinds of ways to make the relationship better.
You'll fill his mind with ideas that burst out all over the place
and you'll also fix his belief system and make sure it's as
awesome and ethical as your own. You're idealistic, so you're
utterly romantic, but you have to do it differently from everyone
else. Love and romance have to be a totally new experience, one
that no one else on this Earth could ever experience. Mind-
boggling dreams keep you sane and keep him fascinated.

what and whom you adore

Electrifying sex, experimental men, avant-garde gurus, computer
whizz kids, technocrats and anarchists. When he surprises you
in the shower.

saturn in aquarius

barriers and defences

You can be so idealistic that your ideas and opinions are more important than your relationship. You guard your ideas and stick by them, but you also lose out on expanding your mind to realize that your man has an opinion which is just as valid as yours. You loathe intense personal discussions and prefer intellectual analysis. You may immediately get defensive about your beliefs and give him ginger tea when he asks for coffee, just because you believe it's better for him. Try to become an expert in human nature as a whole, not just your own desire to be awkward and different. Specialize in what makes him tick. Bring your ideals into the relationship, but be creative with his too.

PISCES PLANETS

If you have planets in Pisces then somewhere you're sensitive, kind and have a powerful imagination. Watery feelings kind of swirl around you and you can't quite get a grip on what you're feeling yourself. Often you're more aware of what others are thinking, feeling or even imagining. And that can get a bit tiresome because you're always having to think of others and not of yourself. You look into his eyes and you instantly know whether he's in love with you. On the other hand, that could mean you find out the truth you don't really want to know. Your relationships are always clouded by dreamy ideas and visions of utter romance that lasts forever. There's nothing wrong with being an all-or-nothing person, all love and poetry, accepting nothing but the best. But you're also elusive and if things are too

intense, you'll escape through the bathroom window rather than
create a scene. You have a constant yearning for love, a longing
for it, but sometimes you feel you have to let go of the very things
or people you love. If you're not living out your Piscean side,
then you might attract those qualities into your life through
experiences, events or people. For example, your lover might be
a dreamer, an alcoholic or even a priest, or you might find
yourself always attracted to men you can't have.

mars in pisces

how you go about getting what you want

Subtly and deceptively. Evasion means you can keep him
guessing and there's a certain passive seduction going on when
you slip out the room without him noticing. Then when he
realizes you're not there, you slip back in again. You don't mean
to tell fibs, but you can exaggerate any story to make yourself
fascinating. When you need to pretend you have feelings,
thoughts or experiences that aren't actually quite you, you play
the part well. That's the actress or the vamp in you. Sometimes
you're totally surprised about what or who turns you on. Stirring
a cocktail, looking as if you've been through ten doomed
relationships or worse, often draws the kind of men who want to
save you. Playing the victim–saviour game works well too. If he
begins to tell his life story, you're involved as quickly as if you
are telling him yours. Even if it's a bit phoney, you'll believe it
yourself anyway. And of course the best way to get what you
want is to be enigmatic. Being mysterious gets you noticed.

who makes you angry

Sexual pragmatists, men who think you're naïve or just lost in a dream, pushy arrogant hustlers, men overloaded with aftershave or hi-tech accessories.

your ideal male image

A cross between Shakespeare and Mel Gibson. A man who has poetry in his head and desire in his eyes. He's got to adore music, dreaming and escaping the rat-race. If he can whistle or hum at least two bars of Berlioz's *Symphonie Fantastique* you'll dance with him until dawn. But he's got to put you to bed when you've crashed out from one too many late nights. Romance has to be in his soul and he has to know he has one in the first place. If he knows the difference between yoga and yoghurt then you'll spoonfeed the latter to him every breakfast. The more he can dream and not scheme and take a few spiritual vitamins rather than physical ones, the deeper you'll let him into your private world.

mercury in pisces

how you communicate

Gently. Your voice is usually streamlined and sympathetic. You listen first, absorb what he's saying and then subtly and slowly reveal little snippets about yourself. But often things come out differently each time you have a conversation, so your mind keeps shifting perspectives of both yourself and him. You often become a kind of verbal chameleon, changing your voice and your diction to mimic him. Sometimes you know what you're saying, other times you don't, and that gives you a reputation for being vague and dithery. You're logical, but it's an intuitive kind of logic. You sense what is going on in his mind, but you can't quite rationalize it.

how you ask for sex

Romantically. You'll have to be in the right location as well – at a candlelit dinner, basking in the sun, dangling your feet in a river or pool. You'll also be elusive with your words. 'Making love is so mysterious isn't it?' is more poetic than a direct question.

jupiter in pisces
your natural talent when you're in love

Being totally kind and generous. You almost have a guardian angel on your shoulder, and even if you feel let down by life's strange twists and turns, you're a miracle-worker when it comes to your relationship. You can be soft and tender, and you're always willing to bear his suffering, his problems and his toothpaste stuck all over the sink. If you don't easily identify with this side of your character, look to see where Saturn is – you might be overloaded with defences that control this very, dare I say it, lucky placement for Jupiter.

what and whom you adore

Magic, drifting into romantic exotica, men who are kind, sensitive artists, poets, dreamers and buskers. The sea, animals and your local vet.

saturn in pisces

barriers and defences

You often deny your sensitivity for fear of being totally absorbed
by it. In relationships you feel the undercurrents and the feelings
swirling about between you, but you don't always know whether
they're your own or his. Rebelling against feeling is easier than
accepting it, so you fear those feelings so much you struggle
against them. You want to enjoy romantic notions, those layers of
the intangible that curve through every relationship, but because
they're not real, not formed, you sink rather than achieve the best
out of your relationship. Giving in seems easier than giving
sometimes. So become an expert in sensitivity and become part
of a loving relationship, rather than always backing away from it.

love
styles

The Moon and Venus in your chart represent two very different feminine aspects of your personality. Venus tells you what you're hunting for in a relationship, in other words what turns you on, your sexual style, what you value in love and the way that you love someone. The Moon tells you about what you need within a relationship to feel comfortable and at home, whether it's literally closeness and a comfortable bed, or freedom and wide-open spaces. Also, the Moon describes how you react to men and the way you feel a relationship should flow. The Moon reflects our instinctive way of behaving and its influence can be so unconscious that we hardly know we are reacting in certain ways.

Sometimes Venus and the Moon are in very different signs. This means their qualities often don't complement each other. So, for example, say you had a Sagittarius Moon and a Taurus Venus. The Venus placement makes you yearn all those very beautiful creature comforts, lots of laid-back sensuality and adds a spot of possessiveness into the bargain. A close binding relationship with one man is what you're hunting for. But the Moon in Sagittarius actually needs freedom to feel safe and secure. Its reactions are fiery, so you'd feel comfortable with big adventures but not necessarily snuggled up in a tête-à-tête in front of the fire. Trying to balance these two very different qualities isn't easy, so you might only be living out one side of your love nature. Perhaps you'll tune into your Moon sign because it's more reactionary, more instinctive. Then developing your Venus in Taurus might take time or you might get very angry with yourself because when you find pleasure in closeness, the Moon keeps nudging you to opt for space and freedom as well.

Look up your Moon and Venus signs in the tables at the end of the book. Then check out your love styles to see how you can work with these different parts of your personality and learn to love them both.

ARIES

venus in aries

you hunt for

Challenging, adrenalin-racing relationships. Lovers who are fiery, impulsive and potent. What you're searching for is passion to motivate you, love that is active, not passive. You crave a man who accepts that you need to be first in everything, whether it's first to take a shower or first to win at strip poker. If you want sex now, you've just got to have it now. Look for men who are sporty, fast and furiously passionate.

what and who turns you on

Sexy men who like to compete with you for who's going to be on top in bed, or who just adores having pillow fights. Danger and excitement give you your biggest adrenalin surges. Ask for sex whenever you feel like it. Sex in daylight gives you total bliss, especially if you imagine he's a stranger you've just met. Try public locations – on an aeroplane, in the shopping mall. The more likely you are to be caught, the better the sex.

the way you love

Fiercely and recklessly. You can get jealous, so check out your Moon sign – if it's in an Air sign, you might find it easier to rationalize your desires. It's all or nothing when it comes to love with this fiery Venus, but you also need lashings of independence and a man who's a champion for you.

moon in aries

you need

To be egocentric, fiercely self-interested and independent. You don't have time for games, but you need to be on the move to keep your feelings sparkling and alive. You must be the centre of attention and can be very demanding. You test yourself and you play to win if you so much as arm-wrestle. But you try to run away from your feelings, because they're alien to your impulsive wilfulness. Feelings just get in the way of that warrior princess image you have in your soul. Sometimes you fight on behalf of other people's emotional security, but you always fight security.

you react

Immediately and impulsively. If he's left half a bottle of
champagne on the table, you'll drink it in one go. If he doesn't
phone you at the office, you'll zip round to his place at midnight
for answers. You have to have a dynamic relationship where you
can express your needs and desires whenever you feel like it.
You feel safest when you're at your most impulsive and
expressive in a relationship, also when you have the space to
come and go as you please. Check out your Venus sign. If it's in
another Fire sign – Leo or Sagittarius – or one of the Air signs –
Libra, Gemini or Aquarius – then it will complement your
emotional needs. If it's in any of the other signs, you might find
you lock swords with yourself. That's when impulse can
override your sensual needs.

TAURUS

venus in taurus

you hunt for

Sensual pleasure. If you aren't rewarded with touch, tenderness
and warmth, you'll seek it elsewhere. You look for lovers who
are gentle, slow to be aroused and will take their time and flow
with your needs. When you're embarking on a new relationship
you seduce him slowly. There's no obvious attempt to throw
yourself in at the deep end. But if he's got money, beautiful
clothes, gorgeous looks and a soft voice, you might leap in before
you realize what you've done.

what and who turns you on

Aesthetically educated men. Dark enticing sensualists. If he's passionate between the sheets and still romantic out of them you're in heaven. Sexually, you want to be inspired by the beauty of his touch, the tenderness of his embrace and the power of his libido. He must be able to massage you all night if you ask and feed you all kinds of romantic but sensual goodies. Aphrodisiacs are *de rigueur*. Passion is a spiritual and materially rich experience.

the way you love

Possessively. You can get jealous and give him all kinds of green-eyed monster looks if he flirts dangerously. You need to feel his eyes are only on you. You're a sensualist, so you love with your body and your touch is like gold dust. But you get very attached to love and that means you find it mega hard to break free from the delight of it, even when things aren't going well. It's an irresistible force, but it can also hurt because you can't let go if it goes wrong.

moon in taurus

you need

To attach yourself to someone for closeness. You generate a magic circle of love around you. Men can't resist your charming, warm and welcoming instinct for seduction. But you're not often aware how possessive you can be and you can become totally attached to those things in your love life which are familiar – like how he eats his eggs, or what kind of socks he prefers, or how many times a week you go out for dinner. If those simple things in your relationship change because he decides to change them, you'll argue over and over again to keep things the same. Watch out you don't become venomously vengeful if you feel betrayed.

you react

Slowly but charmingly. There's a deep compulsion down in your psychological basement to be in control of your feelings, so you often out-seduce him just to stay on the wave of pleasure. The more he riles you, the more you'll put up your emotional guard and play the enchantress instead. If you're let down, the resentment builds up slowly and carefully. Then you'll explode with a fair gush of emotional intensity that often rises up like a volcano. If you have Venus in Earth signs like Virgo, Capricorn or Taurus, then you may find it easier to live out this side of your nature. But if you have Venus in the Fire or Air signs – Aries, Leo, Sagittarius, Gemini, Libra or Aquarius – then conflict between your need for closeness and security and your desire for liberated pleasure could cause you to 'dump' your possessiveness on him by saying, 'He's the possessive, jealous type, not me.'

GEMINI

venus in gemini

you hunt for

Sparkling wit. A man with a sense of humour and a love of words and laughter. He must be able to communicate at any time of day or night, have fun at the same time and be capable of having sex and talking about it, or at least read the papers in two

seconds flat and then be on the mobile to you most of the day.
You're looking for a man who appreciates your restless need for
adventure and for social contact, who can share and bear your
need to gossip, and still make you feel the sexiest woman on
Earth. One minute he must be an explorer, the next an
intellectual wizard. The more outrageous his phone calls and the
more freedom he gives you, the more you'll hunt him.

what and who turns you on

Men who can stimulate your mind first, then your body. You're
in love with words and stories. Hard-to-catch tricksters and
elusive jokers keep you buzzing with desire. Sexually, he must
communicate with his words and his antics and use his lips as
though he means what he says. Your charming, childlike,
lightweight sexuality means you're effervescent and bubbling
like a fishtank airfilter. Romance is a must and you're turned on
by all kinds of surprises, gifts, sexual discoveries and sexy talk
on the phone.

the way you love

Charmingly. You're seductive with your words, suggestive with
your mind and create romance and togetherness through your
conversations. But personal freedom keeps you loving him even
more and companionship is more important than possessiveness.
A good conversation through the night and sparkling,
scintillating romance all day is your very intellectual and multi-
faceted lovestyle. Turn him on with your childlike and flirtatious
manner. You have giggles, jokes and interesting ideas, but you
need room to breathe, explore and expand those ideas with him,
and without him. For you, love is about entertainment – his
and yours.

moon in gemini

you need

To satisfy your curiosity with fascinating conversations and loads of romantic notions. You often fall in love because you trust another person too easily. There's a kind of *naïveté* about your feelings, so the more seriously adult he sounds, the more you'll fall into the net of desire. Yet you feed on words, gestures and ideas, and that means you have to be nurtured by conversation, phone calls and a man who can talk through the night and day on any subject, and every subject. Be careful you don't get cynical. Being so trusting means one day you'll be tricked into believing something because it sounds so enchanting and then be let down.

you react

Quickly and with frightening intelligence. You act with the speed of light when picking up ideas. Your curiosity drives you on. There's nothing you don't want to know and there's really no way you want to close the door because something interesting might just happen if you do so. But you can become mega suspicious of his motives and puzzle over why he wants information from you. Then you can be chronically evasive, dodging out of one question by asking another, thinking that he wants something from you. Denial is easier than telling all, then he won't have control over your feelings, which are very alien to you. Be playfully evasive, but be careful you don't fall into the trap of mistrusting human nature because you're trying to conceal those very feelings you don't understand. Feelings aren't rational, but this kind of game can lead to lies and jest from both of you. If you have Venus in Taurus, Virgo, Capricorn, Pisces, Cancer or Scorpio it will be hard to balance the Moon in Gemini's emotional needs, which by their very placement rely on intellect and information, not feeling.

CANCER

venus in cancer

you hunt for

Emotional closeness. You need to be needed and you need to love. You're looking for a man who can mop up all those stray moods, those feelings which get lost in a day. What gives you most pleasure is to feel secure and you do find it difficult to commit yourself, simply because you loathe the idea of any kind of separation. That's why you need to feel that you own your man, so it's important that he's willing to feel as if he belongs to you. But you also have to dance away sometimes, so you hunt for a relationship where you can be lured and alluring, then loosen your feelings and depart and return again. So you'll act the good cook just to make sure he doesn't slip away, then neglect him so that you have to yearn for him and get close again. Then your tenderness is all.

what and who turns you on

Dynamic, mentally stimulating but passionate men. A man who blows hot and cold, but mostly hot. He must be as unpredictable sexually as he is emotionally. A lover with soul and a heart is preferable to a stick-in-the-mud. If he does want to be mothered then you'll hold him close, but he's got to have an independent side too. Money, possessions and homeliness turn you on, so make sure he agrees to share them with you. Sumptuous surroundings, unlimited affection and a cool approach keep you sane, and unpredictable love-making is essential for your happiness.

the way you love

Tenderly or ruthlessly. You can be the most loving, caring,
sensitive lover and if the mood takes you, you'll be the
unpredictable, light, effervescent romantic and then the deeply
emotional wild woman. Extremes of passion overwhelm you, but
the joy of genuinely caring and supporting another is how you
really make love an art. But you can bend the rules and become
overtly possessive if you don't get your way. Giving him space
gives you space. Then you can both flow with the rhythms and
changes within your relationship.

moon in cancer

you need

To feel very deeply. You're so sensitive to his moods and feelings
that you often feel wrecked by emotional overload, because
you've got your own to get in a panic about as well. It's important
that you have the freedom to care for him and a place and time
for love to work its magic. You're nurtured by knowing he has as
many feelings for you as you do for him. When you are insecure,
you can become overtly jealous for no reason. Then you need
space to retreat into your shell or hide in the kitchen. It's not easy
being so sensitive, so you often act all hard and defiant. But deep
down inside you're often hurting, worrying or feeling much more
than you care to admit to him, or even to yourself.

you react

Oh so sensitively. If he doesn't call you when he says, you'll
either have a sleepless night or pretend you don't care. You're
careful with your feelings and don't like them being invaded,
because you'd rather be looking after him, so you react

defensively or self-protectively. When you're intent on a spot of seduction, your instinct is to circumnavigate the globe if you have to. The more subtle and indirect the approach, the less likely you'll be rejected or humiliated. You're so vulnerable to his opinion and your own insecurity that you'll get manipulative and make him feel guilty if you don't get your own way.

If you have Venus in Gemini, Aries, Aquarius, Libra or Sagittarius, you might find it difficult to integrate your emotional clinginess with those more intellectual or self-centred values.

LEO

venus in leo

you hunt for

A luxurious relationship with connoisseurs of love, men who know how to give you all the sumptuous delights of the flesh, of romance and desire. Luxury and fame, glamour and glitz make you feel loved and the centre of attention. You seek out men who will make you feel number one and numb with admiration. You crave privileged treatment and the best possible arm to hang on to when in public. What makes you feel good is to be treated like a queen or a film star. You desire a relationship where you're centre-stage and adored. You're creative with your feminine mystique and seduce with passion and all the wiles of a wildcat.

what and who turns you on

Celebrities, compliments, being the star in the relationship show. Gladiators or men who will fight a duel for you if they have to. Strength and nobility. Impressive men who run up expense account lunches or buy you a new wardrobe without blinking an eye. Gold bath taps, loads of mirrors, champagne and four-poster beds. If he's got style, sophistication and panache you'll be totally loyal and true.

the way you love

Like silk sheets. Rustled and yummy, you adore your man with such passion that he just wants to fall into bed with you after one look of your eye. You'll shower him with little presents and huge cards every anniversary – for example, last week you went to the country on Sunday, so this Sunday becomes a special day to remember. If he acts as if you're invisible, you'll demand his attention, sulk or go into one of your haughty moods just to provoke him. You have to be the centre of his world and he has to be centre of yours. If you're not feeling as loved and cherished as you desire, you'll make every effort to express yourself and get what you want. Demanding though you are, you're also hugely creative about the way you love and can cook a gourmet meal or drive through hailstorms and lightning if you have to, just to prove your love for him.

moon in leo

you need

To be under the spotlight. You need to be in control of the relationship, so you often choose men who enjoy being dominated. Making all the decisions satisfies your craving for being *numero uno*, but it also often leads to you becoming like bitter chocolate rather than passion fruit, and blaming your man for being weak and senseless, when he just hasn't had a chance to get a word in. Intensely individual, you are nurtured by your image and you must look dramatic and act dramatically. This of course means you must be in a relationship with someone who is either good looking and God's gift to women (well, only a gift to you) or (preferably and) has lashings of success, glamour and money. If you're given the chance to shine independently, you'll offer devotion and dynamic loving. You hate to be taken for granted, so you'll never fall into the trap of remaining the soft pussy cat. After all, tigresses have more fun. And that way your individuality will remain intact.

you react

With style and panache. You love to be recognized as someone special, so you'll react as if you are famous, even if it's only for five minutes. Self-effacing you're not and you expect to be treated as though you have royal blood. Your dignity is important, so if he doesn't admire you and respect your need for special treatment, you'll walk away with your head held high. Later on you might cry your eyes out in the kitchen, get all theatrical and pretend you're in a Shakespearean tragedy. But then you wouldn't be you if you didn't make some kind of horribly dramatic crisis out of anything less than being 'simply the best'. If you have Venus in a sign like Pisces, Cancer, Scorpio or Taurus, then you'll probably win a few Oscars for your *comédies de la nuit*. Histrionics are never taboo with you.

VIRGO

venus in virgo

you hunt for

Communication. And the chance to fit all the pieces of the
puzzle of life together. You look for men who are witty and wise,
who give you the space to be yourself. Self-contained as you are,
you're searching for the subtle aspects of love, good taste,
understanding and someone who respects your knowledge and
your efficiency. Because you want to be skilled in your
relationship, you must find out everything about him before you
let him any closer than a hair's breadth. But you're also in search
of a sensual, earthy man, someone you can really get to know
intimately and who won't leave you after one night. It's not that
you're searching for a sex life filled with tinsel-town passion and
emotional strife, just a meeting of minds.

what and who turns you on

Beautiful health freaks and fitness fanatics. Fiery, irresponsible
jokers, gamblers and reckless rogues. Wild, dashing men who
seem to live life like kids, unstable romantics, musicians and
dreamers. You often get hooked into these kind of relationships
because these men represent all that *joie de vivre* that you won't
allow for yourself. You like sexually experienced men who can
talk all night if you want to discuss a new book. But ultimately
you choose the known, the safe, down-to-earth men. Reliability
seems in the end more of a buzz than unpredictability.

how you love

Discreetly yet sensuously. You want to mould your man into a shape that you know and feel safe with. You're not exactly fire and brimstone material, unless you have the Sun or Moon in Fire sign like Leo, Aries or Sagittarius, so romance for you is a gentle, serene sort of fling. There's no wild being in love with love and gazing longingly at the phone waiting for messages. It's all carefully planned. You'll make dates as though they were business lunches. In a safe, earthy style, you'll follow love's recipe to the letter. Romance is never a very comfortable sensation for you, simply because you mistrust anything which is uncontrollable or unexplainable. The unpredictability of falling in love is unnerving. 'Real' love takes time, it needs cooking like bread, it needs to be kneaded first. Your heart takes a long time to melt, but when you do love, you love for eternity.

moon in virgo

you need

To keep your emotions well hidden. Passion makes you nervous, so you fight against any unpredictable behaviour. You don't make a fuss about your feelings. Yes, they need sorting out, sifting and cultivating, but they have to be rationalized and orderly. Those more chaotic romantic whiffs of emotional tension make your blood run cold. Then you can appear very cool and emotionally invisible. Realism overrides feelings, so it takes you a long time to admit to having any. When you do, though, you'll really, seriously, mean it. Getting edgy and highly strung about your relationship is always your greatest fear, simply because you feel safest when you're intellectually working out life, rather than being worked by it. In other words, letting life be spontaneous can be a problem for you. So, emotions can definitely be a problem, because they are so unpredictable, so unclassifiable.

you react

In a charmingly cool and aloof manner. You don't like drama and theatrics, so you keep your wits about you. If he forgets to phone you, you won't blink an eyelid, simply because you're so realistic you'll think of all the possible reasons why he hasn't, rather than get in a complete tizz about it. Working out why he didn't phone becomes more fascinating than the actual phone call itself. The first time you meet someone, you'll notice every possible flaw and minute detail which you can use as ammunition at a later date if necessary. You react to his voice and listen for bad language, a slip of the tongue and whether he's got his mind straight. Is his tie crooked, what colour are his socks and do they go with his shoes? Noticing those details means if he betrays you at any moment in the relationship, out will come your razor-sharp tongue and you will get critical and sarcastic. If you have Venus in signs such as Aries, Leo or Sagittarius, you could find it difficult to balance your passionate streak with your cool moodiness. In other words, your instinct is to be overtly mistrustful and unwilling to fall further than your own feet. Eventually, when you've worked it all out in your head, you'll respond with total mind-blowing passion.

LIBRA

venus in libra

you hunt for

An ideal relationship. Beautiful men who may be very different, either culturally or age-wise, just because you have to bridge the gap and neutralize differences. It's essential that a man thinks as well as looks the part. He has to be able to agree with you, but also have a mind of his own, solid opinions and few emotional cracks. What you're truly seeking is the perfect relationship, because in your mind you've created an ideal of how it should be. You want the world to be a better place, free from discrimination, bias and intolerance. And love is the way you'll create it, for both of you. Romance is, of course, *de rigueur*. You're one of the most romantic idealists in the world. And socially your man must have good manners and impeccable taste. You desire the best relationship and the purest, most perfectly bliss-inducing love affair imaginable.

what and who turns you on

Charming, seductive men entice you, and you'll entice and charm back if he's got the right clothes, the right smile and is scrumptiously gorgeous. Romance is your ultimate buzz and things like your lipstick, your nail polish and your perfume are all ultra-important accessories that you drool over. Knights in expensive cars or knights on horseback, it doesn't matter as long as your man lives up to your idea of utter dreaminess. The art of seduction itself is one of your greatest turn-ons. Frequent conversations about your relationship and discussing your feelings in a rational way keep you sane. You adore men who don't throw plates but throw you over their shoulder for a night of passionate romantic sex.

how you love

Harmoniously. You have to have peace and companionship at any cost. You often please your man more than you please yourself, just to keep everything in wonderful balance. Fairness keeps you sane and you adore discussing all kinds of fascinating things – as long as there are no arguments. You're capable of spending hours talking to him about your relationship and comparing his past love affairs, without blinking a jealous eye. Mind you, he might not be quite so keen to hear that kind of info from you.

moon in libra

you need

Peace at any cost. If there's a slightest whiff of anger, violence, slamming doors or, horror upon horror, emotional theatrics, you'll be out of the door in a flash. It takes ages for you to return your feelings to balance. It's almost as if you're a walking temperature gauge, because you respond to men with seductive gestures which aim to please, but then fall into the trap of having to retreat or rush off to the loo for a moment to compose yourself again. Sometimes you just have to stop and think to make sure your internal barometer is keeping the needle exactly halfway. It's not that you're hard to get close to, but you like space to breathe, a peaceful life and love that can be talked about as well as felt. Heavy emotional scenes put you in a panic; cosmetics, beauty, romance and a kind of wafting, gently seductive relationship put you in a pleasure dome.

you react

With pleasure. Compromising and placating your man if he's in a mood, or pleasing him and discussing how to make things better. Mind you, you don't always follow through your great ideas and schemes. Because peace is so important, if you can't woo and seduce him into being the sweetest, most romantic and gentlemanly soul you've ever met, you can go to the other extreme and become frigid and warlike if you're pushed too far. Every gesture he makes has to be perfect. If you turn up expecting a romantic dinner for two and find half the street has popped in for a glass of wine, this won't exactly meet your high standards or expectations. Idealism is fine, but sometimes you're so intent on perfection that no one and nothing can give you that sense of contentment. If you have Venus in Scorpio, Pisces or Cancer, you could find it hard to deal with your feelings and deny that you need emotional intensity in your love relationships or always attract utterly impossible men. Then you get that old wounded Libran pattern set up, falling for passionate, maddeningly arrogant, warring or competitive men who can't possibly satisfy your Moon's need for peace.

SCORPIO

venus in scorpio

you hunt for

An all-consuming relationship. 'For love or money' is your battle-cry. Many Venus in Scorpio women merge power and money with sexual desire. Then hidden qualities are revealed, both your own and his. It's an all-or-nothing, totally deep, dark and deadly kind of love you want. In fact, you crave emotional power struggles, erotic bliss and intense unbroken eye contact. The kind of pleasure you're seeking is dangerous and wilful. Secrets and sexual taboos are what you're hunting in a man. And through this kind of deeply mysterious relationship, you want to be possessed and to possess. It's a kind of ownership, menacing and unmentionable. Anything dark and witchy is deliciously seductive, as is forbidden or censored love. Torrid affairs don't scare you, nor do magical trips into the sexual underworld. It's all bittersweet moments, tangled sheets or love in the back row of the cinema while you're watching a horror film.

what and who turns you on

Men who'd die for you. Serious money and seriously rich hustlers and rogues – who are respectful of your own secret hoard. Emotionally honest but powerfully compelling men. Magnetic, mysterious enigmatic encounters. Kissing in the dark. Sex.

the way you love

Powerfully. Nothing will stop you when you fall in love. It has to be the most devouring and intense passion you've ever experienced. Somehow you have to transform your life and bury yourself in sexual euphoria. It's not that you're ruthless, more that you need to be in control, totally, of every experience and to live every moment with drama. Love moves you to court danger, steal other people's husbands, have sex in taboo places like churchyards or be fanatically possessive and jealous. You'll push a relationship to the hilt – just to see if you can win him back or hold him with your erotic, seething sensuality.

moon in scorpio

You need

To know him deeply, madly and thoroughly before you give much away about yourself. So you'll duck and dive and probe every pore of his skin until you believe you can let him close to you. Not that he'll actually ever understand your own depths. If he does, then he's probably got a Scorpio planet somewhere himself. When you finally admit he's got enough soul, class and style, you have to be needed more than you need him. Jealousy and mistrust go hand in hand, and you can't stop it. If he keeps arriving at your place with excuses about being late, you'll check his collar for lipstick, his back for another woman's scratches, his wallet for restaurant receipts and his mobile for unknown numbers. But on the other hand you're fiercely individual and can resort to double standards because you're so strong-willed and vulnerable.

you react

Mysteriously or wilfully. You can become so obsessed about seeing through all his weaknesses and strengths or the events and experiences you share together that you become dangerously close to destroying the mystery and energy of the relationship. But then again, that's often an unconscious way of transforming yourself. To be in a relationship means that at some stage you may have to free yourself from that very bond. Tangled webs are strong recurring patterns in Scorpio Moon relationships. Intimacy must be a shared experience, so that you can put your feelers out and probe the secret recesses of his thoughts and moods. You penetrate those places quickly and professionally, as only a secret agent of love could. When you first set eyes on him, you'll respond invisibly, becoming veiled in a misty enigmatic vapour. You'll avert your gaze and glaze his eyes with desire.

It's an instinctive, animal, sexy reaction, but utterly powerful and utterly mesmerizing.

If you have planets in Gemini, Aquarius or Libra, you may find it difficult to deal with your own deeply emotional nature and will attract men who represent these qualities or accuse your lover of jealousy, possessiveness and emotional manipulation.

SAGITTARIUS

venus in sagittarius

you hunt for

Romantic fantasy. Men who can turn you on instantly, passionately. Men with a knack for sexy, brief but romantic encounters. You dream love, desire sex and think passion. You seek out someone who will spice up your life and give you endless opportunities for adventure. Wild rovers who are always on the move are instant attractions, because they never tie you down. Drama and excitement, dazzle and glamour lure you into all kinds of spontaneous brief relationships. But you're really hunting an ideal, a vision of something which will liberate you from the reality of being an ordinary human, feminine soul with the imagination and fire of a she-dragon. You're restless for the kind of love experiences that mean you're right there where the action is. And being in love gives you hope, optimism and a wild streak. Being out of love gives you the desire to be in it again.

what and who turns you on

Hilarious men, gamblers, philosophers or explorers, preferably all rolled into one. The ultimate sexual experience. Seducing another woman's man. Strangers, foreign countries and wide open spaces. Climbing mountains or being where the rich, the famous and the successful are. Spontaneous sex. Staring at the stars from a sleeping bag, with him beside you of course. Being in love.

how you love

Passionately. Everything has to be now, not later. You're impatient for more of everything and hungry for excitement. Thrills and spills keep you craving more, routines are an instant turn-off. You're spontaneous – likely to pitch up at his office and drag him out to an utterly wild afternoon of adventure and sex. The more exotic the relationship, the longer it will last. Talk all night across the pillow and you'll still be on the mobile or the e-mail at least ten times a day, no matter whether he's married, in a meeting or the world's most eligible bachelor. Doing things your way gives you pleasure and you'll never be possessed or contained. Your belief in any relationship is so infectious you're like a love virus. If he catches it, it's not fatal, it will just mean he's hooked. For as long as you want him to be, of course.

moon in sagittarius

you need

To have honesty and the freedom to be yourself. You thrive on adventure and the imagination. Your feelings are either burning like a forest fire or channelled into activity and sport or taking risks with the unknown and strangers. You don't enjoy deep discussions about your feelings or emotional scenes, you just want fun, spontaneity and wit. Comical behaviour makes your skin tingle, outspokenness and a risk-taking attitude keep you craving more. You live for the future and believe only in future possibilities. The past is not worth considering – you'd rather talk about tomorrow and what you're going to do together than sink into sentimental goo about what you did yesterday. You need communication and you thrive on spirit, energy and vitality. You have to feel you're alive and kicking or at least kick him out of bed when you're ready to pack your bag at a moment's notice. Sensational and conversational, it's images, visions, ideals and words which make you feel nurtured.

you react

Suddenly and impetuously – like a wild horse. If he makes a move towards you first, you'll leap into seductive, tactless and even hilarious action. What you do best is make light of everything, from his flirting technique and his choice of underwear to sex itself. What you do worst is promise the Earth. When he comes round with a bouquet of roses and a reminder that he's booked that flight to Madagascar, as you agreed last week, oh well, you've changed your mind, simply because you made all those wild promises and commitments in the heat of enthusiasm for being in love and there's no way you can commit yourself now. With you there are no half-measures. You either respond with all the feminine wiles you can think of or take the initiative and lead the way. Your restlessness means you want to move on to the next square in the game of relationship faster than anyone else, except an Aries. If you have any planets in Aries, Leo or Sagittarius, it will be almost impossible to keep up with your fiery energy. If he gets all sloppy and sentimental, you'll be on the first bus out of town. If you have planets in Taurus, Virgo or Capricorn, you might find your need for

personal freedom conflicts with your more down-to-earth qualities
and the reality of love doesn't live up to your idealistic needs.

CAPRICORN

venus in capricorn

you hunt for

Serious love and mutual respect. Style, taste, above all class and
sophistication. A relationship that 'works'. Traditional values
and conventional men are of value to you. Maturity is *de rigueur*.
Classic, socially correct men with professions and temperaments
to match will certainly keep you interested longer than many
others. You're ambitious in love, so you'll hunt out the best man.
If it takes you ten years to capture his heart, you have the
patience, the seductive wiles, the sensual arts, the perfume and
the expense account to do so. Status and success walk together
for you, so you seek those men who can make you feel as if
you're the power behind their throne, as well as your own.
Material richness and rich sensuality are lures, and the bait is
often that which could make you an utterly, madly and deeply
successful person in your own right. You seek a man who is as
wise as you are glamorous. But it's not a supermodel glamour, it's
a steely spine, ice-chilling cool allure, mingled with worldly
wise wisdom.

what and who turns you on

Success. Business lunches, gold-diggers or gold brokers.
Professional men who don't have a problem with ambitious

women. To be loved for your discipline and black humour.
Wisdom. Falling into his arms in a scented warm bath. Sensual
luxury, sexual indulgence. Lingerie to die for.

how you love

In an organized way. It takes time, loads of it, for you to trust
anyone. Once you've matured your feelings, like a claret, and
developed your trust, you're delectable, smooth, sophisticated
and very ambitious about your relationship. No one-night stands,
just seriously powerful companionship. You want to improve
your man's life and when you fall in love it's with the best part of
him, the part which has been sculpted into what makes him
genuinely himself. Whatever he's a master or professional at,
that's the bit you love and that's the bit you'll want to develop.
Pragmatism suits you, idealism doesn't, but you'll endure the
rough with the smooth, dare I say it, in a whirl of death-do-us-
part diva-like commitment. But you can become fanatical and if
he doesn't develop that 'real' side of himself you spotted when
you first met, the byte you think will make him famous, rich or
successful, then you'll try to control him in other ways.

moon in capricorn

you need

Emotional honesty. But you tend to surround yourself with an air
of cool, controlled self-effacement. You're guarded, watchful and
let few people close. Sometimes you'll judge someone before you
realize what you're doing, because you can't bear anyone else
having any kind of power over your feelings. Actually, you don't
like emotional outbursts from anyone, let alone your lover. You
often feel vulnerable and would rather face a night alone in
Cinderella style than be a socialite and face everyone's critical

envy of your classic but perfectly stunning new dress. Avoiding relationships can be easier than facing it, warts and all. But isolating yourself from being hurt means you often get hurt. The reality of feeling feels uncomfortable, simply because deep down you're incredibly sensitive and don't actually trust all that chaotic, childlike energy in yourself that you find so attractive in men. You have the power to guide and manipulate, but you also have the greatest gift of all, a gut survival instinct which would put even a lioness to shame.

you react

By controlling those impulsive words or swarms of feelings that rise out of nowhere. You want to work it all out first, not intellectually, but realistically. What are the pros and cons of having a date with X, is there something to be gained by this relationship, how rich is he, what are his bank statements like, what can be improved about him, in fact, is there anything there to be worked on or controlled or gained at all? Like a debutante at a ball, if it's worth bringing out, then you'll do it beautifully. If it's ugly, unkempt, pointless and too animal, then you'll look elsewhere. If you're not in control of the relationship in one way or another, or if the meat and gristle doesn't have any juice, then you'll turn up your nose or go into a sulk. Either way, it's your integrity that's at stake and ultimately your feelings. If you have planets in Aries, Leo or Sagittarius, you may find it hard dealing with this very basic bottom-line earthy survival line. Fiery planets resist being bottled and contained and you might also find you are attracted to fiery, youthful visionaries, but are always getting burnt, because what you really need is a deeply trusting, earthy relationship.

AQUARIUS

venus in aquarius

you hunt for

Originality. A different, eccentric or unusual relationship, or one which gets other people talking or shocked. You often seek out a man radically different from you, from another culture, or with unusual work, or impossible dreams. Idealistic men inspire you and you're drawn to the unattainable, the workaholic or the priest. You quickly fall in love with what's interesting him. What are the ideas or ideals that fascinate him and what makes him tick? Once you have discovered everything about him, have analysed every intimate detail of his psychology and intellect (you're not so interested in his feelings, he can keep those hush-hush), you fear you'll get instantly bored, because you can't bear relationships to become routine. Men who can't deal with astute, clever women should simply stay away from you.

what and who turns you on

Mysterious, unusual or radically brilliant men. Cool customers, intellectuals and fashion-conscious rogues. Designers, hi-tech whizz kids and men who are willing to choose weird food or try a different menu or restaurant every time you go out to eat. Being surprised in bed and surprising him in bed.

how you love

From a distance. Detachment suits you, emotional commitment
brings you out in spots. If your man can't keep part of himself
detached, then you feel trapped. You're seeking a friend first,
lover second and a companion for life after that. If he's
independent and can talk about the universe and everything in it
with rational and objective perception, then maybe, just maybe,
you'll form what you would call a bond. Any words like
'marriage', 'my woman', 'us', 'my partner' or those more gooey
sickly sentiments are like iced buns, better reserved for a vicar's
tea-party. But then don't you just love the idea of shocking a few
parochial villagers or family too?

moon in aquarius

you need

Mental intelligence and a man who has the ability to talk
rationally about everything under the sun. If he's not bright and
breezy, you can become hypocritical and judgemental. So the
more open, independent and honest he is, the more you'll enjoy
having him around. You're best when you're surrounded by social
anonymity, worst when you're faced with an emotional outburst.
Avoid scenes like the plague or you'll become resentful and bitter.
What makes you feel good is to analyse and intellectualize your
feelings. But you're also a truth-addict and sometimes you'll say
exactly what you feel, without caring how your man reacts or
what effect you might have on him. Romantic escapades don't
give you dream-filled nights – more like sleepless nights. Even
though you're a secret romance-freak beneath that cool exterior,
what you'd rather do is concentrate on things of the mind, like
selflessness and perfection. And why he has to eat sausages for
breakfast, when you bought organic yoghurt.

you react

Wickedly. You always want to do exactly what is *not* expected of you. The unpredictable is far more interesting than the norm. But you expect others to conform to your expectations and this sometimes puts you in a difficult spot. If others don't agree, then you'll rant and rave about truth, and life, and then overreact. You want to reform his ideas, his opinions and his way of cutting his toast or shaving his face. So you react by being stubborn or just pulling down the shutters and being unreasonable. When you're approached for the first time you'll be eccentric, amusing, rational and fair. Then you'll analyse why he's so interesting and start to take control of the relationship if you can. Surprise him with tactics he doesn't anticipate and you'll quickly be free of any emotional come-backs. If you have planets in signs like Scorpio, Cancer or Pisces, you might find it difficult to integrate your Moon's needs with your more emotional drives and desires.

PISCES

venus in pisces

you hunt for

Romance. Fantasy and dreams fill your mind, so you're looking for knights in shining armour, sensitive souls, vagabonds, artists and gypsies. You seek the perfectly divine union where love flows with the music and you can adapt to its drifting quality. Inspirational poets, musicians, photographers and designers take your breath away. Your man has to have style and be as idealistic and as compassionate as you. Sometimes you'll go to the other

extreme and hunt out someone dangerously wicked, married to
another woman or simply too hot to handle. Anything deeply
mysterious is alluring – feelings which can't be named or
imagination that has no bounds where love is concerned. The
more elusive he is, the more elusive you'll be. A kind of chaotic,
spiritual existence with one dream man is a lot to desire, but you
fall into love often – and break your own heart often because you
see the dream in virtually any man you meet. You cast an
illusion over him and a spell over yourself. The price you pay is
sacrificing love, surrendering and giving in, or being led astray
by something that is idealistic and perfectly romantic only on the
surface.

what and who turns you on

Romantic films, animals, dreams and poetry. Little cards or
bunches of roses on the doorstep. Unexpected phone calls, sexy
underwear and his body in the shower. Songs which remind you
of the first date. The first date repeated over and over again.
Artists, scoundrels. Fiery, shining, shockingly dangerous men.
Being a saviour, or being a victim so you can escape and return,
then surf a new romantic wave.

the way you love

Enigmatically. There is something elusive and fluid about the
way you enter someone's arms and then leave again. You're
technically always faithful, but because you're so seductive and
seducable, you often develop superficial relationships and
imagine all kinds of other romances, other knights on horseback.
You're attracted first by looks, second by desire and third by
what a man has to offer you. At best you write love songs,
snuggle up together in front of log fires and dream of summer
nights. At worst you wriggle out of dates and are vague about

your feelings, or your moods keep changing with his. When
you're in love you feel something has to be avoided, and that's
usually speaking the truth, simply because you don't really know
what the truth is. You're so sensitive to your partner's moods and
whims that you become him, rather than stay yourself. Dreams
are more important to you than reality. So promising to be there
at eight one day won't always fall in line with your plans the
next. Perhaps yesterday was just a fantasy after all. You're so
romantic that films, music, poetry and lengthy phone calls keep
your dream world intact.

moon in pisces

you need

Protecting and rescuing. Your laser-sharp perception makes you
pick up all his moods and feelings, and caring about him is more
important than caring about yourself. In fact, you live in a kind
of vacuum of everyone else's needs and memories. So it's hard
for you to know whether you really feel things yourself or
whether it's someone else's thoughts and feelings you're picking
up. Being intuitive is a blessing in disguise. You can tune in to
what your lover's thinking, but you have a problem really
knowing what it is that you want yourself. Melt a few barriers
when you first meet if you can, but be careful you don't get into
the habit of always trying to break down the emotional
boundaries between you. You endlessly want to support him, but
at the same time to be cherished and adored. So you can sacrifice
all kinds of daily routines or important commitments or
arrangements for his happiness. And it can get all very unnerving
when being too compassionate means you get too soft and
understanding.

you react

By being charming and seductive. You're always ready to play all
kinds of games with your own feelings and you'll often just
escape out of the room to avoid any confrontation or painful
conversations. You defend yourself by physically or
psychologically disappearing. If he leaves his socks on the
radiator all night, you'll probably drive to the coast alone to
watch the stars, rather than face them in the morning. But you
thrive on fantasy and romance, so if he appears unexpectedly in
your office with a bunch of roses, you'll fall into a kind of poetic
trance. When he first gazes at you across a crowded room, you'll
imagine all kinds of possible scenarios. The more fantastic and
romanticized, the more likely you are to fall in love and bed him
the same night. But the reality of relationships gives you hell and
headaches. He must be able to give you as much as you give him,
and that's often a difficult and dangerous balance to strike.

part

2

him

chemistry

lesson

Now it's time to look at him. The first thing you see when you meet him will probably be his Rising sign. Remember, the Rising sign is how we appear to others and also how we unconsciously want to be seen. We often convey the qualities of our Rising sign without being aware we're doing so. So, check out his Rising sign (see pages 303–60), but remember to look up his planet signs, too, to get a balanced view of his character. You might discover he's living out only certain bytes of his personality. But his Rising sign is the façade or doorway behind which you'll find all the other parts of him.

ARIES RISING

his image

excited ★ dynamic ★ inspiring

Excited, dynamic, inspiring. He's the god of courage and the maestro of self-will. When he wants something, he'll get it, and if it's your attention or your body, he'll move in directly without a thought for anyone other than himself. If you're already hooked up with someone else, he might just even miss that particular bit of reality and assume you'll be immediately available for him anyway. He lives for chances, opportunities and future possibilities. There's a sort of fanaticism abut everything he does or says, but it's not power-motivated, just self-driven. If he doesn't seem to listen to what you're saying, it's because he's absent-minded anyway. He acts naturally and doesn't actually need anyone else on his side. But he loves with passion, frankness and honesty. Action is better for him than comatose languor, so you might find him always jumping up at dawn to go for that run or make love to you, whichever enters his head first. He has to get up and go, and he also likes to wind you up and generate a little steam with a few minor crises, just to get life moving fast and forward.

his charisma

stirring ★ active ★ passionate

Stirring, active and passionate. He'll want to sweep you off your feet, literally. Alternatively, you can't go wrong if you throw yourself straight into his arms. But then be prepared to be a bit of a fox and let him chase you. Whatever you do, be ready for his battle cries and war cries or just his surges of enthusiasm for everything and anything. They all sound very alarming and fanatical, but he's in need of a challenge. If he seems quieter than this, then you've met a mental warrior. He'll be thinking aggressively, even if he isn't talking about it or putting it all into practice. Anything sloppy, slow or complicated just isn't in his nature. When he says he wants sex, or love, or comforting, he means it. But he doesn't believe in total domination. If you put up a fight he'll resist like the cavalier he is, but he'll probably enjoy the conflict, smashing a few plates and driving you crazy just because he thrives on an action-packed relationship.

he falls for

Women he can't have because they're already hitched or they just
don't fancy him. Runaways, women he has to hunt for days or
weeks. If you're cool, beautiful and talented you've got a head
start on anyone else. He's often besotted with the opposite sign to
his Rising sign, which is Libra. He is drawn to that very
unselfish, romantic, perfect style of loving that is so civilized and
so very different from his own sometimes clumsy attempts at
playing the mating game. But if you are attracted to this man,
remember to have your own interests and your own life. He
searches for adventure and physical action, but he's often lured
by earthy, materialistic women who seem to have the power to
put his crusading fantasies and dreams into reality. That's why
he often falls fatally in love with the down-to-earth
determination of women with planets in Virgo, Capricorn and
Taurus. They smell of the real world he imagines he wants for
himself. If he has planets in these signs, then such a committed
relationship might work, but if he has Fire planets (in Leo, Sag
or Aries), then he might come to regret the chase.

he attracts

Very feminine women, who drool over his hunky macho image,
and women who very much depend on a knight in shining
armour to protect them and woo them. If you have the Sun or
Moon in Aries, then you'll be more likely to understand his need
for change and his action-packed desire for challenges every
minute. Women with planets in Leo or Sagittarius will get on
splendidly with him on a physical level, but check out his
planets to make sure he's got a firing range to match. Romantic
dreamers should get along well with him on the surface, but too
much femininity will turn him into a repressed bully. That's why
the Earth signs, Virgo, Taurus and Capricorn, often fall head over

heels for his Don Juan passion, but can't stop themselves from letting their routine realism spoil the romantic party. If you have Mars or the Sun in Aries you'll have an instant physical attraction, but you could end up having more fights than love bites.

TAURUS RISING

his image

swayed by beauty

He's swayed by beauty, is physically sensual and has romantic pragmatism. All these qualities are of course virtues, but they're also difficult to deal with if other planets conflict with this worldly outlook on life. He's easily seduced, because he wants to be lured by the physical, and he wants to have sex often, because it's simply in his nature to indulge in sensual pleasure. Lastly, he treats romance as reality, so what's in front of his eyes is to be loved with horrifying simplicity or married instantly so everything becomes a fairy-tale happy-ever-after ending. He can appear lazy at making the first move. But he'll also sit all night in a bar waiting for you to make it for him. After all, he's not going to budge, or move his stool, when he knows you'll do it. With all that need for self-satisfaction he's still swayed by those things which won't make him quite so happy, like gambling, or daringly outrageous women. He longs for fire in himself and in his relationships, but he also likes to sit in front of it beside his woman with his feet up. He can be possessive, but he's also the strong silent type. Check out his planets to see whether he's genuinely able to be a connoisseur of art, *amour* and happiness. If he has planets in Taurus, Virgo or Capricorn, he probably is.

his charisma

Sensual, physically good-looking, unruffled. There's a certain vanity about him. He's usually elegantly dressed or at least sure of what is good taste and what isn't. Simplicity is important to him, whether it's a simple solution to where you go for dinner or a simple back scrub while he's contemplating his next financial coup. Money is as important to him as love. And the former can buy the latter. He exudes a kind of worldly-wise set of values and what he believes in is founded on what he has in his bank account. He usually knows that to the last penny. But he also derives pleasure from his senses. Music soothes him, poetry usually leaves him cold, but nature stuns him into silent awe. Impress him with your knowledge of the local landscape or where the best nature trails are and you'll be off to the mountains together like a couple of anoraks. And on a mountaintop you'll discover his tenderness, his sexual prowess and his love.

he falls for

Stunningly beautiful women or women with taste, style and sophistication. But he often finds himself drawn to intense mysterious *femmes fatales*, secretive witchy types or sexy damsels in distress. The sign opposite his Rising sign is Scorpio and you often find him besotted by the dark, powerful undercurrents of a Scorpio woman's sexuality. But both are utterly stubborn and making compromises won't be easy unless he has more pliable signs (Virgo, Sagittarius or Libra) behind that fixed façade. Fiery, independent career girls also fascinate him, because they're usually successful and could just be rich. Yes, he does fall in love with money, because he feels it's his destiny to make it, love it or possess it somehow. And why not? The more outrageously passionate, dynamic and restless you are, the more he's liable to fall at your feet and offer you marriage and future bliss – which is, of course, a very fatal attraction for both of you. You want independence and he wants togetherness, and that poses a few problems, unless he has planets in Fire signs or you have some down-to-earth planets to complement his.

he attracts

Extremes of adoring women, from the realistic Virgo, Taurus or Capricorn to the fiery Aries and Leo. If you have the Sun or Moon in Taurus and his planets complement your Rising sign then you could be on to a very long-term relationship. If he's got some planets in Aries, Leo or Sagittarius and you're a fiery independent type, then you might have a longer term relationship than you imagine. The problem with his realistic, practical image of the world is that it can suffocate your dreams and imagination. But of course he's undoubtedly attractive because he exudes mega doses of all those qualities you wish you had yourself. If you have Mars in Taurus, you'll find him physically attractive, but you might end up being as stubborn and uncompromising as he is, and then the conflicts will begin. No movement creates a stagnant relationship.

GEMINI RISING

his image

quick-witted ⋅ flirtatious

Quick-witted, flirtatious and adorable. This man's learnt how to act all kinds of roles to get exactly what he wants. He's a seducer, but he doesn't seduce to gain power just for fun. Like any persuasion, it's a kind of talent that most other men loathe or fear because what is so naïvely charming isn't to be trusted. Women find his company irresistible. He's usually the one who prattles on all night at the bar, while on the phone to his girlfriend at the same time and to his sister in the States. If you catch him without words in his mouth, then he's probably got a load of planets in heavy signs, like Mercury in Scorpio or Saturn in Sagittarius. He appears to be loaded with ideas, live in his head and have little time for emotions. What was that you said? Does he feel like going to a restaurant? No, he 'thinks' it would be a great idea to go. If you ever spend the night with him, he'll probably talk in his sleep and ask you all kinds of questions that are totally irrelevant. He does have a heart, particularly if he's got planets in signs like Taurus, Cancer, Scorpio or Pisces, but he covers it all up so well that at times you wonder if he's a good con-man or just a born-again Houdini. Check out his other planets to make sure he really is the friendly, innocent, fun-loving rogue that he seems.

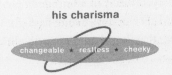

his charisma

changeable ★ restless ★ cheeky

Changeable, restless and downright cheeky. His lively wit and super-speed physical energy, capped by an often very youthful appearance, make him seem like Peter Pan crossed with Romeo. In fact, he's also extremely romantic behind that rational fascination for puns, wit, humour and communication. But he tends to avoid long intense rambling discussions about love and sloppy things. He'd rather slog it down to the coast and spend the day talking on the beach about the latest news, or just take you out to dinner at short notice and talk about the news again.

Well, he does get excited by short-term and often short-lived information. He radiates a kind of genie-like 'now you see him now you don't' aura. Because in fact he's quite devious. If he's in your bed fast, he'll also be out of it at the speed of light in the morning. Deep involvement is difficult for him, unless he has planets in more solid signs, like Taurus, Capricorn or Virgo.

he falls for

Feminine women, gentle but fascinating communicators, travellers, dynamic funny women. He's lured by women who do their own thing, are successful or simply move as fast and as hilariously as he does. The sign opposite his Rising sign is Sagittarius, so he'll be head over heels in love with women who convey an extrovert, freedom-loving persona. Seductive on the surface, he flirts naturally with most women, but he's drawn to those who have volatile hearts, crazy souls and a love for the biggest and widest experiences in life. Strangers in town are compelling and so are foreign women who have travelled the world. But he's also drawn to very feminine, gentle sensitive types and if you're one of these, beware. Unless he has an array of more emotional planets cached away, then he could get bored with long-haul discussions about your feelings, rather than long-haul flights of fantasy.

he attracts

Witty, articulate women with brains, a rational approach and a cool head. If you have the Sun or Moon in Gemini, this could be a very long-lasting relationship, especially if his Sun, Moon or Venus complement your own Rising sign. Watery, sensitive types are also drawn to him, because he appears so level-headed, rational and unfeeling. But that's not exactly true (though it depends on his other planetary placements as well), for the problem with Gemini rising is that he hides his feelings, not only from you, but also from himself. If you're emotionally telepathic then you'll see through this rather fragile façade of objectivity. But he's horrified at talking about anything less banal than the weather. Great if you're in love and understand him totally. But fatal if you're looking for a caring, tender heart. If you have Mars in Gemini you'll probably have an instant physical buzz, but loathe his changeable mind and his moodiness.

CANCER RISING

his image

changeable ★ self-protective

Changeable, self-protective, sensitive to his surroundings. This is one of the hardest masks to wear, because in a way he has to keep changing the costume to keep himself camouflaged. He's cool and unapproachable to begin with, but once you realize that all those moods are just different ways of expressing his inconsistent appearance, then you can learn to appreciate the ambivalence he must maintain as a defence. Beneath the shifting feelings there are depths untold. He may seem as if he needs a home, a family or a clan, but, depending on other planets, he can be far more independent-minded than he appears. He plays different roles in different social occasions. So if you meet him in a bar, he may be warm, funny and radical. But then on your first date he's moody, emotional and jumpy. Then, when you think you really know him well, he gets passionate about politics or ecstatic about travelling to Kathmandu. Sometimes he's withdrawn and needs space, and you really can't understand what that's all about. Then a few days later he's all closeness, comfort and affection. This is a hard outer persona to live with, but if you can understand it's not easy to be as changeable as the tides, as rhythmical as the moon, then you'll probably remain his lover and his mother for life.

his charisma

petulant ★ secretive ★ gentle

Petulant, secretive, gentle. The extremes of Cancer rising show up most when he's put on the spot about your relationship. In some ways he wants to be there, sorting out which restaurant to go to, organizing your phone so that you speak always to him first and being genuinely caring about you and your life. But he's also a secret animal and needs to shield his vulnerable side beneath that rather restless exterior. So what you see isn't always what you get. This is a complex sign and it demands total understanding and total commitment. It's also totally unpredictable, so don't expect to know his routine and do give him a surprise kiss when he comes out of the office. He's usually intuitive enough to avoid any kind of public scene, simply because he feels so vulnerable in the face of other people's opinions. Exposing himself to anything he doesn't trust is fatal. But when he loves, he truly loves – masks, camouflages and hard shells aside. Check out his other planets to see whether he is masking a heart of pure gold (planets in Fire and other Water signs) or is simply going to play the martyred lover, which he is capable of doing to defend a more fragile identity.

he falls for

Successful, ambitious career women or socialites. He's compelled by his opposite sign, Capricorn, and can fall desperately in love with strong, serious women who know where they're going and why. It's also possible he'll end up playing

house-maker, wine-maker or chef, while his partner plays the
bread-winning role. If you're one of these women, take care he
doesn't treat you as a mother figure over and above anything else.
This is, when he's not creatively using his sensitive side and
falling for someone to look after him. Then he'll be drawn to
women who unconsciously allow him to indulge in neediness
rather than happiness. He also falls in love with airy, flirtatious
women, like Geminis, Librans and Aquarians. The very different
quality exuded through Air is one of rational, immediate and
light-hearted coolness. Here he feels safe playing all kinds of
roles without his shell being penetrated. After all, he's actually
very cautious, sensitive and sincere.

he attracts

Women who want to mother him. Caring, sensitive souls, strong,
powerful women and those who love his changeable nature. If
you have the Moon or Sun in Cancer, you could develop a long-
term and successful relationship, especially if his planets
complement your Rising sign too. If you have Mars in Cancer,
you'll probably develop an instant physical attraction to one
another, but you might find you're always trying to test each
other's moods. It may become a battleground of feeling, rather
than a bed of earthy delights. If you have planets in Gemini,
Libra and Aquarius you might find his subtle façade very
challenging. If you have planets in other Water signs, however,
like Scorpio or Pisces, there's a chance you can develop a
wonderful rapport.

LEO RISING

his image

the king of kings ⋆ egotistical

The king of kings – egotistical, straight to the point and a downright show-off. He'll put up a front just to impress you, whether it's wearing the best clothes or the most expensive watch, or simply stylish acting. He must have an audience and be loved for who he is. Majestic, but totally self-centred, he's not going to wait around to woo you. What he wants, he generally gets, and if there's a competitor in the room, then so much more exciting the challenge. It's all crashing contests, the mirror angled just right to make sure he's still looking good and a show-stopping style that outclasses everyone else. 'You're so vain' is a good hook-line for this man's image. He knows it and doesn't much care about it either. He's temperamental, fiery and passionate about life and love. So be warned. He won't be betrayed and he hates time-wasters. If his attention is focused on you, then you'd better be as loyal and as stylish as he is. Love, to him, is a word without inhibitions. It's magical, romantic and mythical. So check out his planets to discover whether he's as loyal and true as he wants you to be.

his charisma

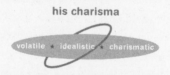

volatile ⋆ idealistic ⋆ charismatic

Volatile, idealistic, very charismatic and not for the faint-hearted. You know he's there because his breath is like dragon-fire and his ideology is so strong he'll move the Earth for you, if not the

pretty bartender from your sight. He's bold, spectacular and likes
to be generous. It's a kind of exotic aura – reds and purples like
royal blood oozing through his pores. Being in love is essential
for his happiness, as it is for all the Fire signs. And of course he
makes the most of his sexiness and his glamorous façade. There's
almost a Napoleonic drama about the way he moves, the way he
speaks and the way he loves to entertain. You can't go to a party
with him unless you're like a sparkling diamond on his arm. But
he can bully you into doing, thinking and saying what he wants,
because if he doesn't trample on a few hearts, then just maybe
someone will trample on his.

he falls for

Independent, glamorous or unusual women. Artists, chic, rich
and stylish career executives. Someone with prestige or fashion
on their mind. Knowledge fascinates him because he usually
believes he knows best. That's why he's often fatally attracted to
his opposite sign, Aquarius, who also has knowledge at her
fingertips and in her head. But the difference between the two is
that she has the mind for knowledge, where he just has the desire
to know everything because he has to be number one. The power
behind a Leonine throne is often an Aquarian woman, but Leo
rising also falls in love with women who are dizzily beautiful or
very feminine sophisticates. Then, of course, he has someone to
show off. He'll also be turned on by women with planets in Leo,
Sagittarius or Aries. Sharing his motivation and fiery visions,
they convey all that vivid imagination and those creatively wild
ideas that he desires and that he often doesn't realize, unless he's
very, very aware, are within himself. Check out his planets to see
whether he's searching for love because he wants to be the centre
of attention or because he believes in it.

he attracts

Women who love the idea of being in love rather than seeing the reality before them. Leo rising makes love affairs magical, so romantic idealists often fall for him, especially those with planets in Libra or Pisces. If you have the Sun or Moon in Leo there's a good chance of a successful long-term relationship, especially if he has planets to complement your Rising sign too. If you have Mars in Leo you'll be instantly attracted to him physically. But you'll both want to be the star of the show and that can mean a mega conflict of self-interest. Earthier women will collapse in heaps around his feet. But that wild, absent-minded lover of life clashes with the user-friendly relationships that those with planets in Taurus, Virgo or Capricorn desire. So take care, unless he's got a suitable array of Earth planets to ground all that fire and brimstone.

VIRGO RISING

his image

reasonable ⋆ communicative

Reasonable, communicative, cool and self-contained. If you want parties every night and sex every morning, this is not your man. He can be infuriatingly organized about love, unless he has more fiery planets to give him a wild, unpredictable side. He's likely to have made the coffee in a percolator and ground the beans before even thinking of kissing you. Work is important to him and love always comes second. But he's generous and can solve all kinds of trivial and major problems without turning it all into a crisis. He is highly strung and worried about his body, diet conscious, smoke aware and terribly obsessed with his muscles. But he's either down the gym every day or thinking about how to give up all those things which are bad for him. He needs some other basis for falling in love than just a sexual one. In fact he doesn't give the appearance of a man with passion on his mind, let alone in his loins. But check out his planets – that cool façade could belie a very sensual sexuality and a truly warm heart.

his charisma

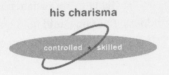

controlled · skilled

Emotionally controlled, socially skilled and intellectually discriminating, he's not exactly about to charge across the bar, fling you over his shoulder and cause a scene. Passion is his biggest fear and any kind of gambling, whether with money or love, is an unknown factor and therefore not just spooky, but utterly terrifying. He will eventually thaw, but it takes him longer than most other signs to look your way or come out with a chat-up line. Of course, when he does it will be the most worked-out line you've ever heard and will convey more than you could ever imagine. His voice resonates as if you were pouring champagne over velvet gloves. Slip him on your hands and you won't be disappointed. He needs someone to make him laugh and that means you have to be willing to accept that relationships are often difficult for him – unless, of course, he sinks into a 'work, sleep, work, sleep' routine with someone equally safe. But there is a wild side to him, it just takes a wild woman to find it and give it back to him. It's a bit of a gamble, but his spirit is always willing.

he falls for

Spontaneous, fiery extroverts, intuitive imaginative artists, poetic women and romantic souls. The unpredictable is scary, so he's often totally fascinated by women who are unreliable, crazy and irresponsible. But if he tries to mould you to fit his ideal image (check his Moon and Venus signs) and if you're Aries, Leo, Sagittarius or Pisces, you're going to feel suffocated. If he warms up and starts spitting fire, then he probably has some more volatile planet placements himself. He's usually attracted, quite fatally, to his opposite sign, Pisces. Both are ultra-sensitive signs, so if you're a Pisces you're likely to appreciate his earthy wit and wisdom, and his kindness. But you could both become so withdrawn, for different reasons, that you never communicate.

he attracts

Usually the other Earth signs, Taurus, Virgo and Capricorn. They see him as an intellectual realist with a dash of sensitivity and a great capacity for fluid thinking and practical planning. But he won't be your rock, unless he has planets in these signs too. However, if you have the Moon or the Sun in Virgo this could be the basis of a very successful long-term relationship, especially if his Moon or Sun complement your Rising sign too. Aries, Leo and Sagittarius might find some short-term excitement with him, especially if they have strong planets in Virgo. Strangely, Gemini women can either be turned right on by him or right off. There's a volatile tension here and often a fatal attraction for both. If you have Mars in Virgo you'll have an instant physical attraction, but you might begin to loathe him for being too pedantic and critical.

LIBRA RISING

his image

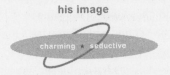

charming ★ seductive

Charming and seductive, he's the 'brute in the Armani suit'.
Always well-dressed at best, vain at worst, he seems to be
looking for someone to indulge in a kind of romantic fairyland,
but of course a very civilized, modern one. He wouldn't be seen
dead with anyone who didn't find him utterly enchanting and
fascinating. Although he's a sucker for a beautiful face, he's also
the most tactful, diplomatic and shrewd operator, so be careful if
you've only just met him. This is a man who wines and dines,
romanticizes and makes all those dreamy phone calls, but then
appears not to be able to commit himself a week later. That's
because he's always looking out for something better – the
perfect relationship, the ultimate romance. He's idealistic and
idyllic, but certainly not someone who wants emotional grenades
lobbed in his direction. No, this man seems to want a peaceful,
harmonious relationship. He appears rational, suave and
sophisticated, but, depending on the planets in his chart,
whether he can live up to this delightfully rational, pleasing
image is another matter.

his charisma

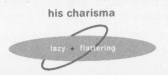

lazy ★ flattering

Lazy, flattering. With a voice and poise like vodka on ice, he can
woo you with a few words, a gesture or just a look. Often his eyes
say more than his body, because they're always shining and
smiling and radiating a sexiness you don't find naturally in many

men. He'll often agree with you, in fact so often that you
eventually wonder when he won't. But he's probably saying one
thing to you and another thing to someone else. He oozes
intellectual brain power and a highbrow taste for fashion. He'll
flatter, zoom in on your good points and forget to mention the
bad, simply because he's such a diplomat. He's genuinely
concerned with what's beautiful, but that means he also
enhances his own best features and hides his worst. Trusting
him seems easy, but don't. It's nice being with someone who's
so pleasant, but he may well be hiding a few beasts and rag-
and-bone emotions behind that idealistic, romantic façade.
Check the rest of his chart to find out.

he falls for

Dangerously assertive women with strong wills and spicy
conversation. The more demonstrative, demanding and
passionate the woman, the more charming and enchanting or
downright compliant he'll be. He falls quickly for daring women,
fiery, sporty glamour kittens, but this may not be the kind of
woman who will be his life-long soul-mate. The opposite sign
from his Rising sign is Aries and women with Aries planets are
often a powerfully magnetic physical draw, for good or ill,
depending on the other planets in his chart. The kind of woman
who lives and breathes fiery impulsive energy is one he might
find ultra-attractive. He looks on the world from a very peaceful,
rational perspective and doesn't live out his own wild side
unless he has many planets in Fire signs. So he'll unconsciously
seek a relationship where the world revolves around a romantic
partnership, but he'll be fascinated by a woman who believes it
revolves around only her.

he attracts

Usually other Air Sun signs, like Gemini, Libra and Aquarius.
There's a good rapport and possible long-term relationship here
if you have the Sun or Moon in Libra and his Sun or Moon
complements your Rising sign. Fiery, assertive self-centred and
passionate women often feel drawn to his very light, charming
'first impressions count' attitude and if he has some Fire planets
and you're an Aries Sun or Moon, for example, this could be a
very physically addictive relationship. Women with Water
planets – in Pisces, Cancer and Scorpio – will find him
compelling company just because he's so gentlemanly, romantic
and charming. But of course that's all in his head and unless he
has a range of planets in Water signs too, he won't *feel* enough,
only think. If you've got Mars in Libra, then you might find him
extraordinarily physically attractive, but hate him for being so
super-smarmy at the same time.

SCORPIO RISING

his image

wicked ★ sexual ★ intense

Wicked, sexual and intense. He's always burning for something,
always aching for the impossible. It's almost as if passion will
turn to obsession if you get close to him. And the 'if' word is
serious. This is a man who keeps his distance and for whom
privacy rules. Whatever else, he's a highwayman. He'll mentally
tie you up, bind and gag you, but give nothing away about
himself. It's not easy playing games, because he knows how to
win them all. Meeting this man for the first time can be a near-
death experience or a fate worst than death. Sexually he oozes

the macabre, the dark, moonlit nights, vampires and werewolves. He's deadly, but he's also powerful and serious and transforms relationships into all-consuming passion. He appears to be secretive, clever, to miss nothing and to have the power to see right through your dress or your façade. There's always something hidden, self-destructive and fanatical about his appearance. If he's interested in you, he won't let it show immediately. But if looks could kill or seduce, then he's got the eyes to do exactly that.

his charisma

burning ★ secretive

Burning, secretive, like bitter chocolate and a bloody Mary. He's so, so sexy that you can't resist him. Meeting him is a kind of magic show or hypnotist's act. There's something mesmeric and frightening about his presence, simply because he's so honestly real, a man with all those bestial qualities unironed, *sauvage*, natural and stark. Emotionally, you'll feel his soul dragging yours out into the open. It seems as though he knows you before you know yourself. He's always one jump ahead and never fails to make shrewd and cutting observations if he needs to prove a point. Erotic, black-lace style moods often overcome him and he's totally self-possessed and possessive. He's jealous and it's all or nothing with him. But remember that everyone has a dark side; the difference is that he can feel them all around him, in every woman and every relationship he begins. So check out his planets to see whether he's quite so deliciously dangerous behind that private façade.

he falls for

Utterly sensual, beautiful romantics. Women who are rich in
money, success or spirit. He has an eye for the impossible, so he
often falls in love with a woman he can't have or someone
dangerously erotic or a nightmare to live with. He's spellbound
by airy, flirtatious women with a head for reason and a flair for
femininity. If they have a dark, wicked side, too, he'll be
obsessed. This might not be his ideal long-term soul-mate, but he
plays on an emotional and sexual knife-edge and is driven by his
instinct and his libido. The sign opposite to his Rising sign will
be a particularly powerful magnet. So women with planets in
Taurus will be heavenly addictive – earthy, materialistic and
naturally wise. This is the kind of woman he'll want to possess.
The problem is, unless you have planets in Scorpio, Taurus, Leo
or Cancer, you won't enjoy the fact that he's ultra-possessive too.

he attracts

Women with planets in Scorpio, Cancer, Taurus or Pisces. If you
have a Sun or Moon in Scorpio, this could be a successful long-
term relationship, especially if his Sun or Moon complements
your own Rising sign. If you have many Air planets you'll
probably find him very cool, dark and remote. A challenge, in
fact. His passionate air will seduce you, but unless he has planets
in Libra, Gemini or Aquarius, he'll be too serious and too crisis-
prone. If you have Mars in Scorpio you'll probably find him
physically compelling, but you'll probably loathe his guts at the
same time. If you have the patience to find a way into the secret
recesses of his heart and soul, then you'll discover a powerful
sexuality and a craving for life that is cherishable and also
perishable.

SAGITTARIUS RISING

his image

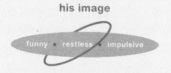

funny ★ restless ★ impulsive

Funny, restless, impulsive and self-centred. He's driven by the desire to explore everything and anyone. So he might come across as the 'archer-seducer', the one who has to be first to make a date, promises and then excuses when he can't live up to his earlier enthusiasm. He's addictive because he lives on his wits and his sexy style. There's little you can do to stop him in his tracks. He moves, breathes, lives and loves for adventure. He's an idealist and his romantic fantasies are the clue to his thirst for excitement. Any whiff of homebound responsibility and he's off. He longs for stability, but fears it too. Back-pack, climb, race or just fall into bed with him and forget about mortgages and fancy linen. He's a bit of a social ligger, too, so if you're famous, successful or simply the centre of acclaim and attention, he'll adore you for it. He appears to be always going and never arriving. In fact, if he comes to stay the night, he'll keep his bag by the bed, just in case he needs to fly.

his charisma

fiery ★ spontaneous ★ sexy

Fiery, spontaneous, like a bubbling geyser and just downright hilariously sexy. His fast-forward ideals are infectious, but you either keep up with his passion for life or get left behind quicker than he picked you up. He is a romantic and proud of it, but he's searching for something so unrealistic that he often prefers to

160

live in his dreams than face the reality of life. His energy is
vibrant, alive and dangerous. He wants to entertain and to be
entertained. Life is for living, loving and romance. So don't make
him angry by talking about commitment and that terrible word
'responsibility' or you'll have plates flying and phones being
slammed down on you. It's fire and brimstone, but it's dynamic,
enthusiastic and mostly humorous. If you can let him laugh with
you or at you, then you have a friend and lover for life. Check out
his other planets to see whether he's just as roguish behind that
devilish façade.

he falls for

Just about any woman who is romantic, fun-loving and mostly
willing to give him his freedom. But if the truth be known, he is
often most attracted to earthy, motherly, down-to-earth types
who give him that sense of stability that he hates so much. If he
has planets in more stable signs like Taurus, Capricorn, Virgo or
Cancer, then he'll probably find the TV watching, gardening,
going to the supermarket on Sundays kind of lifestyle bearable. If
he doesn't, the initial fascination will wear off when he realizes
he's being owned. He adores brainy types with a passion for
talking. He loves phone calls and prefers communicating in bed
to doing anything else. Don't make him dinner more than the
romantic once, as he's hardly got time to eat it, let alone slobber
over the ingredients and worry about the menu for Saturday.
He's spellbound by witty, funny, feminine romantics. The sign
opposite his Rising sign is Gemini and he'll often fall completely
head over heels for this also slightly madcap sign. This may
not be a long-term soul-mate relationship, but it can be a
hilarious one.

he attracts

Women who want to have fun. Also those who are down to earth
and want to do a spot of house-keeping to impress and improve
him. The latter won't last long, though, unless they are very
independent and very gregarious. If you have the Moon, Sun or
Venus in Sagittarius you'll most likely keep him hooked, because
your own freedom is just as much at stake as his. He attracts you
if you're looking for adventure or someone who seems to have a
dynamic and enthusiastic approach to everything he does.
Gemini planets will immediately relate to his restless non-
responsibility style of living and if you have planets in Leo, Aries
or Aquarius, you'll instantly want to be hanging on his arm as he
hikes across the Himalayas. But if you've got Mars in Sagittarius
and no other Saggy planets, you might find an instant fated byte
of love and loathe his judgemental side.

CAPRICORN RISING

his image

overtly conventional

Overtly conventional. Mr classic woolly jumpers and squeaky-
clean shoes. He's rugged, knows what he wants and seems to be
going in the right direction. He's a realist and won't play games,
except power ones. So you won't get romantic ideology spouted
at you across the restaurant table, only real tangible ambition.
His ambition, which usually includes a permanent relationship
in which he knows where his duty and yours lie. If
'responsibility' is a non-word for Sagittarius, it's a 'yes' word for
Capricorn rising. He feels it all the time, so he'll always appear to
know what's best, when's the right time to plan a new scheme

and how to go about grounding it. He's punctual, dedicated and serious about life. Yet he has a real dry humour and spicy wit which he can bring out, albeit carefully, once he knows you're amusing yourself or willing to be amused. Once he's checked out whether you're worthy of his attention, he's also likely to hang around longer than most other signs, depending on his other planets.

his charisma

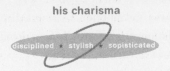

disciplined ⋆ stylish ⋆ sopisticated

Disciplined, stylish, sophisticated and untouchable. He seems emotionless, but is acutely vulnerable behind that tough, business-minded inflexible façade. Don't cross him, as he can be ruthless and fanatical when he gets a bee – or you – in his bonnet. Once hooked, he takes love deadly seriously. There's a kind of hermit-like air about him, but that's because success only comes to those who have had to find it and do it alone. Scratch the diamond and you know there's a secret romantic hidden away. But he won't admit it. He's shrewd, rarely gullible and always reliable. There is a sense of mistrust oozing from his pores, but also an earthy, respectful approach to sex and all that goes with it. His accomplishments seem many, but check out his other planets to see whether he's really so success-driven behind that ambitious, determined façade.

he falls for

Independent, power-behind-the-throne types. He needs to feel you're as committed to his ambition as you are to his traditional values about relationships. But he often falls foul of very opposite types, the emotional wind-maidens who blow hot and then cold, or terrifyingly single-minded women who never give him the respect he deserves. He fears passion and the reason he fears it is because it's not tangible, not a real-life solid structure. Cancer, Scorpio and fiery Aries or Leos often draw him dangerously into affairs. For all his commitment to marriage or long-term relationships, his vulnerable streak often makes him yearn for the ultimate romance and the ultimate pain that goes with it. He'll probably be fatally attracted to Cancerian women, his opposite sign, and he'll either be touched by Cancerian femininity, moodiness and emotional vulnerability or he'll fuse into a love-hate relationship, because he's in demand, needed and can take control of someone's feelings.

he attracts

Other Earth signs – Taurus, Virgo and Capricorn – because he represents stability and structure. But if he's got loads of planets in Sagittarius, Pisces or Gemini, the chances are what you see isn't necessarily what you get. If you have the Sun, Moon or Venus in Capricorn, this could be a successful long-term relationship, especially if his Sun or Moon complements your own Rising sign. He's attractive to women who are in need of a kind of father-figure or backbone support in relationship. If you want commitment, respect and accomplishment, then you'll be instantly in love with his seriously dry humour and will tune in to his sensitive side. If you have Mars in Capricorn, you'll probably fall for his ambitious streak, but also find his defensiveness unbearable.

AQUARIUS RISING

his image

brilliant ★ eccentric

Brilliant but eccentric. A cross between a mad genius and a website. There's something rather innocent about his approach to love, as if he's not sure exactly what it is, so he'll work it out on paper as you go along. Things of the mind seem to be on his mind most of the time. Love, well, that's too complicated and involves those rather irrational things called emotions. He feels, but he won't let you in on the secret unless he's got planets in more fiery, passionate signs like Aries, Sagittarius or Leo. He's shocking but unshockable. The truth, to him, is virtual reality. He appears to live in his head and rarely worries about romance. Love is all about friendship and loyalty. Aquarius rising can be trusted, but make sure you check out his other planets for signs of deception. If he seems genuinely unemotional, don't worry, he does have feelings, he just avoids dealing with them. His interest in you is genuine, because he believes in genius, self-determination and freedom for all.

his charisma

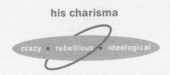

crazy ★ rebellious ★ ideological

Crazy, rebellious and ideological. He thinks up new ideas, new ways to do things all the time. He'll make you feel important and interesting, whether you like it or not. Unpossessive and radical, he's techno-mad, so he'll have all the latest gimmicks or fads or be the first to discover a new fashion. He's ahead of his time and he shocks quite deliberately, just to get a reaction. Then he can analyse for hours about what it is you're thinking, doing, dreaming or feeling. Intellectually infuriating, he'll prefer conversation and ideology to words of love. He loves to stir things up at parties and loves to wind you up on the phone.

he falls for

Independent, fiery, creative women with style and laughter. Falling in love isn't easy for him, because it's against all his so-called principles. And he's so emotionally dishonest with himself that he often falls for feminine, sultry, romantic types who actually represent what he most fears within himself. Covering up his feelings is easier with someone who's a dab-hand at expressing herself. The sign opposite his Rising sign is Leo and he often finds a Leo woman irresistible because she is so self-centred. Her expressiveness is totally dramatic, showy and very unlike his own rather rational, analytical approach. He's an original thinker and if you are, too, so much the better. But check out his other planets to see what he's really like behind that intellectually brilliant façade. He's a secret romantic, so the fiery glamour of love does appeal to him, whatever he says to the contrary.

he attracts

Women with planets in Aquarius will home in on his free-spirited rational side. He's not overtly sentimental, so if you have planets in Cancer, Pisces or Scorpio, take care, unless he has similar watery connections. If you have the Sun or Moon in Aquarius, this could be a good long-term relationship. The other Air signs, Libra and Gemini, will enjoy the friendship aspect of his outlook on life, but be careful you don't fall for someone who's actually deeply emotional under the surface, but just doesn't dare look. Alternatively, if you've got planets in Aries, Leo or Sagittarius, you might discover a den of sexual delights beneath this hi-tech idealist. If you have Mars in Aquarius you'll probably have an instant physical attraction, but you might loathe his highly principled attitude.

PISCES RISING

his image

dazed ⋆ confused ⋆ dreamer

Dazed and confused. He's the dreamer, the victim and the saviour all rolled into one. There's something poetic about the way he talks, but something also rather unrealistic about his view on life and love. He's easily seduced by all kinds of things from a beautiful face to another glass of wine. But he seems detached, far away and belonging really only to himself. This winsome kind of façade may hide a factory of less subtle behaviour. So take care. What you see is not always what you get with this Rising sign, simply because it's a very good disguise for men with something to hide. Pisces rising is elusive and he often has a kind of 'out to lunch' sign in his eyes. But his intuition is astute, his sense of touch extraordinary and he'd probably score 10 out of 10 for telepathy. His allure is his dreamy, romantic attitude to life and the fact that he keeps shifting and changing. Sexually, he's not your meat and two vegetables kind of man, more likely champagne on ice for breakfast overlooking the sea. But many women find his kind of slippery, roguish, child-like behaviour intensely attractive. And, of course, he knows it.

his charisma

Imaginative, soft, compassionate. He's the most unchauvinistic of companions. At a party, he'll be the one who chatters away and subtly flirts with you in the most natural, genuinely caring way. Take care, though, that you don't fall into the trap and think it's all going to be music, candlelit dinners and sensual bliss. He gives the appearance of all this, but once the initial wooing is over, he can resort to passive manipulation. He's a charmer, a seducer and sometimes doesn't realize he's working on you to prop himself up in one way or another. Many Pisces rising men go to extremes, simply because they cannot tolerate their own moods, feelings and sensitivity. Then they'll become martyrs to feeling or turn into henchmen or playboys to compensate for their softness. He'll often play the victim or work up all kinds of sympathy from motherly types or strong women who love to protect him. But he actually has a pretty emotionally bullet-proof vest beneath that sensitive, nonchalant, carefree outer casing. Check out his planets to see whether he's an extremist or merely a joker. Pisces rising is often an illusion unto himself and if he has Earth or Fire planets, he might turn out to be a victim of his own deceptive tactics without even knowing it.

he falls for

Rational, realistic, powerful women. Fated attraction is how he'd describe his feelings towards the many women he falls for, gets involved with and then slips away from before it all gets too painful or too demanding. If you're successful, witty and awfully wise, he'll be in love in seconds. But watch out, he can fall in love over and over again in the same day, simply because to him,

women are goddesses. His dreams are filled with visions of
women who pamper him, wear erotic underwear and are always
on top. He thrives on women in power, because then he can be
passive and maintain that neutral tone to his feelings. He adores
you if you're feminine, clever but tough. The Leos, Aries, Scorpios
and Virgos of this world are usually his chosen many. Check out
his other planets carefully. Beneath that dreamy passive façade
may lie a woman-eater or a genuinely committed, trusting soul.

he attracts

Sleeping beauties, women who love romance and dreams. If your
Sun or Moon is in Pisces, this could be a long-term relationship,
especially if his Sun or Moon complements your own Rising
sign. Extremes of women fall for this man. The other Water signs,
Cancer and Scorpio, will click into his strange emotionally
barren but acutely sensitive attitude to life. Rational, vibrant,
buzzing socialites and successful power-hungry executives will
adore that visionary, artistic approach to love. If you have Mars
in Pisces, you'll find there's an instant physical attraction
between you, but you might detest his victim–saviour games
once the romance begins to wear thin.

don't take it
personally

Now you know what kind of image your man projects onto the world and how he wants (usually unconsciously) to be seen, it's time to face the facts! What's the rest of his character like? Look up his Mars, Jupiter, Saturn and Mercury in the tables at the end of the book and then read on. Remember, though, he might not be living out all these different bytes of his personality. So handle with care and be tolerant of his vulnerabilities, defences and weaknesses. After all, he's only human. And we're all fraught with the same limitations and fears.

MARS

mars in aries

how he goes about getting what he wants

Usually directly, impulsively and without a thought for anyone else. Mars is at its most 'natural' in Aries, which also means it's instinctive – an almost raw, uncultured impulse to go after something. If he's spotted you in the corridor, the first thing he'll do is act without thinking. That means he'll either throw you a few chat-up lines or throw you over his shoulder and cart you off to bed and to hell with work, life and the fact you might already have a lover tucked away. This is direct, spontaneous, caveman-like energy. Sure he's egocentric, but then he also has more fighting spirit and guts than an urban guerrilla. He'll aim straight for what's turning him on and that's often a woman with a gentler nature than his own. But he can be blatantly selfish, simply because he has to strike now or never. Putting off the impulse for even a nano-second means he might just give up the whole idea until someone else comes along.

his libido

Pretty rampant – and he's usually direct and honest enough to admit it too. He won't kid you about his needs. If you phone him in the office at midday and say you're in the mood for sex, then he's likely to drop everything – meetings, important phone calls, even his trousers – just to keep his sex drive active. Someone once said that men go around thinking about sex every five minutes of the day. Perhaps that's an exaggeration, but it's certainly true of a man with Mars in Aries. If he doesn't, then he might have another planet blocking this innate lust-and-must drive from operating.

performance

Fast, dynamic and passionate.

desire

Spontaneous, thrilling and a bit like a blockbuster film without the credits.

mars in taurus

how he goes about getting what he wants

Carefully and in a beautifully controlled way, or perhaps making a complete U-turn and returning when you least expect it. There's a force to be reckoned with here. Don't expect a sudden gush of romantic passion, flowers and a seductive dance. He's the passively aggressive type. He plays hard to get and then when you're seriously interested he'll steam in full throttle. But it all has to be done with the skill of a craftsman. He's not propelled into action by a dream or a fantasy of what he wants, but of the reality behind the dream. That's why he needs to bring it all down to earth first. If he's fixated on you, then your make up, your body language and your beauty become important factors. So will how much you've got in your bank account or your purse. Sometimes he'll resort to financial tactics to impress you – he'll mention how much he's liable to earn next month or how successful his shares or current business investments are. He feeds you slowly with the grand practicalities of life, testing the ground so that he won't fall into any emotional traps. Then he'll move the Earth for you.

his libido

Sensual, placid and reliable. You can be sure he's got one – there's something very physically fleshy about his sex drive. This is a meat and potatoes man, and he adores sex because it's a basic earthy need. His lust factor is high, but he doesn't make a song and dance about it, unless he's got Mercury in Aries and likes to brag a little. But he'll always play the anticipation game smoothly but surely. His sexuality depends on slow arousal, plenty of touch, massage and lengthy foreplay. If you're in bed, smelling of perfume and eating strawberries doused in

champagne, that's the kind of realistic visual turn-on that will
fire his impulse. For him, the gradual intentional build up is far
more arousing than climax. He may not be a three times a night
man, but just one long session with him is enough to faze you out
of your mind.

performance

Strong, physical and nakedly brazen.

desire

Like Ravel's *Bolero*, slow and intensifying, and always sure of
the crescendo-like ending.

mars in gemini

how he goes about getting what he wants

With all kinds of wily and sometimes cunning ways. But he often
thinks so fast that he can't keep up with himself. Clowning
around is one thing, but when he's after you, remember he's
planning and plotting how to undress you, and sometimes how
to get up in the morning and leave as quickly as possible without
disturbing you. But mostly he's thinking up the kind of antics
you can both enjoy. Be careful, though, devious methods are
sometimes used. You may be deep in conversation with his best
friend and really fancy him, but he's not exactly pulling his
weight, or pulling you. Then Mars in Gemini, in true
mischievous fashion, starts to join in, offers you a drink, plays
with words as if they were juggler's balls (excuse that kind of
Gemini *double entendre*, but that's what he's also good at) and
basically makes you laugh so much that you start to find him far

more amusing, wicked and flirtatious than dear old best friend. Wit and words give him a buzz, and even though all men communicate, it's his passion to connect with you and make playful evasions and mental twists and turns to get himself out of tedious fixes – and into sexy ones.

his libido

Never easy to fathom. Light and laid-back, he doesn't exactly ooze Schwarzenegger-like masculinity or advertise that he's a walking sex-bomb. But there's a youthful, unstoppable, restless sex drive behind that charming smile. As well as the sweetness, the quick tongue and razor-sharp mind, he has a passion for sexy dialogue and erotic phone calls, and an unpredictable libido which is like greased lightning. Make sure you're not the jealous type. He's flirtatious and of course he adores women or he wouldn't have chosen you. But he does enjoy sexy teasing. When he gets playful, you'll be the first to know what he really wants. He might talk about sex to other women, but it's usually in jest, not in desire.

performance

Now you see him, now you don't, but when you do, he has the words, the wit and a few magic tricks up his sleeve that you'd never have dreamt possible.

desire

Erratic, charming, crazy and seductive.

mars in cancer

how he goes about getting what he wants

In a very roundabout way. Interested in you? He's hardly likely to
admit it. In fact, he's unlikely to take direct action, or even the
initiative, so if he fancies you, you won't know it. Cool and
remote as he may seem on the surface, he's actually terribly
sensitive about being rejected or made a fool of, so he never puts
himself in a position where it could possibly happen. That's why
he circles, hovers and walks sideways, but never, never goes for a
direct hit. You may see him across the bar, but you can't be sure
whether he's seen you. He doesn't look your way, he doesn't
even glance in your direction. But he works on you in a very
uncanny way. It's almost as if he's adapting the atmosphere,
soaking it up and becoming part of it. He becomes the bar on
which your beautiful hands are placed, he is the music to which
your sexy ears are attuned. He's manipulating you from the
wings, subtly working on your feelings, but it's instinctual,
charming and totally unpremeditated. There is very little
plotting and scheming involved in his seduction, unlike that of
some other signs. When he finally senses the moment is right,
he'll probably move slightly nearer, or spill his drink on the bar,
or ask you for a light. But it's never ever calculating and he's
never ever aware that he's manipulating the atmosphere to
enable him to get what he desires in the first place! He's a
complex man, a man of moods and moves. But he'll get it
just right.

his libido

Restless, swinging from high to low. One minute he's constant as
the sunrise, the next as changeable as the moon. If you catch him
when he's feeling sexy, he's the most tender, rampant and yet

inspiring lover. He reacts to the roots of beauty and love. He makes sure he absolutely trusts the moment and you. He's not into direct, aggressive, animal sex. Yes, he's a superb love-maker; yes, he's a man; but he's a man who's aware of his body *and* his feelings. If he has most of his planets in the Air signs – Libra, Aquarius and Gemini – he may find it difficult to combine the feelings behind his sexuality with his more rational outlook on life.

performance

Ultra-stylish, not the crab of the zodiac, more sidewinder with a mission.

desire

Chaotic, cautious but compelling.

mars in leo

how he goes about getting what he wants

Creatively and usually with panache and drama. Boldly going where no man has gone before. He's looking for someone who will make him feel special, love him for his spirit and adore him for his sexiness. Direct and to the point, he'll stage the whole hunt, chase or mere chat up, with the art of an actor turned film director. He's so idealistic that he assumes that he won't be rejected or turned down. He zooms in with persuasion, seduction and a camera lens big enough to record the whole flamboyant act. It's all romantic flurries of passion and he'll put you on the spot in the most dramatic and spicy of ways. It's a kind of 'now or never' approach. He's the king and you'd better be ready to be his queen. His optimism is infectious and when he drags you on the dance-floor or whirls you around at the party, he's basically stating you're part of his kingdom. And he'll assume you've already fallen among the angels because you're besotted with him. Be careful, his ego-centred desire is more important to him than anything else and he'll rarely share the stage with a woman who's more dramatic and show-stopping than he is. Two stars are one too many.

his libido

Spectacular, uninhibited and magical. He'll make you feel as if you're the only person in the world to be loved. But he can assume he knows the only way to turn you on or that his favourite sex techniques and style are more important than yours. He's aroused quickly and there's little you can do to resist him when he's on form. Quite frankly, unless he's got a wodge of planets in something like Cancer, he's going to be the kind of hunk who wants sex on a pretty regular basis. It's not the slow sensual crafting of Taurus, but it's lust pure, undiluted and basically insatiable, wild and potent.

performance

Uninhibited, larger than life, or just large.

desire

Charismatic, irresistible. Lust equates with romance.

mars in virgo

how he goes about getting what he wants

Realistically. He sorts out all the options, gathers the facts about who you are, where you've come from and whom you know, and works out if you're the kind of woman who's, well, basically, reliable. His cool approach springs from the fact he wants something useful to come out of desiring you, whether it's a working relationship, a friendship or just good sex. There must be a purpose behind his desire. When he slides into the right gear and feels romance isn't as bad or as chaotic and mysterious as he reckoned, then he'll probably discuss all kinds of useful information with you, rather than use witty amusing chat-up lines (unless he has Mercury in Gemini or Libra). He wants to get what he sees, so it's a sensible, cautious but direct approach, motivated by your wit, your humour and your ability to realize that life and love aren't just games but are to be worked at and taken seriously. But if you're fiery, spontaneous and, God forbid, funny, then his earthy sensual side will take over. That's when he's often hooked before he knows it. Loosening up comes after the tight, controlled mental approach. That's when you know his coolness is just a cover-up for a very sensitive and delicate kind of love.

his libido

It's said to be styled on textbook techniques and to follow the instructions to the letter. But there are Mars in Virgo men out there who are super-studs and super lovers, simply because they believe practice makes not so much perfect as it does sense. Mars in Virgo has a sex drive that's probably equally as gutsy as the notorious Mars in Sagittarius or Scorpio, but he doesn't like to admit it. His body is a very sensitive zone and therefore it must

work for its pleasure. The sensuous side of his nature is often
locked away, because passion, sex drives and libidos are all
rather mysterious, rather like things that go bump in the night.
And the darkness is a place he'd rather not be. When he warms
up, he becomes hotter than hot, wilder than his own imaginings,
but getting there takes courage and, whether he likes it or not,
involves his emotions. Those are bits of clutter he'd rather keep
hidden away under the laundry basket, thanks very much.

performance

Usually sleek, sophisticated and breathtaking.

desire

Controlled, aloof and restrained.

mars in libra

how he goes about getting what he wants

Strategically and romantically. It won't be obvious, but he'll suss
out your virtues first, because he loves to flatter, loves to charm
and mostly loves to seduce. But it's a passive seduction. He
wants to be wanted more than he wants you. Then there comes
the romantic bit, the tactical chit-chat, the romance with
romance, the flowers, the phone calls. He'll even de-seed your
figs if he's still trying to win you. That way, he gets you to think
he's the most lovely, gentle considerate man in town. You're
fascinated by his eyes and his voice. The rearview mirror is
exactly at the right angle, so that he can see himself and you in it
together. The ideal he's searching for is almost real and
believable. But then again, if he's planning a major campaign to

win your heart, he'll often resort to quite ruthless, though usually unconscious tactics, like playing you off against someone else. OK, so you've just met, gazed at each other and fallen into a sexy cauldron of chemical reactions you can't stop. Then your friend walks in. 'Hey,' he says, kidding but not kidding, 'isn't she stunning? Wow, she's beautiful.' Maybe, just maybe, he should ask her out one night. Of course, he hasn't temporarily gone barmy and jumped out of the cauldron, but it's dangerously hot, because he's hooked and he's not so sure about you. So this is his way of gaining approval, affection and making sure you really fancy him.

his libido

Strangely potent. Mars in Libra is a bit of a paradox. When you first meet him, he's gentle, refined and has the grace of a sophisticate, but beneath that harmonious peace-loving strategy lurks a sex drive unmatched by many. Because he lives in his head and because he 'thinks' love rather than feels it (unless he has the majority of planets in Water signs), all that emotion is repressed and often the only release for anger, resentment and then the subsequent guilt about feeling anything less than nice feelings is through his sex life. It's all quite lovely stuff if you want a man who'll make love every night and every morning. And doesn't that sound like an ideal *homme*, rather than an ideal home? The downside to all this romantic idealism is that you have to maintain that beautiful face and that perfect body to match, otherwise his libido just sort of slithers away in the night. Only the beautiful turns him on. Mud-packs and knickers left stranded in the bathroom are turn-offs. Then his libido is nil and you're left wondering.

performance

Don Juan himself.

desire

Romantic impresario.

mars in scorpio

how he goes about getting what he wants

Subtly, but hypnotically. When this enigmatically wicked man
sets eyes on you, there's little that will stop him. He'll have you,
if it kills him. Probing is his business and he does it so well that
you'll either feel he's burned his way into your soul with his gaze
or has undressed you a million times in one minute. Then there's
the compelling feeling that you're being drawn to him. He
exudes not so much crude sexuality as an erotic and deeply
moving experience that you have no choice but to submit to.
He'll be devious too. When you disappear to the loo and leave
your drink, book or mobile on the bar, he'll sneakily browse
through your things and discover all your secrets. Then he has
plenty of ammunition for later, he's one up on you and in
control. When he wants you, it's a form of possession. So take
care, because he can get pretty fanatical. The force is with him
and it's powerful one which he can use for good or ill. The Mars
in Scorpio man commits his body, mind, soul and emotions into
having what he wants. And that's you.

his libido

Erotic, intense and darkly passionate. Notoriously sexy, but neither blatant nor macho, he prefers to play the game almost in silence. He's got big opinions about what passion is anyway and about when he wants sex. Private parts are really private to this man. Sure, he's as steamy, potent and volatile as any fiery lover. But his energy is controlled and contained. He takes his time and when he's being aroused he likes to feel he can dominate, tangle the sheets and involve all of his feelings. He enjoys taboo sex, but that's only because it's the atmosphere, the images and the traces of the hidden, unwelcome aspects of sexuality that he's curious about. He's looking for a mysterious experience, not a quick shag over the office desk. His libido rises as fast as that famous Scorpio sting in the tail. But it's full-blown passion, so make sure you're as serious about his body and his emotions as he is.

performance

Vivid, compelling, stunning.

desire

Soulful, mysterious and unrelenting – if you can take it.

mars in sagittarius

how he goes about getting what he wants

With all the seductive charm of an arch-persuader and the hustling instinct of a entrepreneur of love. He's unstoppable and knows he's lovable. When he aims for you across the other side of the room, he'll be there before any other zodiac sign, except perhaps a Mars in Aries. But then a little healthy competition gives him more to get excited about, so if you want to wind him up, make sure you've a few racy male friends parked conveniently outside in their fast cars. His kind of romance is about action, impulse and danger. The more difficult you are to woo, the more you'll have him chasing you. The hunt is what matters. He thinks big and he laughs a lot too. He's even capable of making the whole pick up, chat up a total circus or just downright hilarious. He'll probably promise you the Earth and persuade himself that he will deliver. But he's a romantic roamer, so take care with your heart. That crazy character is very easy to fall for. And he knows it. He'll leap in quickly, but he can also leap out again with just as much speed, unless he has planets in more stable signs like Capricorn or Virgo.

his libido

Dynamic, active, assertive and comedy in motion. He'll laugh about his body, express his sexual needs without embarrassment and have sex on his mind at least half the day. What about the night? That's play time. So watch out if you're a slow sensual type, as he's after basic fiery imaginative sex, not serious emotional closeness. This man's libido rises at dawn and is usually unfailingly pointed towards you for most of the day, with a dash of fun and most of all romantic bravado. He considers his body to be magnificent and often struts around as if he's naked and doesn't care what anyone thinks of him. When he is literally naked, you can't be one of those women who likes to have sex beneath the bedcovers with the lights out. He prefers the great outdoors and sex in dangerously public locations, like trains, country lanes and planes.

performance

Exhibitionist and hilarious.

desire

Excessive and free-ranging.

mars in capricorn

how he goes about getting what he wants

Tenaciously and conventionally. In fact, he'll want to master you, rule you and if he has to fight for you all the way, so much the better. When he sets his eyes on you and decides you're the one for him, he'll rarely deviate from his plans. If he feels challenged, he'll push slowly, creating a vacuum into which you fall and can't escape. Be warned, though, he has been known to drop women as soon as he's wooed them, bedded them and wined and dined them, simply because the feat of mastering and winning is over. Then he needs another challenge, in other words another woman, to capture and control. Now not all Mars in Capricorns are like this, but success can go to their head and that's when they think they're a little god-like. On the other hand, this man's gift is that if you're worthy of his total commitment and his seriousness about relationships, then he'll stick. When he spots you at that cocktail party, all those conventional tactics will come into play – the polite conversation, the offer to get you a drink, and so on. Of course, he knows the etiquette required, like giving you his work phone number just in case you might want to discuss some professional matters, and reminding you that he's single, ambitious and certainly not gay, poor or a time-waster.

his libido

Powerful, heroic, very masculine. Sexually, he needs emotional closeness, but he can also go to the other extreme and run a few physical relationships without any commitment when he's feeling horny. He means business and takes his libido seriously. So must you. His body is a kind of temple and if you respect every hair on his chest and every surge of his sex drive, then he'll make the Earth move for you too. He's sensual and has mastered the arts of passion. There's a great deal of lust surging around in his loins, so don't think behind that cool, controlled conventional energy he's not sexual dynamite. He is, but he'll take his time to show you.

performance

Focused, seriously dynamic.

desire

Cautious, controlled, dedicated to you.

mars in aquarius

how he goes about getting what he wants

Logically, often with icy precision, in a very aloof, unpredictable way. The thing is, when he's in pursuit, it's not hot, passionate desire driven by simple basic biology. He's driven by an idealistic vision of how love *should* be. And that little word 'should' is one that often boils down to how principled he's feeling at the time. Then he's either going to pursue you to the ends of the Earth in dashing style or take more unpredictable action, like surprising you with a direct question, a crazy gesture or an analysis of your virtues. It's all fuelled by the fact that he's a secret romantic, but at the same time he detests sentiment, including his own feelings. So he'll act in a very rational way. In fact, he'll probably start discussing anything from God to the media in his attempt to suss out whether you're as freedom-loving and equality-minded as he is. You're more likely to chat him up than vice versa. After all, love and desire are free enterprises. Social convention doesn't matter when he so chooses. And of course, he's going to remain independent and rebellious if it kills him, even when all those swirling unknown urges surge up inside him because he wants something, but isn't quite sure what it is. Sex, love? Well, they're indefinable. But certainly worth pursuing out of a very bizarre Aquarian fascination.

his libido

Unpredictable and unique. He needs to be different, to stand out, to not be just the normal macho type who whirls you around the bedroom for all-night sexual romps. The kind of marathons he has in his head are conversational ones. Sex comes when it's least expected. So don't even for one minute think you can judge when he's feeling horny, because he'll always be one step ahead of you. Just when you think he's not interested is when he probably is. And just when you think he is, his mind is on far more abstract or important matters, depending on where his other planets are too. His is a complex sex drive. But if you want to swing from chandeliers or listen to Chopin and have sex in the bath, he'll be there. As long as it's his idea first.

performance

Zany, shockingly experimental at times.

desire

Unconventional and idealistic.

mars in pisces

how he goes about getting what he wants

In a meandering, rather laid-back kind of way. There's something
very tenuous and elusive about his attraction to you. Because
he's often surprised himself by who actually turns him on,
women in general are highly attractive to him. He's not going to
charge in with passion steaming from his boots and macho one-
liners. In fact, he's going to want to be charmed first by your
seductive skills, because that way he's not responsible for the
romantic feelings which pound through his body and his heart.
The man with Mars in Pisces is like a deep-sea diver. He's
searching for something quite profound, but he's not always sure
what it is. The problem is, he doesn't really feel comfortable with
his gentleness, because it doesn't conform to social and
collective expectations, and that's why he often resorts to
extremes. Either he'll play the passive victim – yes, it's you who
led him astray and stopped him from finishing that work of art
because desire got in the way of his artistic flow – or he'll go after
women who are strong and powerful and then slip out of the loo
window when he's feeling dominated. Actually, he doesn't really
know what he wants and that's why he's usually fooling himself
into relationships which he can't handle. His way of hunting you
is not to hunt. But he's beautifully deep beneath that rather
pliable surface and if he meets you halfway and realizes you're
feminine, sensitive and as emotionally torn as him, his desire
will become love.

his libido

Enigmatic, romantically aroused. He's instinctual and gifted as a lover, and yet his libido is driven by a profound sensitivity towards the other person. His needs often come second. But his feelings and his sexual habits are elusive and changeable, and they're certainly not cageable. Try to pin him down to sex every night and every morning, and he'll fall out of love as quickly as he fell in. Romance turns him on, and like water running through your fingers, when he's there, take the moment and really live it. When he's not with you, he's probably living in his imagination. He's always sexually yearning and never quite has that complete profound experience he desires. But then he's a dreamer and that makes him irresistible.

performance

Sensitive, romantic, shimmering.

desire

Silky, erratic, all-consuming.

HIS OTHER PLANETS

Now for some snippets of insight into how to handle your man's communication style, beliefs and defences. Remember, you're building up a portrait which is very complex. If, for example, he has many planets in the same sign it might be easier for you to recognize or reconcile those qualities. But often, even with an 'easy' chart, he might be only living out certain dynamics of his personality. The love bytes he consciously owns may be very different from the ones he doesn't admit to. Then you get a distorted or warped sense of that quality and it might surface as shadowy behaviour – all those things that he complains about in someone else or that make him feel in some way responsible, guilty or furious.

his way with words: mercury

mercury in aries

Assertive, impatient and quick off the mark, he's actually much more intuitive than he knows. His mind is sparked by ideas that are so fast and furious that he doesn't have time to analyse or be logical about them. He's the man with a hunch and that's what matters. What was it you just said, did you actually dare to disagree with him? He'll turn it into a major disaster or a Holocaust or just be downright angry. That's fine if you're capable of taking the flack without getting defensive. But he'll often push your emotional buttons without realizing he's doing so. Take a few psychology lessons and be brave, then you can deal with all that fire and brimstone without taking it all personally.

He wants to rile you, because he needs excitement, spontaneity and passion. His words are never empty, they always mean something, so listen carefully or you might miss the point, which is often over so quickly you've hardly had time to draw breath. He can be outrageously impatient and also incredibly selfish. If he asks you to be at the restaurant at eight and you're one minute late, that temper can come out like a brandished sword. When he wants something done, it must be done now, immediately and flawlessly.

You know you washed the dishes in a moment of romantic impulse, but when he says you missed the spot of ketchup on the plate, it takes on gigantic proportions in his head. Don't say I didn't tell you so, when he gets all in a flap because you don't instantly wash it off for him. Tolerance must be your ally.

mercury in taurus

He takes in information slowly and will only give it out if he's sure he knows all the facts well and deeply. His mind thrives on peace, beauty and the quality behind the words you express or the information he wants to divulge. If he's a Gemini or Aries Sun sign, he could get awfully impatient with his own slowness or get into the habit of repeating everything twice, just to make sure it sinks in. On the other hand, if whatever he says makes sense, then he may just want to hear it again because he likes the sound of it. This is where your patience is required, because what can appear as laziness is often just his ability to go so deeply into everything that's being said.

His mind focuses on the things he loves and he'll tell you the most amazing things if you give him a chance to get going. And, of course, he's realistic. So if you come out with all kinds of combustible ideas and romantic fairy-tale schemes, he's likely to be pragmatic enough to stay in control of those thoughts which make him feel uncomfortable. So there you are, getting all enthusiastic about moving to the country or to the Andes, because you hate city life and how inspiring the mountains and staring at the sea from a wild romantic beach can be. Then he's likely to remind you that you don't get much work or money living in the middle of nowhere and it takes hours to commute. And quite honestly, living in Peru is really very unrealistic when you don't even speak the lingo or know anything about it. He's down to earth and proud of it.

mercury in gemini

At best he's loquacious, witty and will talk about anything under the sun, as if he knows it all intimately. This is often a ploy, because he's actually clever enough to skim the surface of every subject, but not necessarily skin it. He's a hoot and he's chatty and vivacious. At worst, he's also very cunning and don't put it past him to tell a few tall stories, exaggerate and bluff to get himself out of trouble or into your bed. That wicked child-like conversation makes him seem fabulously intelligent. Well, he is, up to a point, and somehow gets away with being professionally known for his writing, speaking or merely gossiping. He also probably has at least two mobile phones, two computers and has been through more newspapers and magazines on Sunday mornings than you've read in a month. He needs to talk and can often split his mind between two different subjects and still talk about them simultaneously.

Mercury is at home in Gemini, so he's off to a good start. He's a born communicator. But, like any sign, there is a catch. He's the artful dodger when it comes to giving anything away about himself. Sure, he's crazy about finding out all kinds of interesting facts about you, but giving away his own, well, you'd better be ready for some fairly sharp and sometimes wounding remarks if you try to probe too deeply. Either that or he'll just be totally evasive and cleverly turn the subject round to why you've never gone deep-sea diving or smoked cigarettes.

mercury in cancer

The past is his favourite subject and he can seem incredibly sentimental when he's in one of those reminiscing moods. But he's always gentle, sensitive about what he says and also about what others say to him. That's why it takes a long time for him to open up. He sieves the information through his feelings and his mind before actually coming straight to the point. So be careful, what he says may not always be exactly what he means. Instinctively he'll remember all those things he said or admitted in the past and either makes sure he doesn't say them again if they brought any kind of rejection or intuitively feel that what he says will go down the right way.

He's also horrifyingly subtle. So when you start panicking about how you can lose half a stone in a week, he'll rarely say, 'Go on a carrot diet,' rather, 'Losing weight has to come from your heart as well as what you eat.' But the downside is that sometimes he just doesn't want to talk at all. And that's because he resents being the nice, sensitive, always helping you out in a crisis soul that he is. Then he become bitter, hyper-critical and ruthlessly bitchy. OK, he's not always like that, but watch out when he gets judgemental. He's just protecting himself, but it can hurt.

mercury in leo

He really does want to be the king of communication. If he comes across as a know-it-all, then listen, because he can also be incredibly inspiring and creative with words. He talks with the voice of passion and with style and confidence. You just can't help noticing his voice. It purrs like a cat and growls luxuriously with feline warmth. He wants to tell you everything, and he's really and truly generous with his information and seems genuinely interested in you – as long, of course, as you're interested in him. That's the only snag. At best he'll entertain you over dinner with a million ideas, dreams, jokes and 'important information', at worst he'll want to be admired, adored and by golly, never be told he's wrong.

He thinks of future possibilities rather than dwelling on the past. And when he starts telling you how to improve your image, or change your life, or forget about X, because he really was out to lunch, then you have little choice but to listen. He needs an audience, I'm afraid. But he also gets a very large boost to his ego when you're flexible enough to agree with every word he says, even if you don't. His know-it-all quality can get a little exhausting, he does like to interfere and you have to expect some grand operatic arguments, which, of course, he will always win. He's the king after all. But he's wild.

mercury in virgo

He's clever, witty, awfully wise and realistic. There's little that you can get away with, because he spots flaws in arguments and synthesizes everything to make sure he understands it completely and perfectly. He can be unnervingly accurate about the smallest detail and then forget about the wider implications of the subject. When you're in the middle of one of those serious discussions about changing the bathroom decor or whether you should move in together, he'll be analysing every colour chart, holding up swatches in daylight, candlelight, any old light, until he decides on the right shade. Moving in together? Ah, now that involves articulating all the useful things that might come out of a joint venture. Like who is going to do the washing or clean the car.

This a shrewd man, so take care you don't assume his quiet, undemanding conversations aren't loaded with hyper-sensitivity and highly-strung thoughts. They are, but he listens to reason and logic and won't stand for slanging matches or plate-flying. The downside to all this is that he can be so obsessed with the right words, right tone of your voice or correct information that he can become pedantic and hyper-critical. Spontaneous ideas

flowing from your fiery imaginative brain might sound good in
the abstract, but can you actually put it down on paper and make
it useful? The unknown scares the pants off him, so he'll
probably pretend he had all those ideas himself and they didn't
work, so how could they work for you?

mercury in libra

The diplomatic voice of the zodiac, always charming, always
talking about the nicer things of life, he's actually quite a
flatterer. And when he tells you you're looking scrumptious, he
probably does mean it. But he is also known to pass compliments
just for the sake of making his life peaceful and easy. He can be
lazy with words, but he can also be highly articulate. What
makes him want to talk through the night are romantic
connotations, beautiful dreams and ideals and thoughts that
don't send you plummeting into the hell-fire disputes or slanging
matches that some other signs thrive on. He can be peculiarly
indecisive when talking on the phone. But it's only because he's
weighing up all the pros and cons and viewing all the options
from both sides of the fence. And really, if you make the
decision, then everyone will be happier, won't they? When
things aren't in place, for example your hair, your bags in his hall
or simply your feelings, he's constantly rectifying the situation to
make it all wonderfully good and ideal again – in his mind
anyway.

But the other side of all this obliging sweetness and light is that
he can get so swept away by his notion of a perfect conversation
or a perfect negotiation that when the reality of life hits him,
probably involving his feelings, he may well end up saying the
most ghastly thing to you at the most inappropriate moment. Say
you're at a party together and you really have made an effort to
look flawless and are actually attracting all kinds of male

attention. He won't admit to anything like possessiveness or fear of rejection, he'll just come out with something like, 'That dress really is too short and maybe you should have done your hair differently. No wonder everyone's looking at you. It's so unflattering.' Remember, he needs to find a middle way. Extremes scare him and that's why the fine line in the middle becomes his straw.

mercury in scorpio

At best he's skilled at telling you every bit of information about a highly complex subject. At worst he finds all kinds of obscure and enigmatic ways to say the simplest of things. How he loves the way you look tonight will probably come out as, 'It's the mystery between two people that is so compelling, so intensely fascinating, and don't you think you're beginning to find yourself wearing clothes that bring the best out of our relationship?' When he calls you to make a date, he's more than likely to arrange a secret rendezvous where no one else knows you. Then he'll whisper from behind the boardroom door about how much money it's going to cost and then get highly passionate about how he's going to survive the next two hours without you. He's got a dead sexy voice, too. But he's actually not averse to using different tones when speaking to you, or other women I'm afraid, than when he's talking business, family or simply politics.

The deeper you can plummet the depths of your soul together (and he's unlikely to give anything away about his own), the more he'll be fascinated. Superficial, gossipy conversations, silly jokes and lukewarm contact are not going to make pillow-talk easy. He can seem very cynical, but he needs to keep in control of the conversation, which is why he doesn't easily open up his own bag of tricks. It's safer to stay mysterious and give away nothing. Watch out if he ever starts generalizing. He's known to never acknowledge you have your own mouth and own opinions. He's not happy with facts, because he feels first, then processes those feelings into words. You have to ride a few waves to get to the bottom of his mystery, but it's deep, dark and tantalizingly dangerous communication.

mercury in sagittarius

The joker of the zodiac, punchlines just fall out his mouth at the rate of nano-seconds. Hilarious and never known to pause for breath, he's totally tactless and appears not to give a hoot what he says, or when or to whom. He's the eternal optimist, but he's also the eternal enthusiast, who's been to the latest film before everyone else, who knows the sister of someone glamorous and famous, and who's always going to have the last laugh and tell the funniest stories. Gesticulating like a baboon, he's up when you're down. He's always full of surprise phone calls, great ideas, dreams and fantasies that roll off his tongue like champagne. Put the phone down on him, though, and he'll probably come round, smash a few plates and then laugh. If you want to talk politics, famine problems, how the cosmos was made or whether God exists, then he's your man. But watch out when you return to his place from the off-license and he's been left to fend for himself for ten minutes. He'll probably have picked up his mobile phone and started calling all those ex-girlfriends who still owe him a tenner. Discreet? Never. But at least you know where you stand. Basically he's honest, but if he has the Sun in Scorpio, you could find his chit-chat has a twist to its tail.

And is there a downside to this witty, optimistic entertainer? I'm afraid so. He often doesn't think before he speaks. So you get the wonderful wild enthusiasm – 'Yes, I'll put up those shelves for you tomorrow', 'Sure, I'll meet you in Paris on Xmas Day' – but will he actually show up or put up those dust-gathering pine

units? The chances are usually nil, because what he promises
now may well have fluttered away in the heat of the moment.
He's sure he's convinced himself, and you, at the time, but then
that was yesterday and the past rarely matters in his future-
oriented mind. Talking about tomorrow is always more exciting,
more inspiring than putting plans into practice. Don't forget,
when Mercury in Sagittarius speaks, he's a persuader, a seducer –
if not of you, then of himself.

mercury in capricorn

This is a serious thinker and a man who acquires wisdom and
achievement through using his mind. He takes his time to come
up with answers, and questions, and they have to be exactly the
right ones. His mind is organized, not in the way Virgo sifts and
finds use for the words, but so that he can master the facts, so
that he can be in control of the conversation. That's why he's
mastered the art of a very dry and sometimes black kind of
humour. When you first meet him, he'll give the appearance of a
light and merry conversationalist. His wry look at the world is
very infectious and entrancing. But underneath there's a serious
approach to every subject. He's so shrewd that there's little you
can get away with when you try to explain why you didn't turn
up for his business dinner. He's cautious and suspicious of other
people's motives, and often cynical and sceptical, because he's
always controlling everything that might erupt from his own
psychological cellar. Respect his advice and he'll begin to warm
to you. Trust in his wisdom and there's a chance that he'll
respect you back.

All that disciplined thinking is hard to maintain, but it does
suggest that when he says he loves you he means it. There are no
regrets, no wishing he hadn't blurted out such ridiculous things
when he'd had a few glasses too many. He's never gushing, a

sentimental romantic slop. If he really does think he loves you, then he does. Words are serious things and the little word 'love' the most serious of all. Of course he can go to the other extreme and be totally cynical about romance and the future with you. Then again he can get fanatical about his pet subjects and ruthless when he wants to convince you of what's best for you. If he can see that talking silly is just as valuable as talking serious, then he'll realize both can give him the true wisdom he's seeking.

mercury in aquarius

Rational and quick to spot a hole in your argument, this is a man whose eccentric thinking and original conversations are always fascinating and always logical. That is, if you're an intellectual type and don't mind being analysed every time you open your mouth. Mercury is very powerful here and so this is a man with a mission to speak. He won't gabble away like a Gemini, but he'll speak with absolute authority about the things which truly fascinate him and with complete conviction that he's right. That's the catch. Talking back to someone who makes such intelligent sense all the time can seem like facing an exam every breakfast. So you have to have a degree in human psychology or at least a sense of humour to get past why that egg hasn't boiled as quickly or as firmly as the others. And whether there's a way of changing the shape of an egg to fit an egg-cup.

He is full of innovative ideas and he's fabulously funny in a very eccentric, perverse way. But he's also stubborn and won't be moved by sentiment or anything short of his most brilliant thoughts, which of course you can't contradict. He's so idealistic in his thinking that if your thoughts don't live up to his thoughts, he can be incredibly principled. The real problem is that he may know everything about hi-tech living or about how the world is going to be run by ants in 3,000 years, but he knows very little about himself. Human nature? Yes, he knows all about that, too, but on an intellectual level only. Feelings are like aliens, to be analysed and dissected. Even if he has the Sun in Pisces, he'll still be unpredictable, although perhaps a little more tolerant. His mind finds it hard to negotiate the romance of life, but at least he is the most original thinker on Earth.

mercury in pisces

Meandering at worst, intuitive at best, he's a bit of a slippery rogue when he turns conversations into vague ramblings just to slip out of making any kind of commitment. But it's all done with a gentle, dreamy kind of voice and a few sad twinges from the soul. He thinks the world, quite frankly, is a bit of a pig. He's also good at making up all kinds of excuses if he doesn't want to do something or if he's forgotten to meet you for lunch. But always in a very nice and charming way, so he usually gets away with it. 'Oh, did we arrange to meet? I thought it was tomorrow, and anyway, there was a terrible traffic jam on the motorway, and I left my mobile in the office and couldn't call you.' He is slightly absent-minded, but for Mercury in Pisces, it's often easier to dream than be realistic.

He soaks up all the different kinds of moods you're going through, though, and, horrors upon horrors, often knows exactly what you're thinking. It's not that he's a mind-reader, more a mind-mimic. Argumentative he's not and he's more likely to fall in with your plans than make up his own. It's so much easier to speak softly, or take off your previous boyfriend's voice on the phone just to fool you, even if he's only heard it once. His imagination is vast, but he struggles with the practicalities of making his ideas reality. So when he rambles on about all those dreams he has of writing that film script, or the great musical, or painting a huge canvas, the following week the chances are he hasn't even begun thinking about it, let alone put his ideas on paper. But his psychic ability is frighteningly accurate. And listen carefully, because he does have a habit of talking in his sleep and what he says could well be more revealing than what he says in broad daylight.

the lover he imagines himself to be: jupiter

Jupiter informs us of what we can do best and what gives us joy. But more importantly, its placement describes what we imagine ourselves to be. This doesn't always correspond to the persona we project onto the world (our Rising sign) or who we think we are on the surface (a *mélange* of other planets).

So, what sort of lover might he imagine himself to be? This may not be obvious. The fantasy he has of himself may be nothing like his behaviour. Don't forget, the birthchart is very complex and so, for example, someone with Jupiter in Aries, who gets maximum joy from being impulsive, assertive and challenging, and imagines himself to be a warrior of love, may have loads of planets in Taurus, Virgo, Cancer, Capricorn or Libra and find it difficult to 'access' his Jupiter.

Use the information to bring out the best in him – it will make for better understanding and better relationships.

jupiter in aries

He imagines he's a knight in shining armour or a crusading, romantic lover, never tied to routine sex, the ultimate warrior of love and desire. Passionate, rampant and explosive, he sees himself as the best, the most desirable and the most dynamic

lover since Casanova. The more challenges he has in love, the
happier he feels. Lob a few physically seductive grenades at him
and he'll be in heaven, or just throw caution to the wind and
suggest sex in outrageous places to bring his wild side alive.

jupiter in taurus

He imagines he's the most sensual, indulgent seducer, a kind of
snuggled up and snogging maestro of the flesh. All those soft
lights, wine and sexy foods give him the maximum of pleasure
trips. He wants to caress you all night and doze all day in your
arms. Delicious sex and complete and utter indulgence in your
body are his fantasies. He sees nothing wrong in indulging in a
gourmet banquet in bed, especially if you cooked it. Bring out
his sensuous side by massaging him with your breasts, hair, toes
or lips.

jupiter in gemini

He imagines he's the genie with the magic lamp to light your way
to bed. Wicked and teasing, he believe he can excite your mind
first and your body will just follow on naturally. The more
conversational and light-hearted sex is, the more he'll be turned
on. He adores role-playing and he'll play an assortment of
different lovers. One minute he's passion personified, the next
submissive. Make erotic phone calls, play sexual forfeits and
you'll draw out his love of playful sex.

jupiter in cancer

He imagines he's the most tender, caring and sensitive lover in
the world. He sees himself holding you close in his arms with all
those romantic glazed longings as you look into each other's
eyes, before even touching. Hesitant, slowly arousing and

emotionally bonding sex is a seriously mood-inducing pleasure.
He has a repertoire of love-making to suit any time or location.
Be giddily in love with him, gentle and ultra-romantic, and he'll
swoon into your arms or, better still, let you fall into his.

jupiter in leo

He imagines he's the king of lovers, a regal, heroic, dashing and
idealistic lover who will conquer your heart and ravish your
body before you've had a chance to surrender. He sees himself as
the adventurer, the action-packed blockbusting film star whose
passionate desire for the heroine puts him in the most dangerous
of situations. Sex is a fiery, imaginative mythical experience,
where you're the goddess and he's the god. Bring out his
dramatic self-empowering side and have sex surrounded
by mirrors.

jupiter in virgo

He imagines he's a foreign correspondent or an athlete who can
teach you all kinds of sexy ideas or physical techniques. He sees
himself as a lover whose words and wisdom can improve your
mind and your body. He's obsessed with the details of how to
arouse you and how to make love to you the best possible way.
Sensual and earthy, he wants passion to be real, not just a
mission with an outcome. Admire his mind and his body, and
you'll bring out his joy of combining mind with body sensations.

jupiter in libra

He imagines he's the perfect lover, a kind of jewel thief or suave
sophisticate, someone who can dance his way past every woman
at the party just to be at your side. It's all romantic and light,
beautiful words and knowing gestures across the restaurant table.

He sees himself as the lover who knows how to greet you in the morning with fresh flowers or a Buck's Fizz. Sex is not bodies writhing, it's bodies connecting in a magical embrace where warts and bodily fluids don't exist. Bring out his romantic side and always wear beautiful lingerie.

jupiter in scorpio

He imagines he's a god from the underworld, a probing sex therapist or an erotic, brooding sensualist. Sexy and intensely passionate, he sees himself as sexy, hypnotic and at ease with the darkest, most taboo areas of sexuality. And he will exude an incredible sexiness, laced with wicked thoughts and wicked deeds. He wants to be the lover who ravishes you across the dining table in candlelight or beneath a full moon with wolves howling. Make love while watching a horror film or in the back row of the cinema and you'll bring out his dark wild side.

jupiter in sagittarius

He imagines he's a lover who's larger than life. Romanticism goes to his head and he believes so fiercely in his sexual prowess that he won't take no for an answer. Volatile and risky, he sees himself as an adventurer, an explorer who's sexually dynamite. Grounding all that vision into real-life flesh and blood can seem an impossibility. He sees so much fiery drama and lives such perfect fantasies about knights in shining armour and space missions that he won't be tamed. Bring out his freedom-loving side and have sex in the great outdoors.

jupiter in capricorn

He imagines he's the oil magnet or the rich industrialist in the penthouse suite. He wants gold taps and considered sex, at the right place, the right time. He has a real serious commitment to sex and a duty to himself to work hard to be the best lover. He imagines sexual skill is the key to joy and the more experiences he notches up on his bedhead, the more stylish, suave and sophisticated his image. He sees himself as self-willed, but also knows he has the ability to keep his sex-drive firmly under control. Let him be that secret romantic he really is and tell him your erotic fantasies while you make love.

jupiter in aquarius

He imagines he's a sexual guru, an idealistic lover or totally and utterly original. His style has to be different from anyone else's. Experimental sex thrills him, in his head anyway. He wants to be shocking, surprising and anti any kind of conventional sexual assumptions. He sees himself as way out, rebellious and eccentric, a joker, an inventor and a whizz kid about town. Bring out his zany sexual side by suggesting all kinds of new sexy techniques and toys, and never play by the rules of the sexual game.

jupiter in pisces

He imagines he's the most generous, romantic and exotic lover, maybe a sex photographer or a love poet, but always the guardian angel of your needs and desires. Sometimes he imagines himself as a martyr, the one who has saved you, scooped you up from your dull, boring sexual existence and taught you the mysteries of love and life. He sees himself as the ultimate dreamboat, gentle, sensitive and almost spiritual. If you adore romance and live in a world of sexy dreams and gentle embraces, you'll bring out his celestial side.

his barriers and defences: saturn

We all have barriers and defences, and once you know what your man is guarding, or building walls around, you'll have a better idea of how to handle his moods, drive and energies. On one hand this means you're one up on him and that could make you feel that you have some kind of power over him. So you might say things like, 'Well, you've got Saturn in Aries, that's why you're so defensive about your personal space.' But it's not 'why' he is, Saturn is just a reflection of certain qualities that we either fear, doubt or feel limited by in our personality. It's safer and wiser not to use that kind of one-upmanship to win battles or prove points. If you do, you're really falling into your own shadowy trap and maybe you have to look a little more closely at your own chart!

But if you at least have some inkling about how he can work with what he might be denying in himself (and this is not often something he's even aware he's doing, or you for that matter, so always check your own Saturn sign too), you'll be able to navigate that 'stern' side of him. After all, it's really only a defence of the place where he's most vulnerable.

Getting to know more about astrology can bring you power, but it can also bring you happiness. It just depends upon how you use this knowledge and how well you know your own chart and yourself too.

saturn in aries

This man battles against his own will-power. He has an all-or-nothing drive, but he feels limited by outer experiences and people. Yet it's actually his own inner resistance that is the strongest limitation. He sometimes feels as if the world is against him personally. So he can be very defensive about his personal space – who comes into it, who doesn't. When he desires something, it can be very hard for him to go for it. The fear of being assertive, courageous and daring overrides the energy of his warrior side. That spark of adventure he feels inside could be dangerous, it could spill him out of his safety net.

He has to learn the rules of personal will – that he can have what he wants without challenging others or feeling challenged himself. And he could feel threatened if you don't back him up when he wants to do something impulsive, like eat doughnuts for breakfast or prove that he was right about your best friend being a bit of a bitch behind your back. If you argue, he's likely to respond by closing down the fire and hurling insults at himself. He imagines the worst, if he doesn't work very hard to imagine the best.

saturn in taurus

He feels a deep responsibility for everything and everyone around him. He thinks it's his fault if you're not happy, his fault if the grass isn't growing this week because there isn't any rain and maybe the weather's his fault, too. That doesn't mean he's obsessed with weeding or tending the flowers, but he will be working hard on other people's behalf, rather than his own. He fears his own creative ability and often resents those who are apparently 'more talented' than he is, or more beautiful in his eyes. In fact he might even make himself look less attractive, because that way he's got no reason to compete. How could he, such a scruffy, untalented individual, ever get to the top anyway? Alternatively, he'll compensate by being seen with only the most glamorous women or wearing the most ridiculously expensive suits and designer gear, just to prove he's got it.

Falling in love with your beauty or your talent can generate all
kinds of frustrations for him. He has to learn to cultivate his own
creativity, not rely on the gifts of others. He's threatened by
beauty and has to work very hard to concentrate on himself and
accept that his values and desires are no less genuine than
anyone else's.

saturn in gemini

Cynical at worst, he builds a wall to keep out new ideas and
defends himself from other people with powerful beliefs.
Gradually, he'll decide which ideas he'll agree to take in and
which he won't. But sometimes when he's suspicious and
mistrustful of your ideas, he'll say things he doesn't mean and
the rules of conversation get broken easily. Then when he says
things just to be clever, witty and one up on you to defend
himself, he's often misunderstood, misquoted and disliked for
being a smart-arse. 'Mmmm,' he mumbles into his coffee mug
wisely, 'of course I've had more affairs than you've had hot
dinners, and so I know how relationships work, and that's not
very often.' Or you get the true sceptic: 'Astrology? What a joke.
Let me tell you why it doesn't work.' All this sneering, doubting
and pessimism is really only a battle with his own curiosity,
fascination and gullibility, which he just can't bear to face. He's
threatened by knowledge and in his rush to defend himself, he
often forgets that the one thing we fear in others is usually what
we haven't yet accepted in ourselves.

saturn in cancer

Emotional and material security is a serious business for him. He
feels contained by those things which make him feel secure, but
he also feels trapped by them. He's so vulnerable that he needs
emotional safety at all costs. Now this can make him threatened

by anyone that tries to get close to him, so he desensitizes himself. Then he only has relationships that are non-committed and guards his vulnerable side with chauvinistic or macho materialism which he thinks brings him security he can handle, or he searches for relationships where he can hide his feelings away. He'll play cool, remote and unfeeling on the surface, but underneath he's hurting, trapped, unable to feel truly safe, because it's not love, just a protection racket he's got himself involved in. He hates to be alone, but he wants to be alone. This is where he needs to find a balance, otherwise his resentment is often the resulting compensation. Then he'll begin to judge and criticize. What he needs to learn is to find safety within himself, to recognize he can't hang all that naked vulnerability act on another person and to respect his own sensitivity.

saturn in leo

Personal performance is everything to this man and it's his greatest test and challenge. If he's not the star of the show he can get mean. But it's a meanness built around his fear of not being the best. This can sometimes lead to 'no negotiation is better than some'. That's when you come up against a brick wall of arrogance or disdain. If he's learnt to use all that creative, shining, self-interest well, then there's no one who does it better. In intimate relationships this gives him the chance to be magnanimous, but it also can make him assume that you're merely an extension of him and his creativity. He's threatened by other people being more creative than he is. And when threatened, he'll use others' creativity for himself and truly believe that their knowledge is really his. Say you've suddenly developed a taste for archaeology or anthropology. Well, what a coincidence, that's a subject he knows everything about!

He needs to learn that to shine, you have to do it properly, and that means not being vulnerable or fearful of other people's impressiveness and trying to out-impress – or gaze into your vanity-mirror every time it pops out of your handbag at that party.

saturn in virgo

Obsessive and critical at worst, he's not going to be easy to unbend. Improving himself comes first. He might be a gym-freak, health-freak or workaholic, but whatever gives him that sense of ritual will keep him sane, believe me! The problem is that, although critical of others, he is the one who is most vulnerable to criticism. Once threatened, he simply retaliates with the same tactics. It may be a touch of emotional blackmail, as in 'You're always so wrapped up in your work, you never have time for me,' or an obsession, maybe with your untidiness. Never mind his own chaos. His biggest defence is to mentally attack, often by demanding that you tell him exactly what you mean. 'You didn't make yourself clear' is a favourite response of Saturn in Virgo. Alternatively, he may criticize your logic: 'I don't understand your reasoning.' The details are essential, not the bigger philosophical picture, he can do without that, thank you. He tends to know it all anyway. Not like Saturn in Leo, who needs to feel he's top cat, but because he is actually terrified of his own unpredictability and chaos. The test for him is to learn to be perceptive and to pay attention so that his critical judgement doesn't isolate him from that inner world, whether he feels comfortable with it or not.

saturn in libra

His greatest desire is for a relationship, but he's so idealistic that he often finds others just can't live up to his expectations. The test for him is to find a balance between his need for approval, because he just doesn't have much admiration for himself, and his need to love. He also has to learn to juggle with three balls, not just two, in finding a balance between his ideals, your ideals and reality. His biggest defence against his insecurity about loneliness is to play the charmer and the flatterer. It's all about strategy, and it's a very manipulative and subtle one. Yes, you're the most beautiful, stunning woman he's ever met, but then the next day he's as cool and remote as a block of ice. And after that he flirts with your best friend and stages all kinds of scenarios playing you off against his ex.

This is all because relationship is his greatest desire but his greatest fear too. A relationship implies reality, human flaws and weaknesses, not the ideals of perfection he lives by. So the more people who love him, the greater his sense of worth, because a one-to-one long-term relationship seems hellishly fraught with illusions, and disillusions. He has to learn that love isn't just about being adored by others, it's overcoming the desire simply to be loved and to work at learning how to love. It's hard work and often painful on the way, so he has problems finding those moments of perfection in the imperfectness of relationship. A man who's conscious of his idealism, realizes that his search for the perfect relationship is a paradox and actually likes himself without relying on a gaggle of adoring women to do it for him has a head start here.

saturn in scorpio

He takes power, money, sex and magic seriously. And I mean seriously. If Saturn is where we have to keep paying attention to ourselves, where we have to work to become an expert, rather than a busker, then this man has to really come to terms with the most vulnerable side of himself. Emotional commitment is a serious business for him and any kind of betrayal cuts more deeply than you can imagine. So he's not going to let you get any closer than he wants, not for one minute. The boundary is fixed, high, wide and deep, and it's rare that he'll let anyone through.

His fear of his own feelings means he often compensates by either denying he has any or becoming rigidly defensive or jealous, but never admitting it. Then he drowns in negative feelings. If he doesn't realize they're his own, he will project them onto you and accuse you of all kinds of vindictiveness. Does he get suspicious when you're late for a date? Yes, of course. Secretly you're betraying him, meeting someone else. And he'll resent your mild flirtation with his best friend and use it against you when you least expect it. Then even his seething becomes your fault. You're the one who's jealous, possessive, treacherous even. He can also make sweeping generalizations about why women are always seductive, two-faced or manipulative.

Saturn in Scorpio, when handled right, can make a man an expert in human relationships, in feeling and in passion. But working at it is not easy, simply because it's underground, hidden work, not something that's easy to bring out into the light of day and discuss mildly over a curry. Take care with this one, but care about him too.

saturn in sagittarius

He's compelled to find a belief system to run his life by, but he's also fearful of being committed to it. So, when other people's ideas, dreams and visions seem to be based in some kind of reality, they become threatening, especially if he hasn't developed his own. He'll compensate by turning cynical, by taking sides or by perfecting the art of name-dropping, just to convince himself that he has some claim to success and so that others might see him as more like those he's hanging around with. He's so fearful of failure, it's often easier to perch on someone else's fame or notoriety than his own. Yes, he knows film stars, rock stars, all about the stars, and yes, he's been there done it, seen it, you name it, he's been there.

Saturn in Sagittarius has to believe in something. Life and love have to have *some* kind of meaning. But he can get very defensive about what he believes in, so you get the scenario where he's always rising to the bait when others criticize him. Then he can get fanatical, especially if Jupiter is in a passionate sign like Aries. However, when he realizes that grounding his visions is not as frightening as he believes, he can become an expert in philosophy, in ideas and in himself.

saturn in capricorn

He needs to develop some gravitas and a real serious sense of personal achievement, otherwise he can wallow in depression and self-disgust. The more he's got to focus on, the better. And personal success does come to him, but it often takes longer than most people have patience for. That's why he can get very defensive about his ambitions, his work and his career. Time, money and success are all taken incredibly seriously and he can become quite ruthless in his desire to achieve more than anyone else. Breaking the rules of the game isn't on. He usually knows it, but if he doesn't, he may have to pay a high price. One of the rules of relationships he is often tempted to break is trying to change you into something you're not. That's because he gets so fanatical about what he believes is right for you that any opposition just makes it more of a challenge for him to prove his point and never budge. Of course, he's being defensive because he's had to really work hard and discipline himself to get where he is, or even get onto the road at all. So why shouldn't everyone else, including you?

His greatest fear is not being in control of himself – of his emotions mostly. And that's why he'll perhaps try to control you too. Emotional feelings muddle up his great visions and romance isn't easy, because it's wild, mysterious and uncontrollable. When he sees meat and potatoes on his plate that gives him pleasure, but a curdling mass of exotica just makes him furious because it's so chaotic. He will become an expert in something, because that is how he'll defend his vulnerable side, but just make sure he's not an expert in fanaticism.

saturn in aquarius

Idealistic at best, egocentric at worst, his biggest fear is that he's only human after all. With such vision and intellectual awareness, he can seem as if he rules the world, or at least know which politics will be in vogue in 400 years' time. The problem is that he thinks ahead and at tangents, and that means he has very little time to be merely human, which would involve accepting the flaws of life, love and himself. He is genuinely concerned with the welfare of everyone else, as long as they conform to his ideals, but his visions and high principles can make you tear your hair out. And because he always seems fair and duty bound and ultra-conscious of what others want, he'll often accuse you of being so principled that *you're* the one who's being unfair.

Romance is in his head, but not so often in his arms. That human warmth that he desperately needs is often lacking in himself and he has to learn that your opinions matter just as much as his. When you love your job but he asserts, 'You can't possibly work in that office, it really isn't the right environment for you, what you need is fresh air and politics, not small-talk and air-conditioning,' then remember, it's just because he'd really like to be a human being too.

saturn in pisces

Of course he's ultra-defensive about his sensitive side, but what
he fears most is his own gullibility, his own gentleness and his
own compassion. He doesn't want to be easily led astray, to be
shapeshifting, one day feeling one thing, the next another. So
he'll build a few high walls around this and become martyrish,
or play the victim. Then it's always everyone else's fault that he's
angry, or it's your fault he's feeling so damned hurt, because you
didn't call when you said and, unlike him, you're always making
up excuses.

Deep down it hurts him to have to achieve the things which are
expected of him, because then he can't go on dreaming about
them. That's why he'll sometimes give up on things, like
relationships, his work or even his visions, because his
confidence is actually a very subtle thread in his emotional seam
and can easily be unpicked. That's when you get the moodiness
and the accusations: 'Find another man who'll make a success of
his life' or 'Leave me alone, I'm not worth worrying about.'

Those Saturn in Pisces men who were born in the 1960s with
Pluto and Uranus in Virgo find this a particularly hard road.
They're having to work through not only a personal barrier, but
also a social one. They have the feeling that they have to build
some kind of tangible sense of achievement for themselves, yet
they must rebel against the authority they meet in the big wide
world. But let Saturn in Pisces find his own authority and he'll
become an expert in compassion and understanding.

chemical
reaction

HIS VENUS AND MOON

Now that you know so much about your man, you're bound to be
curious about what he imagines you to be and what he actually
projects onto you. His Moon and Venus signs tell you exactly
that. The Moon is also how he 'experiences' you, but just because
he has the Moon in Libra, for example, you don't have to be a
Sun Libra or have other planets in Libra for him to see you this
way. However, if you do, then that's a bonus, because you will
share the values, qualities and traits which he's searching for in a
woman. Remember, it's his Moon, his experience and his need.
It's his Venus, his loves and his values. The only catch is that
he'll often experience and imagine you to be like this, even if
you're totally the opposite! This is simply because we project all
kinds of stuff onto the person we fall in love with. That's why
when you first meet, he has a kind of idealized image of his
perfect woman, just as you have an idealized image of your

perfect man. It's not necessarily something you're both conscious of, but you both carry this image in your mind and soul.

The chances are there are many qualities in you that reflect his Moon or Venus and it's not necessarily because you have planets in that sign. That's where astrology gets more complex than there's space for in this book. But if you can cross that bridge and realize what it is that he likes, responds to and warms to, then you can be that woman for him, as long as there's a part of you that is willing and able and tolerant of those needs. Once you get past the first date you both usually know if something clicks between you or not. And often it's the magical hook of idealized images that keeps you fascinated with each other.

The most difficult scenarios are when his Moon and Venus are in very different signs, say, for example, Cancer and Aquarius. Aquarius is all mind and ideas, emotionally repressive and resistant to change. Cancer, on the other hand, is all feelings, restless and sensitive. How does he align these two very different sides to his nature? He might side with his Aquarian Venus and place great value on companionship, intellectual chit-chat and experimental sex and might project all his Moon stuff onto you. Then he sees you, rather than himself, as restless, changeable and over-reactionary. You might actually have some Cancerian planets and then he can really hook into this side of your personality. What he does then is either to admire these qualities in you or accuse you of being possessive, insecure and manipulative, the shadow side of his Moon in Cancer. Then he'll have trouble merging his Cancerian Moon into his ideal feminine image and will perhaps never feel that he's met the right woman.

Another problem occurs when, for example, he has the Moon in restless Sagittarius and all your planets are basically homely ones, so the thought of jumping on the next flight to San

Francisco at the crack of dawn sends shivers of fear down your spine rather than pangs of excitement. Then, however much you try to be his Moon experience for him, you'll never feel comfortable with yourself, because you're just not being yourself. Read Chapter 8 for more on contacts between charts.

his venus/moon in aries

If you can keep him guessing, gushing, diving and hunting, and drive him wild, he'll be in heaven, for a while at least. Support his passion for sport, whether sexual or at the local sky-diving club, and keep the romance sparkling. Sentimental gooey romance? Never. He values the drama of it all and sees you as the vixen, the huntress and the princess waiting to be rescued, or to at least have someone to catch her when she climbs out of that ivory tower herself. He'll imagine unrequited love and dash around in hot pursuit like a Formula One racing driver. That kind of romance keeps him inspired, Romeo-like and full of passion.

Where sex is concerned, he's gallant, impulsive and unrestrained. But watch out for battle zones, if you're just as feisty. If you're merely pretending to be the unpredictable, independent woman of his dreams, he'll soon catch on to your game and see right through you, especially if he has the Moon in Aries, because what's in your heart will be very vivid to him. This is a man with intuition and a mission. Fire-queens are one thing, but damp squibs are soon forgotten. If you tell him how to run his life, or his business, he'll get angry. No one tells him what to do and he doesn't like being bossed around. But he does want a motivated woman who's dynamic, fast-paced and assertive about her own life. He enjoys rising to a challenging conversation and hurling a few plates around, but he'll loathe having a slanging match just because he's forgotten which day of the week it is. Today is hardly worth thinking about, tomorrow is everything and yesterday, well, it just doesn't exist.

He sees you as a woman with confidence, panache and above all the ability to do her own thing. An ordinary existence just doesn't work. There have to be fantasies, dreams and schemes, and no pruning hedges in the suburbs, that's really out to lunch. If he's actually doing anything as mundane as that, then perhaps it's the women in his life who are living out his wild side for him!

What you have to be is the ultimate heroine in his blockbuster movie. The warrior, the huntress, the daring romantic, whichever you are, he'll still want to hunt you too. Sex is an adventure and a fantasy. He's passionate and provocative, but he's not after sensuality, just pillow fights and sexual sparring. Don't try to tame him or control him and always be that motorbike freak or hang-glider in his head, even if not in real life. If you have planets in Aries, then you'll probably be able to live up to this image and if you have Aries rising you'll have qualities which match.

his venus/moon in taurus

First he needs to know where he stands and second, how much you value the good things in life. To him, the quality of everything really matters, whether it's the car you drive, the clothes you wear or your perfume you use. Quantity is irrelevant, but if you have an eye for beautiful things, taste that doesn't depend on fashion *per se* and you know that the price of everything is relative, then he'll admire and respect you. For him, that's more important than merely falling into a comatose in-loveness without worrying about the size of the bed and whether the mattress is worth its weight in gold.

It's like living with a department store. He acquires beautiful
things, whether antiques, clothes or a scented garden, and
anything which gives his eye pleasure gives his heart pleasure
too. So look good and don't fall into the trap of thinking that he's
an easy catch. Sporting rollers, looking a mess and wearing
ancient tatty knickers frankly doesn't turn him on. Never get
caught with anything less than your most beautiful lingerie or
naked persuasion. He sees you as the most gorgeous thing he's
ever set eyes on, so make sure you stay that way. And he's
reliable, so you must be equally self-reliant and able to prove
you're not going to walk out of that door when the going
gets tough.

Nature is just as important to him as materialism, and often more
so. That's because money and possessions are things he can see,
touch and feel, but the value he places on the sound of a lark, the
fields covered in dew at dawn or the last sunrise are equally if
not more important. If you love music, nature, art, beauty and
anything sensual, then you'll be an instant hit. And don't forget
he loves to be seduced and to seduce. Venus rules Taurus and
like the ultra self-indulgent goddess herself, he adores sensual
eroticism and all the games and art of seduction. If you have
planets in Taurus yourself, you'll respond to his sensual values,
his need for permanence and material security. If his Venus is in
Taurus, but his Moon is in a more fiery sign, like Aries, Leo or
Sagittarius, then be prepared to be slightly wild one moment and
down to earth and practical the next! Your dreams and your
values matter, so make sure you have them and can put them
into practice.

Financial matters can be the hub of his life, so make sure you
know where you stand with your own money. But he's just as
likely to want to trip around the hills, stumble across some
mountain hideaway and live like a hermit with you for at least a

few days. After that, civilization haunts him and the train, the
bus, the car and the lure of a good life with no worries usually
bring him back to reality.

his venus/moon in gemini

Wit, intelligence and the ability to change your mind make him
feel comfortable. And if you're as equally fascinated by life,
words, communication and what makes other people tick as he
is, he'll find you incredibly sexy. Holding a conversation in bed
across the pillows is far more erotic to him than holding a glass
of champagne to his lips. If you're always on the phone rather
than ironing, always scribbling love letters or e-mails rather than
dreaming of that novel you'll one day write, you'll be his star. He
needs conversation to stimulate his mind and a light, sparkling
approach to the routines and rigours of life. He thinks rather than
feels, and that means you have to be pretty smart and clever to
always be reasonable, rather than reactionary. If you have planets
in Gemini, you're off to a head start. But remember, playing the
game and pretending you're a witty, restless, adaptable woman,
when in fact you'd rather not budge from your sofa except to put
the chips on is like playing with a born-again Houdini. He'll be
out of the bathroom window very quickly if he senses any
complacency, pushiness or malingering.

Socially, you must be able to talk to anyone and also look good.
He's happiest with very feminine, flirty independent types who
give him as much freedom as he respects in them. He hates being
tied down and although he has a penchant for being tied up
occasionally, it's always in fun. Now 'fun' is a word you have to
love and laugh about. Distract him with a new idea, a joke, a
change of subject and he's happiest. Snuggle up in front of the
TV every night and he'll get bored. Think humour and light

conversations and you'll woo him, especially if you can seduce him over the phone at the office and talk about any subject under the sun. He can certainly sit down and talk about feelings, emotions and anything, even in depth, as long as it's not about himself. If Venus is in Gemini and his Moon in a more sensitive sign, like Scorpio, Cancer or Pisces, he might project all that emotional side of his nature on you. Then, when he's feeling moody, grim or emotional, he'll tell you you're too sentimental, too moody or too intense. Check where your planets are to see whether he's liable to hook his Moon onto you in this way. Alternatively, if he has the Moon in Gemini, not Venus, he might start accusing you of being flippant and lightweight, when in fact really it's him.

Sharpness of mind, amusement of body and a woman who can talk her way out of an awkward social corner will thrill him. Be scintillating, even if it kills you. Then you'll be sure he's breathless because you're stunning everyone else – and he's definitely a man who likes to be with a woman who can impress.

his venus/moon in cancer

He imagines you to be sensuous, sensitive and caring. He's sentimental and deeply emotional, particularly if he has the Moon rather than Venus in Cancer. This can make him either very soft and protective, or, if he represses his feelings, he'll be looking for all those homely, cosy, security blankets in you. He likes you to be as sincere about your feelings as he is about his. The one big factor you have to consider, even if he's not aware of it, or won't admit to it, is that Mother plays an awfully big role in his life. Now, if you're the motherly, warm, protective type, you'll have little problem, but he also imagines you to be a little like his own mother. This is when it gets complicated, because

some Moon Cancer men hate their mothers and some adore
them. Be careful how you deal with the subject of his mum,
because it's a deep issue, not something to bring lightly to the
dinner table on your first date.

But he also sees you as strong, independent, changeable, restless
and able to swap plans and drop schemes at a drop of a hat.
That's because he's so moody and imaginative himself. If you
don't feel the feeling that he gets, the one when he says, 'I've got
a feeling we should go to the party, not the film tonight,' then
you'll be in for a very hard shell-like experience of his Cancer
streak. This is when he can be so fearful of his own emotional
dependency that he snaps, manipulates and plays the macho
image for all it's worth, just to avoid his vulnerable side. And
when he accuses you of being possessive, clingy and moody, he's
projecting all his own vulnerable side onto you. That's why
you've got to be a bit of a good drinking pal in his eyes and be
ready to hang out with his friends when he's feeling in need of
male company. He's money conscious, too, not in the material
way of the Earth signs, but in a very clingy, evasive way. And he
expects you to be as careful and shrewd about your finances as
he is.

He can over-romanticize Mother, too, so that she does no wrong.
Then he'll either imagine you can never live up to her cooking,
her way of bringing up children, her glamour, her mystique and
her beauty, or he'll see it all written in indelible ink on your
forehead. You are Supermum, sophisticated, wise and secure as a
rock. Tender and gentle, he'll look into your eyes and see his
own sensitivity, and then you'll move him, because he's so easily
moved by anything that resembles himself and his own inner
battle with his insecurity. He sees you as special, totally
dedicated to his needs and someone who'll rescue him from his
mother, whether he's devoted to her or hates the ground she

walks on. He needs to free himself somehow from the spell she has over him and you'll be the one who does it. If you have planets in Cancer, you won't find it difficult to be Wonder Woman, but if you've Fire or Air planets, you could start feeling as though you're caught in quicksand.

his venus/moon in leo

He imagines you to be the queen of his dreams and as starry-eyed about him as he is about you. Glamorous women appeal to him and make him feel comfortable because he values the best. Anything less won't do. So if you have planets in Leo, you're off to a good start. He's looking for the special creative qualities in you that make him feel good about himself. That's why if you naturally have an air of authority, creativity and regality, he'll feel that he's got someone on his arm who will make him feel special. Your professional and social status count, and if you're the kind of woman who adores a spot of drama in your life, you'll have considerable pulling power. Being successful and outrageously glamorous helps a bit too. Secretly he wants to impress everyone else, so the more daring, brilliant and striking you are, the better. It's not so much that you have to be a supermodel, but if you can walk like one, smile at everyone as if you're a film star and act a bit, too, he'll be in heaven.

He admires women with egos – and battle tactics. So if you're not prepared to rant and rave a bit, or show how queenly you are when it comes to who's going to demean themselves and put the rubbish out when you've just got dressed up in your glad-rags, then he might accuse you of being vain and selfish. If you have planets in Leo, Aries or Sagittarius, you should be able to handle his passionate streak. He likes a woman who can toss her head and steam off in a temper rather than one who sulks and throws herself on the bed in despair. The catch is, you have to be willing to accept his rather temperamental nature too. But he can make you feel as though you're wearing the cat's pyjamas. He excels at making you feel good, so that he feels good. A sexually passionate, demanding and yet dramatic woman makes him feel comfortable with his own sex drive. Which is usually pretty dynamic. But he's also looking for someone who can provide all that down-to-earth reality of poaching eggs perfectly and still looking as if they've been at the beauty parlour all morning. Vitality, colour and living life to the full are part of his fiery package, and you'd better keep up with it all, or else. You have to have total faith in him and then he'll have faith in you. But his stubborn pride can sometimes result in all kinds of scenarios, especially if you ever make him feel stupid in public. He's a gallant, dashing figure who wants a glamorous companion he can sweep off her feet. Let him, and always tell him he's the best, and he'll be yours for life.

his venus/moon in virgo

He imagines you to be smart, intelligent and most of all hard-working. The more useful the job you do and the more intelligent you are, the sexier he'll find you. What he sees in you is ambition, logic and body-awareness. That's why you have to keep yourself in good shape and worry about whether you bought enough organic yoghurt, rather than about how many fizzy drinks you've downed in a day. Cool, unemotional behaviour makes him feel comfortable, particularly if he has the Moon in Virgo. That's because he's not comfortable with his own feelings, which are all very mysterious. So, be natural, reasonable and realistic about your hopes, dreams and expectations. And be fussy about your clothes, your make up and your bathroom, and keep it squeaky clean and smelling fresh.

That way he'll realize you have the same values as he does. What
he wants is not so much perfection – that's Libran territory – but
a sense of discrimination. So he sees that there's a use for that
new-fangled grape de-seeder, not that it's hanging on the kitchen
wall like a work of art. If what is of use, what is real and what is
practical all come together in your kitchen, that's far more
satisfying to him than trying to perfect soufflés. Getting idealistic
notions about how to please him with brilliant white floors and
never a fingermark on the walls is perfectionism, and that's not
actually a Virgo trait. But discrimination is. Watch out, though, if
he has one or other of these two planets in Libra, as then he *will*
expect the glasses to be gleaming and the grass to be greener than
anyone else's.

Venus in Virgo values the sensuous side of sex, but also the
privacy of it. So, be cool in public, even if it kills you. No kissing,
snogging or fondling under the restaurant table, please. On the
other hand be willing to be the erotic vamp beneath the sheets.
Crisp white linen would be nice, too.

Be politically correct when it comes to your work, or he won't
take you seriously. He sees that you are clever enough to know
how to survive in this world, that you're not just a pretty face or
a glamour queen, that you've got a head and you know how to
use it. But he also imagines you need him at a very down-to-
earth level. Because he likes to feel useful himself, don't forget.
And if you don't have the same ideas about working together on
any kind of project, whether it's mending the leaky tap or
building a tree house for a mini-retreat, then he'll get sharp and
critical. How could your views be different from his? Accusing
you of nit-picking and criticism is really his defence, because he
loathes those traits in himself.

However, if you can be a calm, cool and collected woman who doesn't forget the phone bill, drop coffee on the floor or leave your tights on the bath, then he'll let you in on his romantic streak. The reality that he's so obsessed with is only the one he sees before him. The other reality, which is that relationships do have a magical, mysterious side, is the one he really has to learn to trust through you.

his venus/moon in libra

He's always drawn to beauty, a pretty face and a soft feminine voice. He imagines you to be romantic through and through. It has to be all rosebuds, poetry and beautiful bodies merging in gorgeous surroundings. He's looking for a woman with taste, who can appreciate his own vanity too. Yes, he's very fond of gazing at himself in the mirror and can preen himself in the bathroom for longer than even you. He sees you as someone who always looks wonderful and never turns into a raging she-wolf, never has spots on her face and certainly doesn't walk around in tatty underwear. He has to have harmony and that means no rows, no complaints and no jealous tantrums. That's why you have to appreciate his desire to watch other beautiful women or his comments about how beautiful your best friend is. It's not that he's comparing you, it's just that he needs to be adored so much, he often unconsciously riles you so as to get you swooning at his feet again. Venus or Moon in Libra values and feels better around a goddess-like partner. You don't have to be Venus herself, though that would do very nicely, but you do have to be a lady, and above all charming, ultra-feminine and willing to please him.

Romantic sex, pretty lingerie, beautiful surroundings and light-hearted teasing turn him on. But he wants you to be perfect, which is a pretty hard ideal for any human being to live up to, especially as it includes being willing to sit and discuss your relationship with complete reason, rationale and logic. Love must be discussed, not brought down to silly manipulative games. Not that he's beyond those, but the more willing you are to agree you're 50 per cent to blame for the misunderstanding, the more he'll listen and the less evasive he'll be.

You have to want to be a good companion too. And that means sleeping, eating, living and doing all kinds of things together. If you're a more independent soul, beware. He'll talk about 'us' and if you prefer to talk about 'me', then think carefully whether this is the right man for you. He imagines you'll always share his ideals, never explode with rage or be irrational, or set off on a mountain bike without him. If you have planets in Libra, you'll find this harmony easy to appreciate. But if you have planets in more temperamental signs, like Aries, Cancer, Scorpio or Leo, then you might find he shatters a few of his own dreams himself and starts to play hard to get. Check out his Venus, if it's not in Libra and his Moon is. That will give you a clue as to whether he can handle a more volatile relationship. If Venus is in a sign like Taurus, Gemini, Virgo or Pisces, then he's definitely a peace-lover and won't want his dreams trampled on. So, love his dreams, let him escape into the ether for a while and then he'll be the ultimate romantic.

his venus/moon in scorpio

He's looking for the most passionate, intense woman who can share his emotional need for sex and intimacy. He imagines you to be a kind of all-or-nothing soulful lover, a *femme fatale* who's sexually mysterious and knows all about the taboo side of love. He's going to be pretty secretive about his own sex drive, too.

That is, until he's sure he's probed deeply enough into your psyche to be sure he can trust you with his secret weapon: sex. His own libido is all about tangled sheets and locked doors. He assumes you won't reveal your bedroom secrets to anyone, and if you do, he'll probably have left the neighbourhood before you've had time to phone and apologize.

You have to be private, intimate and passionate about him and no one else. This man can get pretty jealous if you even look at another male torso. This is fine if you've got planets in Scorpio or it is your Rising sign. Then you'll be able to handle this kind of intense love, intense possessiveness and deeper well of insecurity. If you have Air or Fire planets, in Aries, Gemini, Leo, Sagittarius, Libra or Aquarius, however, you might find his dedication to the dark a little intimidating. If you're squeaky clean and would rather talk all night than raise his pulse-rate, beware. This man takes sex very seriously, even if he's cool and remote on the surface. He sees you as a mistress rather than a wife, or as a woman who is waiting for a potent transformative love that will be all-consuming. There's always something rather weird about Scorpio relationships. They change everything about your life on a subtle level. And that's ultimately what he wants – transformation. He's longing for some kind of almost mystical sexual experience that normal human relationships can rarely provide. That's why he's never lukewarm, always either consumingly hot or frighteningly cold.

Take great care he doesn't complain you're too possessive or jealous. This is when you know you're in danger of not getting through to him. He's acutely sensitive to his own feelings of possessiveness and has to take some kind of control, even if it's by instigating a few deadly emotional dramas. He also has a tendency to feel that he owns you, but beware of ever admitting that you want to own him, even though he can sometimes bring out all kinds of accusations about how you do. 'Don't keep telling me I owe you anything, you're so possessive, so demanding' is really a projection of his own deep fear of being betrayed or walked over.

Ultimately he's looking for the deep experience, the profound unknown something that he sees in you. So smoulder away with care. If you have Water planets – planets in Cancer, Scorpio or Pisces – you'll respect and understand his depth of feeling and his desire for the most erotic, moving experience. There are really no half-measures with him. Be adored, loved and possessed, and you'll really know it.

his venus/moon in sagittarius

He imagines you to be a wild, laughing companion, who'll travel on impulse and find romance and excitement more intimate than a warm cosy sofa. You have to be freedom-loving and independent enough to fit in with his own rather crusading spirit. He sees you as being frank, outspoken and self-confident. Unpack your toothbrush, but never leave tell-tale accessories to give you the option of a return visit. The 'I forgot my ear-rings, I'm sure they're under your bed' excuse to phone him will go right over his head. And he'll see right through your ruse. Commitment, promises and pressure aren't what he's looking for. But fun, craziness and a little exotica are. Be daring, but do it without manipulating his need for space. When he suggests a weekend break skiing, don't rush out and book it as a surprise present. The chances are he won't even remember the enthusiastic chit-chat the next day, let alone turn up at the airport. But he does like a woman who does her own thing. So play it the other way. Book your own skiing holiday and he'll pitch up in your chalet when you least expect it.

Honesty is something he admires in you. So make sure when you really want to tell him how you feel, it's the truth. No silly mind or emotional games, only wilder sexy ones. If you have planets in Sagittarius or Sagittarius rising, you should be able to handle his sense of adventure and that restless wandering side that he sees in you too. He'll also assume you're prepared to talk about your ex-lovers with the same kind of enthusiasm as he talks about his. He won't usually be jealous, unless his Moon or Venus are in a very different sign like Scorpio or Cancer. Then he'll flounder between extremes of passionate possessiveness and his own need for freedom. Whichever he doesn't admit to, he'll probably hang on you. Then you'll get the 'Give me some space and don't be so needy' or 'Look, you're so free and easy, I don't know where I stand' syndrome.

Be exotic, be sexy, be daring. Be natural, independent and a bit street-wise. Those are the qualities he respects and loves in you. Socially, it helps to know the right places to be seen in and to know the right people. And of course, you have a nose for sniffing out where the next 'in' restaurant is. Not because it has good food – that doesn't really matter – but because it's good to be seen there.

Give him space and freedom, be positive about life and love, and he'll give you the space and the freedom to do exactly the same. Make sure you truly want that kind of open relationship, though, before you leap into his kind of fire.

his venus/moon in capricorn

He imagines you to be like the Rock of Gibraltar – solid, reliable and with a bit of interesting history. If you have family connections or have inherited vats of money or even just good

breeding, he'll be totally immersed in you. You don't *have* to be
an aristocrat or know a member of a royal family, but you do
have to be seriously status-oriented and have more class and
style than chit-chat. He especially admires innate qualities of
sophisticated worldliness and stylish classic womanliness.
Organize your wardrobe like a military parade, don't wear tights
when you could be wearing real silk stockings and always be
self-assured at any dinner party, and he'll probably marry you.
Yes, traditional values are *de rigueur*. So if you're actually more
concerned with independence or an alternative lifestyle, or tell
him you'll meet him in Venezuela in two years' time, he simply
won't be there. But if you are professional, diplomatic and
dedicated to both his success and your own, then he'll meet you
in the kitchen at midnight. The boardroom meetings you've both
been attending all day will become a focus of conversation.
Ambition is a plus point. He sees you as ruthless and determined
where your work is concerned, and doesn't expect you to be the
kind of woman who'd rather flit around the shopping mall every
day gossiping to pals than be out making your career into
something valuable and stable.

He'll fall for you if you're serious about life, love and work. He
feels comfortable with cool conversations and controlled
affection, particularly in public. If he has Venus in Capricorn, he
sees you as mature and wise enough to never argue with him and
always support him. In front of his colleagues or if he's out
socializing to make contacts, you have to be squeaky clean and
never flirt with another man. You are the flagship of his
reputation, so you have little choice but to behave like one, as
well as being the perfect wife, PA, lover and diplomat. Then he'll
give you all the attention, love and smouldering passion that
lurks beneath that practical composed smile.

If you think you can be the chic, confident working wife of his dreams, you'll find him the most committed and perennial of men. He might think you're too fanatical about your work, too unemotional and uncaring, or too disciplined and wilful, but that's when he's denying certain bytes in himself and projecting them onto you. He's not easy to get close to, unless he has either Venus or the Moon in a more sensitive sign like Pisces, Cancer or Scorpio, and he's more likely to fall for your stylish, sophisticated aura if you have planets in Capricorn, too. Then you can be sure of being bonded and never betrayed for life.

his venus/moon in aquarius

He imagines you to be the most independent, unusual woman, one who acts differently and thinks differently from everyone else. What he feels comfortable with is when you're frank, free, uncommitted and liberated enough to have one of those 'open' relationships. Of course it's best if he gets most of the freedom. But he admires and values you if you have your own space too. He sees you as slightly crazy, always unpredictable and willing to go to any lengths to be a little bit unconventional. He wants a woman who won't tie him down, but also one who'll be there as a friend when he needs one. That word 'friend' is very important, because he'll have lots of his own, both men and women. So if you're a possessive type who wants to keep him to yourself, trouble could brew. Give him loads of rope, plenty of bizarre and slightly surprising ideas and experiences, and he'll probably be able to commit himself in a very non-committal way. That doesn't mean he'll move in with you like a shot, but he will give you the kind of love he values, which is honest, frank and free.

Emotions aren't things he'll want to discuss. He might analyse you and psycho-babble away at you, but it's the love of the mind

which is important to him, not his feelings. The less emotional
you are, the longer you'll keep him fascinated. He wants to find
out everything about you, so keep a few bits secret, and always
appear to be detached, progressive and willing to rationalize
everything he does. Being prepared for his rather open approach
to relationships means you won't be surprised when he turns up
for dinner with one of his ex-girlfriends. Not that he's likely to
call anyone 'my ex' – they're just his friends and that's that. If
you can join in his need to make up the rules and make changes
when he feels – or rather thinks – it's time to do so, you'll get
along splendidly. Live your life and never try to live his for him.
He can accuse you of being too principled and judgemental, but
that's often a cover up for his own assumptions.

However much he sees you as free, easy and unconventional,
though, he needs that liberty to be himself. If you have planets in
Aquarius you'll probably find it easy. If you have planets in less
experimental signs, like Taurus, Virgo, Capricorn or Cancer,
you'll find it difficult to live up to his rather wild, erratic sense of
what a relationship is. In a way he's also very idealistic about
any relationship and that's why he finds it difficult to live within
the binding legalities of marriage or even within assumptions
about one-to-one partnerships. But if you are original, exciting
and inspiring, you might find he's around a lot longer than you
thought. That kind of freedom does have its bonuses, for both of
you.

his venus/moon in pisces

He sees you as the ultimate romantic, a woman who needs
rescuing or who will rescue him from the reality of life. You're
beautiful, gentle, sensitive and protean in his eyes. He'll want to
write you poetry, play you music and scrawl love messages on

your windscreen or mirror. He may even hang out in bars waiting
for you with flowers and misty eyes. He imagines you to be
mysterious and sensuous. Dreamy and distant, you're very
ephemeral, coming and going, elusive and evasive. With Venus
in Pisces he'll probably have amazing fantasies and imagine
you're the most perfect, understanding woman on Earth. He
values the feminine qualities that you exude, but be careful, as
he can also get disillusioned if you're don't live up to his
imagination. Dirty laundry, mortgages and pensions aren't
exactly what he's looking for in a woman. Romantic sex, gazing
longingly into the sunset together and loads of trips to art
galleries, concerts and the sea are. He's also sure you'd give up
your job, your career or your husband for him. He's that
idealistic. And when he gets carried away with some fantasy
about how much of a martyr you are or how you put up with the
realities of life, make sure you give him the feeling he's being
saved from the harshness of life too.

If you have planets in Pisces, you'll respond to this kind of
victim–saviour co-dependency quite well. And if he has a more
down-to-earth Venus or Moon, you could find he's a lot more
dependable and stable himself. Then he might well project all
that dreamy elusive stuff onto you. That's when he'll say things
like, 'You're always looking lost, as if everyone's victimizing you'
or 'Why don't you write that novel, all it takes is discipline.' This
is really about himself, of course.

His sensitivity might be alien to the expectations that society or
his family have placed on him to be 'a man'. Then he can harden
himself against his own feelings and seem quite the opposite.
That's when you become the fantasy lover, the woman he can
never have. He often actually falls in love with unattainable
women, just so he can feel secretly rejected and then play the
martyr himself. There's always one end of a Piscean relationship

which needs helping or rescuing. That's fine if you're both into a spot of mutual redemption, but love for him is not financial knots and materialism, or taking out credit on a car together. It's about the romance and beauty of falling in love and never believing that it has to change. That's why he often disappears into the night before it all gets too real and shatters his dreams. If he stays, it's because you're both living the romance and the spiritual closeness that he so desperately needs.

part

3

together

working it out

The compatibility chart, or 'synastry', as it's known in astrological circles, basically gives you both your and your boyfriend's chart to compare and analyse, to see what you have in common and what could be a problem between you. It looks at your personalities to see whether you have a chance of long-term happiness or just a short sexy fling. Of course, the latter might be what you're looking for anyway. The outer wheel is usually his and the inner wheel is usually yours, so you can easily see where the planets make contact. Astrologers look at both charts individually and then put them together to form one chart, as you are about to do. There's also something known as a 'composite chart', because for professional astrologers there's much more to it than just looking at the planetary contacts between charts. There's also the relationship itself which is created by merging the two charts into one, the composite.

Professional synastry looks not only at the inter-aspects between charts but also the house positions, the signs, affinities and the current transit of planets relating to both charts.

This book gives you a simplified version of the real thing, but one which will still enable you to discover far more about your relationship than just looking at your two charts separately.

So this is where you have to start doing some practical work.

CREATING THE COMPATIBILITY CHART

Obviously, working out your exact Rising sign is the most difficult thing, simply because the time changes of your birth date and the place where you were born can make a lot of difference. But use the chart at the end of the book to see which is your closest Rising sign and read both descriptions if you are on the cusp of one sign and another or don't know your exact time of birth. If you really have no idea of your time of birth, ask a friend to work out which Rising sign fits you most.

The best solution is of course to get a chart done in a flash through the Internet or computer-aided astrology services, which will give you the exact Rising sign, as long as you have a birth time.

To draw up the compatibility chart, use the blank chart on the facing page or copy it and make your own.

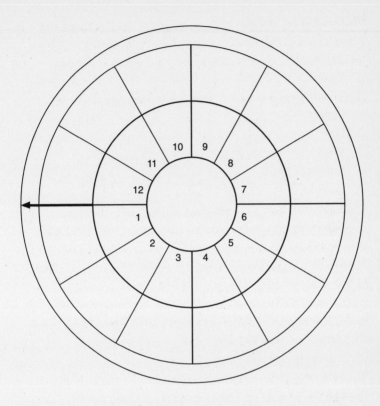

First you need to enter your Rising sign. Your Rising sign starts from the arrow on the left of the chart. This is the sign that was rising over the Eastern horizon at the moment of your birth. So write either the glyph for the sign or just the name in the segment marked 1. Then place all the other signs in the order shown below, but make sure you go in an anti-clockwise direction, following the numbers. So, for example, if your Rising sign is Cancer, then the sign that goes into the second segment would be Leo, and so on.

Here's the order of signs:

♈ Aries
♉ Taurus
♊ Gemini
♋ Cancer
♌ Leo
♍ Virgo
♎ Libra
♏ Scorpio
♐ Sagittarius
♑ Capricorn
♒ Aquarius
♓ Pisces

Next place the planets in the corresponding sections of each sign in the inner ring. Use the glyphs as shown below or just write in the names.

☉ Sun
☽ Moon
☿ Mercury
♀ Venus
♂ Mars
♃ Jupiter
♄ Saturn
♅ Uranus
♆ Neptune
♇ Pluto

For example, say you have the Moon in Aries, Jupiter in Libra and the Sun in Virgo and your Rising sign is Aries, the chart would look like this:

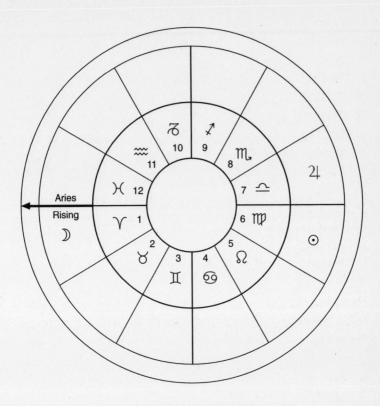

Fill in your other planets accordingly. This is not a professionally finished chart by the way, but it is a quick and easy way to check your man's planets in relation to yours.

Now look up all your man's planets and place them in the correct section of the outermost band. So, for example, carrying on with the same chart from above, if he has the Moon in Libra and Virgo rising, the chart will now look like this:

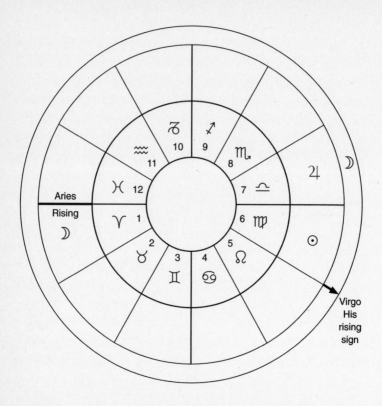

Gradually fill in all his planets and add his Rising sign last. Just draw a thick line through the outer band where his Rising sign starts, as in the above example. With Virgo rising, his Virgo starts at segment 6 (because that's where your Virgo sign starts), so draw the line at the beginning of segment 6 and write 'His Rising sign' next to it.

Once you have all the planets filled in, your chart should resemble something like this:

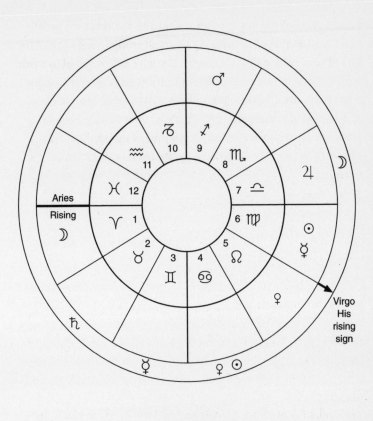

HOW TO USE THE CHART

Astrological compatibility is actually very complex. Normally, if a professional astrologer does a compatibility chart for you, they will look at the contacts that are very close by counting the degrees between the planets. But what you're going to discover here is the main points of contact between you and your man based on the signs that click into place or don't get on together. These are basically the plus contacts and the less easy ones.

I don't ever believe any contact is negative, but there are pitfalls and conflicts that often arise if you aren't really living out certain bits of your personality. Of course, if you're not prepared to work with understanding your different traits, then wherever planets don't naturally click into place there will be some kind of clash or a feeling of incompatibility. That's when we really have to work hard to ease the tension, or we project our shadow side onto others, or qualities become exaggerated or distorted in ourselves.

planetary contacts: good and not so good

Obviously, if you have planets in the same sign as your partner, you're going to feel comfortable with whatever those planets represent. This is particularly true of the personal planets, the Sun, Mercury, Venus, Mars and the Moon. But it can be more complicated if the sign also contains outer planets. *(See Chapter 9 for more information on generation differences and the outer planets.)*

So, for example, in our above chart, Jill has a Sun Virgo and John's rising Sign is Virgo, which is a very important and often long-term connection. They have a great deal in common in their outlook and outward behaviour in life.

But also look at signs which are *opposite* each other in the chart. For example, he has the Moon in Libra, which is a very sexy placement for her Jupiter in Libra. He's looking for a romantic harmonious relationship and her natural talent when she's in love is to be seductive and wildly romantic.

But his Moon is also opposite her Moon. That could mean there is a conflict between what makes them feel at their most comfortable. An Aries Moon instinctively rushes headlong into things alone. So Jill's reactions are quick, impulsive and quite self-willed. John, on the other hand, wants to share all decisions, do everything together and always think things through, rather than leaping in at the deep end. There's already a little clash of Moon signs here and it's likely that although these people will be attracted by their very different emotional needs, they could also get into all kinds of arguments – which her Aries Moon and Aries rising might actually enjoy, but which his Libran Moon and Virgo rising will just loathe.

Opposite signs are easy to spot, but signs that are *three away* from each other also create tensions. For example, count after her Moon in Aries, taking Taurus as one, Gemini as two and Cancer as three. Her Moon Aries will make his Sun Cancer feel insecure. Cancer Sun needs security, a clan, a family and home-cooking. Her Moon Aries is impatient and self-centred and the last thing she will want to do is cook the dinner when she could be out at every party. Also, her realistic Sun in Virgo would prefer to be taken out to dinner at the best restaurant than slave over a hot stove.

Beneficial contacts occur between planets in the same sign and those which are four signs apart. So again count after Virgo, taking Libra as one, Scorpio as two, Sagittarius as three and Capricorn as four. Neither Jill nor John have any planets in Capricorn, but if you count back in the same way from Virgo, you get back to Taurus and John has Saturn in Taurus, which could be a very binding contact for her Virgo Sun.

checklist of contacts

The simplest way to check all the contacts between your chart and his is to make two columns with your name and his at the top of each as shown below. Start with your Sun and see if there are any contacts between your Sun and his planets, then look at his Sun and see if there are any contacts with your planets, and so on. Finally you will have a list that looks something like this:

JOHN	JILL	
♄	☉	Easy
☉	♃	Clash
☉	☽	Clash
Rising	☉	Easy
☽	☽	Clash

etc.

OK, so it all sounds complicated! But once you've found some contacts between your charts and listed them, read the relevant sections in the next chapter and your relationship will become clearer.

counting elements

As a quick way of checking how compatible you are, count up the elements. This means counting how many planets you both have in the four elements, Fire, Air, Earth and Water.

The three Fire signs are: Aries, Leo and Sagittarius
The three Earth signs are: Taurus, Virgo and Capricorn
The three Air signs are: Gemini, Libra and Aquarius
The three Water signs are: Cancer, Scorpio and Pisces

If you have mostly planets in any one group, then you can consider yourself a fiery person or an airy person, a watery person or an earthy person. Of course, you may have a good balance of the four elements and that makes it easier for you to navigate all the other types, as long as you can access the different flavours of your personality in yourself.

Basically, the more planets you both have in the same element, or compatible elements, the more likely you are to make a good match.

Fire and Air are traditionally compatible, as are Earth and Water. So, if you both have planets mostly in Fire and Air, there's a strong dynamic link. Alternatively, if you both have mostly planets in Earth and Water you'll understand each other's needs and realistic view about life.

planets mostly in fire and air

This makes for pretty exciting times. You'll both want adventure and thrills and spills every minute. You'll live on caffeine highs and sexy escapades fuelled by high adrenalin levels. There's nothing stopping you. You're motivated and both need to chat, laugh and generally keep that enthusiasm and passion for tomorrow alive and kicking. Tomorrow is always far more inspiring and interesting than today. This is a very dynamic partnership and if you have time to sit down and toast crumpets in front of a log fire, you'll probably be eating them *en route* to an all-night party.

You both like to discuss the world and each other, and analyse and gossip about life. This is a mentally stimulating relationship and you don't have time for emotional scenes and weepy movies. Your ideas are important and you prefer a hectic social life to a static home life. The more you communicate, the more you're alive. Phone calls will take up most of your time, and friends and good company are just as important as your sex life. This is a very reasoning liaison based on discussions, imagination, future possibilities and light-hearted fun. You value intelligence and you usually fall for each other's minds.

planets mostly in earth and water

What you share are the practicalities of life and being useful. Stability is a high factor and you both like to know where you stand before you commit yourself. But commit yourself you will if it feels right. This is a very mature, materialistic relationship and you'll focus on your finances and your possessions, make killings on the stock markets and get back to nature when the mood takes you. You develop habits and are very reliable together, because everything has to be real, true and comfortable. Your sense of solidity means you're pretty impregnable as a unit, but you'll be both stubborn and controlling if pushed.

This relationship is also about feelings, sensitivity and romantic longings. Passion is deep and moving, intimacy is secretive and soulful, and love is anything from jealous imaginings to gut-rendering heartaches. You'll unburden your thoughts and feelings in a very emotional way, and you won't give in to reason and logic if it kills you. You can accuse each other of being irrational on the one hand, or of being possessive and demanding on the other. Your relationship is full of passion laced with moods and manipulation or all very clandestine, cloak and dagger stuff and very, very moving.

game or match?

By looking at the contacts between your two charts you can
start to build up a picture of the kind of impact you will have on
one another – anything from the problems you may encounter in
communication to the sexual undercurrents that flow between you
when you first meet. These contacts give you a clue to your long-term
prospects together and how you can work together to improve or at
least be aware of the differences and difficulties between you. The
more binding or easy contacts you have, obviously the better. But
difficult contacts can help to provide a more lively and stimulating
relationship, if you're both prepared to work with the energy and make
it into a positive force between you. Read the relevant contact
sections and discover if this is going to be just a game played between
the sheets, a short-term fun-loving love affair or a match made in
heaven.

Any contacts between your mutual Sun, Venus, Mars and Moon
are very important, as well as any contacts between your Rising
sign and his planets, or his Rising sign and your planets. Saturn
contacts, too, are very important long-term binders in a chart. If
you have good Sun–Moon contacts, Rising sign compatibilities

and just one Saturn contact, you'll probably find there's an instant click that you may never have felt with anyone else before.

Remember, when comparing charts, to look at all the possible contacts, not just the ones you think are 'good'. For example, Saturn shows where we have to work extra hard to become an expert in our relationships, yet Saturn contacts with other planets in your charts serve as anchors, hooks and stabilizers. His Saturn and your Sun, Moon or Venus, for example, can make for a lot of work on his part, because he has to learn about the rules of the sign Saturn is in, but for you it just comes naturally. So you feel there's a bond, a connection. But there's also a wall between you, with fascinating chinks and windows through which he can see bits of himself. Likewise, his barriers and boundaries will give you a window on yourself. If you have Saturn in Libra, for example, and he has a Libran Moon, he'll be drawn to romantic, feminine women. But a Saturn in Libra woman works hard to create a peaceful, idealistic partnership and often learns the hard way, perhaps through a series of disastrous relationships, so that she strives to become an expert in Libran ways. For her, balance, relationship, harmony and mutual adoration become mega important. So he'll hook into your serious need to develop all that within yourself. And you'll find it comes so naturally for him to want peace, love and a good companion that you're attracted by that too.

When you're younger, you may not be conscious of your need to 'bring out' Saturn in yourself, as you have to grow into it. In the Libran example above, he will react naturally to harmony, peace, finding a balance and keeping the needle halfway. Then you will catch glimpses of your own personality through his instinctive behaviour and, over time, will learn 'how to do it'.

Sometimes we don't like what we see in someone's personality because it unconsciously echoes something we don't like about our own. For many psychological reasons we may have also become hugely defensive about our Saturn side. But on the whole, whether we're drawn to Saturn contacts with another person or not, with Saturn involved there's usually a strong bond and a lasting connection on a very profound level.

THE CONTACTS

A reminder: Easy contacts are those in the same sign and four signs away. Clash contacts are those in signs directly opposite each other and three signs away. Remember to count the sign following your planet's sign as one.

sun/sun

easy

Co-operative and naturally appreciative of each other's drive and purpose in life, you understand each other's highs and lows. Both of you feel optimistic in the other's presence and you know that you complement each other. There's a natural warmth and strong affinity for the same kinds of experiences. But you can be quite competitive together. A lively light-hearted rivalry often strengthens your Sun-sign focus, but it also makes you both very subjective. You both believe adamantly about creating the same kind of lifestyle, so you'll always boost each other's confidence and give and receive loads of useful feedback. If this is a same-sign Sun contact and you're birthdays are close, be careful you don't fall into the trap of being so similar that you don't 'work' any other area of your chart because it's so easy playing the Sun-sign role with your partner. The mirror image is perfect, so you don't look at the background or the details of your or your partner's personality.

clash

A Sun/Sun clash is always fascinating but dangerous, simply because you have such very different motivations and potentials. For example, if you are Sun Aries and he's a Sun Libra, then you're all for 'me' and he's all for 'we'. Yet there's often a highly magnetic attraction between opposite Sun signs, simply because in a way that sign represents a side of you that lives in the shadows. When it comes hurtling at you across a party, you are drawn to it, because it brings all that dark hidden stuff in yourself out into the light, right there in front of you. You can't help but be attracted or repelled by it. If this is a three sign away clash, the pressure can be enormous. You are walking down very different roads and you can feel as if you're always being held up, frustrated and stuck in a rut. Mutual respect is needed and obstacles *can* become stepping-stones. But it's not easy unless you have other, more harmonious contacts.

sun/moon

easy

If it's your Sun and his Moon it's almost like one of those soul-mate feelings. Whatever he imagines you to be, you actually are, even if your Sun sign isn't as obvious to him as your Rising sign. You're both able to express yourselves clearly and he finds it easy to co-operate with your decisions and desires. If it's your Moon and his Sun, there's an innate kind of understanding about

how you feel and how he focuses on life. True companionship is
a distinct long-term possibility, but check out other contacts to
get a broader picture of where any work has to be done.
Otherwise you could become the proverbial couple who walk
round in matching jumpers or who never go anywhere without
each other. Nothing wrong in that, if you like that kind of 'close-
knit' relationship, but it can mean your co-dependency actually
weakens your sense of who you are as individuals, rather than
strengthens it.

clash

Misunderstandings can occur between you and each of you can
cause the other to feel some kind of self-doubt. If it's your Sun
and his Moon, there may be problems around your sexual
expression. You could end up worrying about how attractive you
are and he may begin worrying about his masculinity. Points of
view, principles and feelings all come over as mixed messages
and sometimes he thinks you're like his mother and you think
he's like your father. If you had any problems with your parents,
then the same patterns of behaviour will start to emerge between
the two of you. Then friction can result. If you have easy contacts
elsewhere, you'll probably just feel a nagging kind of frustration
with one another, rather than get into disputes.

sun/mercury

easy

What is valued here is the communication between you. If it's
your Sun and his Mercury, you might be attracted to how he
thinks, talks or expresses himself. His ideas will give you
inspiration and your optimism will develop his mind in all kinds
of ways. This isn't a 'sexy' attraction or contact, but it can make

for good communication and understanding of what you need to develop in your life to make you truly yourself. If it's your Mercury and his Sun, you'll fire him with all kinds of enthusiasm for life and he'll be fascinated by your self-expression. Rather than 'lust factor', this is 'wit factor'. Your questions will always get the right answers and his answers will always give you new ideas to play with. It makes for good companionship, but look to see whether other contacts will give the relationship a less platonic feel.

clash

With this contact, whatever one of you says becomes riddled with all kinds of hidden agendas. If it's your Mercury, he could be fascinated initially by your way of expressing yourself, but it won't actually fit very well with his life purpose. Then he could see you as a challenge, rather than a partner. He'll feel deflated rather than elated and confused rather than enthused. If his Mercury is compatible with yours, you might on the surface share the same interests and ideas and communicate well. But there'll be an underlying sense that what one of you is saying is not really in tune with the purpose of this relationship.

sun/venus

easy

This is a classically romantic contact and there's usually a feeling of sexiness and sensuality around you when you're together which others will notice, though not necessarily comment on! Each of you is able to seduce the other with a twinkle in your eye or a touch across the restaurant table. If it's your Venus, this could be one of those love-at-first-sight relationships and if other contacts suggest stability (good Saturn contacts, for example), then this can be a very long-term connection. Money and possessions will be crucial issues, but you'll also find you can build something together and that you have the same kind of dreams. If it's his Venus and your Sun, you may be the driving force in the relationship and he might feel protected by your strength. This contact can lead to a mutual lazy attitude towards life, but there's usually a wonderful sense of harmony and creativity within the relationship.

clash

Very irritating. It's like being bitten by a mosquito and waiting for the first itch. It's actually a very sexy attraction to begin with. You both think you're going to find what you're looking for in a partner, but then you don't and that's when it all gets frustrating. Then you feel it's your fault, that you're not beautiful or seductive enough, or are flawed in some way, and he makes you feel vulnerable, while he's finding he prefers the company of his pals to the difficult atmosphere when he's with you. This is often a very short-term attraction. It's fine for a fling or an affair, but not a good contact for a long-term relationship.

sun/mars

easy

Whether it's your Mars and his Sun, or his Mars and your Sun, this is a very sexy liaison. It can also be a very competitive relationship, but chances are that the testing, challenging spirit behind the scenes will be played out between the sheets. This is a very tactical, sporty, goal-oriented contact. So you'll probably both share the same objectives and lead a high-energy, lust-for-life existence. Emotionally, you'll probably wind each other up, particularly if the planets are in Fire signs, like Aries, Leo or

Sagittarius. Then you'll probably be burning candles – and each other's toes – through the night. If Mars and the Sun are in Water signs (Cancer, Pisces or Scorpio), this will be an emotionally-heightened sexual relationship – lots of tangled sheets and passionate rendezvous.

clash

Usually a very sexual attraction to begin with, especially if it's your Mars and his Sun. There's tremendous vigour, passion and desire here, but unless other contacts suggest strong bonds, this is usually a relationship fraught with who can better the other or who can score emotional and sexual points. If it's your Sun and his Mars this could be a very impulsive and daring relationship. There's a feeling of vibrancy and power-tripping, and there are many ego battles to be fought. Sexy, romantic beginnings could turn into a war of nerves. Take care, unless other contacts suggest long-term commitment.

sun/jupiter

easy

With this contact, optimism, hope and energy will fill any kind of holes in your relationship. This is a tremendously exciting contact and there's a great magnetic surge of energy between you. But take care, because it can either give you both the feeling you're free together or that you need more space apart, particularly if it's your Jupiter and his Sun. Still, there's a kind of healthy competitive spirit when you're together and luck will play a great part in all kinds of life projects. Capitalize on life's rewards together, as you've really got the chance to pursue great wealth or greater knowledge of life and love. And you'll always choose wisely. Travel plans are often talked about and there's a

restless need for adventure, risks and even a spot of gambling.
This is a very expansive relationship, but remember to respect
each other's need for personal space, particularly if this contact
is between Fire or Air signs.

clash

This shows that one of you will be judgemental and highly
principled and accuse the other of being morally, ethically or
personally on the wrong track. The danger here is that if it's your
Sun you might feel that your own values and self-worth are being
taken for granted at the expense of his personal philosophy or
the relationship itself. If it's your Jupiter, you might find it all
exciting and amusing on the surface, but there will be an inner
frustration about not really being able to reach the other person.
This can end up with big banner-waving, self-righteous wrangles
because you're both trying to outwit each other.

sun/saturn

easy

A powerful connection that may seem seriously ambitious to
outsiders. You both have a sense of the importance of your
potential together. Goals, ideals and the ability to build a future
based on trust and achievement become important issues. You'll
help each other out in all kinds of practical ways and even if you
have this contact in an Air or Fire sign like Gemini, Libra,
Sagittarius or Aries, you'll still feel grounded and down to earth
when you're together. If it's your Saturn and his Sun, be prepared
to have to learn how to do whatever his Sun is doing. Now, if
he's not conscious of his Sun-sign potential, then he may
unconsciously see it all in you. Again, if it's his Saturn, he's
going to have to work hard to develop those qualities he finds so

binding in you. This is a powerful link and one that can bring extraordinary success, security and long-lasting happiness. Check out other contacts to support this.

clash

This can cause very powerful unconscious feelings to rise to the surface in a rather insidious way. It's a bit like a pressure cooker that needs release. Both of you will feel locked in a prison. You may actually be building all kinds of defensive walls around yourself to stop yourself from being hurt. Then you get the classic scenario of blame, guilt and manipulation. If it's your Sun, you may feel cheated out of being exactly who you want to be. You may also feel as if you're repeating a difficult relationship with a parent and this brings obstacles and limitations within your territory. You'll see him as preventing you from going your own way or he'll seem to begrudge the fact you have a mind of your own. But there can be something enduring if it's your Saturn, simply because he'll begin to feel a sense of responsibility through the serious side of your nature. He may eventually accept your differences, but it would take a great deal of maturity and commitment for you both to do so. This is a learning-curve contact and can flow smoothly only if you have plenty of easier contacts to take the pressure off.

moon/moon

easy

You intuitively feel or will reach out towards each other's moods, emotions and sexual needs. That will bring an immediate sense of security, rapport and physical harmony. But although this is a good contact for a creative and comfortable emotional flow, it can also mean you're never able to stabilize each other in moments when you're both feeling down or depressed, because your feelings tend to rub off on each other. If your Moons are both in Fire signs you'll be very intuitive and imaginative at the same time. If both your Moons are in Air, you'll want to discuss your feelings rationally. If they're both in Water, you'll be able to suss out exactly what the other is feeling. In Earth, you'll stay in the real world, instinctively knowing the right time to make plans, ground ideas and start schemes together.

clash

A very sexy relationship on the surface, but the undercurrents of your very different emotional needs will make feelings very fraught for one or both of you. If your Moons are opposite each other, there will be a great physical attraction, so that you both unconsciously aim to find the balance through your intimate relationship. This often results in a very sexual and highly passionate relationship. But when feelings start worming their way into the equation, great intensity and friction can bubble up. Excitement is one thing, but the build up of such frantic energy can also lead to problems because, in the end, you have such different emotional needs. Moons three signs away from each other will create a tension that isn't quite so volatile on the surface, but one of you could start playing all kinds of underhand games because you feel isolated by not having your emotional needs met. Look to see whether your Moons make any other, easier contacts to reflect more mutual understanding.

moon/mercury

easy

Here there's good communication between mind and heart. If it's your Mercury, he'll respond naturally because he feels comfortable with the way you air your views and understand his problems. He'll feel happy expressing his needs and wants, and you'll both have the honesty and openness to get away with a few mind games too. There's often a childlike, sweet but smart quality to your relationship. In fact you'll probably go around like a couple of kids, laughing and joking about life and love. This is useful if you have other easy contacts, but not a sign of long-lasting compatibility if you have too many clashes.

clash

In this case, feelings and thoughts are contrary. You will both have trouble communicating and understanding what the other is really expressing. This is particularly difficult if it is your Moon and his Mercury. Then resentment can build up around your Moon's need for secrecy, privacy and emotional expression, and his for analysis and cool, controlled conversations. If it's your Mercury, you might start to resent the fact that he's imagining you to be something your mind can't rationalize. If you have easier contacts, you might be able to work this one through. But it will cause you both to have inner doubts and insecurities and be unable to relate with complete honesty.

moon/venus

easy

This doesn't indicate a volatile sexy relationship, more one of sensual understanding and gentle, harmonious living. If other contacts between you are good, this makes for a sensitivity and an ability for either of you to express yourself without feeling vulnerable. You'll feel especially comfortable discussing music, art and the pleasurable things in life. If it's your Venus, he might feel as if you're a cross between a motherly type and a *femme fatale.* Keeping up that kind of image and feeling responsible for the relationship can give you headaches, though. If it's his Moon, he could see you as the strength behind the relationship. You are seductive, he is reflective. Better if it's your Moon and his Venus, but either way this is generally a very luxurious, opulent kind of relationship and can lead to long-term companionship if other contacts are compatible too.

clash

This can bring a moody, childish attitude to the relationship. If it's your Venus, you'll always feel you're competing with his mother, or the image he has of her. If it's your Moon, then feelings from your past get tangled up with his values and style of loving. There's often great tension between you and you'll rarely be able to see each other as you really are, simply because the images you carry of the feminine aspects of your personality will be so very different. If, for example, your Moon is in Aries and his Venus is in Cancer, you feed on emotional independence and need to be the boss. But he values and has an image of a woman who is tender, caring and protective. He wants you to be all this, but your Moon rejects that because the contact between you sets off an underlying fear in your Moon nature and a compensatory need to be free-spirited. The Cancerian values of homely domesticity are far from your Moon's demand never to be tied down. If you have planets in Cancer, you'll find this pushes even more psychological buttons around your own Moon. So you get resentment, anger and fear appearing in the relationship in the form of manipulation.

moon/mars

easy

This indicates a very sexy, vibrant relationship, where you feel immediately hypnotized by each other's presence. If it's your Moon, you instinctively know what turns him on, feel moved to take chances and have the knack of developing a great sense of spirited co-operation. Impulsive and dynamic, neither of you lets feelings get in the way of progress. You feel stimulated by each other's company and want to get out and be daring, adventurous and take a few sexy risks. If it's your Mars, you'll probably lead him astray first. It's a bit like 'Dangerwoman Meets her Match'. But that makes it all exciting and stimulating, and you'll probably drag each other round your favourite haunts like a pair of roving wolves. Just take care you don't burn each other out if these planets are in Fire signs.

clash

Sexual attraction is a high priority at first. You hook into each other on a very physical level. But there is an underlying sense of tension because one of you has needs which are very different from the drives and desires of the other's ego. If it's your Moon, passion, friction and sexual power-tripping will become a big bone of contention between you. If it's your Mars, you could unconsciously create situations and experiences to try to be in control. For example, if his Moon is in Pisces and your Mars is in Sagittarius, he'll start to feel he's being rescued by you and the last thing you want is to feel as though you're saving him. Then you'll start making all kinds of promises to which you can't commit yourself and he'll play the victim and use his elusive tactics to keep you on your toes. This is not good for long-term bonding, unless you have very strong contacts between the Sun and Moon, Rising sign and Moon or Venus and Mars.

moon/jupiter

easy

You both feel your love is limitless. And in fact, valuing the other's spirit means your emotional rapport is dynamic, open and carefree. This is great as a supplementary contact to other, more bonding ones in the chart, but the excessive nature of this energy might need something more solid, like a Saturn click with your Sun, to make it more committed – if that's what you both want. But there's so much optimism and *joie de vivre* between you, it's very unlikely that much will keep you apart. This isn't an intense sexy contact, no torrid nights and tear-stained pillows, unless you've got a clash between your Moons. But it is liberating, mind-expanding and scintillating. You feel warmth and tenderness mingled with daring, progressive ideas and liberated sexuality. If it's your Moon, you'll be able to tune into exactly what he adores about life and love, and also what turns him on. If it's your Jupiter, it will feel lovely, romantic and enchanting. You'll both be wooing and cooing, rushing around, travelling and making plans for the future.

clash

If it's his Jupiter and your Moon, there's a conflict between his ideals and romantic notions and your sensitivity and emotional needs. In fact he'll feel slightly claustrophobic about the relationship and will seek more freedom than you're prepared to give. You'll sense a kind of irresponsible side to him and that makes you feel rejected and insecure. Then he'll think you're too sensitive and reactionary and will push harder to give himself more time and space to himself. If it's your Jupiter, you'll probably have strong differences of opinion and many disputes which will be difficult to resolve. Check to see whether you have other contacts which can take the burden off this freedom/closeness dilemma.

moon/saturn

easy

A very stabilizing contact, this will bring a binding, strong
committed feel to your relationship. If it's your Moon, he'll be
drawn to you on a very subtle emotional level. He feels
responsible for learning how to do those things which are natural
to you and will work at understanding your feelings, needs and
comforts. If it's his Moon, he might feel he has to give in to
feminine seduction and commit himself. Feeling slightly
overawed, it will be impossible for him to let go of his feelings
for you. There's a kind of mutual possessiveness between you,
whether it's your Moon or his, and for a long-term relationship
this is a very profound solidifying contact. Your relationship will
grow slowly and very deeply, and be rooted in your feelings,
memories and reactions. There can be a very powerful and
compelling force between you which matures like oaked wine,
smooth, refined and dignified. In fact outsiders to the
relationship might see you as untouchable.

clash

Be careful with this contact. There's a very powerful attraction
and it's initially very compelling, just because of the very
different energies involved. On the one hand the stern self-
judgemental side of the Saturn person can't resist trying to
control what is essentially not in its nature, that is, the sensitive,
rhythmical reactions and natural flow of the other person's
Moon. This relationship can mature slowly into something
valuable, but the problem is, if it's your Moon, your needs and
comforts are very alien to his struggle to make something that
works for himself. You might feel dominated and forced into
acting against your nature. Then you have to make compromises
which don't feel right and the discomfort of not being in tune

with your own feelings makes any real communication difficult.
If it's his Moon, he may see you as a mother figure or assume you
behave like his mother and only see the authoritative, parental
side that you come to represent. Then you start to act out, or
appear to act out, this kind of serious, heavy, resentful mother
figure, because he's hung all that stuff on you. Not easy unless
you're both very aware of your differences.

mercury/mercury

easy

You both think the same way and could almost talk to each
other as if you were talking to yourself. This is a mirroring
contact and it gives you both the opportunity to say exactly what
you want without upsetting the other. You're both like a couple
of kids and your conversations will be light-hearted and logical.
Both of you are in tune with the same kind of reasoning and
have a spontaneous understanding of what the other is talking
about. An excellent rapport and good for long-term relationships.

clash

Mental opposition can produce a steamy relationship, but it's not
the kind of wrangling and debating for the faint-hearted. Here
you're both thinking and reasoning in very different ways. In fact
so contrary are your thought processes that whatever either of you
says is usually misinterpreted and misunderstood. The problem is
you're both so attached to your own ways of communicating that
you rarely open your mind to being objective. So you both become
more and more subjective and the arguments and tiffs turn into
major slanging matches. If you have more compatible contacts,
then you might enjoy the fireworks – at least until you both tire of
having to explain yourself or listen to yet another accusation.

venus/mercury

easy

You share common interests and can talk about them freely and warmly. There are no power-trips, just good exchanges of conversation. You'll have a common bond of understanding. If it's your Venus, you'll probably be in love with his mind. If it's his Venus, he'll be infatuated by your voice, your wit and your childlike behaviour in his company. This is a gentle contact, useful if you want a romantic light-hearted relationship with no strings. It's hardly bonding, but it does give you both the chance to communicate and listen with fairness, truth and belief.

clash

Little real communication here as you'll both feel that intellect is trying to overcome love. If it's your Venus, you're discovering love through his mind, not through his heart. That can hurt and be a very fragile wound which takes a long time to heal. The problem is that if it remains a shadow in your relationship you'll end up resenting him for having no feelings, or always telling you what not to do, or always accusing you of caring more about yourself than him. These little love bytes often surface when you're not aware of the inner battles that are being waged between you. So remember, if you do have a clash here, make sure you learn to make your communication an art, rather than a fart.

venus/venus

easy

One of the most creative and beautiful contacts between two people. This is excellent for an enduring and harmonious relationship. You both have the same feelings about what you want from love, so you usually flow into the things that you value and cherish without feeling you have to make compromises. You both understand what the other wants and there's great kindness, sexual happiness and pleasurable companionship. For example, you might both have Venus in Taurus, so you're both happy to linger over wonderful food, drive to the country and count sheep or merely tumble into bed with sex, music and champagne. This is a great contact for long-lasting relationship as you'll be able to reflect your feelings through each other.

clash

A great magnetism between you keeps you sane, because there's always an hypnotic, haunting quality about such very different signs where you unconsciously struggle to find a balance. The chances are this is a very physically active relationship where sexual needs become more important than anything else. But because Venus is seductive and skilled in the art of self-love, there can be an awful lot of vanity from you both, with each trying to be the fairest of them all. So, as a social couple, expect an awful lot of flirting to attract each other's attention or scoring points about who's getting more attention from the other sex. There's no dynamic challenge with this contact, however, except for the fact you both have very different tastes and values. So, in an attempt to maintain your sexual values, neither of you will be satisfied at the same time and that's where you run into conflict. You might adore slow sensual massages and lengthy foreplay, while he might prefer romping round the countryside, or sex in public places. A testing contact, but short-term fun guaranteed.

venus/mars

easy

This a classic sign of compatibility in astrology. Well, physical
compatibility at least. The assertive, dynamic potency of Mars
mingles with the seductive wiles of Venus. If it's your Venus and
his Mars, there's a very strong sexual attraction and you'll have a
creative, passionate and inspiring relationship. If it's your Mars,
sparks will be flying, but the heat is often so intense it evokes all
kinds of dynamics between you. If the planets are in the same
sign, you're able to relate to each other's values and desires
instinctively. If they're in Fire signs, then you'll be radiating
sexiness wherever you go; if they're in Earth, you'll be sensual
sensationalists; if they're in Water, you'll be dreamy lovers; if
they're in Air, erotic pillow talk will keep you up all night. This
makes for a long-lasting sexy bond, but look to other contacts for
commitment and friendship. Mars and Venus can produce a very
volatile relationship, even when they're in easy aspect to each
other, so watch out.

clash

You'll have good intentions to start off with, but this is usually a
complex relationship, based on sexual attraction and power-
struggles in and out of the bedroom. If it's your Venus, there's
less tension, but you're always struggling to maintain your
independence and may feel dominated. Then you get indifferent,
play hard to get or use manipulative games to prove you're still
adored. There may be many misunderstandings between you,
because you're so locked into your female role, which is totally
distorted by his very male Don Juan-like role when he's with
you. If it's your Mars, there's almost a role reversal between you.
Sexy and volatile, you push each other to the limits.
Unconsciously you take on an aggressive spirited approach to

the relationship, while he takes on a more passive, submissive one. Then you end up secretly resenting each other for being not what you expected at the outset. This is a notorious fated attraction and often based solely on indiscreet meetings, affairs and love triangles where sex seems to be the sole purpose of the liaison. It can be very dangerous, exciting and feisty, but lack compassion unless other contacts suggest a more serious understanding of each other's needs.

venus/jupiter

easy

Unless other contacts are to the contrary, you'll have an optimistic and harmonious partnership, where sex is beautiful but not the only thing in your life. Creating new values, establishing joint objectives and goals, and enjoying a feeling of mutual generosity make you feel at home with one another. You can be mega indulgent together, but if you're practical, realistic and aware of your progressive energy, you can achieve great things. If this contact involves Earth signs (Taurus, Virgo or Capricorn), you might end up creating a mind-expanding lifestyle or simply travel the world together, never having to worry about money. This is in fact considered a very lucky contact, so make the most of it. The rich experiences between you are worth their weight in gold. You feel free in each other's company and the power of love gives you both the kind of magic that keeps it real.

clash

If it's your Jupiter, you may feel uncomfortably possessed by his very seductive nature. This means you're caught in something that resembles a Venus fly-trap, where you like the taste of his

values, his possessiveness and his stability, but can't swallow
them for fear they'll poison your free spirit. Then he starts to
become more demanding and more compromising just to keep
you close. The driven feeling behind this contact awakens your
need for independence and puts you into a situation where you
can't develop your own beliefs and talents because he's too
suffocating. If it's your Venus, there's less tension, but he's more
like a rogue with a mission or a knight on a crusade while you're
left waiting around to clean up after him. If there are other, more
stable contacts between you, then there's a chance you'll both
accept the Jupiter person's need for space, but the problem is the
Jupiter person rarely sees the full value of what's being offered.

venus/saturn

easy

Like other easy Saturn contacts this can bring long-lasting love
and a genuine caring relationship. If it's your Venus, you may
feel as if he offers the kind of strength and responsibility of a
father figure or gives the kind of authority and commitment to
the relationship which allows you to be yourself. If it's your
Saturn, he'll feel drawn to your ability to work hard at being
yourself and the seriousness you put into the relationship as a
whole. If this contact is in Fire signs you'll probably draw out a
world of imagination and progressive ideas for your future
together; in Earth, materialistic aims and joint career moves will
be the focus of attention; in Air, ideals, ideas, communication
and harmony will be valued; in Water, feelings and emotional
stability will be crucial to you both. Commitment and enduring
love are the centre of this energy. But check out other contacts
which might contradict this very valuable dynamic between you.

clash

With this contact, there's a feeling of coldness and distance from Saturn's sign. If it's your Saturn, then however much you try to project some warmth into the relationship, he will always feel there's a wall between you. Love is not easily expressed here, because what you are trying to become an expert in is contrary to his Venusian values. This often means you both feel frustrated, blocked out by and yet bound to each other in a very unsatisfying way. Similarly, if it's his Saturn, the value you place on your own style of loving and the ways in which you express your love will feel very uncomfortable to him. Then he will retreat or try to change you or mould you into what he believes is best for you. This makes for a difficult relationship, often compelling and emotionally tiring. But if there are better contacts in the chart this can add a depth of wisdom if both of you are willing to negotiate about what you hope to achieve from the relationship.

mars/mercury

easy

An active, lively and stimulating relationship. If it's your Mars, you'll be fascinated by his wit, humour and conversation, because it makes you feel good to be you. He also makes you confident about expressing your desires, both sexually and objectively. This is a great contact for ideas and action. The more you can actually do together, the more joy you will have. Reason and progress are competitively inspiring, and although you may disagree on some points, you energize his mind and he boosts your sense of identity. If it's your Mercury, then you mind will stimulate his libido, so sexual expression will be healthy, but not the sole purpose of this contact. Your joint energy here is for mutual understanding and you can both get wealthy and wise if you learn to discriminate together.

clash

Here you unconsciously try to demean one another by pointing out each other's faults and weaknesses. There's a conflict of intellect versus sexuality and if it's your Mercury, he might feel that you're too clever, too smart and too bright for him. Then for the sake of protecting his male libido, he'll accuse you of being unsexy, too wise and too unfeminine. If it's your Mars, you may seem to condemn his ideas, thoughts and youthful approach to life. Then one of you will start to get defensive and build on the other's weaknesses. But in the end you can end up hurting yourselves, because the games get too complex for you to realize you're even playing them. A very difficult contact for long-term commitment.

mars/mars

easy

Actually this is never easy, but is usually exciting, stimulating and dynamic. The only downside is that you might lose your feminine qualities at the expense of keeping up with the competitive nature of this contact. There's often a brotherly rivalry and each of you will push each other to do your best. This is a great contact if you've also got more gentle contacts between you, because it can add a feeling of adventure, expressiveness and drive to an otherwise passive relationship. But if you both have Mars in a Fire sign, or you have loads of fiery, spicy contacts, this can put you into overdrive, so you're both trying to win a race before you even know where the finish line is. Sexually, this can be a very challenging contact, but if you do get into power struggles in the bedroom, be careful this doesn't defuse a strong physical bond.

clash

Your ego needs really clash here and although it might start out as a spot of fun and rivalry, or arm-wrestling across the pillow, tempers can run high and battles turn into full-scale wars. If your Mars are in opposite signs, it will feel like a tug of war. You have to assert yourself in a way that stretches you to your limits, and for every one of your actions or reactions, there's a force to be reckoned with from his reactions. This is a powerful sexual attraction, but often it's so overwhelming that you feel you have to back down and submit to the needs of his ego, which could mean you're giving up on your own.

mars/jupiter

easy

You'll discover you have a mutual interest in sport, travel or just indulging in the good things in life. This is a genuinely supportive, but quite intense relationship, where you stimulate each other in turn. It's also a very sexy relationship, but you can burn each other out if too many sparks are flying! You might both actually feel like jet-planes passing in the night because there's so much uncontrolled enthusiasm for sex you don't even truly experience it when it's there. If it's your Mars, then you give him the impetus to develop the many ideas he has for the future. If realistic goals are your focus, then there's great opportunity here for you both to achieve something. You'll have a great deal of activity and movement, and if it's your Jupiter, he'll inspire you with wonderful plans and schemes. In the end equality of minds and spirits is what counts.

clash

A feeling of impatience pervades your relationship and each of you feels frustrated by the other's go-it-alone attitude. Individuality runs high and it can be quite a battle between your will (if it's your Mars) and his sense of freedom and adventure (his Jupiter). Whatever the case, there can be very strong differences of opinion and you'll both feel compelled to worry about your own personal identity rather than creating a smooth, loving relationship. There's a strong sexual attraction here, but it's more about excessive energies and impulsive gestures than a deeply moving experience. Very difficult unless you have more gentle, loving and harmonious contacts elsewhere.

mars/saturn

easy

If it's your Saturn, then you seem like an anchor and a controlling force in his life. This is often a relationship where a roving hunk gets stopped in his tracks, married and tamed before he has time to think about it. But this is a very powerful connection and if both of you work to achieve something together, it can also bring you long-term success. The only downside is that if it's his Mars, he'll feel bound to you, but he can also feel as if his sexuality has been suppressed. The fact is you become the controlling factor in the relationship. Again, if it's your Saturn, then this is where you need to work at yourself. The defensive nature of the sign Saturn is in will tell you how you can best grow into his Mars energy and ego needs without demeaning his sense of masculinity. His vitality feels threatened by the power of your Saturn, but in a way it also challenges him to be himself. If it's your Mars, you'll feed his sense of duty and responsibility with lively, youthful energy. Your impulses

and personal identity will give him the opportunity to break
down his own barriers and begin to accept himself, warts and
all. A good link, often very long-term, but can be frustrating
at times.

clash

There's a sense here of irresponsibility versus control. If it's your
Saturn, he will see you as trying to prevent him from being the
self-willed person he wants to be. He thrives on personal
conquests and his independence and has to be his own boss. You
want to stick to the rules, make him conform to your way of life
and to be the boss. If it's his Saturn, he will unconsciously want
to control your impulses and ego needs and drives. The more one
of you tries to limit the other, the more you learn that it's
impossible to ever control someone else. Then usually this
relationship breaks up because you can only gain your self-worth
by setting the other free. The unconscious dynamics of this very
tense contact often bring out the worst qualities in you both.
There's a push from one end and a pull from another, and often
one of you will feel as if you're driving with the brakes on and
not getting very far. A very difficult contact for long-term
happiness, unless there are very strong supportive connections
between your other planets.

jupiter/mercury

easy

You both have the ability to share all kinds of ideas and progress
with schemes and plans. This is not a particularly bond-forming
contact, but it does lighten up your relationship with good
conversation and the ability to communicate your deepest
desires and dreams. If it's your Jupiter, you find it easy to

persuade him to do exactly as you want, and if it's your Mercury, you enjoy playing a few mental games with him. The pillow talk will be funny, the humour will be outrageous and you'll stimulate each other's minds to give you both an enthusiastic, spirited approach to life and love.

clash

Communication problems abound here, mainly because what he considers meaningful (if it's his Jupiter) won't necessarily have any importance to you. Then you resist each other and argue until one of you breaks. The difficulty here is that if it's your Mercury, he might come across as a know-it-all or self-righteous and that just makes you feel very insecure about your lighter mental approach. Then you get defensive and start to wonder what the truth of the whole matter is anyway. If it's your Jupiter, he seems unable to communicate about the kind of things which are so important to you. Then your views simply clash. This contact is not good for a long-term relationship, but can prove stimulating and often so irritating that you just keep locking horns for the sake of it.

jupiter/jupiter

easy

You both have the same ideals and philosophical outlook on life. If your Jupiters are in the same sign, you're probably close to each other in age and share the same mind-expanding ideas of your generation. There's optimism, hope and lightness when you're together, and you can freely discuss ideas without being too emotionally involved. This is a good contact for enjoying life to the full and for developing joint interests and future objectives. It doesn't necessarily seal a relationship, but it can

give you both generosity of spirit and a genuine feeling of
freedom of mind and spirit.

clash

Because you have such very different views about life and love,
you'll probably spend so much time fighting about those ideas
that you won't have time for any other kind of communication.
In fact any physical attraction between you will become less
important than the differences of opinion you share. This is a
very difficult contact to have because each of you is disillusioned
by the other's very different philosophy of life. Also, what gives
one of you joy and optimism always feels depressing to the other.
So you're always trying to persuade each other that you are right
and they are wrong. Check other contacts for more stabilizing
and balancing factors.

jupiter/saturn

easy

This is one of those very binding contacts, where if it's your
Saturn, he'll feel you offer him some stability and loyalty to his
cause. However crusading he is for his own beliefs and
convictions, you do stand by him and give him the feeling that
whatever he does is viable and justifiable. You give him a sense
of responsibility and dignity, and his panache and optimism
make you feel you can admire and honour his achievements and
progressive outlook on life. If it's your Jupiter, you feel he can
show you how to make your goals and objectives reality. There's
a chance here that you can achieve something very worthwhile
together. This is not a relationship about fixing the roof, more
about bringing you both some kind of worldly reward if you're
looking for success.

clash

This contact can often involve ethnic or cultural differences
and it can take a lot of guts and effort to overcome the very
different beliefs and traditional concepts that you both hold. If
it's your Jupiter, he may have very conservative attitudes which
weigh heavily on your lighter beliefs and hopes for the future.
He wants structure, stability and a serious commitment; you
want freedom, independence and space. The problems arise
because he wants time to stand still and you want time to move
forward. Then you get locked into all kinds of arguments about
who is right and wrong. If it's his Jupiter, he might resent your
intrusion into his life, even though he's attracted to you in other
ways. He has to do things his own way and could become
outrageously self-opinionated when you try to make him
conform to the kind of relationship that feels safe or contained.
This is a very limiting contact, unless you have easier contacts
to negate the differences of social and personal beliefs and
boundaries.

saturn/mercury

easy

With this contact, whoever asks the questions gets the kind of
answers that they want. This is a very teacher–pupil kind of
relationship. If it's your Mercury, then although he may withhold
a lot of his deeper insecurities from you, you somehow have a
direct line through to his vulnerable side and can ask and talk
about all the right things without making him feel
uncomfortable. If it's your Saturn, he loosens you up with his
childlike enthusiasm, so that you have the space to understand
how your boundaries and barriers can yield something real and
valuable. This isn't a bonding contact as such, but it can give you

both the feeling that you're in tune and can accept those things which are hidden beneath the surface.

clash

There can be a very hidden war of nerves here, as you both try to assert some kind of authority over the other. If it's your Saturn, you'll feel responsible every time he doesn't agree with you, and that's when you'll retreat into your Saturn defences (check Chapter 2 for how your Saturn operates) as a way to test him or provoke him. If it's your Mercury, there's a strong conflict between your need for free expression and his need for caution when it comes to communicating with you. If it's your Saturn, he'll see you as bigoted and one-sided, and you'll see him as fickle, scattered and incapable of having any inner authority. A very difficult contact, where you may end up trying to impress each other just for the sake of argument.

saturn/saturn

easy

When your Saturns are both in the same sign, then you're either about the same age or there's a big age gap of about 28 years. In either case, you both have the same boundaries and defences, and you mould to each other, because you can sense the underlying fears and vulnerabilities you both share. This can be a powerful bond, if other contacts back it up. If your Saturns are four signs apart, then you'll both feel the need to struggle and work towards the same goals and objectives. Although you might make slow progress together, it will feel comfortable and workable. You know this is someone you can trust. But the harmony you feel might be so covert and unexpressed that you take it for granted. So it becomes important for you to reveal your sincerity towards each other. Learning 'how to do' your mutual Saturn signs becomes a focus of the relationship and gradually you can both break down those barriers.

clash

You're both concerned with the practicalities and the reality of your relationship, but it's very hard work, because you've both got very different boundaries and barriers to get through. If your Saturns are in opposition, this means you're about 14 years apart in age. Although there may be a heavy attraction at first, because you have such opposing psychological limitations, it can seem as though an immovable object has met an unstoppable force. There's a great deal of friction here and however hard you both try to fix the resistance you feel and give out towards one another, there's a feeling that you'll always be challenged. You're certainly aware of the validity of each other's sense of structure, but it is so alien to your own that the chances are you won't make any compromises, simply because your sense of insecurity is so acute in the other's presence.

your outer planets

This chapter describes how the slow-moving planets in your chart represent something of your generation rather than just something personal about you. This 'collective' influence also has a great clash or match with your personal planets, and can add an unbelievable attraction to someone you wouldn't normally think you'd fall for, often a much older or younger person. By 'older', don't imagine I'm talking about a difference of a few years, but a much wider age gap, anything from 10 to 30 years, which gives you a feeling you've fallen in love with someone from a totally different generation. A father-figure or an eternal youth are two distinct types which some women seem destined to fall for. Psychological underlying motives aside, it's a pattern that is repeated just as often as falling for someone who's already attached or a man who will never want any kind of commitment.

THE OUTER PLANETS

Uranus, Neptune and Pluto are the planets which represent
generational and collective differences. Look up your own outer
planets in the section below and then read about what they mean
for you first, before looking up your partner's. If your mutual
outer planets are in the same sign, then they still might make
contact with your personal planets, so read the sections for more
compatibility clues and descriptions.

the outer planet dates

Uranus in Taurus: 1 January 1940–6 August 1941

Uranus in Gemini: 7 August 1941–29 August 1948

Uranus in Cancer: 30 August 1948–24 August 1955

Uranus in Leo: 25 August 1955–9 September 1962

Uranus in Virgo: 10 August 1962–28 September 1968

Uranus in Libra: 29 September 1968–7 September 1975

Uranus in Scorpio: 8 September 1975–15 November 1981

Uranus in Sagittarius: 16 November 1981–onwards

Neptune in Virgo: 1 January 1940–2 August 1942

Neptune in Libra: 3 August 1942–24 December 1955

Neptune in Scorpio: 25 December 1955–5 January 1970

Neptune in Sagittarius: 6 January 1970–3 May 1970

Neptune in Scorpio: 4 May 1970–5 November 1970

Neptune in Sagittarius: 6 November 1970–20 January 1984

Neptune in Capricorn: 21 January 1984–onwards

Pluto in Leo: 1 January 1940–10 June 1958

Pluto in Virgo: 11 June 1958–5 October 1971

Pluto in Libra: 6 October 1971–5 November 1983

Pluto in Scorpio: 6 November 1983–18 May 1984

Pluto in Libra: 19 May 1984–27 August 1984

Pluto in Scorpio: 28 August–onwards

uranus

Uranus describes the ideals and visions of a generation. It also shows what that generation has to wake up to, experiment with and sometimes break up, and how it will shock other generations.

uranus in taurus

Your generation has already woken up society to the materialism of the world and how important it has become to us all. But you have to break through the issues surrounding your own need to make radical changes in the industrial world and personally fight for new values and break away from your traditions and roots. You're often attracted to people or cultures very different from your own.

uranus in gemini

You have to experiment with words, conversations and ideas. Your generation has a different way of playing relationship games. The rules are there to be broken, so you enjoy twisting things round and making up ideas and notions which others can't understand. Cultural boundaries really begin to shift and you're fascinated by spreading your wings, learning shocking or unusual ideas, or teaching new and outrageous thoughts.

uranus in cancer

Your generation has to wake up to the fact that your family life
has to be different from that of past generations, that there are
different ways of looking after yourself. You won't rest easily or
comfortably in your own family origins and you'll have to create
a different kind of family from what is considered traditional or
normal. When this works, you create a unit which is free and
individual; when it doesn't work, there's a feeling of insecurity
and a sense that you don't have any kind of clan or belong to
anything.

uranus in leo

Your generation has to experiment with personal freedom and
self-expression, shake up other people's views of personal
autonomy and live life just for yourself. You have to follow your
heart, no matter what anyone else says. Your creative expression
is shaken and stirred so that you develop extraordinary images of
what freedom really means to you, particularly within your
relationships.

uranus in virgo

Your generation experiments with routines and rituals, with how
you can be useful in very radically different ways from anyone
else. There's a personal quest to break the normal way of things,
so that nature, patterns of behaviour and all kinds of assumed
ways of doing and thinking have to be changed. There is a sense
that there is important work to be done, but you often can't
achieve it, so you break up your own realistic ideas with
unpredictable patterns of behaviour.

uranus in libra

Relationships have to be different for you. Your generation looks for new ways to develop your intimate relationships and they won't follow the patterns or expectations of those in the past. Your values, your judgement and your principles have to be experimented with, and you have to keep the wind changing in relationships, so that they stay unpredictable, original and unformed.

uranus in scorpio

Your generation has to change the underlying hidden depths of your feelings and your sense of power. It has to be broken apart so that those darker qualities can be pushed into the light of day or radically transformed into something worthwhile. You're experimenting with your emotions and your sense of danger.

uranus in sagittarius

You are on a quest to discover new forms of meaning and deeper truths. Your generation is still so young that the long-term consequences aren't yet apparent, but it's likely you'll experiment with unusual ideas, weird philosophies and original imaginative ideas.

neptune

Neptune describes the longings, dreams and fantasies of a generation.

neptune in virgo

Your generation dreams of doing something useful, so that you can cultivate your talents and gifts. You dream of order and the ability to work things out discriminately. Nothing's ever black and white, but you long for harmony and the discreet, simple pleasures of nature and gentle, realistic relationships.

neptune in libra

Your generation dreams of the perfect relationship. There is always a battle between harmony and strife, and you long for beauty to overcome suffering. Your idea of what love is makes you vulnerable, but it also makes you alive and lures you on to find an answer to the mystery of love which seems so unsolvable.

neptune in scorpio

Your generation dreams of some kind of transformation through intense emotional encounters or relationships. But you feel caught up in dangerous emotions and your sense of identity feels as if it will be lost if you really get too involved. You're always feeling as if you're touched by something deep and profound in your relationships.

neptune in sagittarius

Your generation dreams of adventure and excitement. You long to escape and be free, and you actually believe yourself into situations because you have such wild faith in the future. Your fantasies are about finding a meaning in life and exploring unknown ways of relating to one another.

pluto

Pluto describes bottom-line survival – what weapon a generation and an individual reaches for for defence, so that on both a personal and collective level you can almost literally rise from the ashes.

pluto in cancer

Your generation wants to disrupt and transform all the ideals and notions of family life. There's a sense of wild abandon and your basic sense of security is threatening in itself. So your bottom-line survival is to be acutely sensitive and defensive about your personal comforts and those of other people.

pluto in leo

Your generation stirs up ideas about what an individual is or isn't. The bottom-line survival here is the self. It's very wilful and very self-protective. This is a generation of egotists, whose gut survival strategy is to think of themselves first and everyone else second.

pluto in virgo

Your generation stirs up the changes that must be made to improve the world, both in nature and in your own physical space. You have to unearth all the details and classify and sift everything to feel comfortable. Your weapon is knowledge and the more you cultivate yourself, the more protected you feel.

pluto in libra

You generation stirs up the balance and harmony between individuals, and the feelings within you as an individual. The bottom-line survival instinct is for harmony. You seek peace, beauty and truth, and nothing will stop you from finding it or mastering it.

pluto in scorpio

Ultimately, your generation must stir up those dark, unknown and often dangerous feelings within yourselves and the world as a whole. You have to look at the dark side of yourself and plummet the depths emotionally to defend yourself. Your bottom-line survival instinct is to change or regenerate yourself when the going gets tough.

Now plot your outer planets onto your chart, then do your partner's. You might find you have the same generational planets, but it's important that you still read the following sections for how your personal planets might conflict or collude.

OUTER PLANET CONTACTS WITH PERSONAL PLANETS

When it comes to contacts between your outer planets and his personal planets, very strange things happen. If it's your outer

planet, say Neptune, making a contact with his Sun, then your
collective longings are going to either sit very neatly or clash
very messily with the true nature and potential of his Sun.
Say you have Neptune in Libra and he has a Libran Moon,
and say his Neptune is in Scorpio (he is 15 years younger than
you), contacting your Mars in Scorpio. In this case all those
generational longings of the perfect relationship, harmony,
romance and companionship gel very nicely. And his yearning
for something all-consuming, transformative and deeply binding
is stimulated by your Mars. Generational qualities can be just as
magnetic attractions as the personal planet links between two
people.

Below are some of the most potent connections between the
outer planets and personal planets. The Sun, Moon, Venus and
Mars are the most personal and potent. If you are always falling
for younger or older men, look to see whether either of you has
outer planets making contact with the other's personal planets. If
you have the same outer planets, then the potency will feel less
intense.

URANUS

Uranus is neither a good nor bad contact. It's neutral, but it can
change you and break up relationships, awaken you to other
ideas and get you out of conventional expectations. It challenges
and makes a spirited and sometimes frustrating atmosphere
between two people, but it's never passive.

If you both have Uranus in the same sign, then you'll be able to deal with the excitement and vivacity that this contact induces in you both. If you have it in different signs, then your generational ideals will be very different, but also very seductive. This isn't always a good contact for long-term relationships, as Uranus, by its very nature, is unstable, but it can wake you up to knowing who you are.

uranus/sun

easy

If it's your Uranus, then you'll feel sparkling, zesty and unconventional in each other's company. If your Uranus is in a different sign from his Uranus, then he may be attracted to you because your collective ideals are so contrary to his personal sense of himself. This is an animated, lively and electrifying rapport, with loads of surprises and shocks. But you might find that you want to change his natural desire to do his own thing into a different goal for you both.

clash

If you have Uranus in different signs, and if it's his Uranus and your Sun, you could find he wants to control you or change your ideas into something more progressive and idealistic. You will be fascinated by the things he wants to break up, or wake you up to. But they may be very contrary to your own personal goals and potential in life.

uranus/moon

easy

Very sexy and often a very sudden attraction, this is an exciting encounter. It is usually inspirational, electric and dynamic to begin with, especially if there is a generational difference here too. If it's your Moon, then he'll respond to your spontaneity and your instincts and idealize your femininity. Be careful, though, if you have a generational difference, as then his Uranus might also contradict your own Moon's needs.

clash

A long-lasting rapport is difficult here because you're both unpredictable. If it's your Uranus and his Uranus is in a different sign, he might find it very difficult to understand your spontaneity, wilfulness and desire for freedom. If you're both mature enough to be aware of your personal differences, then this can be a very mind-expanding contact. But sexuality may lack fulfilment and security. If it's your Moon, then you'll feel uncomfortable with his need to experiment with those qualities you instinctively respond to.

uranus/venus

easy

An adventurous and unpredictable relationship. If it's your Venus, he'll be your vitality, your energy and your buzzing sex-god. There is a great electricity between you, and if you have a generational difference then the attraction will become eccentric, unusual and intellectually focused. However, the spark between you depends a lot on your sexual originality and on his ability to change his style of loving to suit yours.

clash

If it's your Uranus, the attraction can become so intense one minute and scattered and rebellious the next that a bond will be difficult to form. This could be a relationship that never seems to flow, because you're both feeling so insecure in the other's company. Then, however magnetic and compelling the attraction, especially if it's your Uranus, neither of you will feel comfortable with the erratic behaviour that blazes between you.

uranus/mars

easy

This makes for stimulating and buzzing romance. There is often a direct attraction to begin with. If it's your Mars, you'll feel excited and spontaneous in his company. If you have different Uranus signs, then you might find his behaviour, ideals and habits so totally different from your own that you want to force him to do things your way. If it's your Uranus, the more detached you are, the more he'll be fascinated by you. This contact is good for short-term sexy flings and is often a sudden attraction, as if you're compelled to kiss this person on the first date. But it's hardly bonding and often can break up as quickly as it woke you up.

clash

An extremely volatile relationship. There is little stability between you because you're both on edge. If it's your Uranus, there'll be an immediate excitement between you, but you'll seem to have a changeable sexuality and play unexpected games or experience unusually irritating behaviour from one another. If it's his Uranus, then you won't like the feeling that he's so self-

centred, when you are trying to change the relationship to your
needs and desires. This means neither of you plays fair, and
there's little give and take between you. Challenging and
stimulating, but not usually bonding.

NEPTUNE

Because Neptune both longs for something but also makes it
seem impossible to ever grab hold of anything, contacts between
Neptune and the personal planets give a misty, seductive feel to a
relationship and make us live in a kind of haze of romantic
longing. But they can also make us feel we have to sacrifice
something to have what we want and we can live under all kinds
of illusions and self-deception about the reality of the
relationship too.

If your Neptunes are in different signs and if one of your
Neptunes is in contact with the other's personal planets, you may
find peace and fulfilment, because the dream you have is there
before you in the eyes or behaviour or values of the other person.
With difficult contacts, however, you never really know the
other's true identity, because Neptune makes you idealize what
the other person represents.

neptune/sun

easy

You bring out each other's sensitivity and can be highly intuitive
about each other's longings and dreams. If you both have realistic

goals, then as long as you are caring and understanding, you will probably attain them. But, as with any Neptune contact, be careful you aren't imagining that the other person possesses qualities they don't have. The relationship can be light, sparkling and romantic, as long as you don't deceive yourselves about its reality. If your Neptunes are in different signs, then whoever's Sun contacts the other Neptune will feel as if they represent all the longings and dreams of the Neptune person.

clash

Although you'll be totally fascinated by each other, if it's your Sun you might not be able to totally trust him. Promises and commitments will seem double-edged and although there'll be a lot of charm and mystical feelings between you, there will also be a sense that you can never really understand each other. The sensual and sexual attraction between you will be powerful, but if it's your Neptune he'll probably feel he's lost in a kind of misty dream world. If your Neptunes are in different signs and it's your Sun, you might have to fight for your individuality.

neptune/moon

easy

A deeply sensuous and almost mystical attraction. You both feel as if you've known each other before and there's an almost uncanny psychic link between you. The sensitivity between you is acute and if other contacts indicate harmony, then this can add a very powerful mystical energy to a long-term relationship. You both feel comfortable in each other's presence and although you can both spend a lot of time idealizing the other, there is a grounding from the Moon person which brings a mellow, even peace between you. Beautifully compelling and usually compassionate, warm and romantic.

neptune/moon

clash

You'll find it difficult to express your true feelings to one another. If it's your Moon, your moods, emotions and sensitivity will be very different from the idealized vision he has of romantic involvement. He seeks a sensitivity that your Moon is totally opposed to. If it's your Neptune, he may seem to be always evading and escaping romance and never really being open about his feelings. Then you'll feel disappointed because it seems as if he's not really there for you. This is not easy, because whether it's your Moon or your Neptune, your feelings and dreams can start to seem hopeless and the relationship can take on a rather cold, chilling feel.

neptune/venus

easy

A romantic, beautifully creative combination, especially if it's your Venus. If your Neptunes are in different signs and it's his Venus, then you'll both flow intuitively to each other's romantic yearnings. If it's your Venus, this will be a memorable romantic involvement, but not necessarily a long-term relationship, unless you have other contacts which are more stabilizing and down to earth. This is a very dream-like relationship, where you live a cocoon-like existence – highly seductive, beguiling and utterly romantic.

neptune/venus

clash

If it's your Venus, then the ideal image he has of romantic bliss
will be defused by your sensual and sexual values. Somehow
you don't quite fit the bill and although he'll be drawn to you
sexually and romantically, he will begin to feel he has to give you
up in order to feel comfortable with his own dream. If it's your
Venus, then you're chasing a dream which isn't your dream. The
more you long for him, the more you lose part of your identity
and wish you were alone, or were back to square one without
him. This is very difficult for a long-term relationship, but often
compelling and sacrificial on both sides.

neptune/mars

easy

Harmony isn't easy, but there is a sense that you must find a
balance between the excessive desire energy of Mars and the
dissolving effects of that desire from Neptune. If it's your Mars,
it's easier, simply because you activate all the dreams and desires
that are instinctive in your partner. If it's your Neptune, you may
feel he's pushing you, making you move into situations and
commitments which may be too seductive and illusory. But the
two totally different energies can create a very powerful
combination, if you can achieve more realistic expectations from
each other.

clash

This can result in lies, deception and dishonesty. If it's your
Mars, he will begin to resent your energy and assertiveness. Then
he'd rather drift away into a fantasy world. The more you desire

progress and movement, the more he'll try to escape back into his private world. Because the energies are so different – Mars is about desire, Neptune about dissolving desire – one of you will always feel the other is never really there for you. There is a great lack of communication and mutual purpose, and unless you have other very concrete rock-solid contacts in your chart, long-term happiness may prove very difficult to achieve.

PLUTO

A transformative quality always pervades any contact between Pluto and a personal planet, for better or worse. There's often a powerfully compelling pull and if there are generational differences, the passion between you will be volatile, especially as your bottom-line survival instincts will be ultimately very different. Easy contacts aren't always as easy as they seem, but the force and power between you will be tremendous. How you live out this binding contact is another thing. Clash contacts will be tricky, but they can also be torrid, sexual and highly magnetic lures at the beginning of a relationship.

pluto/sun

easy

The best and the worst of everything in a relationship is emphasized, especially if it's your Pluto. This is highly compulsive and sexually dynamite. Handled right, you can both transform and begin to seriously understand the power between you. Handled wrongly, this can be explosive, temperamental and passionate in the extreme. If it's your Sun, you may feel you have been plundered and taken down into the underworld. But it can make for a relationship where you begin to find the depths within yourself, whether you like it or not.

clash

A strong sexual attraction, but a very difficult one to sustain. If it's your Sun, there is a great distance between your purpose in life and his instinctive, animal nature. If you have Pluto in the same sign, then you might also recognize the dichotomy in yourself, but being prepared to work with it takes maturity and strength. If it's his Sun, you have a constant battle between your deeper, unconscious needs and behaviour, and his higher goals and sense of self. Whatever else, this can be a deep, dark regenerative relationship, but it is rarely easy for love to endure.

pluto/moon

easy

With this highly charged energy, darkness and light merge into a feeling that emotions are deeper and there's always something left unsaid or undone. There's a great sexual attraction here and a feeling that you cannot resist one another. The relationship is incredibly intense and profound, and can be extremely dynamic, active and transformative. The intensity of the passion between you will keep you together long enough to realize how binding your relationship is on many other, deeper levels.

clash

Power struggles are inevitable here, but are usually hidden and appear as manipulative or jealous behaviour. There's a volatile sexual relationship between you. If it's your Moon, you feel as if you have to break away from your family and roots or make sweeping changes in your life which may be contrary to your personal needs. Arguments will often arise and lead to tearful scenes, breaks or separations. The challenging nature of this contact makes for emotional overkill and intense and often angry scenarios. Very difficult for a long-term relationship.

pluto/venus

easy

A highly compelling attraction, particularly if it's your Pluto. You'll experience great sexual desire for each other and this makes for a very instinctive, sexy, passionate relationship. It could also be a very secretive, clandestine liaison. Powerful and transformative, you'll both feel as if this is the relationship to beat all relationships. Intense and fertile, it has lust, storms and beauty, and if it's your Venus, you'll feel like the queen of the underworld in his presence. Dark and exciting, this can, with other good contacts, produce a very deeply rewarding relationship.

clash

Destructive and intense, there's a feeling here that you have to let go of the things you love most to be with him, especially if it's your Venus. Sexual attraction is high, but the friction between you will be equally intense, and that's where power struggles, jealousy and possessiveness will start to seep into the relationship. Take care with this one, as it's very hypnotic at the outset, but the upheavals and turmoil involved will be very testing.

pluto/mars

easy

Passion personified and a complex but highly irresistible affair.
There's a strong, gutsy animal feel to your sexual relationship
and there's also a deeper underlying strength between you. You
both act as a dynamic transformative force and you feel that you
are motivated by each other's presence. There's excitement and
an urge to make changes in your life. If it's your Pluto, you may
have to experience upheavals in your family life to cope with the
dynamic and progressive feelings that will keep you together
through thick and thin.

clash

Your survival instincts clash totally, especially if your Plutos are
in different signs. Turbulent and often ruthless, one of you will
want to get the better of the other, so sexual power games and
intense battle of wills can result, and fights, break-ups and
passion rule. This can be very challenging and hardly makes for
a peaceful life. We are often drawn into this type of self-
destructive relationship when we can't accept the shadowy sides
of our nature and project them onto others unknowingly. Then
we end up fighting who we actually are. It's dangerously erotic,
yet disturbingly attractive – a pure fatal attraction.

how to look up the planets and rising sign in your chart

the planets

The tables over the next few pages give you a list of all the planets and the dates they changed sign. Obviously this can vary depending on where you were born in the world, because of different time changes and local daylight-saving times. But if you can't get a chart down by a professional astrologer or over the Internet, then these tables will give you a pretty good idea of the planets' signs. Under the year of your birth in the appropriate tables, find your date of birth. For example, you may have been born on 5th September 1960. If you look at your date of birth in the Venus table you will see that Venus was in the sign of Libra from the 3rd to 26th September.

When looking up your planet placements, you may find that you were born on the day that one of them has just moved into a sign, or a day when the planet moves out of a sign. This is known as being born on the cusp. It is possible, due to time variations throughout the world, that the planets may be actually positioned in either the preceding or following sign. For example, say you were born on 3rd September 1960. If you look in the table for Venus placements, you will see that on that day Venus moved into Libra. However, it is possible that your Venus placement might be in the preceding sign of Virgo. Also, if you were born at the end of a given period, for example, on the 26th September 1960, Venus was at the end of Libra, and it may just be that Venus moved into Scorpio before your actual time of birth. If this is the case, the simplest solution is to read the adjacent sign, as well as the given one, and you should be able to determine which you feel is most like you. Or ask a friend for a very objective opinion. Remember, this is only important if you were born on a day when a planet has just moved into a sign, or the last day a planet is in a sign, before it moves into the next. For all other dates, the planets will be in the right signs regardless of where you were born in the world, and whatever time.

rising signs

For the Rising sign look up the nearest possible date and time to your own birth. On the whole this should be pretty accurate, but remember if you were born in a time zone ahead of or behind Greenwich Mean Time, then you will either have to add or subtract the time differences accordingly before using the times for Rising signs here. For example, if you were born in a time zone that is five hours ahead of Greenwich Mean Time, then you will have to subtract five hours to get back to GMT. If you were born in a time zone five hours behind Greenwich Mean Time, then add five hours to get you to GMT. Remember, If you were born in the summer you may also have to take into account local daylight saving time.

The time is very important, and if you don't have a rough idea, then you are better off using midday on the date you were born as a rough guide. But again, time differences and the place where you were born have an effect on your rising sign, so only use this as a general guide to discovering your rising sign. If you think the Rising-sign description doesn't 'fit' your character, then read the signs preceding and after the one given, and see if they match up better. Again, if in real doubt, consult a professional astrologer or one of the Internet sites suggested in the appendix.

To use the table, find your birth date in the list on the left and run across the page until you find your exact time of birth. The zodiac sign at the top of the column is your rising sign.

astrology web sites

There are many astrology web sites available that offer free horoscopes and new sites are appearing all the time. Here are a few that I recommend:

http://www.astro.com

http://www.stariq.com

http://www.Astropro.com

sun

mth	day	sign
JAN	1	CAP
JAN	21	AQU
FEB	19	PIS
MAR	20	ARI
APR	20	TAU
MAY	21	GEM
JUN	21	CAN
JUL	23	LEO
AUG	23	VIR
SEP	23	LIB
OCT	23	SCO
NOV	22	SAG
DEC	21	CAP

mercury

mth	day	sign
JAN	1	SAG
JAN	6	CAP
JAN	25	AQU
FEB	11	PIS
MAR	4	ARI
MAR	8	PIS
APR	17	ARI
MAY	6	TAU
MAY	21	GEM
JUN	4	CAN
JUN	26	LEO
JUL	21	CAN
AUG	11	LEO
AUG	29	VIR
SEP	14	LIB
OCT	3	SCO
DEC	9	SAG
DEC	29	CAP

venus

mth	day	sign
JAN	1	AQU
JAN	18	PIS
FEB	12	ARI
MAR	8	TAU
APR	4	GEM
MAY	6	CAN
JUL	5	GEM
AUG	1	CAN
SEP	8	LEO
OCT	6	VIR
NOV	1	LIB
NOV	26	SCO
DEC	20	SAG

mars

mth	day	sign
JAN	1	PIS
JAN	4	ARI
FEB	17	TAU
APR	1	GEM
MAY	17	CAN
JUL	3	LEO
AUG	19	VIR
OCT	5	LIB
NOV	20	SCO

saturn

mth	day	sign
JAN	1	ARI
MAR	20	TAU

jupiter

mth	day	sign
JAN	1	ARI
MAY	16	TAU

moon

DAY	JAN	FEB	MAR	APR	MAY	JUN	JUL	AUG	SEP	OCT	NOV	DEC	DAY
1	10.44	SCO	SAG	07.13	01.56	ARI	TAU	CAN	12.57	LIB	10.21	CAP	1
2	LIB	01.37	15.02	AQU	PIS	10.46	05.15	CAN	VIR	23.12	SAG	CAP	2
3	14.36	SAG	CAP	19.16	14.52	TAU	GEM	01.21	12.55	SCO	12.23	03.12	3
4	SCO	09.27	CAP	PIS	ARI	20.49	12.10	LEO	LIB	23.54	CAP	AQU	4
5	20.12	CAP	01.07	PIS	ARI	GEM	CAN	02.50	13.16	SAG	18.03	11.35	5
6	SAG	19.23	AQU	08.10	03.12	GEM	16.12	VIR	SCO	SAG	AQU	PIS	6
7	SAG	AQU	13.07	ARI	TAU	04.05	LEO	03.52	15.36	03.28	AQU	23.26	7
8	03.33	AQU	PIS	20.38	13.34	CAN	18.44	LIB	SAG	03.45	ARI	ARI	8
9	CAP	06.58	PIS	TAU	GEM	09.00	VIR	05.46	20.46	10.45	PIS	ARI	9
10	12.42	PIS	02.01	TAU	21.33	LEO	21.07	SCO	CAP	AQU	16.13	12.27	10
11	AQU	19.49	ARI	07.32	CAN	12.41	LIB	09.27	CAP	21.18	ARI	TAU	11
12	AQU	ARI	14.44	GEM	CAN	VIR	LIB	SAG	04.51	PIS	ARI	TAU	12
13	00.05	ARI	TAU	16.05	03.22	15.43	00.07	15.15	AQU	PIS	05.13	00.08	13
14	PIS	08.38	TAU	CAN	LEO	LIB	SCO	CAP	15.25	09.50	TAU	GEM	14
15	12.57	TAU	01.53	21.44	07.17	18.32	04.05	23.08	PIS	ARI	17.00	09.21	15
16	ARI	19.10	GEM	LEO	VIR	SCO	SAG	AQU	PIS	22.47	GEM	CAN	16
17	ARI	GEM	09.57	LEO	09.40	21.34	09.17	AQU	03.43	TAU	GEM	16.16	17
18	01.15	GEM	CAN	00.35	LIB	SAG	CAP	09.11	ARI	TAU	02.52	LEO	18
19	TAU	01.46	14.15	VIR	11.12	SAG	16.22	PIS	16.44	10.59	CAN	21.35	19
20	10.32	CAN	LEO	01.23	SCO	01.44	AQU	21.15	TAU	GEM	10.38	VIR	20
21	GEM	04.19	15.20	LIB	13.00	CAP	AQU	ARI	TAU	21.18	LEO	VIR	21
22	15.35	LEO	VIR	01.33	SAG	08.15	01.58	ARI	05.05	CAN	16.11	01.37	22
23	CAN	04.11	14.47	SCO	16.35	AQU	PIS	10.17	GEM	CAN	VIR	LIB	23
24	17.10	VIR	LIB	02.47	CAP	17.56	14.01	TAU	14.57	04.51	19.25	04.30	24
25	LEO	03.29	14.33	SAG	23.19	PIS	ARI	22.13	CAN	LEO	LIB	SCO	25
26	17.12	LIB	SCO	06.50	AQU	PIS	ARI	GEM	21.09	09.09	20.44	06.36	26
27	VIR	04.13	16.31	CAP	AQU	06.13	02.56	GEM	LEO	VIR	SCO	SAG	27
28	17.43	SCO	SAG	14.39	09.39	ARI	TAU	06.53	23.41	10.37	21.18	08.58	28
29	LIB	07.54	21.59	AQU	PIS	18.52	14.04	CAN	VIR	LIB	SAG	CAP	29
30	20.17		CAP	AQU	22.18	TAU	GEM	11.31	23.46	10.25	22.50	13.09	30
31	SCO		CAP		ARI		21.32	LEO		SCO		AQU	31

306

sun

mth	day	sign
JAN	1	CAP
JAN	20	AQU
FEB	19	PIS
MAR	21	ARI
APR	20	TAU
MAY	21	GEM
JUN	21	CAN
JUL	23	LEO
AUG	23	VIR
SEP	23	LIB
OCT	23	SCO
NOV	22	SAG
DEC	22	CAP

mercury

mth	day	sign
JAN	1	CAP
JAN	16	AQU
FEB	3	PIS
MAR	7	AQU
MAR	16	PIS
APR	12	ARI
APR	28	TAU
MAY	13	GEM
MAY	29	CAN
AUG	6	LEO
AUG	21	VIR
SEP	6	LIB
SEP	28	SCO
OCT	29	LIB
NOV	11	SCO
DEC	3	SAG
DEC	22	CAP

venus

mth	day	sign
JAN	1	SAG
JAN	13	CAP
FEB	6	AQU
MAR	2	PIS
MAR	27	ARI
APR	20	TAU
MAY	14	GEM
JUN	7	CAN
JUL	2	LEO
JUL	27	VIR
AUG	21	LIB
SEP	15	SCO
OCT	10	SAG
NOV	6	CAP
DEC	5	AQU

mars

mth	day	sign
JAN	1	SCO
JAN	4	SAG
FEB	17	CAP
APR	2	AQU
MAY	16	PIS
JUL	2	ARI

saturn

mth	day	sign
JAN	1	TAU

jupiter

mth	day	sign
JAN	1	TAU
MAY	26	GEM

moon

DAY	JAN	FEB	MAR	APR	MAY	JUN	JUL	AUG	SEP	OCT	NOV	DEC	DAY
1	20.35	ARI	ARI	08.06	01.56	LEO	11.17	22.49	CAP	AQU	ARI	TAU	1
2	PIS	ARI	12.23	GEM	CAN	00.38	LIB	SAG	11.39	00.18	ARI	22.01	2
3	PIS	04.41	TAU	19.45	11.34	VIR	14.33	SAG	AQU	PIS	03.18	GEM	3
4	07.35	TAU	TAU	CAN	LEO	05.17	SCO	01.17	17.52	09.37	TAU	GEM	4
5	ARI	17.09	01.12	CAN	18.06	LIB	16.13	CAP	PIS	ARI	15.54	10.23	5
6	20.28	GEM	GEM	04.26	VIR	07.14	SAG	04.33	PIS	20.52	GEM	CAN	6
7	TAU	GEM	12.04	LEO	21.12	SCO	17.21	AQU	02.29	TAU	GEM	21.43	7
8	TAU	02.58	CAN	09.22	LIB	07.23	CAP	09.51	ARI	TAU	04.26	LEO	8
9	08.27	CAN	19.19	VIR	21.34	SAG	19.36	PIS	13.32	09.23	CAN	LEO	9
10	GEM	09.07	LEO	10.54	SCO	07.31	AQU	18.14	TAU	GEM	15.46	07.12	10
11	17.34	LEO	22.51	LIB	20.47	CAP	AQU	ARI	TAU	21.54	LEO	VIR	11
12	CAN	12.22	VIR	10.31	SAG	09.42	00.43	ARI	02.04	CAN	LEO	13.46	12
13	23.39	VIR	13.51	SCO	21.03	AQU	PIS	05.32	GEM	CAN	00.29	LIB	13
14	LEO	14.07	LIB	10.07	CAP	15.33	09.34	TAU	14.09	08.29	VIR	16.53	14
15	LEO	LIB	LIB	SAG	CAP	PIS	ARI	18.09	CAN	LEO	05.23	SCO	15
16	03.46	15.52	00.03	11.38	00.15	PIS	21.30	GEM	23.36	15.36	LIB	17.10	16
17	VIR	SCO	SCO	CAP	AQU	01.32	TAU	GEM	LEO	VIR	06.40	SAG	17
18	07.00	18.37	01.08	16.32	07.36	ARI	TAU	05.37	LEO	18.54	SCO	16.26	18
19	LIB	SAG	SAG	AQU	PIS	14.09	10.08	CAN	05.29	LIB	05.53	CAP	19
20	10.04	22.55	04.25	AQU	18.34	TAU	GEM	14.15	VIR	19.25	SAG	16.53	20
21	SCO	CAP	CAP	01.07	ARI	TAU	21.15	LEO	08.17	SCO	05.11	AQU	21
22	13.18	CAP	10.34	PIS	ARI	02.44	CAN	19.53	LIB	19.00	CAP	20.33	22
23	SAG	05.01	AQU	12.36	07.26	GEM	CAN	VIR	09.23	SAG	06.46	PIS	23
24	17.01	AQU	19.30	ARI	TAU	13.51	05.48	23.21	SCO	19.40	AQU	PIS	24
25	CAP	13.18	PIS	ARI	20.11	CAN	LEO	LIB	10.24	CAP	12.09	04.24	25
26	22.06	PIS	PIS	01.22	GEM	22.55	12.03	LIB	SAG	23.02	PIS	ARI	26
27	AQU	23.54	06.39	TAU	GEM	LEO	VIR	01.48	12.44	AQU	21.26	15.43	27
28	AQU	ARI	ARI	14.13	07.36	LEO	16.41	SCO	CAP	AQU	ARI	TAU	28
29	05.34		19.13	GEM	CAN	06.03	LIB	04.13	17.17	05.51	ARI	TAU	29
30	PIS		TAU	GEM	17.16	VIR	20.09	SAG	AQU	PIS	09.18	04.27	30
31	16.02		TAU		LEO		SCO	07.18		15.38		GEM	31

sun

mth	day	sign
JAN	1	CAP
JAN	20	AQU
FEB	19	PIS
MAR	21	ARI
APR	20	TAU
MAY	21	GEM
JUN	22	CAN
JUL	23	LEO
AUG	23	VIR
SEP	23	LIB
OCT	24	SCO
NOV	22	SAG
DEC	22	CAP

mercury

mth	day	sign
JAN	1	CAP
JAN	9	AQU
MAR	17	PIS
APR	5	ARI
APR	20	TAU
MAY	5	GEM
JUL	12	CAN
JUL	29	LEO
AUG	13	VIR
AUG	31	LIB
NOV	7	SCO
NOV	25	SAG
DEC	14	CAP

venus

mth	day	sign
JAN	1	AQU
APR	6	PIS
MAY	6	ARI
JUN	2	TAU
JUN	27	GEM
JUL	23	CAN
AUG	17	LEO
SEP	10	VIR
OCT	4	LIB
OCT	28	SCO
NOV	21	SAG
DEC	15	CAP

mars

mth	day	sign
JAN	1	ARI
JAN	11	TAU
MAR	7	GEM
APR	26	CAN
JUN	14	LEO
AUG	1	VIR
SEP	17	LIB
NOV	1	SCO
DEC	15	SAG

saturn

mth	day	sign
JAN	1	TAU
MAY	8	GEM

jupiter

mth	day	sign
JAN	1	GEM
JUN	10	CAN

moon

DAY	JAN	FEB	MAR	APR	MAY	JUN	JUL	AUG	SEP	OCT	NOV	DEC	DAY
1	16.41	LEO	LEO	LIB	SCO	CAP	AQU	ARI	20.40	17.03	LEO	VIR	1
2	CAN	18.57	03.07	19.55	06.04	15.58	03.46	ARI	GEM	CAN	LEO	18.55	2
3	CAN	VIR	VIR	SCO	SAG	AQU	PIS	01.48	GEM	CAN	01.19	LIB	3
4	03.31	VIR	08.23	21.04	06.04	19.14	09.12	TAU	09.01	05.36	VIR	LIB	4
5	LEO	01.19	LIB	SAG	CAP	PIS	ARI	12.54	CAN	LEO	09.22	00.07	5
6	12.42	LIB	11.51	22.42	07.57	PIS	18.22	GEM	21.15	16.13	LIB	SCO	6
7	VIR	05.56	SCO	CAP	AQU	02.12	TAU	GEM	LEO	VIR	13.27	01.34	7
8	19.48	SCO	14.28	CAP	12.44	ARI	TAU	01.31	LEO	23.34	SCO	SAG	8
9	LIB	09.07	SAG	01.56	PIS	12.16	06.11	CAN	07.32	LIB	14.48	01.06	9
10	LIB	SAG	17.09	AQU	20.32	TAU	GEM	13.39	VIR	LIB	SAG	CAP	10
11	00.25	11.19	CAP	07.18	ARI	TAU	18.51	LEO	15.05	03.46	15.18	00.57	11
12	SCO	CAP	20.30	PIS	ARI	00.13	CAN	LEO	LIB	SCO	CAP	AQU	12
13	02.33	13.28	AQU	14.49	06.37	GEM	CAN	00.10	20.18	06.11	16.49	02.57	13
14	SAG	AQU	AQU	ARI	TAU	12.50	07.08	VIR	SCO	SAG	AQU	PIS	14
15	03.07	16.51	01.09	ARI	18.15	CAN	LEO	08.31	23.57	08.14	20.29	08.04	15
16	CAP	PIS	PIS	00.19	GEM	CAN	18.08	LIB	SAG	CAP	PIS	ARI	16
17	03.52	22.47	07.42	TAU	GEM	01.18	VIR	14.38	SAG	11.01	PIS	16.18	17
18	AQU	ARI	ARI	11.37	06.49	LEO	VIR	SCO	02.49	AQU	02.30	TAU	18
19	06.44	ARI	16.39	GEM	CAN	12.34	03.02	18.36	CAP	15.05	ARI	TAU	19
20	PIS	07.57	TAU	GEM	19.21	VIR	LIB	SAG	05.27	PIS	10.37	02.48	20
21	13.08	TAU	TAU	00.11	LEO	21.04	LIB	20.46	AQU	20.36	TAU	GEM	21
22	ARI	19.48	04.02	CAN	LEO	LIB	SCO	CAP	08.34	ARI	20.35	14.47	22
23	23.18	GEM	GEM	12.21	06.07	LIB	11.58	22.08	PIS	ARI	GEM	CAN	23
24	TAU	GEM	16.33	LEO	VIR	SAG	AQU	12.57	03.52	GEM	CAN	24
25	TAU	08.15	CAN	22.03	13.22	SCO	12.38	23.55	ARI	TAU	08.18	03.35	25
26	11.43	CAN	CAN	VIR	LIB	03.09	CAP	PIS	19.35	13.19	CAN	LEO	26
27	GEM	19.07	04.06	VIR	16.32	SAG	12.37	PIS	TAU	GEM	21.09	16.10	27
28	GEM	LEO	LEO	03.50	SCO	02.32	AQU	03.38	TAU	GEM	LEO	VIR	28
29	00.03		12.36	LIB	16.39	CAP	13.49	ARI	05.05	01.00	LEO	VIR	29
30	CAN		VIR	05.59	SAG	02.00	PIS	10.29	GEM	CAN	09.30	02.45	30
31	10.38		17.36		15.43		17.55	TAU		13.48		LIB	31

sun

mth	day	sign
JAN	1	CAP
JAN	20	AQU
FEB	19	PIS
MAR	21	ARI
APR	20	TAU
MAY	21	GEM
JUN	22	CAN
JUL	23	LEO
AUG	24	VIR
SEP	23	LIB
OCT	24	SCO
NOV	23	SAG
DEC	22	CAP

mercury

mth	day	sign
JAN	1	CAP
JAN	3	AQU
JAN	27	CAP
FEB	15	AQU
MAR	11	PIS
MAR	28	ARI
APR	12	TAU
APR	30	GEM
MAY	26	TAU
JUN	14	GEM
JUL	6	CAN
JUL	20	LEO
AUG	5	VIR
AUG	27	LIB
SEP	25	VIR
OCT	11	LIB
OCT	30	SCO
NOV	18	SAG
DEC	8	CAP

venus

mth	day	sign
JAN	1	CAP
JAN	8	AQU
FEB	1	PIS
FEB	25	ARI
MAR	21	TAU
APR	15	GEM
MAY	11	CAN
JUN	7	LEO
JUL	7	VIR
NOV	9	LIB
DEC	8	SCO

mars

mth	day	sign
JAN	1	SAG
JAN	26	CAP
MAR	8	AQU
APR	17	PIS
MAY	27	ARI
JUL	7	TAU
AUG	23	GEM

saturn

mth	day	sign
JAN	1	GEM

jupiter

mth	day	sign
JAN	1	CAN
JUN	30	LEO

moon

DAY	JAN	FEB	MAR	APR	MAY	JUN	JUL	AUG	SEP	OCT	NOV	DEC	DAY
1	09.39	23.15	07.19	18.27	04.39	TAU	17.23	LEO	18.33	SCO	13.01		1
2	SCO	CAP	CAP	PIS	ARI	00.29	CAN	LEO	LIB	SCO	03.37	AQU	2
3	12.33	23.10	08.56	21.17	09.57	GEM	CAN	00.45	LIB	17.03	CAP	15.36	3
4	SAG	AQU	AQU	ARI	TAU	10.45	05.39	VIR	04.20	SAG	07.09	PIS	4
5	12.35	23.07	09.54	ARI	17.16	CAN	LEO	12.51	SCO	22.11	AQU	19.00	5
6	CAP	PIS	PIS	01.37	GEM	23.03	18.45	LIB	11.38	CAP	10.16	ARI	6
7	11.42	PIS	11.41	TAU	GEM	LEO	VIR	22.40	SAG	CAP	PIS	23.30	7
8	AQU	01.00	ARI	08.41	03.17	LEO	VIR	SCO	16.13	AQU	13.10	TAU	8
9	12.03	ARI	15.53	GEM	CAN	12.03	06.44	SCO	CAP	AQU	ARI	TAU	9
10	PIS	06.17	TAU	19.03	15.39	VIR	LIB	05.08	18.18	03.44	16.32	05.32	10
11	15.21	TAU	23.39	CAN	LEO	23.22	15.40	SAG	AQU	PIS	TAU	GEM	11
12	ARI	15.25	GEM	CAN	LEO	LIB	SCO	08.09	18.46	05.12	21.31	13.46	12
13	22.22	GEM	GEM	07.39	04.21	LIB	20.37	CAP	PIS	ARI	GEM	CAN	13
14	TAU	GEM	10.51	LEO	VIR	06.59	SAG	08.36	PIS	07.26	GEM	CAN	14
15	TAU	03.25	CAN	19.59	14.44	SCO	22.07	AQU	ARI	TAU	05.22	00.37	15
16	08.39	CAN	23.41	VIR	LIB	10.36	CAP	08.06	21.14	12.07	CAN	LEO	16
17	GEM	16.18	LEO	LEO	21.19	SAG	21.46	PIS	TAU	GEM	16.27	13.22	17
18	20.53	LEO	LEO	05.41	SCO	11.29	AQU	08.32	TAU	20.28	LEO	VIR	18
19	CAN	LEO	11.43	LIB	SCO	CAP	21.30	ARI	02.42	CAN	LEO	VIR	19
20	CAN	04.20	VIR	12.04	00.33	11.33	PIS	11.39	GEM	CAN	05.21	01.55	20
21	09.44	VIR	21.21	SCO	SAG	AQU	23.08	TAU	12.10	08.12	VIR	LIB	21
22	LEO	14.30	LIB	15.56	02.00	12.36	ARI	18.34	CAN	LEO	17.19	11.46	22
23	22.03	LIB	LIB	SAG	CAP	PIS	ARI	GEM	CAN	21.10	LIB	SCO	23
24	VIR	22.25	04.23	18.39	03.23	15.52	TAU	GEM	LEO	00.34	LIB	17.44	24
25	VIR	SCO	SCO	CAP	AQU	ARI	TAU	05.07	LEO	VIR	02.09	SAG	25
26	08.47	SCO	09.23	21.21	05.58	21.52	12.04	CAN	13.30	08.38	SCO	20.25	26
27	LIB	03.59	SAG	AQU	PIS	TAU	GEM	17.49	VIR	LIB	07.35	CAP	27
28	16.51	SAG	13.05	AQU	10.16	TAU	23.04	LEO	VIR	17.14	SAG	21.21	28
29	SCO		CAP	00.36	ARI	06.27	CAN	LEO	00.56	SCO	10.43	AQU	29
30	21.34		15.57	PIS	16.25	GEM	CAN	06.47	LIB	23.14	CAP	22.17	30
31	SAG		AQU		TAU		11.43	VIR		SAG		PIS	31

sun

mth	day	sign
JAN	1	CAP
JAN	21	AQU
FEB	19	PIS
MAR	20	ARI
APR	20	TAU
MAY	21	GEM
JUN	21	CAN
JUL	22	LEO
AUG	23	VIR
SEP	23	LIB
OCT	23	SCO
NOV	22	SAG
DEC	21	CAP

mercury

mth	day	sign
JAN	1	CAP
FEB	12	AQU
MAR	3	PIS
MAR	19	ARI
APR	3	TAU
JUN	11	GEM
JUN	27	CAN
JUL	11	LEO
JUL	28	VIR
OCT	5	LIB
OCT	22	SCO
NOV	10	SAG
DEC	1	CAP
DEC	23	SAG

venus

mth	day	sign
JAN	1	SCO
JAN	3	SAG
JAN	28	CAP
FEB	21	AQU
MAR	17	PIS
APR	10	ARI
MAY	4	TAU
MAY	29	GEM
JUN	22	CAN
JUL	17	LEO
AUG	10	VIR
SEP	3	LIB
SEP	28	SCO
OCT	22	SAG
NOV	16	CAP
DEC	11	AQU

mars

mth	day	sign
JAN	1	GEM
MAR	28	CAN
MAY	22	LEO
JUL	12	VIR
AUG	29	LIB
OCT	13	SCO
NOV	25	SAG

saturn

mth	day	sign
JAN	1	GEM
JUN	20	CAN

jupiter

mth	day	sign
JAN	1	LEO
JUL	26	VIR

moon

DAY	JAN	FEB	MAR	APR	MAY	JUN	JUL	AUG	SEP	OCT	NOV	DEC	DAY
1	PIS	TAU	00.06	CAN	23.04	LIB	SCO	14.42	AQU	14.30	TAU	15.17	1
2	00.34	17.17	GEM	02.54	VIR	LIB	23.38	CAP	04.14	ARI	01.28	CAN	2
3	ARI	GEM	08.38	LEO	VIR	06.32	SAG	17.10	PIS	13.46	GEM	21.53	3
4	04.58	GEM	CAN	15.49	11.39	SCO	SAG	AQU	03.27	TAU	05.04	LEO	4
5	TAU	02.40	20.19	VIR	LIB	14.27	04.42	17.35	ARI	14.59	CAN	LEO	5
6	11.44	CAN	LEO	VIR	22.18	SAG	CAP	PIS	03.28	GEM	12.44	08.04	6
7	GEM	14.20	LEO	04.22	SCO	19.41	07.14	17.43	TAU	19.56	LEO	VIR	7
8	20.48	LEO	09.18	LIB	SCO	CAP	AQU	ARI	06.13	CAN	23.59	20.28	8
9	CAN	LEO	VIR	15.12	06.27	23.12	08.39	19.19	GEM	CAN	VIR	LIB	9
10	CAN	03.08	21.55	SCO	SAG	AQU	PIS	TAU	12.47	05.03	VIR	LIB	10
11	07.57	VIR	LIB	SCO	12.33	AQU	10.18	23.38	CAN	LEO	12.45	08.42	11
12	LEO	15.54	LIB	00.02	CAP	01.58	ARI	GEM	22.50	17.04	LIB	SCO	12
13	20.38	LIB	09.12	SAG	17.10	PIS	13.16	GEM	LEO	VIR	LIB	18.50	13
14	VIR	LIB	SCO	06.56	AQU	04.41	TAU	07.03	LEO	VIR	00.48	SAG	14
15	VIR	03.24	18.31	CAP	20.35	ARI	18.11	CAN	11.00	05.55	SCO	SAG	15
16	09.29	SCO	SAG	11.46	PIS	07.52	GEM	17.08	VIR	LIB	11.02	02.22	16
17	LIB	12.15	SAG	AQU	23.03	TAU	GEM	LEO	23.48	18.03	SAG	CAP	17
18	20.27	SAG	01.13	14.28	ARI	12.11	01.21	LEO	SCO	19.20	07.44	18
19	SCO	17.33	CAP	PIS	ARI	GEM	CAN	05.00	LIB	SCO	CAP	AQU	19
20	SCO	CAP	04.55	15.35	01.15	18.28	10.51	VIR	12.11	04.50	CAP	11.39	20
21	03.53	19.27	AQU	ARI	TAU	CAN	LEO	17.45	SCO	SAG	01.47	PIS	21
22	SAG	AQU	05.59	16.29	04.26	CAN	22.24	LIB	23.16	13.48	AQU	14.42	22
23	07.26	19.09	PIS	TAU	GEM	03.24	VIR	LIB	SAG	CAP	06.18	ARI	23
24	CAP	PIS	05.42	18.59	10.04	LEO	VIR	06.13	SAG	20.19	PIS	17.24	24
25	08.09	18.31	ARI	GEM	CAN	14.58	11.08	SCO	07.55	AQU	08.57	TAU	25
26	AQU	ARI	06.01	GEM	19.04	VIR	LIB	16.52	CAP	23.53	ARI	20.26	26
27	07.48	19.36	TAU	00.49	LEO	VIR	23.16	SAG	13.10	PIS	10.22	GEM	27
28	PIS	TAU	08.58	CAN	LEO	03.40	SCO	SAG	AQU	PIS	TAU	GEM	28
29	08.15	TAU	GEM	10.36	06.58	LIB	SCO	00.12	14.58	00.54	11.55	00.44	29
30	ARI		15.59	LEO	VIR	15.10	CAP	PIS	PIS	ARI	GEM	CAN	30
31	11.07		CAN		19.37		SAG	03.44		00.45		07.19	31

sun

mth	day	sign
JAN	1	CAP
JAN	20	AQU
FEB	19	PIS
MAR	20	ARI
APR	20	TAU
MAY	21	GEM
JUN	21	CAN
JUL	23	LEO
AUG	23	VIR
SEP	23	LIB
OCT	23	SCO
NOV	22	SAG
DEC	22	CAP

mercury

mth	day	sign
JAN	1	SAG
JAN	14	CAP
FEB	5	AQU
FEB	23	PIS
MAR	11	ARI
MAY	16	TAU
JUN	4	GEM
JUN	18	CAN
JUL	3	LEO
JUL	26	VIR
AUG	17	LEO
SEP	10	VIR
SEP	27	LIB
OCT	15	SCO
NOV	3	SAG

venus

mth	day	sign
JAN	1	AQU
JAN	5	PIS
FEB	2	ARI
MAR	11	TAU
APR	7	ARI
JUN	4	TAU
JUL	7	GEM
AUG	4	CAN
AUG	30	LEO
SEP	24	VIR
OCT	19	LIB
NOV	12	SCO
DEC	6	SAG
DEC	30	CAP

mars

mth	day	sign
JAN	1	SAG
JAN	5	CAP
FEB	14	AQU
MAR	25	PIS
MAY	2	ARI
JUN	11	TAU
JUL	23	GEM
SEP	7	CAN
NOV	11	LEO
DEC	26	CAN

saturn

mth	day	sign
JAN	1	CAN

jupiter

mth	day	sign
JAN	1	VIR
AUG	25	LIB

moon

DAY	JAN	FEB	MAR	APR	MAY	JUN	JUL	AUG	SEP	OCT	NOV	DEC	DAY
1	LEO	12.46	LIB	SCO	19.40	AQU	PIS	TAU	CAN	LEO	10.08	04.43	1
2	16.49	LIB	LIB	03.08	CAP	15.25	00.28	11.23	CAN	17.34	LIB	SCO	2
3	VIR	LIB	08.32	SAG	CAP	PIS	ARI	GEM	03.19	VIR	22.28	17.30	3
4	VIR	01.22	SCO	13.51	04.06	18.51	03.04	15.23	LEO	VIR	SCO	SAG	4
5	04.44	SCO	20.45	CAP	AQU	ARI	TAU	CAN	11.36	04.16	SCO	SAG	5
6	LIB	12.57	SAG	21.28	09.21	20.23	05.20	20.52	VIR	LIB	11.18	05.23	6
7	17.13	SAG	SAG	AQU	PIS	TAU	GEM	LEO	21.48	16.24	SAG	CAP	7
8	SCO	21.28	06.37	AQU	11.25	21.15	08.10	LEO	LIB	SCO	23.35	15.34	8
9	SCO	CAP	CAP	01.10	ARI	GEM	CAN	04.24	LIB	SCO	CAP	AQU	9
10	03.55	CAP	12.40	PIS	11.24	23.02	12.43	VIR	09.48	05.17	CAP	23.20	10
11	SAG	02.12	AQU	01.38	TAU	CAN	LEO	14.21	SCO	SAG	09.59	PIS	11
12	11.28	AQU	14.50	ARI	11.12	CAN	19.58	LIB	22.37	17.33	AQU	PIS	12
13	CAP	03.52	PIS	00.40	GEM	03.20	VIR	LIB	SAG	CAP	17.05	04.15	13
14	15.57	PIS	14.32	TAU	12.51	LEO	VIR	02.24	SAG	CAP	PIS	ARI	14
15	AQU	04.12	ARI	00.31	CAN	11.07	06.13	SCO	10.11	03.07	20.24	06.30	15
16	18.27	ARI	13.54	GEM	17.57	VIR	LIB	14.56	CAP	AQU	ARI	TAU	16
17	PIS	05.05	TAU	03.13	LEO	22.06	18.28	SAG	18.19	08.34	20.48	07.03	17
18	20.21	TAU	15.04	CAN	LEO	LIB	SCO	SAG	AQU	PIS	TAU	GEM	18
19	ARI	08.01	GEM	09.52	02.56	LIB	SCO	01.31	22.19	10.09	20.02	07.27	19
20	22.48	GEM	19.31	LEO	VIR	10.36	06.36	CAP	PIS	ARI	GEM	CAN	20
21	TAU	13.42	CAN	20.03	14.43	SCO	SAG	08.32	23.11	09.30	20.14	09.30	21
22	TAU	CAN	CAN	VIR	LIB	22.27	16.28	AQU	ARI	TAU	CAN	LEO	22
23	02.35	21.58	03.32	VIR	LIB	SAG	CAP	12.05	22.53	08.49	23.12	14.44	23
24	GEM	LEO	LEO	08.15	03.21	SAG	23.16	PIS	TAU	GEM	LEO	VIR	24
25	08.05	LEO	14.11	LIB	SCO	08.14	AQU	13.30	23.32	10.11	LEO	23.45	25
26	CAN	08.13	VIR	20.52	15.11	CAP	AQU	ARI	GEM	CAN	05.59	LIB	26
27	15.33	VIR	VIR	SCO	SAG	15.36	03.26	14.34	GEM	14.55	VIR	LIB	27
28	LEO	19.57	02.15	SCO	SAG	AQU	PIS	TAU	02.38	LEO	16.18	11.43	28
29	LEO		LIB	08.56	01.24	20.51	06.07	16.47	CAN	23.12	LIB	SCO	29
30	01.09		14.50	SAG	CAP	PIS	ARI	GEM	08.47	VIR	LIB	SCO	30
31	VIR		SCO		09.35		08.28	21.00		VIR		00.32	31

sun

mth	day	sign
JAN	1	CAP
JAN	20	AQU
FEB	19	PIS
MAR	21	ARI
APR	20	TAU
MAY	21	GEM
JUN	22	CAN
JUL	23	LEO
AUG	23	VIR
SEP	23	LIB
OCT	24	SCO
NOV	22	SAG
DEC	22	CAP

mercury

mth	day	sign
JAN	1	SAG
JAN	9	CAP
JAN	29	AQU
FEB	15	PIS
MAR	4	ARI
APR	1	PIS
APR	16	ARI
MAY	11	TAU
MAY	27	GEM
JUN	10	CAN
JUN	27	LEO
SEP	3	VIR
SEP	19	LIB
OCT	7	SCO
OCT	30	SAG
NOV	20	SCO
DEC	13	SAG

venus

mth	day	sign
JAN	1	CAP
JAN	22	AQU
FEB	15	PIS
MAR	11	ARI
APR	5	TAU
APR	29	GEM
MAY	24	CAN
JUN	18	LEO
JUL	13	VIR
AUG	9	LIB
SEP	7	SCO
OCT	16	SAG
NOV	8	SCO

mars

mth	day	sign
JAN	1	CAN
APR	22	LEO
JUN	20	VIR
AUG	9	LIB
SEP	24	SCO
NOV	6	SAG
DEC	17	CAP

saturn

mth	day	sign
JAN	1	CAN
AUG	2	LEO

jupiter

mth	day	sign
JAN	1	LIB
SEP	25	SCO

moon

DAY	JAN	FEB	MAR	APR	MAY	JUN	JUL	AUG	SEP	OCT	NOV	DEC	DAY
1	SAG	05.23	AQU	09.16	TAU	06.29	LEO	12.05	SCO	SAG	10.36	04.30	1
2	12.11	AQU	20.25	ARI	20.03	CAN	20.45	LIB	17.31	14.29	AQU	PIS	2
3	CAP	11.32	PIS	09.56	GEM	07.39	VIR	21.23	SAG	CAP	20.32	12.05	3
4	21.38	PIS	23.23	TAU	20.23	LEO	VIR	SCO	SAG	CAP	PIS	ARI	4
5	AQU	15.38	ARI	10.25	CAN	11.57	03.21	SCO	06.24	02.27	PIS	15.48	5
6	AQU	ARI	ARI	GEM	23.04	VIR	LIB	09.36	CAP	AQU	03.29	TAU	6
7	04.47	18.47	01.08	12.21	LEO	19.57	13.41	SAG	17.41	11.09	ARI	16.30	7
8	PIS	TAU	TAU	LEO	LIB	SCO	22.23	AQU	PIS	04.49	GEM	8
9	09.56	21.45	03.12	16.37	04.57	LIB	SCO	CAP	AQU	16.05	TAU	15.50	9
10	ARI	GEM	GEM	LEO	VIR	07.04	02.20	CAP	01.46	ARI	05.07	CAN	10
11	13.25	GEM	06.29	23.20	13.53	SCO	SAG	09.23	PIS	18.20	GEM	15.46	11
12	TAU	00.59	CAN	VIR	LIB	19.50	15.05	AQU	06.49	TAU	05.15	LEO	12
13	15.42	CAN	11.14	VIR	LIB	SAG	CAP	17.41	ARI	19.37	CAN	18.09	13
14	GEM	04.50	LEO	08.13	01.08	SAG	CAP	PIS	10.03	GEM	06.53	VIR	14
15	17.32	LEO	17.32	LIB	SCO	08.39	02.17	23.37	TAU	21.23	LEO	VIR	15
16	CAN	10.03	VIR	19.03	13.46	CAP	AQU	ARI	12.45	CAN	11.05	00.07	16
17	20.04	VIR	VIR	SCO	SAG	20.16	11.15	ARI	GEM	CAN	VIR	LIB	17
18	LEO	17.36	01.40	SCO	SAG	AQU	PIS	03.59	15.42	00.35	18.12	09.43	18
19	LEO	LIB	LIB	07.30	02.42	AQU	17.59	TAU	CAN	LEO	LIB	SCO	19
20	00.40	LIB	12.04	SAG	CAP	05.43	ARI	07.22	19.13	05.35	LIB	21.48	20
21	VIR	04.05	SCO	20.29	14.31	PIS	22.35	GEM	LEO	VIR	03.58	SAG	21
22	08.31	SCO	SCO	CAP	AQU	12.19	TAU	10.06	23.38	12.33	SCO	SAG	22
23	LIB	16.41	00.30	CAP	23.39	ARI	TAU	CAN	VIR	LIB	15.44	10.50	23
24	19.40	SAG	SAG	07.56	PIS	15.56	01.18	12.38	VIR	21.41	SAG	CAP	24
25	SCO	SAG	13.18	AQU	PIS	TAU	GEM	LEO	05.40	SCO	SAG	23.29	25
26	SCO	05.01	CAP	15.54	05.05	17.07	02.44	15.54	LIB	SCO	04.40	AQU	26
27	08.27	CAP	23.51	PIS	ARI	GEM	CAN	VIR	14.12	09.03	CAP	AQU	27
28	SAG	14.34	AQU	19.45	07.03	17.10	03.57	21.15	SCO	SAG	17.30	10.43	28
29	20.18		AQU	ARI	TAU	CAN	LEO	LIB	SCO	21.59	AQU	PIS	29
30	CAP		06.26	20.31	06.54	17.47	06.32	LIB	01.32	CAP	AQU	19.31	30
31	CAP		PIS		GEM		VIR	05.49		CAP		ARI	31

312

sun

mth	day	sign
JAN	1	CAP
JAN	20	AQU
FEB	19	PIS
MAR	21	ARI
APR	20	TAU
MAY	21	GEM
JUN	22	CAN
JUL	23	LEO
AUG	24	VIR
SEP	23	LIB
OCT	24	SCO
NOV	23	SAG
DEC	22	CAP

mercury

mth	day	sign
JAN	1	SAG
JAN	3	CAP
JAN	21	AQU
FEB	8	PIS
APR	16	ARI
MAY	4	TAU
MAY	18	GEM
JUN	2	CAN
AUG	10	LEO
AUG	26	VIR
SEP	11	LIB
OCT	1	SCO
DEC	7	SAG
DEC	26	CAP

venus

mth	day	sign
JAN	1	SCO
JAN	5	SAG
FEB	6	CAP
MAR	5	AQU
MAR	30	PIS
APR	25	ARI
MAY	20	TAU
JUN	13	GEM
JUL	8	CAN
AUG	2	LEO
AUG	26	VIR
SEP	19	LIB
OCT	13	SCO
NOV	6	SAG
NOV	30	CAP
DEC	24	AQU

mars

mth	day	sign
JAN	1	CAP
JAN	25	AQU
MAR	4	PIS
APR	11	ARI
MAY	21	TAU
JUL	1	GEM
AUG	13	CAN
OCT	1	LEO
DEC	1	VIR

saturn

mth	day	sign
JAN	1	LEO

jupiter

mth	day	sign
JAN	1	SCO
OCT	24	SAG

moon

DAY	JAN	FEB	MAR	APR	MAY	JUN	JUL	AUG	SEP	OCT	NOV	DEC	DAY
1	ARI	GEM	20.59	LEO	19.24	SCO	SAG	PIS	ARI	GEM	CAN	1
2	01.06	13.38	CAN	08.30	LIB	18.54	13.03	AQU	12.02	02.15	17.32	02.30	2
3	TAU	CAN	23.00	VIR	LIB	SAG	CAP	19.49	ARI	TAU	CAN	LEO	3
4	03.26	14.01	LEO	12.39	02.35	SAG	CAP	PIS	20.10	07.44	20.03	04.23	4
5	GEM	LEO	LEO	LIB	SCO	06.51	01.50	PIS	TAU	GEM	LEO	VIR	5
6	03.28	14.42	00.46	18.56	12.09	CAP	AQU	06.20	TAU	11.47	22.55	08.14	6
7	CAN	VIR	VIR	SCO	SAG	19.38	14.03	ARI	02.18	CAN	VIR	LIB	7
8	02.53	17.39	03.51	SCO	23.55	AQU	PIS	14.43	GEM	14.41	VIR	14.24	8
9	LEO	LIB	LIB	04.12	CAP	AQU	PIS	TAU	06.12	LEO	02.42	SCO	9
10	03.45	LIB	09.51	SAG	CAP	07.47	00.34	20.17	CAN	16.47	LIB	22.49	10
11	VIR	00.28	SCO	16.08	12.41	PIS	ARI	GEM	08.03	VIR	08.02	SAG	11
12	07.54	SCO	19.34	CAP	AQU	17.34	08.12	22.49	LEO	19.31	SCO	SAG	12
13	LIB	11.15	SAG	CAP	AQU	ARI	TAU	CAN	08.51	LIB	15.33	09.14	13
14	16.15	SAG	SAG	04.51	00.20	23.45	12.16	23.06	VIR	23.45	SAG	CAP	14
15	SCO	SAG	08.00	AQU	PIS	TAU	GEM	LEO	10.16	SCO	SAG	21.16	15
16	SCO	00.12	CAP	15.47	08.56	TAU	13.14	22.49	LIB	SCO	01.37	AQU	16
17	04.03	CAP	20.35	PIS	ARI	02.23	CAN	VIR	14.11	06.53	CAP	AQU	17
18	SAG	12.38	AQU	23.25	13.51	GEM	12.34	VIR	SCO	SAG	13.45	09.59	18
19	17.10	AQU	AQU	ARI	TAU	02.32	LEO	00.04	21.49	17.14	AQU	PIS	19
20	CAP	22.57	06.57	ARI	15.51	CAN	12.19	LIB	SAG	CAP	AQU	21.37	20
21	CAP	PIS	PIS	03.56	GEM	02.06	VIR	04.44	SAG	CAP	02.16	ARI	21
22	05.37	PIS	14.23	TAU	16.27	LEO	14.33	SCO	08.58	05.39	PIS	ARI	22
23	AQU	06.57	ARI	06.27	CAN	03.01	LIB	13.34	CAP	AQU	12.53	06.11	23
24	16.23	ARI	19.29	GEM	17.18	VIR	20.41	SAG	21.38	17.45	ARI	TAU	24
25	PIS	13.08	TAU	08.22	LEO	06.51	SCO	SAG	AQU	PIS	20.06	10.47	25
26	PIS	TAU	23.16	CAN	19.50	LIB	SCO	01.31	AQU	PIS	TAU	GEM	26
27	01.10	17.47	GEM	10.44	VIR	14.17	06.40	CAP	09.24	03.31	23.55	12.03	27
28	ARI	GEM	GEM	LEO	VIR	SCO	SAG	14.18	PIS	ARI	GEM	CAN	28
29	07.45		02.26	14.15	00.54	SCO	19.01	AQU	18.58	10.16	GEM	11.41	29
30	TAU		CAN	VIR	LIB	00.46	CAP	AQU	ARI	TAU	01.31	LEO	30
31	11.52		05.22		08.42		CAP	02.03		14.36		11.47	31

sun

mth	day	sign
JAN	1	CAP
JAN	21	AQU
FEB	19	PIS
MAR	20	ARI
APR	20	TAU
MAY	21	GEM
JUN	21	CAN
JUL	22	LEO
AUG	23	VIR
SEP	23	LIB
OCT	23	SCO
NOV	22	SAG
DEC	21	CAP

mercury

mth	day	sign
JAN	1	CAP
JAN	14	AQU
FEB	2	PIS
FEB	20	AQU
MAR	18	PIS
APR	9	ARI
APR	25	TAU
MAY	9	GEM
MAY	28	CAN
JUN	28	GEM
JUL	11	CAN
AUG	2	LEO
AUG	17	VIR
SEP	3	LIB
SEP	27	SCO
OCT	17	LIB
NOV	10	SCO
NOV	29	SAG
DEC	18	CAP

venus

mth	day	sign
JAN	1	AQU
JAN	18	PIS
FEB	11	ARI
MAR	8	TAU
APR	4	GEM
MAY	7	CAN
JUN	29	GEM
AUG	3	CAN
SEP	8	LEO
OCT	6	VIR
NOV	1	LIB
NOV	26	SCO
DEC	20	SAG

mars

mth	day	sign
JAN	1	VIR
FEB	12	LEO
MAY	18	VIR
JUL	17	LIB
SEP	3	SCO
OCT	17	SAG
NOV	26	CAP

saturn

mth	day	sign
JAN	1	LEO
SEP	19	VIR

jupiter

mth	day	sign
JAN	1	SAG
NOV	15	CAP

moon

DAY	JAN	FEB	MAR	APR	MAY	JUN	JUL	AUG	SEP	OCT	NOV	DEC	DAY
1	VIR	02.26	17.41	CAP	AQU	15.55	10.40	GEM	LEO	SCO	SAG	PIS	1
2	14.10	SCO	SAG	23.17	19.44	ARI	TAU	07.20	18.20	04.30	18.10	09.16	2
3	LIB	10.26	SAG	AQU	PIS	ARI	17.48	CAN	VIR	LIB	SAG	CAP	3
4	19.51	SAG	03.50	AQU	PIS	01.43	GEM	08.13	17.35	04.58	23.39	17.32	4
5	SCO	21.30	CAP	11.56	07.28	TAU	21.07	LEO	LIB	SCO	CAP	AQU	5
6	SCO	CAP	16.14	PIS	ARI	08.06	CAN	07.32	18.34	07.55	CAP	AQU	6
7	04.40	CAP	AQU	23.28	16.48	GEM	21.53	VIR	SCO	08.41	04.46	7
8	SAG	09.59	AQU	ARI	TAU	11.28	LEO	07.30	22.52	14.31	AQU	PIS	8
9	15.41	AQU	04.53	ARI	23.20	CAN	22.03	LIB	SAG	CAP	20.34	17.30	9
10	CAP	22.36	PIS	08.58	GEM	13.11	VIR	09.56	SAG	CAP	PIS	ARI	10
11	CAP	PIS	16.33	TAU	GEM	LEO	23.31	SCO	06.56	00.42	PIS	ARI	11
12	03.54	PIS	ARI	16.20	03.38	14.49	LIB	LIB	SAG	17.58	AQU	09.12	ARI	05.09	12
13	AQU	10.36	ARI	GEM	CAN	VIR	LIB	SAG	17.58	13.03	ARI	TAU	13
14	16.35	ARI	02.40	21.41	06.39	17.33	03.28	SAG	AQU	PIS	20.24	13.44	14
15	PIS	21.08	TAU	CAN	LEO	LIB	SCO	00.51	AQU	PIS	TAU	GEM	15
16	PIS	TAU	10.45	CAN	09.14	22.03	10.11	CAP	06.26	01.36	TAU	19.01	16
17	04.44	TAU	GEM	01.16	VIR	SCO	SAG	12.02	PIS	ARI	05.02	CAN	17
18	ARI	04.56	16.14	LEO	12.07	SCO	19.13	AQU	19.02	12.54	GEM	22.03	18
19	14.42	GEM	CAN	03.30	LIB	04.28	CAP	AQU	ARI	TAU	11.11	LEO	19
20	TAU	09.09	18.58	VIR	15.56	SAG	CAP	00.23	ARI	22.15	CAN	LEO	20
21	21.01	CAN	LEO	05.16	SCO	12.51	06.02	PIS	06.45	GEM	15.32	00.19	21
22	GEM	10.07	19.42	LIB	21.22	CAP	AQU	13.05	TAU	GEM	LEO	VIR	22
23	23.23	LEO	VIR	07.49	SAG	23.15	18.13	ARI	16.40	05.21	18.48	LIB	23
24	CAN	09.22	20.01	SCO	SAG	AQU	PIS	ARI	GEM	CAN	VIR	LIB	24
25	23.00	VIR	LIB	12.31	05.08	AQU	PIS	01.03	23.46	10.10	21.33	06.39	25
26	LEO	09.05	21.49	SAG	CAP	11.23	08.57	TAU	CAN	LEO	LIB	SCO	26
27	21.56	LIB	SCO	20.21	15.31	PIS	ARI	10.40	CAN	12.53	LIB	11.29	27
28	VIR	11.24	SCO	CAP	AQU	23.56	18.34	GEM	03.35	VIR	00.19	SAG	28
29	22.29	SCO	02.46	CAP	AQU	ARI	TAU	16.34	LEO	14.16	SCO	17.47	29
30	LIB		SAG	07.16	03.46	ARI	TAU	CAN	LEO	LIB	03.52	CAP	30
31	LIB		11.34		PIS		03.01	18.41		15.31		CAP	31

314

sun

mth	day	sign
JAN	1	CAP
JAN	20	AQU
FEB	18	PIS
MAR	20	ARI
APR	20	TAU
MAY	21	GEM
JUN	21	CAN
JUL	23	LEO
AUG	23	VIR
SEP	23	LIB
OCT	23	SCO
NOV	22	SAG
DEC	22	CAP

mercury

mth	day	sign
JAN	1	CAP
JAN	6	AQU
MAR	14	PIS
APR	1	ARI
APR	16	TAU
MAY	2	GEM
JUL	10	CAN
JUL	25	LEO
AUG	9	VIR
AUG	28	LIB
NOV	3	SCO
NOV	22	SAG
DEC	11	CAP

venus

mth	day	sign
JAN	1	SAG
JAN	13	CAP
FEB	6	AQU
MAR	2	PIS
MAR	26	ARI
APR	19	TAU
MAY	14	GEM
JUN	7	CAN
JUL	1	LEO
JUL	26	VIR
AUG	20	LIB
SEP	14	SCO
OCT	10	SAG
NOV	6	CAP
DEC	6	AQU

mars

mth	day	sign
JAN	1	CAP
JAN	4	AQU
FEB	11	PIS
MAR	21	ARI
APR	30	TAU
JUN	10	GEM
JUL	23	CAN
SEP	7	LEO
OCT	27	VIR
DEC	26	LIB

saturn

mth	day	sign
JAN	1	VIR
APR	3	LEO
MAY	29	VIR

jupiter

mth	day	sign
JAN	1	CAP
APR	12	AQU
JUN	27	CAP
NOV	30	AQU

moon

DAY	JAN	FEB	MAR	APR	MAY	JUN	JUL	AUG	SEP	OCT	NOV	DEC	DAY
1	02.07	PIS	15.35	TAU	GEM	00.35	VIR	SCO	12.05	01.13	PIS	ARI	1
2	AQU	09.04	ARI	22.03	12.43	LEO	13.22	SCO	CAP	AQU	05.34	01.22	2
3	12.58	ARI	ARI	GEM	CAN	04.53	LIB	01.25	19.37	11.19	ARI	TAU	3
4	PIS	21.57	04.33	GEM	19.11	VIR	16.22	SAG	AQU	PIS	18.37	13.28	4
5	PIS	TAU	TAU	07.10	LEO	07.57	SCO	06.35	AQU	23.27	TAU	GEM	5
6	01.40	TAU	16.05	CAN	23.11	LIB	19.45	CAP	05.26	ARI	TAU	23.31	6
7	ARI	08.40	GEM	12.59	VIR	10.13	SAG	13.34	PIS	ARI	06.55	CAN	7
8	14.03	GEM	GEM	LEO	VIR	SCO	SAG	AQU	17.13	12.26	GEM	CAN	8
9	TAU	15.22	00.21	15.32	01.07	12.23	00.02	22.45	ARI	TAU	17.35	07.27	9
10	23.31	CAN	CAN	VIR	LIB	SAG	CAP	PIS	ARI	TAU	CAN	LEO	10
11	GEM	18.00	04.33	15.48	01.54	15.40	06.09	PIS	06.12	01.02	CAN	13.31	11
12	GEM	LEO	LEO	LIB	SCO	CAP	AQU	10.20	TAU	GEM	02.00	VIR	12
13	04.57	LEO	05.24	15.27	02.57	21.26	15.01	ARI	18.47	11.51	LEO	17.45	13
14	CAN	VIR	VIR	SCO	SAG	AQU	PIS	23.18	GEM	CAN	07.42	LIB	14
15	07.08	17.44	04.40	16.23	05.57	AQU	PIS	TAU	GEM	19.35	VIR	20.13	15
16	LEO	LIB	LIB	SAG	CAP	06.38	02.43	TAU	04.51	LEO	10.35	SCO	16
17	07.52	18.53	04.25	20.16	12.19	PIS	ARI	11.23	CAN	23.42	LIB	21.32	17
18	VIR	SCO	SCO	CAP	AQU	18.45	15.35	GEM	11.04	VIR	11.18	SAG	18
19	09.03	22.49	06.30	CAP	22.26	ARI	TAU	20.15	LEO	VIR	SCO	23.00	19
20	LIB	SAG	SAG	03.59	PIS	ARI	TAU	CAN	13.34	00.48	11.15	CAP	20
21	11.59	SAG	12.04	AQU	PIS	07.30	02.57	CAN	VIR	LIB	SAG	CAP	21
22	SCO	05.50	CAP	15.08	11.02	TAU	GEM	01.07	13.41	00.18	12.19	02.24	22
23	17.09	CAP	21.10	PIS	ARI	18.20	10.52	LEO	LIB	SCO	CAP	AQU	23
24	SAG	15.26	AQU	PIS	23.42	GEM	CAN	02.55	13.20	00.08	16.24	09.20	24
25	SAG	AQU	AQU	04.01	TAU	GEM	15.19	VIR	SCO	SAG	AQU	PIS	25
26	00.21	AQU	08.50	ARI	TAU	02.01	LEO	03.24	14.21	02.10	AQU	20.05	26
27	CAP	02.54	PIS	16.41	10.27	CAN	17.35	LIB	SAG	CAP	00.35	ARI	27
28	09.26	PIS	21.41	TAU	GEM	07.00	VIR	04.19	18.07	07.50	PIS	ARI	28
29	AQU		ARI	TAU	18.38	LEO	19.20	SCO	CAP	AQU	12.18	08.58	29
30	20.26		ARI	03.48	CAN	10.27	LIB	07.00	CAP	17.21	ARI	TAU	30
31	PIS		10.29		CAN		21.44	SAG		PIS		21.13	31

315

sun

mth	day	sign
JAN	1	CAP
JAN	20	AQU
FEB	19	PIS
MAR	21	ARI
APR	20	TAU
MAY	21	GEM
JUN	21	CAN
JUL	23	LEO
AUG	23	VIR
SEP	23	LIB
OCT	23	SCO
NOV	22	SAG
DEC	22	CAP

mercury

mth	day	sign
JAN	1	AQU
JAN	15	CAP
FEB	14	AQU
MAR	7	PIS
MAR	24	ARI
APR	8	TAU
JUN	14	GEM
JUL	2	CAN
JUL	16	LEO
AUG	2	VIR
AUG	27	LIB
SEP	10	VIR
OCT	9	LIB
OCT	27	SCO
NOV	15	SAG
DEC	5	CAP

venus

mth	day	sign
JAN	1	AQU
APR	6	PIS
MAY	5	ARI
JUN	1	TAU
JUN	27	GEM
JUL	22	CAN
AUG	16	LEO
SEP	10	VIR
OCT	4	LIB
OCT	28	SCO
NOV	21	SAG
DEC	14	CAP

mars

mth	day	sign
JAN	1	LIB
MAR	28	VIR
JUN	11	LIB
AUG	10	SCO
SEP	25	SAG
NOV	6	CAP
DEC	15	AQU

saturn

mth	day	sign
JAN	1	VIR
NOV	20	LIB

jupiter

mth	day	sign
JAN	1	AQU
APR	15	PIS
SEP	15	AQU
DEC	1	PIS

moon

DAY	JAN	FEB	MAR	APR	MAY	JUN	JUL	AUG	SEP	OCT	NOV	DEC	DAY
1	GEM	22.34	08.30	VIR	11.37	21.27	09.19	PIS	02.19	GEM	CAN	21.53	1
2	GEM	LEO	LEO	00.40	SCO	CAP	AQU	07.03	TAU	GEM	05.38	VIR	2
3	06.56	LEO	12.25	LIB	10.50	23.18	13.51	ARI	14.45	10.59	LEO	VIR	3
4	CAN	02.37	VIR	00.34	SAG	AQU	PIS	18.06	GEM	GEM	14.21	04.29	4
5	13.58	VIR	14.00	SCO	11.08	AQU	22.25	TAU	GEM	21.40	VIR	LIB	5
6	LEO	05.19	LIB	00.37	CAP	04.57	ARI	TAU	02.54	LEO	19.10	07.19	6
7	19.06	LIB	14.55	SAG	14.22	PIS	ARI	06.44	CAN	LEO	LIB	SCO	7
8	VIR	07.50	SCO	02.29	AQU	14.44	10.13	GEM	12.34	04.54	20.29	07.17	8
9	23.08	SCO	16.37	CAP	21.34	ARI	TAU	18.27	LEO	VIR	SCO	SAG	9
10	LIB	10.51	SAG	07.25	PIS	ARI	23.02	CAN	18.55	08.29	19.51	06.16	10
11	LIB	SAG	20.07	AQU	PIS	03.12	GEM	CAN	VIR	LIB	SAG	CAP	11
12	02.28	14.45	CAP	15.38	08.18	TAU	GEM	03.36	22.28	09.31	19.25	06.34	12
13	SCO	CAP	CAP	PIS	ARI	16.05	10.33	LEO	LIB	SCO	CAP	AQU	13
14	05.16	19.57	01.52	PIS	20.59	GEM	CAN	10.03	LIB	09.44	21.14	10.10	14
15	SAG	AQU	AQU	02.32	TAU	GEM	19.52	VIR	00.27	SAG	AQU	PIS	15
16	08.06	AQU	09.59	ARI	TAU	03.45	LEO	14.31	SCO	10.55	AQU	17.58	16
17	CAP	03.11	PIS	15.00	09.52	CAN	LEO	LIB	02.12	CAP	02.38	ARI	17
18	12.07	PIS	20.21	TAU	GEM	13.37	03.05	17.49	SAG	14.27	PIS	ARI	18
19	AQU	13.01	ARI	ARI	21.50	LEO	VIR	SCO	04.49	AQU	11.39	05.09	19
20	18.41	ARI	ARI	03.54	CAN	21.31	08.34	20.36	CAP	20.53	ARI	TAU	20
21	PIS	ARI	08.32	GEM	CAN	VIR	LIB	SAG	08.59	PIS	23.08	17.49	21
22	PIS	01.12	TAU	16.02	08.06	VIR	12.27	23.23	AQU	PIS	TAU	GEM	22
23	04.37	TAU	21.28	CAN	LEO	03.09	SCO	CAP	15.09	05.59	TAU	GEM	23
24	ARI	14.03	GEM	CAN	15.50	LIB	14.55	CAP	PIS	ARI	11.38	06.18	24
25	17.08	GEM	GEM	01.51	VIR	06.19	SAG	02.53	23.22	17.03	GEM	CAN	25
26	TAU	GEM	09.17	LEO	20.26	SCO	16.39	AQU	ARI	TAU	GEM	17.45	26
27	TAU	01.03	CAN	08.30	LIB	07.26	CAP	08.02	ARI	TAU	00.13	LEO	27
28	05.43	CAN	18.04	VIR	22.01	SAG	18.55	PIS	TAU	GEM	LEO	LEO	28
29	GEM		LEO	11.25	SCO	07.48	AQU	15.44	TAU	GEM	12.02	03.41	29
30	15.50		23.01	LIB	21.43	CAP	23.19	ARI	22.26	18.03	LEO	VIR	30
31	CAN		VIR		SAG		PIS	ARI		CAN		11.20	31

sun

mth	day	sign
JAN	1	CAP
JAN	20	AQU
FEB	19	PIS
MAR	21	ARI
APR	20	TAU
MAY	21	GEM
JUN	22	CAN
JUL	23	LEO
AUG	23	VIR
SEP	23	LIB
OCT	24	SCO
NOV	23	SAG
DEC	22	CAP

mercury

mth	day	sign
JAN	1	CAP
FEB	9	AQU
FEB	28	PIS
MAR	16	ARI
APR	2	TAU
MAY	1	ARI
MAY	15	TAU
JUN	9	GEM
JUN	24	CAN
JUL	8	LEO
JUL	27	VIR
OCT	2	LIB
OCT	19	SCO
NOV	8	SAG
DEC	1	CAP
DEC	12	SAG

venus

mth	day	sign
JAN	1	CAP
JAN	7	AQU
JAN	31	PIS
FEB	24	ARI
MAR	21	TAU
APR	15	GEM
MAY	11	CAN
JUN	7	LEO
JUL	8	VIR
NOV	9	LIB
DEC	8	SCO

mars

mth	day	sign
JAN	1	AQU
JAN	22	PIS
MAR	1	ARI
APR	10	TAU
MAY	21	GEM
JUL	3	CAN
AUG	18	LEO
OCT	5	VIR
NOV	24	LIB

saturn

mth	day	sign
JAN	1	LIB
MAR	7	VIR
AUG	13	LIB

jupiter

mth	day	sign
JAN	1	PIS
APR	21	ARI

moon

DAY	JAN	FEB	MAR	APR	MAY	JUN	JUL	AUG	SEP	OCT	NOV	DEC	DAY
1	LIB	01.16	SAG	AQU	PIS	02.33	GEM	CAN	VIR	LIB	05.20	CAP	1
2	15.58	SAG	09.29	22.44	11.26	TAU	GEM	03.07	VIR	18.23	SAG	15.45	2
3	SCO	02.52	CAP	PIS	ARI	14.03	08.27	LEO	05.32	SCO	06.40	AQU	3
4	17.38	CAP	12.11	PIS	20.46	GEM	CAN	14.18	LIB	21.48	CAP	18.08	4
5	SAG	04.04	AQU	05.16	TAU	GEM	21.00	VIR	11.49	SAG	08.43	PIS	5
6	17.32	AQU	15.45	ARI	TAU	02,31	LEO	23.34	SCO	SAG	AQU	23.18	6
7	CAP	06.29	PIS	13.52	07.51	CAN	LEO	LIB	16.11	00.30	12.23	ARI	7
8	17.35	PIS	21.16	TAU	GEM	15.12	08.36	LIB	SAG	CAP	PIS	ARI	8
9	AQU	11.43	ARI	TAU	20.13	LEO	VIR	06.24	19.06	03.20	17.52	07.04	9
10	19.56	ARI	ARI	00.41	CAN	LEO	18.04	SCO	CAP	AQU	ARI	TAU	10
11	PIS	20.33	05.33	GEM	CAN	02.46	LIB	10.31	21.11	06.46	ARI	16.54	11
12	PIS	TAU	TAU	13.04	08.49	VIR	LIB	SAG	AQU	PIS	01.07	GEM	12
13	02.05	TAU	16.36	CAN	LEO	11.31	00.20	12.18	23.21	11.20	TAU	GEM	13
14	ARI	08.18	GEM	CAN	19.44	LIB	SCO	CAP	PIS	ARI	10.15	04.22	14
15	12.11	GEM	GEM	01.18	VIR	16.17	03.03	12.53	PIS	17.37	GEM	CAN	15
16	TAU	20.51	05.06	LEO	VIR	SCO	SAG	AQU	02.47	TAU	21.27	17.05	16
17	TAU	CAN	CAN	11.07	03.05	17.26	03.14	13.52	ARI	TAU	CAN	LEO	17
18	00.36	CAN	16.44	VIR	LIB	SAG	CAP	PIS	08.41	02.22	CAN	LEO	18
19	GEM	08.01	LEO	17.13	06.23	16.38	02.41	16.58	TAU	GEM	10.12	05.52	19
20	13.06	LEO	LEO	LIB	SCO	CAP	AQU	ARI	17.47	13.42	LEO	VIR	20
21	CAN	16.43	01.40	19.56	06.44	16.04	03.29	23.26	GEM	CAN	22.35	16.41	21
22	CAN	VIR	VIR	SCO	SAG	AQU	PIS	TAU	GEM	CAN	VIR	LIB	22
23	00.12	23.01	07.21	20.40	06.07	17.49	07.21	TAU	05.34	02.25	VIR	23.38	23
24	LEO	LIB	LIB	SAG	CAP	PIS	ARI	09.27	CAN	LEO	08.09	SCO	24
25	09.26	LIB	10.36	21.20	06.41	23.13	15.07	GEM	18.08	14.01	LIB	SCO	25
26	VIR	03.31	SCO	CAP	AQU	ARI	TAU	21.44	LEO	VIR	13.32	02.27	26
27	16.46	SCO	12.40	23.32	10.05	ARI	TAU	CAN	LEO	22.25	SCO	SAG	27
28	LIB	06.49	SAG	AQU	PIS	08.17	02.07	CAN	05.05	LIB	15.20	02.24	28
29	22.04		14.51	AQU	16.53	TAU	GEM	10.11	VIR	LIB	SAG	CAP	29
30	SCO		CAP	04.13	ARI	19.51	14.42	LEO	13.08	SCO	15.22	01.36	30
31	SCO		18.02		ARI		CAN	21.00		SCO		AQU	31

sun

mth	day	sign
JAN	1	CAP
JAN	21	AQU
FEB	19	PIS
MAR	20	ARI
APR	20	TAU
MAY	21	GEM
JUN	21	CAN
JUL	22	LEO
AUG	23	VIR
SEP	23	LIB
OCT	23	SCO
NOV	22	SAG
DEC	21	CAP

mercury

mth	day	sign
JAN	1	SAG
JAN	13	CAP
FEB	3	AQU
FEB	20	PIS
MAR	7	ARI
MAY	14	TAU
MAY	31	GEM
JUN	14	CAN
JUN	30	LEO
SEP	7	VIR
SEP	23	LIB
OCT	11	SCO
NOV	1	SAG

venus

mth	day	sign
JAN	1	SCO
JAN	2	SAG
JAN	27	CAP
FEB	21	AQU
MAR	16	PIS
APR	9	ARI
MAY	4	TAU
MAY	28	GEM
JUN	22	CAN
JUL	16	LEO
AUG	9	VIR
SEP	3	LIB
SEP	27	SCO
OCT	22	SAG
NOV	15	CAP
DEC	10	AQU

mars

mth	day	sign
JAN	1	LIB
JAN	20	SCO
AUG	27	SAG
OCT	12	CAP
NOV	21	AQU
DEC	30	PIS

saturn

mth	day	sign
JAN	1	LIB

jupiter

mth	day	sign
JAN	1	ARI
APR	28	TAU

moon

DAY	JAN	FEB	MAR	APR	MAY	JUN	JUL	AUG	SEP	OCT	NOV	DEC	DAY
1	02.11	19.51	TAU	07.39	04.12	VIR	LIB	SAG	09.03	PIS	06.58	GEM	1
2	PIS	TAU	12.36	CAN	LEO	12.26	05.25	22.27	AQU	19.34	TAU	GEM	2
3	05.42	TAU	GEM	20.11	16.57	LIB	SCO	CAP	09.00	ARI	11.02	03.08	3
4	ARI	04.55	23.40	LEO	VIR	20.19	10.27	22.41	PIS	21.05	GEM	CAN	4
5	12.43	GEM	CAN	LEO	VIR	SCO	SAG	AQU	08.57	TAU	18.12	13.23	5
6	TAU	16.44	CAN	08.40	03.39	SCO	12.02	22.05	ARI	TAU	CAN	LEO	6
7	22.42	CAN	12.30	VIR	LIB	00.21	CAP	PIS	10.48	01.15	CAN	LEO	7
8	GEM	CAN	LEO	18.56	10.49	SAG	11.54	22.33	TAU	GEM	04.56	01.57	8
9	GEM	05.36	LEO	LIB	SCO	01.46	AQU	ARI	16.06	09.16	LEO	VIR	9
10	10.34	LEO	00.51	LIB	14.50	CAP	11.59	ARI	GEM	CAN	17.47	14.35	10
11	CAN	18.02	VIR	02.13	SAG	02.26	PIS	01.46	GEM	20.50	VIR	LIB	11
12	23.19	VIR	11.16	SCO	17.09	AQU	13.56	TAU	01.24	LEO	VIR	LIB	12
13	LEO	VIR	LIB	07.08	CAP	04.00	ARI	08.36	LEO	LEO	05.57	00.39	13
14	LEO	05.00	19.20	SAG	19.14	PIS	18.45	GEM	13.38	09.51	LIB	SCO	14
15	12.00	LIB	SCO	10.41	AQU	07.29	TAU	18.52	LEO	VIR	15.18	07.00	15
16	VIR	13.45	SCO	CAP	22.05	ARI	TAU	CAN	LEO	21.44	SCO	SAG	16
17	23.19	SCO	01.15	13.43	PIS	13.11	02.37	CAN	02.41	LIB	21.33	10.17	17
18	LIB	19.42	SAG	AQU	PIS	TAU	GEM	07.19	VIR	LIB	SAG	CAP	18
19	LIB	SAG	05.19	16.40	02.07	21.03	13.05	LEO	14.41	07.11	SAG	12.02	19
20	07.44	22.49	CAP	PIS	ARI	GEM	CAN	20.23	LIB	SCO	01.40	AQU	20
21	SCO	CAP	07.55	19.56	07.29	GEM	CAN	VIR	LIB	14.12	CAP	13.45	21
22	12.23	23.48	AQU	ARI	TAU	07.04	01.20	VIR	SCO	00.43	SAG	04.52	22
23	SAG	AQU	09.39	ARI	14.37	CAN	LEO	08.42	SCO	19.28	AQU	16.30	23
24	13.39	AQU	PIS	00.15	GEM	19.02	14.24	LIB	08.33	CAP	07.55	ARI	24
25	CAP	00.01	11.34	TAU	GEM	LEO	VIR	19.11	SAG	23.28	PIS	20.46	25
26	13.06	PIS	ARI	06.40	00.06	LEO	VIR	SCO	14.06	AQU	11.09	TAU	26
27	AQU	01.11	15.05	GEM	CAN	02.54	SCO	CAP	AQU	ARI	TAU	TAU	27
28	12.45	ARI	TAU	16.06	11.59	VIR	LIB	02.53	17.24	02.23	14.54	02.48	28
29	PIS	05.02	21.36	CAN	CAN	20.18	13.04	SAG	AQU	PIS	TAU	GEM	29
30	14.33		GEM	CAN	LEO	LIB	SCO	07.24	18.52	04.34	19.53	10.53	30
31	ARI		GEM		00.57		19.37	CAP		ARI		CAN	31

sun

mth	day	sign
JAN	1	CAP
JAN	20	AQU
FEB	18	PIS
MAR	20	ARI
APR	20	TAU
MAY	21	GEM
JUN	21	CAN
JUL	23	LEO
AUG	23	VIR
SEP	23	LIB
OCT	23	SCO
NOV	22	SAG
DEC	22	CAP

mercury

mth	day	sign
JAN	1	SAG
JAN	6	CAP
JAN	25	AQU
FEB	11	PIS
MAR	2	ARI
MAR	15	PIS
APR	17	ARI
MAY	8	TAU
MAY	23	GEM
JUN	6	CAN
JUN	26	LEO
JUL	28	CAN
AUG	11	LEO
AUG	30	VIR
SEP	15	LIB
OCT	4	SCO
OCT	31	SAG
NOV	6	SCO
DEC	10	SAG
DEC	30	CAP

venus

mth	day	sign
JAN	1	AQU
JAN	5	PIS
FEB	2	ARI
MAR	14	TAU
MAR	31	ARI
JUN	5	TAU
JUL	7	GEM
AUG	4	CAN
AUG	30	LEO
SEP	24	VIR
OCT	18	LIB
NOV	11	SCO
DEC	5	SAG
DEC	29	CAP

mars

mth	day	sign
JAN	1	PIS
FEB	8	ARI
MAR	20	TAU
MAY	1	GEM
JUN	14	CAN
JUL	29	LEO
SEP	14	VIR
NOV	1	LIB
DEC	20	SCO

saturn

mth	day	sign
JAN	1	LIB
OCT	22	SCO

jupiter

mth	day	sign
JAN	1	TAU
MAY	9	GEM

moon

DAY	JAN	FEB	MAR	APR	MAY	JUN	JUL	AUG	SEP	OCT	NOV	DEC	DAY
1	21.17	VIR	VIR	05.19	SAG	14.44	00.08	10.57	GEM	18.53	VIR	LIB	1
2	LEO	VIR	11.41	SCO	SAG	AQU	PIS	TAU	03.30	LEO	VIR	21.30	2
3	LEO	05.31	LIB	14.58	03.55	18.12	02.22	15.10	CAN	LEO	01.51	SCO	3
4	09.41	LIB	23.31	SAG	CAP	PIS	ARI	GEM	13.05	06.40	LIB	SCO	4
5	VIR	17.21	SCO	22.29	09.12	21.01	05.22	21.59	LEO	VIR	14.12	08.09	5
6	22.36	SCO	SCO	CAP	AQU	ARI	TAU	CAN	LEO	19.28	SCO	SAG	6
7	LIB	SCO	09.20	CAP	12.46	23.41	09.42	CAN	00.47	LIB	SCO	16.33	7
8	LIB	02.20	SAG	03.29	PIS	TAU	GEM	07.16	VIR	LIB	01.06	CAP	8
9	09.44	SAG	16.10	AQU	14.49	TAU	15.54	LEO	13.29	07.56	SAG	22.59	9
10	SCO	07.32	CAP	05.49	ARI	03.03	CAN	18.33	LIB	SCO	10.18	AQU	10
11	17.14	CAP	19.37	PIS	16.12	GEM	CAN	VIR	LIB	19.19	CAP	AQU	11
12	SAG	09.16	AQU	06.19	TAU	08.17	00.28	VIR	02.05	SAG	17.31	03.46	12
13	20.55	AQU	20.17	ARI	18.29	CAN	LEO	07.08	SCO	SAG	AQU	PIS	13
14	CAP	08.58	PIS	06.31	GEM	16.29	11.28	LIB	13.32	04.51	22.17	07.06	14
15	21.57	PIS	19.39	TAU	23.16	LEO	VIR	19.43	SAG	CAP	PIS	ARI	15
16	AQU	08.30	ARI	08.29	CAN	LEO	VIR	SCO	22.21	11.34	PIS	09.22	16
17	22.07	ARI	19.44	GEM	CAN	03.36	00.04	SCO	CAP	AQU	00.35	TAU	17
18	PIS	09.51	TAU	13.53	07.47	VIR	LIB	06.30	CAP	14.55	ARI	11.29	18
19	23.08	TAU	22.35	CAN	LEO	16.16	12.17	SAG	03.30	PIS	01.15	GEM	19
20	ARI	14.29	GEM	23.29	19.31	LIB	SCO	13.53	AQU	15.29	TAU	14.40	20
21	ARI	GEM	GEM	LEO	VIR	LIB	21.59	CAP	05.06	ARI	01.54	CAN	21
22	02.20	22.47	05.29	LEO	VIR	03.57	SAG	17.29	PIS	14.47	GEM	20.22	22
23	TAU	CAN	CAN	11.53	08.16	SCO	SAG	AQU	04.30	TAU	04.31	LEO	23
24	08.21	CAN	16.14	VIR	LIB	12.47	04.06	18.12	ARI	15.04	CAN	LEO	24
25	GEM	10.05	LEO	VIR	19.32	SAG	CAP	PIS	03.44	GEM	10.40	05.24	25
26	17.07	LEO	LEO	00.40	SCO	18.29	07.03	17.46	TAU	18.24	LEO	VIR	26
27	CAN	22.51	05.04	LIB	SCO	CAP	AQU	ARI	05.01	CAN	20.41	17.11	27
28	CAN	VIR	VIR	11.52	04.08	21.51	08.07	18.10	GEM	CAN	VIR	LIB	28
29	04.06		17.51	SCO	SAG	AQU	PIS	TAU	09.56	01.55	VIR	LIB	29
30	LEO		LIB	20.52	10.17	AQU	08.56	21.07	CAN	LEO	09.06	05.43	30
31	16.35		LIB		CAP		ARI	GEM		13.04		SCO	31

319

sun

mth	day	sign
JAN	1	CAP
JAN	20	AQU
FEB	19	PIS
MAR	21	ARI
APR	20	TAU
MAY	21	GEM
JUN	21	CAN
JUL	23	LEO
AUG	23	VIR
SEP	23	LIB
OCT	23	SCO
NOV	22	SAG
DEC	22	CAP

mercury

mth	day	sign
JAN	1	CAP
JAN	18	AQU
FEB	4	PIS
APR	13	ARI
APR	30	TAU
MAY	14	GEM
MAY	30	CAN
AUG	7	LEO
AUG	22	VIR
SEP	8	LIB
SEP	29	SCO
NOV	4	LIB
NOV	11	SCO
DEC	4	SAG
DEC	23	CAP

venus

mth	day	sign
JAN	1	CAP
JAN	22	AQU
FEB	15	PIS
MAR	11	ARI
APR	4	TAU
APR	28	GEM
MAY	23	CAN
JUN	17	LEO
JUL	13	VIR
AUG	9	LIB
SEP	6	SCO
OCT	23	SAG
OCT	27	SCO

mars

mth	day	sign
JAN	1	SCO
FEB	9	SAG
APR	12	CAP
JUL	3	SAG
AUG	24	CAP
OCT	21	AQU
DEC	4	PIS

saturn

mth	day	sign
JAN	1	SCO

jupiter

mth	day	sign
JAN	1	GEM
MAY	24	CAN

moon

DAY	JAN	FEB	MAR	APR	MAY	JUN	JUL	AUG	SEP	OCT	NOV	DEC	DAY
1	16.39	CAP	CAP	PIS	ARI	GEM	CAN	VIR	22.48	18.41	CAP	AQU	1
2	SAG	15.38	02.07	15.40	01.42	12.46	02.16	VIR	SCO	SAG	CAP	14.38	2
3	SAG	AQU	AQU	ARI	TAU	CAN	LEO	03.14	SCO	SAG	00.22	PIS	3
4	00.45	18.03	04.32	14.43	01.06	16.34	08.56	LIB	11.32	07.04	AQU	19.34	4
5	CAP	PIS	PIS	TAU	GEM	LEO	VIR	15.03	SAG	CAP	07.34	ARI	5
6	06.09	19.14	04.40	14.40	02.30	LEO	18.53	SCO	23.10	16.45	PIS	21.23	6
7	AQU	ARI	ARI	GEM	CAN	00.06	LIB	SCO	CAP	AQU	10.42	TAU	7
8	09.43	20.47	04.32	17.29	07.29	VIR	LIB	03.32	CAP	22.17	ARI	21.16	8
9	PIS	TAU	TAU	CAN	LEO	10.59	07.04	SAG	07.31	PIS	10.48	GEM	9
10	12.27	23.54	06.06	CAN	16.23	LIB	SCO	14.20	AQU	23.58	TAU	21.06	10
11	ARI	GEM	GEM	00.05	VIR	23.30	19.19	CAP	11.55	ARI	09.50	CAN	11
12	15.10	GEM	10.37	LEO	VIR	SCO	SAG	21.54	PIS	23.32	GEM	22.48	12
13	TAU	05.10	CAN	10.03	04.03	SCO	SAG	AQU	13.22	TAU	09.59	LEO	13
14	18.29	CAN	18.17	VIR	LIB	11.37	05.40	AQU	13.45	ARI	23.10	CAN	14
15	GEM	12.34	LEO	21.57	16.42	SAG	CAP	02.17	13.45	GEM	13.03	03.54	15
16	23.01	LEO	LEO	LIB	SCO	22.05	13.19	PIS	TAU	GEM	LEO	VIR	16
17	CAN	22.00	04.22	LIB	SCO	CAP	AQU	04.37	14.55	00.50	19.52	12.51	17
18	CAN	VIR	VIR	10.32	04.53	CAP	18.33	ARI	GEM	CAN	VIR	LIB	18
19	05.24	VIR	15.57	SCO	SAG	06.26	PIS	06.26	18.13	05.41	VIR	LIB	19
20	LEO	09.14	LIB	22.55	15.49	AQU	22.07	TAU	CAN	LEO	06.02	00.43	20
21	14.14	LIB	LIB	SAG	CAP	12.37	ARI	08.56	CAN	13.45	LIB	SCO	21
22	VIR	21.43	04.26	SAG	CAP	PIS	ARI	GEM	00.04	VIR	18.13	13.34	22
23	VIR	SCO	SCO	10.11	00.48	16.43	00.52	12.50	LEO	VIR	SCO	SAG	23
24	01.30	SCO	16.56	CAP	AQU	ARI	TAU	CAN	08.11	00.12	SCO	SAG	24
25	LIB	10.00	SAG	19.02	07.08	19.09	03.30	18.22	VIR	LIB	07.01	01.40	25
26	14.03	SAG	SAG	AQU	PIS	TAU	GEM	LEO	18.11	12.11	SAG	CAP	26
27	SCO	19.58	03.55	AQU	10.31	20.41	06.41	LEO	SCO	19.24	12.00	27
28	SCO	CAP	CAP	00.22	ARI	GEM	CAN	01.45	LIB	SCO	CAP	AQU	28
29	01.42		11.37	PIS	11.33	22.34	11.10	VIR	05.52	00.59	CAP	20.09	29
30	SAG		AQU	02.08	TAU	CAN	LEO	11.12	SCO	SAG	06.19	PIS	30
31	10.26		15.16		11.41		17.50	LIB		13.36		PIS	31

sun

mth	day	sign
JAN	1	CAP
JAN	20	AQU
FEB	19	PIS
MAR	21	ARI
APR	20	TAU
MAY	21	GEM
JUN	22	CAN
JUL	23	LEO
AUG	23	VIR
SEP	23	LIB
OCT	24	SCO
NOV	23	SAG
DEC	22	CAP

mercury

mth	day	sign
JAN	1	CAP
JAN	10	AQU
MAR	17	PIS
APR	6	ARI
APR	22	TAU
MAY	6	GEM
JUL	13	CAN
JUL	30	LEO
AUG	14	VIR
SEP	1	LIB
NOV	8	SCO
NOV	27	SAG
DEC	16	CAP

venus

mth	day	sign
JAN	1	SCO
JAN	6	SAG
FEB	6	CAP
MAR	4	AQU
MAR	30	PIS
APR	24	ARI
MAY	19	TAU
JUN	13	GEM
JUL	8	CAN
AUG	1	LEO
AUG	25	VIR
SEP	18	LIB
OCT	13	SCO
NOV	6	SAG
NOV	30	CAP
DEC	24	AQU

mars

mth	day	sign
JAN	1	PIS
JAN	15	ARI
FEB	26	TAU
APR	10	GEM
MAY	26	CAN
JUL	11	LEO
AUG	27	VIR
OCT	13	LIB
NOV	29	SCO

saturn

mth	day	sign
JAN	1	SCO

jupiter

mth	day	sign
JAN	1	CAN
JUN	13	LEO
NOV	17	VIR

moon

DAY	JAN	FEB	MAR	APR	MAY	JUN	JUL	AUG	SEP	OCT	NOV	DEC	DAY
1	01.56	14.02	GEM	08.20	VIR	20.54	15.33	CAP	15.23	05.46	19.23	05.46	1
2	ARI	GEM	22.40	LEO	VIR	SCO	SAG	22.52	PIS	ARI	GEM	CAN	2
3	05.24	16.36	CAN	14.31	04.26	SCO	SAG	AQU	21.24	08.52	20.11	06.07	3
4	TAU	CAN	CAN	VIR	LIB	09.23	04.29	AQU	ARI	TAU	CAN	LEO	4
5	07.04	19.28	02.48	22.33	15.04	SAG	CAP	08.04	ARI	10.59	22.20	08.50	5
6	GEM	LEO	LEO	LIB	SCO	22.21	16.18	PIS	01.36	GEM	LEO	VIR	6
7	08.00	23.43	08.09	LIB	SCO	CAP	AQU	15.00	TAU	13.23	LEO	14.48	7
8	CAN	VIR	VIR	08.38	03.19	CAP	AQU	ARI	04.58	CAN	02.36	LIB	8
9	09.41	VIR	15.20	SCO	SAG	10.30	02.08	20.03	GEM	16.41	VIR	23.59	9
10	LEO	06.33	LIB	20.41	16.19	AQU	PIS	TAU	08.01	LEO	09.15	SCO	10
11	13.43	LIB	LIB	SAG	CAP	20.32	09.33	23.33	CAN	21.11	LIB	SCO	11
12	VIR	16.38	01.04	SAG	CAP	PIS	ARI	GEM	11.02	VIR	18.12	11.33	12
13	21.15	SCO	SCO	09.40	04.29	PIS	14.20	GEM	LEO	VIR	SCO	SAG	13
14	LIB	SCO	13.13	CAP	AQU	03.24	TAU	01.50	14.33	03.13	SCO	SAG	14
15	LIB	05.07	SAG	21.20	13.53	ARI	16.43	CAN	VIR	LIB	05.17	00.23	15
16	08.14	SAG	SAG	AQU	PIS	06.50	GEM	03.33	19.35	11.23	SAG	CAP	16
17	SCO	17.33	02.01	AQU	19.21	TAU	17.30	LEO	LIB	SCO	17.59	13.19	17
18	21.01	CAP	CAP	05.28	ARI	07.36	CAN	05.57	LIB	22.07	CAP	AQU	18
19	SAG	CAP	12.47	PIS	21.12	GEM	18.03	VIR	03.18	SAG	CAP	AQU	19
20	SAG	03.33	AQU	09.29	TAU	07.15	LEO	10.33	SCO	SAG	06.58	01.02	20
21	09.09	AQU	19.45	ARI	20.56	CAN	20.06	LIB	14.11	10.52	AQU	PIS	21
22	CAP	10.09	PIS	10.29	GEM	07.36	VIR	18.37	SAG	CAP	18.01	10.05	22
23	18.58	PIS	23.09	TAU	20.33	LEO	VIR	SCO	SAG	23.33	PIS	ARI	23
24	AQU	14.06	ARI	10.24	CAN	10.26	01.16	SCO	03.01	AQU	PIS	15.33	24
25	AQU	ARI	ARI	GEM	21.52	VIR	LIB	06.03	CAP	AQU	01.47	TAU	25
26	02.11	16.46	00.31	11.09	LEO	16.55	10.19	SAG	15.07	09.37	ARI	17.33	26
27	PIS	TAU	TAU	CAN	LEO	LIB	18.57	SCO	AQU	PIS	05.27	GEM	27
28	07.19	19.24	01.42	14.09	02.16	LIB	22.24	CAP	AQU	15.46	TAU	17.17	28
29	ARI		GEM	LEO	VIR	03.04	SAG	CAP	00.12	ARI	06.11	CAN	29
30	11.06		04.05	19.58	10.08	SCO	SAG	06.35	PIS	18.30	GEM	16.36	30
31	TAU		CAN		LIB		11.18	AQU		TAU		LEO	31

sun

mth	day	sign
JAN	1	CAP
JAN	21	AQU
FEB	19	PIS
MAR	20	ARI
APR	20	TAU
MAY	21	GEM
JUN	21	CAN
JUL	22	LEO
AUG	23	VIR
SEP	23	LIB
OCT	23	SCO
NOV	22	SAG
DEC	21	CAP

mercury

mth	day	sign
JAN	1	CAP
JAN	4	AQU
FEB	2	CAP
FEB	15	AQU
MAR	11	PIS
MAR	28	ARI
APR	12	TAU
APR	29	GEM
JUL	6	CAN
JUL	21	LEO
AUG	5	VIR
AUG	26	LIB
SEP	29	VIR
OCT	11	LIB
OCT	31	SCO
NOV	18	SAG
DEC	8	CAP

venus

mth	day	sign
JAN	1	AQU
JAN	17	PIS
FEB	11	ARI
MAR	7	TAU
APR	4	GEM
MAY	8	CAN
JUN	23	GEM
AUG	4	CAN
SEP	8	LEO
OCT	6	VIR
OCT	31	LIB
NOV	25	SCO
DEC	19	SAG

mars

mth	day	sign
JAN	1	SCO
JAN	14	SAG
FEB	28	CAP
APR	14	AQU
JUN	3	PIS
DEC	6	ARI

saturn

mth	day	sign
JAN	1	SCO
JAN	12	SAG
MAY	14	SCO
OCT	10	SAG

jupiter

mth	day	sign
JAN	1	VIR
JAN	18	LEO
JUL	7	VIR
DEC	13	LIB

moon

DAY	JAN	FEB	MAR	APR	MAY	JUN	JUL	AUG	SEP	OCT	NOV	DEC	DAY
1	17.31	LIB	SCO	SAG	CAP	PIS	ARI	11.15	23.14	08.24	22.24	12.59	1
2	VIR	13.34	SCO	04.37	01.27	PIS	22.26	GEM	LEO	VIR	SCO	SAG	2
3	21.44	SCO	08.09	CAP	AQU	07.04	TAU	13.32	23.20	10.01	SCO	22.36	3
4	LIB	SCO	SAG	17.24	13.15	ARI	TAU	CAN	VIR	LIB	04.56	CAP	4
5	LIB	00.13	20.32	AQU	PIS	13.22	02.26	13.27	VIR	13.19	SAG	CAP	5
6	06.00	SAG	CAP	AQU	22.05	TAU	GEM	LEO	00.04	SCO	14.24	10.15	6
7	SCO	13.08	CAP	04.37	ARI	16.09	03.20	12.50	LIB	19.46	CAP	AQU	7
8	17.32	CAP	09.19	PIS	ARI	GEM	CAN	VIR	03.26	SAG	CAP	22.57	8
9	SAG	CAP	AQU	12.46	03.24	16.42	02.42	13.50	SCO	SAG	02.19	PIS	9
10	SAG	01.52	20.11	ARI	TAU	CAN	LEO	LIB	10.46	05.48	AQU	PIS	10
11	06.34	AQU	PIS	18.03	06.00	16.45	02.34	18.20	SAG	CAP	14.51	10.37	11
12	CAP	12.52	PIS	TAU	GEM	LEO	VIR	SCO	21.46	18.09	PIS	ARI	12
13	19.19	PIS	04.26	21.29	07.21	18.03	04.54	SCO	CAP	AQU	PIS	19.15	13
14	AQU	21.48	ARI	GEM	CAN	VIR	LIB	03.00	CAP	AQU	01.36	TAU	14
15	AQU	ARI	10.32	GEM	08.52	21.58	10.56	SAG	10.28	06.25	ARI	TAU	15
16	06.47	ARI	TAU	00.15	LEO	LIB	SO	14.47	AQU	PIS	09.12	00.06	16
17	PIS	04.48	15.11	CAN	11.40	LIB	20.38	CAP	22.34	16.35	TAU	GEM	17
18	16.17	TAU	GEM	03.00	VIR	05.03	SAG	CAP	PIS	ARI	13.45	01.52	18
19	ARI	09.50	18.47	LEO	16.25	SCO	SAG	03.38	PIS	ARI	GEM	CAN	19
20	23.11	GEM	CAN	06.17	LIB	14.55	08.40	AQU	08.47	00.07	16.17	02.11	20
21	TAU	12.50	21.31	VIR	23.26	SAG	CAP	15.47	ARI	TAU	CAN	LEO	21
22	TAU	CAN	LEO	10.36	SCO	SAG	21.28	PIS	17.01	05.28	18.10	02.56	22
23	03.05	14.10	23.53	LIB	SCO	02.43	AQU	PIS	TAU	GEM	LEO	VIR	23
24	GEM	LEO	VIR	16.44	08.46	CAP	AQU	02.29	23.25	09.23	20.32	05.39	24
25	04.20	15.05	VIR	SCO	SAG	15.26	09.50	ARI	GEM	CAN	VIR	LIB	25
26	CAN	VIR	03.00	SCO	20.11	AQU	PIS	11.23	GEM	12.27	VIR	11.09	26
27	04.06	17.20	LIB	01.25	CAP	AQU	20.54	TAU	04.00	LEO	00.11	SCO	27
28	LEO	LIB	08.18	SAG	CAP	03.54	ARI	17.59	CAN	15.09	LIB	19.20	28
29	04.17	22.45	SCO	12.44	08.52	PIS	ARI	GEM	06.49	VIR	05.34	SAG	29
30	VIR		16.56	CAP	AQU	14.43	05.40	21.51	LEO	18.10	SCO	SAG	30
31	06.56		SAG		21.09		TAU	CAN		LIB		05.37	31

sun

mth	day	sign
JAN	1	CAP
JAN	20	AQU
FEB	18	PIS
MAR	20	ARI
APR	20	TAU
MAY	21	GEM
JUN	21	CAN
JUL	23	LEO
AUG	23	VIR
SEP	23	LIB
OCT	23	SCO
NOV	22	SAG
DEC	22	CAP

mercury

mth	day	sign
JAN	1	CAP
FEB	12	AQU
MAR	4	PIS
MAR	20	ARI
APR	4	TAU
JUN	12	GEM
JUN	28	CAN
JUL	12	LEO
JUL	30	VIR
OCT	6	LIB
OCT	23	SCO
NOV	11	SAG
DEC	2	CAP
DEC	28	SAG

venus

mth	day	sign
JAN	1	SAG
JAN	12	CAP
FEB	5	AQU
MAR	1	PIS
MAR	25	ARI
APR	19	TAU
MAY	13	GEM
JUN	6	CAN
JUL	1	LEO
JUL	26	VIR
AUG	20	LIB
SEP	14	SCO
OCT	10	SAG
NOV	5	CAP
DEC	6	AQU

mars

mth	day	sign
JAN	1	ARI
JAN	28	TAU
MAR	17	GEM
MAY	4	CAN
JUN	21	LEO
AUG	8	VIR
SEP	24	LIB
NOV	8	SCO
DEC	23	SAG

saturn

mth	day	sign
JAN	1	SAG

jupiter

mth	day	sign
JAN	1	LIB
FEB	19	VIR
AUG	7	LIB

moon

DAY	JAN	FEB	MAR	APR	MAY	JUN	JUL	AUG	SEP	OCT	NOV	DEC	DAY
1	CAP	12.20	PIS	23.11	13.47	CAN	13.23	LIB	SAG	CAP	09.18	05.56	1
2	17.24	PIS	PIS	TAU	GEM	04.45	VIR	01.00	21.05	14.04	PIS	ARI	2
3	AQU	PIS	06.31	TAU	19.08	LEO	15.16	SCO	CAP	AQU	22.00	17.48	3
4	AQU	00.42	ARI	07.30	CAN	06.59	LIB	06.47	CAP	AQU	ARI	TAU	4
5	06.04	ARI	17.20	GEM	22.53	VIR	19.10	SAG	07.50	02.17	ARI	TAU	5
6	PIS	11.37	TAU	13.37	LEO	09.45	SCO	15.23	AQU	PIS	09.38	03.00	6
7	18.23	TAU	TAU	CAN	LEO	LIB	SCO	CAP	20.04	14.57	TAU	GEM	7
8	ARI	19.34	02.03	17.24	01.37	13.41	01.20	CAP	PIS	ARI	19.09	09.16	8
9	ARI	GEM	GEM	LEO	VIR	SCO	SAG	02.01	PIS	ARI	GEM	CAN	9
10	04.26	23.39	07.45	19.13	03.57	19.09	09.34	AQU	08.45	02.48	GEM	13.23	10
11	TAU	CAN	CAN	VIR	LIB	SAG	CAP	14.02	ARI	TAU	02.24	LEO	11
12	10.44	CAN	10.12	20.08	06.48	SAG	19.43	PIS	20.57	13.01	CAN	16.28	12
13	GEM	00.19>LEO	LEO	LIB	SCO	02.36	AQU	PIS	TAU	GEM	07.36	VIR	13
14	13.05	23.17	10.20	21.45	11.13	CAP	AQU	02.46	TAU	20.55	LEO	19.23	14
15	CAN	VIR	VIR	SCO	SAG	12.23	07.32	ARI	07.26	CAN	11.07	LIB	15
16	12.50	22.50	09.59	SCO	18.13	AQU	PIS	15.00	GEM	CAN	VIR	22.34	16
17	LEO	LIB	LIB	01.43	CAP	AQU	20.14	TAU	14.49	01.59	13.25	SCO	17
18	12.03	LIB	11.16	SAG	CAP	00.16	ARI	TAU	CAN	LEO	LIB	SCO	18
19	VIR	01.06	SCO	09.08	04.12	PIS	ARI	00.51	18.31	04.23	15.17	02.30	19
20	12.55	SCO	15.55	CAP	AQU	12.46	07.58	GEM	LEO	VIR	SCO	SAG	20
21	LIB	07.23	SAG	19.53	16.20	ARI	TAU	06.48	19.11	05.03	17.52	07.47	21
22	17.02	SAG	SAG	AQU	PIS	23.38	16.34	CAN	VIR	LIB	SAG	CAP	22
23	SCO	17.27	00.34	AQU	PIS	TAU	GEM	08.51	18.33	05.31	22.29	15.19	23
24	SCO	CAP	CAP	08.23	04.34	TAU	21.05	LEO	18.40	07.33	CAP	AQU	24
25	00.52	CAP	12.17	PIS	ARI	07.07	CAN	08.26	LIB	SCO	CAP	AQU	25
26	SAG	05.42	AQU	20.22	14.43	GEM	22.16	VIR	SCO	SAG	06.16	01.41	26
27	11.32	AQU	AQU	ARI	TAU	11.00	LEO	07.41	21.27	12.41	AQU	PIS	27
28	CAP	18.25	01.00	ARI	21.47	CAN	21.59	LIB	SAG	CAP	17.16	14.13	28
29	23.42		PIS	06.18	GEM	12.31	VIR	08.45	SAG	21.32	PIS	ARI	29
30	AQU		12.55	TAU	GEM	LEO	22.20	SCO	03.59	AQU	PIS	ARI	30
31	AQU		ARI		02.05		LIB	13.07		AQU		02.37	31

sun

mth	day	sign
JAN	1	CAP
JAN	20	AQU
FEB	19	PIS
MAR	21	ARI
APR	20	TAU
MAY	21	GEM
JUN	21	CAN
JUL	23	LEO
AUG	23	VIR
SEP	23	LIB
OCT	23	SCO
NOV	22	SAG
DEC	22	CAP

mercury

mth	day	sign
JAN	1	SAG
JAN	14	CAP
FEB	6	AQU
FEB	24	PIS
MAR	12	ARI
APR	2	TAU
APR	10	ARI
MAY	17	TAU
JUN	5	GEM
JUN	20	CAN
JUL	4	LEO
JUL	26	VIR
AUG	23	LEO
SEP	11	VIR
SEP	28	LIB
OCT	16	SCO
NOV	5	SAG

venus

mth	day	sign
JAN	1	AQU
APR	6	PIS
MAY	5	ARI
JUN	1	TAU
JUN	26	GEM
JUL	22	CAN
AUG	16	LEO
SEP	9	VIR
OCT	3	LIB
OCT	27	SCO
NOV	20	SAG
DEC	14	CAP

mars

mth	day	sign
JAN	1	SAG
FEB	3	CAP
MAR	17	AQU
APR	27	PIS
JUN	7	ARI
JUL	21	TAU
SEP	21	GEM
OCT	29	TAU

saturn

mth	day	sign
JAN	1	SAG

jupiter

mth	day	sign
JAN	1	LIB
JAN	13	SCO
MAR	20	LIB
SEP	7	SCO

moon

DAY	JAN	FEB	MAR	APR	MAY	JUN	JUL	AUG	SEP	OCT	NOV	DEC	DAY
1	TAU	04.40	CAN	06.01	LIB	02.53	CAP	12.11	ARI	TAU	08.09	LEO	1
2	12.23	CAN	18.77	VIR	16.14	SAG	19.44	PIS	19.24	14.50	CAN	LEO	2
3	GEM	07.37	LEO	05.54	SCO	05.23	AQU	23.14	TAU	GEM	17.02	05.18	3
4	18.22	LEO	19.15	LIB	16.43	CAP	AQU	TAU	TAU	GEM	LEO	VIR	4
5	CAN	08.11	VIR	05.16	SAG	10.35	03.57	ARI	08.07	02.00	22.45	09.31	5
6	21.23	VIR	18.35	SCO	19.23	AQU	PIS	12.04	GEM	CAN	VIR	LIB	6
7	LEO	08.23	LIB	06.07	CAP	19.24	15.18	TAU	18.22	09.50	VIR	11.28	7
8	22.59	LIB	18.35	SAG	CAP	PIS	ARI	TAU	CAN	LEO	01.16	SCO	8
9	VIR	10.03	SCO	10.00	01.29	PIS	ARI	00.16	CAN	13.49	LIB	12.02	9
10	VIR	SCO	20.56	CAP	AQU	07.20	04.09	GEM	00.41	VIR	01.30	SAG	10
11	00.52	14.11	SAG	17.41	11.27	ARI	TAU	09.25	LEO	14.44	SCO	12.46	11
12	LIB	SAG	SAG	AQU	PIS	20.12	15.46	CAN	03.19	LIB	01.03	CAP	12
13	04.02	20.55	02.36	AQU	23.58	TAU	GEM	14.43	VIR	14.11	SAG	15.38	13
14	SCO	CAP	CAP	04.38	ARI	TAU	GEM	LEO	03.44	SCO	01.54	AQU	14
15	08.49	CAP	11.28	PIS	ARI	07.31	00.15	17.07	LIB	14.09	CAP	22.12	15
16	SAG	05.51	AQU	17.23	12.50	GEM	CAN	VIR	03.49	SAG	05.53	PIS	16
17	15.13	AQU	22.41	ARI	TAU	16.04	05.31	18.17	SCO	16.23	AQU	PIS	17
18	CAP	16.39	PIS	ARI	TAU	CAN	LEO	LIB	05.16	CAP	13.56	08.45	18
19	23.22	PIS	PIS	06.16	00.14	22.04	08.41	19.50	SAG	22.04	PIS	ARI	19
20	AQU	PIS	11.17	TAU	GEM	LEO	VIR	SCO	09.13	AQU	PIS	21.38	20
21	AQU	05.02	ARI	18.03	09.23	LEO	11.11	22.48	CAP	AQU	01.28	TAU	21
22	09.41	ARI	ARI	GEM	CAN	02.22	LIB	SAG	16.03	07.19	ARI	TAU	22
23	PIS	18.05	00.16	GEM	16.14	VIR	13.57	SAG	AQU	PIS	14.30	10.09	23
24	22.03	TAU	TAU	03.46	LEO	05.41	SCO	03.38	AQU	19.10	TAU	GEM	24
25	ARI	TAU	12.20	CAN	21.00	LIB	17.25	CAP	01.33	ARI	TAU	20.33	25
26	ARI	05.52	GEM	10.44	VIR	08.30	SAG	10.28	PIS	ARI	03.00	CAN	26
27	10.56	GEM	21.53	LEO	23.55	SCO	21.53	AQU	13.07	08.07	GEM	CAN	27
28	TAU	14.17	CAN	14.40	LIB	11.11	CAP	19.25	ARI	TAU	13.51	04.33	28
29	21.47		CAN	VIR	LIB	SAG	CAP	PIS	ARI	20.49	CAN	LEO	29
30	GEM		03.45	16.06	01.33	14.32	03.52	PIS	01.58	GEM	22.41	10.41	30
31	GEM		LEO		SCO		AQU	06.35		GEM		VIR	31

324

sun

mth	day	sign
JAN	1	CAP
JAN	20	AQU
FEB	19	PIS
MAR	21	ARI
APR	20	TAU
MAY	21	GEM
JUN	22	CAN
JUL	23	LEO
AUG	23	VIR
SEP	23	LIB
OCT	24	SCO
NOV	23	SAG
DEC	22	CAP

mercury

mth	day	sign
JAN	1	SAG
JAN	10	CAP
JAN	30	AQU
FEB	17	PIS
MAR	5	ARI
MAY	12	TAU
MAY	28	GEM
JUN	11	CAN
JUN	28	LEO
SEP	5	VIR
OCT	21	LIB
OCT	9	SCO
OCT	31	SAG
NOV	25	SCO
DEC	13	SAG

venus

mth	day	sign
JAN	1	CAP
JAN	7	AQU
JAN	31	PIS
FEB	24	ARI
MAR	20	TAU
APR	14	GEM
MAY	10	CAN
JUN	6	LEO
JUL	8	VIR
SEP	20	LEO
SEP	25	VIR
NOV	9	LIB
DEC	7	SCO

mars

mth	day	sign
JAN	1	TAU
FEB	10	GEM
APR	10	CAN
JUN	1	LEO
JUL	20	VIR
SEP	5	LIB
OCT	21	SCO
DEC	3	SAG

saturn

mth	day	sign
JAN	1	SAG
JAN	5	CAP

jupiter

mth	day	sign
JAN	1	SCO
FEB	10	SAG
APR	24	SCO
OCT	5	SAG

moon

DAY	JAN	FEB	MAR	APR	MAY	JUN	JUL	AUG	SEP	OCT	NOV	DEC	DAY
1	15.21	SCO	08.33	22.42	11.58	ARI	TAU	07.23	LEO	22.08	SCO	20.11	1
2	LIB	03.11	SAG	AQU	PIS	16.37	12.05	CAN	08.31	LIB	10.02	CAP	2
3	18.42	SAG	12.05	AQU	22.19	TAU	GEM	17.09	VIR	23.54	SAG	20.35	3
4	SCO	06.29	CAP	06.23	ARI	TAU	GEM	LEO	12.56	SCO	10.05	AQU	4
5	20.55	CAP	17.16	PIS	ARI	05.35	00.03	LEO	LIB	SCO	CAP	AQU	5
6	SAG	10.40	AQU	16.33	10.39	GEM	CAN	00.29	15.53	00.54	12.14	00.16	6
7	22.50	AQU	AQU	ARI	TAU	17.44	10.08	VIR	SCO	SAG	AQU	PIS	7
8	CAP	16.50	00.25	ARI	23.34	CAN	LEO	05.56	18.20	02.38	17.35	07.59	8
9	CAP	PIS	PIS	04.32	GEM	CAN	18.15	LIB	SAG	CAP	PIS	ARI	9
10	01.52	PIS	09.54	TAU	GEM	04.19	VIR	09.59	21.04	06.12	PIS	18.56	10
11	AQU	01.55	ARI	17.25	11.57	LEO	VIR	SCO	CAP	AQU	02.10	TAU	11
12	07.39	ARI	21.37	GEM	CAN	12.50	00.26	12.58	CAP	12.06	ARI	TAU	12
13	PIS	13.47	TAU	GEM	22.40	VIR	LIB	SAG	00.43	PIS	13.04	07.22	13
14	17.10	TAU	TAU	05.48	LEO	18.42	04.33	15.18	AQU	20.20	TAU	GEM	14
15	ARI	TAU	10.30	CAN	LEO	LIB	SCO	CAP	05.54	ARI	TAU	20.00	15
16	ARI	02.39	GEM	15.55	06.38	21.38	06.42	17.53	PIS	ARI	01.16	CAN	16
17	05.33	GEM	22.28	LEO	VIR	SCO	SAG	AQU	13.16	06.40	GEM	CAN	17
18	TAU	13.50	CAN	22.27	11.06	22.14	07.42	21.59	ARI	TAU	13.56	07.58	18
19	18.16	CAN	CAN	VIR	LIB	SAG	CAP	PIS	23.12	18.40	CAN	LEO	19
20	GEM	20.38	07.22	VIR	12.22	22.01	09.05	PIS	TAU	GEM	CAN	18.29	20
21	GEM	LEO	LEO	01.19	SCO	CAP	AQU	04.51	TAU	GEM	02.04	VIR	21
22	04.47	LEO	12.28	LIB	11.51	23.00	12.42	ARI	11.16	07.22	LEO	VIR	22
23	CAN	02.06	VIR	01.34	SAG	AQU	PIS	14.58	GEM	CAN	12.08	02.29	23
24	12.12	VIR	14.27	SCO	11.22	AQU	19.53	TAU	23.49	19.03	VIR	LIB	24
25	LEO	04.29	LIB	00.59	CAP	03.09	ARI	TAU	CAN	LEO	18.42	07.00	25
26	17.12	LIB	14.53	SAG	13.09	PIS	ARI	03.18	CAN	LEO	LIB	SCO	26
27	VIR	06.14	SCO	01.32	AQU	11.28	06.43	GEM	10.36	03.48	21.21	08.15	27
28	20.54	SCO	15.31	CAP	18.42	ARI	TAU	15.33	LEO	VIR	SCO	SAG	28
29	LIB		SAG	04.55	PIS	23.11	19.23	CAN	18.04	08.42	21.12	07.38	29
30	LIB		17.49	AQU	PIS	TAU	GEM	CAN	VIR	LIB	SAG	CAP	30
31	00.05		CAP		04.18		GEM	01.33		10.14		07.15	31

325

sun

mth	day	sign
JAN	1	CAP
JAN	21	AQU
FEB	19	PIS
MAR	20	ARI
APR	20	TAU
MAY	21	GEM
JUN	21	CAN
JUL	22	LEO
AUG	23	VIR
SEP	23	LIB
OCT	23	SCO
NOV	22	SAG
DEC	21	CAP

mercury

mth	day	sign
JAN	1	SAG
JAN	4	CAP
JAN	23	AQU
FEB	9	PIS
APR	16	ARI
MAY	4	TAU
MAY	19	GEM
JUN	2	CAN
JUL	1	LEO
JUL	6	CAN
AUG	10	LEO
AUG	27	VIR
SEP	12	LIB
OCT	1	SCO
DEC	7	SAG
DEC	27	CAP

venus

mth	day	sign
JAN	1	SCO
JAN	2	SAG
JAN	27	CAP
FEB	20	AQU
MAR	16	PIS
APR	9	ARI
MAY	3	TAU
MAY	28	GEM
JUN	21	CAN
JUL	16	LEO
AUG	9	VIR
SEP	2	LIB
SEP	27	SCO
OCT	21	SAG
NOV	15	CAP
DEC	10	AQU

mars

mth	day	sign
JAN	1	SAG
JAN	14	CAP
FEB	23	AQU
APR	2	PIS
MAY	11	ARI
JUN	20	TAU
AUG	2	GEM
SEP	21	CAN

saturn

mth	day	sign
JAN	1	CAP

jupiter

mth	day	sign
JAN	1	SAG
MAR	1	CAP
JUN	10	SAG
OCT	26	CAP

moon

DAY	JAN	FEB	MAR	APR	MAY	JUN	JUL	AUG	SEP	OCT	NOV	DEC	DAY
1	AQU	00.39	18.18	GEM	CAN	16.38	08.46	SCO	CAP	22.12	ARI	TAU	1
2	09.19	ARI	TAU	GEM	21.59	VIR	LIB	02.04	12.35	PIS	15.27	07.01	2
3	PIS	09.16	TAU	01.46	LEO	VIR	15.08	SAG	AQU	PIS	TAU	GEM	3
4	15.21	TAU	05.08	CAN	LEO	01.31	SCO	03.25	13.51	01.46	23.46	17.52	4
5	ARI	20.58	GEM	14.01	08.59	LIB	17.42	CAP	PIS	ARI	GEM	CAN	5
6	ARI	GEM	17.37	LEO	VIR	06.20	SAG	03.21	16.26	07.09	GEM	CAN	6
7	01.22	GEM	CAN	LEO	16.30	SCO	17.34	AQU	ARI	TAU	10.26	06.21	7
8	TAU	09.37	CAN	00.02	LIB	07.31	CAP	03.42	21.46	15.16	CAN	LEO	8
9	13.45	CAN	05.25	VIR	20.07	SAG	16.43	PIS	TAU	GEM	22.59	19.12	9
10	GEM	21.08	LEO	06.35	SCO	06.48	AQU	06.21	TAU	GEM	LEO	VIR	10
11	GEM	LEO	14.45	LIB	20.55	CAP	17.19	ARI	06.31	02.18	LEO	VIR	11
12	02.23	LEO	VIR	10.01	SAG	06.23	PIS	12.36	GEM	CAN	11.24	06.10	12
13	CAN	06.35	21.19	SCO	20.50	AQU	21.07	TAU	18.10	14.55	VIR	LIB	13
14	13.59	VIR	LIB	11.37	CAP	08.17	ARI	22.29	CAN	LEO	21.07	13.12	14
15	LEO	13.55	LIB	SAG	21.51	PIS	ARI	GEM	CAN	LEO	LIB	SCO	15
16	LEO	LIB	01.37	13.01	AQU	13.42	04.48	GEM	06.46	02.40	LIB	16.07	16
17	00.03	19.24	SCO	CAP	AQU	ARI	10.43	LEO	VIR	02.53	SAG		17
18	VIR	SCO	04.37	15.32	01.23	22.33	15.40	CN	18.07	11.32	SCO	16.16	18
19	08.12	23.12	SAG	AQU	PIS	TAU	GEM	23.17	VIR	LIB	05.17	CAP	19
20	LIB	SAG	07.12	19.55	07.55	TAU	GEM	LEO	VIR	17.06	SAG	15.49	20
21	13.59	SAG	CAP	PIS	ARI	09.46	04.09	LEO	02.58	SCO	06.02	AQU	21
22	SCO	01.39	10.10	PIS	17.00	GEM	CAN	10.41	LIB	20.16	CAP	16.45	22
23	17.02	CAP	AQU	02.23	TAU	22.10	16.46	VIR	09.18	SAG	07.04	PIS	23
24	SAG	03.42	14.02	ARI	TAU	CAN	LEO	20.09	SCO	22.28	AQU	20.34	24
25	17.59	AQU	PIS	10.50	03.55	CAN	LEO	LIB	13.42	CAP	09.49	ARI	25
26	CAP	06.04	19.29	TAU	GEM	10.51	04.31	LIB	SAG	CAP	PIS	ARI	26
27	18.19	PIS	ARI	21.16	16.06	LEO	VIR	03.23	16.54	00.57	14.51	03.30	27
28	AQU	10.38	ARI	GEM	CAN	22.53	14.33	SCO	CAP	AQU	ARI	TAU	28
29	19.56	ARI	03.12	09.22	CAN	VIR	LIB	08.19	19.32	04.26	22.00	13.01	29
30	PIS		TAU	CAN	04.50	VIR	21.55	SAG	AQU	PIS	TAU	GEM	30
31	PIS		13.32		LEO		SCO	11.09		09.11		GEM	31

sun

mth	day	sign
JAN	1	CAP
JAN	20	AQU
FEB	18	PIS
MAR	20	ARI
APR	20	TAU
MAY	21	GEM
JUN	21	CAN
JUL	23	LEO
AUG	23	VIR
SEP	23	LIB
OCT	23	SCO
NOV	22	SAG
DEC	22	CAP

mercury

mth	day	sign
JAN	1	CAP
JAN	14	AQU
FEB	1	PIS
FEB	24	AQU
MAR	18	PIS
APR	10	ARI
APR	26	TAU
MAY	10	GEM
MAY	28	CAN
AUG	4	LEO
AUG	18	VIR
SEP	4	LIB
SEP	27	SCO
OCT	22	LIB
NOV	10	SCO
NOV	30	SAG
DEC	20	CAP

venus

mth	day	sign
JAN	1	AQU
JAN	5	PIS
FEB	2	ARI
JUN	5	TAU
JUL	7	GEM
AUG	3	CAN
AUG	29	LEO
SEP	23	VIR
OCT	18	LIB
NOV	11	SCO
DEC	5	SAG
DEC	29	CAP

mars

mth	day	sign
JAN	1	CAN
FEB	5	GEM
FEB	7	CAN
MAY	6	LEO
JUN	28	VIR
AUG	17	LIB
OCT	1	SCO
NOV	13	SAG
DEC	24	CAP

saturn

mth	day	sign
JAN	1	CAP

jupiter

mth	day	sign
JAN	1	CAP
MAR	15	AQU
AUG	12	CAP
NOV	4	AQU

moon

DAY	JAN	FEB	MAR	APR	MAY	JUN	JUL	AUG	SEP	OCT	NOV	DEC	DAY
1	00.23	LEO	14.13	LIB	SCO	CAP	AQU	ARI	05.52	CAN	LEO	VIR	1
2	CAN	07.48	VIR	16.36	05.25	17.45	02.52	16.19	GEM	CAN	06.17	03.08	2
3	12.54	VIR	VIR	SCO	SAG	AQU	PIS	TAU	15.00	09.43	VIR	LIB	3
4	LEO	19.27	01.21	22.34	08.40	19.50	04.13	23.04	CAN	LEO	18.42	13.30	4
5	LEO	LIB	LIB	SAG	CAP	PIS	ARI	GEM	CAN	22.45	LIB	SCO	5
6	01.48	LIB	10.24	SAG	11.24	23.23	10.01	GEM	03.01	VIR	LIB	20.24	6
7	VIR	04.51	SCO	02.52	AQU	ARI	TAU	08.56	LEO	VIR	04.40	SAG	7
8	13.31	SCO	17.04	CAP	14.23	ARI	17.27	CAN	16.05	11.04	SCO	SAG	8
9	LIB	11.01	SAG	06.03	PIS	04.38	GEM	20.59	VIR	LIB	11.51	00.31	9
10	22.09	SAG	21.19	AQU	17.56	TAU	GEM	LEO	VIR	21.19	SAG	CAP	10
11	SCO	13.50	CAP	08.31	ARI	11.40	03.13	LEO	04.33	SCO	16.59	03.11	11
12	SCO	CAP	23.29	PIS	22.25	GEM	CAN	10.00	LIB	SCO	CAP	AQU	12
13	02.40	14.13	AQU	10.55	TAU	20.50	14.56	VIR	15.23	05.21	20.59	05.41	13
14	SAG	AQU	AQU	ARI	TAU	CAN	LEO	22.45	SCO	SAG	AQU	PIS	14
15	03.41	13.53	00.26	14.16	04.34	CAN	LEO	LIB	23.54	11.24	AQU	08.45	15
16	CAP	PIS	PIS	TAU	GEM	08.16	03.55	LIB	SAG	CAP	00.18	ARI	16
17	02.55	14.41	01.32	19.55	13.17	LEO	VIR	09.45	SAG	15.37	PIS	12.39	17
18	AQU	ARI	ARI	GEM	CAN	21.13	16.39	SCO	05.42	AQU	03.10	TAU	18
19	02.32	18.21	04.25	GEM	CAN	VIR	LIB	17.45	CAP	18.10	ARI	17.46	19
20	PIS	TAU	TAU	04.50	00.45	VIR	LIB	SAG	08.43	PIS	06.03	GEM	20
21	04.26	TAU	10.32	CAN	LEO	09.32	03.04	22.07	AQU	19.35	TAU	GEM	21
22	ARI	01.51	GEM	16.43	13.38	LIB	SCO	CAP	09.36	ARI	09.59	00.50	22
23	09.51	GEM	20.23	LEO	VIR	18.51	09.42	23.25	PIS	21.07	GEM	CAN	23
24	TAU	12.49	CAN	LEO	VIR	SCO	SAG	AQU	09.40	TAU	16.20	10.26	24
25	18.50	CAN	CAN	05.31	01.18	SCO	12.28	23.02	ARI	TAU	CAN	LEO	25
26	GEM	CAN	08.48	VIR	LIB	00.05	CAP	PIS	10.42	00.24	CAN	22.29	26
27	GEM	01.34	LEO	16.34	09.34	SAG	12.41	22.49	TAU	GEM	02.01	VIR	27
28	06.23	LEO	21.30	LIB	SCO	02.00	AQU	ARI	14.32	07.03	LEO	VIR	28
29	CAN		VIR	LIB	14.11	CAP	12.13	ARI	GEM	CAN	14.25	11.26	29
30	19.05		VIR	00.27	SAG	02.18	PIS	00.37	22.19	17.30	VIR	LIB	30
31	LEO		08.21		16.20		12.56	TAU		LEO		22.42	31

sun

mth	day	sign
JAN	1	CAP
JAN	21	AQU
FEB	19	PIS
MAR	21	ARI
APR	20	TAU
MAY	21	GEM
JUN	21	CAN
JUL	23	LEO
AUG	23	VIR
SEP	23	LIB
OCT	23	SCO
NOV	22	SAG
DEC	22	CAP

mercury

mth	day	sign
JAN	1	CAP
JAN	7	AQU
MAR	15	PIS
APR	3	ARI
APR	18	TAU
MAY	3	GEM
JUL	11	CAN
JUL	26	LEO
AUG	10	VIR
AUG	29	LIB
NOV	5	SCO
NOV	23	SAG
DEC	12	CAP

venus

mth	day	sign
JAN	1	CAP
JAN	21	AQU
FEB	14	PIS
MAR	10	ARI
APR	3	TAU
APR	28	GEM
MAY	23	CAN
JUN	17	LEO
JUL	12	VIR
AUG	8	LIB
SEP	7	SCO

mars

mth	day	sign
JAN	1	CAP
FEB	1	AQU
MAR	12	PIS
APR	19	ARI
MAY	28	TAU
JUL	9	GEM
AUG	22	CAN
OCT	11	LEO

saturn

mth	day	sign
JAN	1	CAP
JAN	3	AQU

jupiter

mth	day	sign
JAN	1	AQU
MAR	25	PIS

moon

DAY	JAN	FEB	MAR	APR	MAY	JUN	JUL	AUG	SEP	OCT	NOV	DEC	DAY
1	SCO	21.09	06.38	20.42	06.12	17.40	06.19	LEO	03.02	SCO	SAG	14.26	1
2	SCO	CAP	CAP	PIS	ARI	GEM	CAN	07.57	LIB	SCO	01.17	AQU	2
3	06.22	22.57	09.53	20.41	06.49	21.56	13.55	VIR	15.47	09.40	CAP	19.53	3
4	SAG	AQU	AQU	ARI	TAU	CAN	LEO	20.17	SCO	SAG	09.02	PIS	4
5	10.24	22.53	10.16	20.25	08.16	CAN	LEO	LIB	SCO	19.35	AQU	23.17	5
6	CAP	PIS	PIS	TAU	GEM	05.22	00.22	LIB	03.26	CAP	13.53	ARI	6
7	12.00	22.50	09.33	22.00	12.28	LEO	VIR	08.56	SAG	CAP	PIS	ARI	7
8	AQU	ARI	ARI	GEM	CAN	16.12	12.48	SCO	12.20	02.20	15.45	00.59	8
9	12.53	ARI	09.40	GEM	20.35	VIR	19.48	CAP	AQU	ARI	TAU	02.07	9
10	PIS	00.35	TAU	03.12	LEO	VIR	SAG	17.26	PIS	05.29	15.45	02.07	10
11	14.34	TAU	12.35	CAN	LEO	04.51	01.05	SAG	AQU	PIS	TAU	GEM	11
12	ARI	05.18	GEM	12.36	08.11	LIB	SCO	03.17	19.02	05.40	15.43	04.20	12
13	18.02	GEM	19.25	LEO	VIR	16.45	11.00	CAP	PIS	ARI	GEM	CAN	13
14	TAU	13.20	CAN	LEO	21.01	SCO	SAG	07.07	18.33	04.43	17.49	09.20	14
15	23.42	CAN	CAN	00.57	LIB	SCO	17.33	AQU	ARI	TAU	CAN	LEO	15
16	GEM	CAN	05.56	VIR	LIB	02.01	CAP	08.17	18.02	04.50	23.40	17.59	16
17	GEM	00.03	LEO	13.53	08.43	SAG	21.07	PIS	TAU	GEM	LEO	VIR	17
18	07.39	LEO	18.33	LIB	SCO	08.30	AQU	08.25	19.29	08.05	LEO	VIR	18
19	CAN	12.26	VIR	LIB	18.02	CAP	23.00	ARI	GEM	CAN	09.33	05.41	19
20	17.50	VIR	VIR	01.37	SAG	12.49	PIS	09.20	GEM	15.30	VIR	LIB	20
21	LEO	VIR	07.28	SCO	SAG	AQU	PIS	TAU	00.26	LEO	21.58	18.18	21
22	LEO	01.20	LIB	11.27	01.08	15.59	00.34	12.28	CAN	LEO	LIB	SCO	22
23	05.53	LIB	19.28	SAG	CAP	PIS	ARI	GEM	09.07	02.31	LIB	SCO	23
24	VIR	13.36	SCO	19.20	06.31	18.43	02.57	18.34	LEO	VIR	10.33	05.33	24
25	18.53	SCO	SCO	CAP	AQU	ARI	TAU	CAN	20.31	15.11	SCO	SAG	25
26	LIB	23.47	05.48	CAP	10.29	21.34	06.57	CAN	VIR	LIB	21.43	14.19	26
27	LIB	SAG	SAG	01.08	PIS	TAU	GEM	03.30	VIR	LIB	SAG	CAP	27
28	06.53	SAG	13.47	AQU	13.15	LEO	13.00	LEO	09.08	03.48	SAG	20.42	28
29	SCO		CAP	04.40	ARI	01.09	CAN	14.36	LIB	SCO	07.00	AQU	29
30	15.59		18.43	PIS	15.17	GEM	21.20	VIR	21.49	15.19	CAP	AQU	30
31	SAG		AQU		TAU		LEO	VIR		SAG		01.20	31

sun

mth	day	sign
JAN	1	CAP
JAN	20	AQU
FEB	19	PIS
MAR	21	ARI
APR	20	TAU
MAY	21	GEM
JUN	22	CAN
JUL	23	LEO
AUG	23	VIR
SEP	23	LIB
OCT	24	SCO
NOV	23	SAG
DEC	22	CAP

mercury

mth	day	sign
JAN	1	CAP
JAN	2	AQU
JAN	20	CAP
FEB	15	AQU
MAR	9	PIS
MAR	26	ARI
APR	9	TAU
MAY	3	GEM
MAY	10	TAU
JUN	14	GEM
JUL	4	CAN
JUL	18	LEO
AUG	3	VIR
AUG	26	LIB
SEP	16	VIR
OCT	10	LIB
OCT	28	SCO
NOV	16	SAG
DEC	6	CAP

venus

mth	day	sign
JAN	1	SCO
JAN	6	SAG
FEB	5	CAP
MAR	4	AQU
MAR	30	PIS
APR	24	ARI
MAY	19	TAU
JUN	12	GEM
JUL	7	CAN
JUL	31	LEO
AUG	25	VIR
SEP	18	LIB
OCT	12	SCO
NOV	5	SAG
NOV	29	CAP
DEC	23	AQU

mars

mth	day	sign
JAN	1	LEO
JUN	3	VIR
JUL	27	LIB
SEP	12	SCO
OCT	25	SAG
DEC	5	CAP

saturn

mth	day	sign
JAN	1	AQU

jupiter

mth	day	sign
JAN	1	PIS
APR	4	ARI

moon

DAY	JAN	FEB	MAR	APR	MAY	JUN	JUL	AUG	SEP	OCT	NOV	DEC	DAY
1	PIS	TAU	21.39	CAN	LEO	00.09	SCO	SAG	AQU	PIS	00.42>TAU	GEM	1
2	04.48	16.03	GEM	14.45	06.13	LIB	SCO	03.12	AQU	13.48	23.48	10.45	2
3	ARI	GEM	GEM	LEO	VIR	12.38	08.11	CAP	01.37	ARI	GEM	CAN	3
4	07.33	20.40	02.08	LEO	17.42	SCO	SAG	11.25	PIS	13.50	GEM	12.20	4
5	TAU	CAN	CAN	00.20	LIB	SCO	19.03	AQU	03.52	TAU	00.08	LEO	5
6	10.14	CAN	09.15	VIR	LIB	01.01	CAP	16.46	ARI	13.58	CAN	17.26	6
7	GEM	03.06	LEO	11.49	06.16	SAG	CAP	PIS	05.02	GEM	03.24	VIR	7
8	13.41	LEO	18.34	LIB	SCO	12.07	03.36	20.07	TAU	16.01	LEO	VIR	8
9	CAN	11.36	VIR	LIB	18.42	CAP	AQU	ARI	06.46	CAN	10.14	02.21	9
10	19.01	VIR	VIR	00.14	SAG	21.22	09.53	22.37	GEM	20.54	VIR	LIB	10
11	LEO	22.18	05.35	SCO	SAG	AQU	PIS	TAU	10.08	LEO	20.07	14.04	11
12	LEO	LIB	LIB	12.48	06.13	AQU	14.16	TAU	CAN	LEO	LIB	SCO	12
13	03.07	LIB	17.51	SAG	CAP	04.20	ARI	01.06	15.30	04.34	LIB	SCO	13
14	VIR	10.38	SCO	SAG	15.51	PIS	17.15	GEM	LEO	VIR	07.57	02.53	14
15	14.05	SCO	SCO	00.27	AQU	08.46	TAU	04.39	22.47	14.24	SCO	SAG	15
16	LIB	22.57	06.27	CAP	22.32	ARI	19.27	CAN	VIR	LIB	20.40	15.21	16
17	LIB	SAG	SAG	09.34	PIS	10.54	GEM	09.17	VIR	LIB	SAG	CAP	17
18	02.35	SAG	17.35	AQU	PIS	TAU	21.45	LEO	08.00	01.52	SAG	CAP	18
19	SCO	09.00	CAP	14.53	01.47	11.44	CAN	15.40	LIB	SCO	09.23	02.29	19
20	14.20	CAP	CAP	PIS	ARI	GEM	CAN	VIR	19.10	14.32	CAP	AQU	20
21	SAG	15.23	01.21	16.30	02.21	12.46	01.15	VIR	SCO	SAG	20.51	11.28	21
22	23.23	AQU	AQU	ARI	TAU	CAN	LEO	00.25	SCO	SAG	AQU	PIS	22
23	CAP	18.17	05.04	15.51	01.53	15.44	07.06	LIB	07.50	03.21	AQU	17.41	23
24	CAP	PIS	PS	TAU	GEM	LEO	VIR	11.39	SAG	CAP	05.32	ARI	24
25	05.14	19.05	05.37	15.06	02.29	21.56	16.02	SCO	20.15	14.20	PIS	20.57	25
26	AQU	ARI	ARI	GEM	CAN	VIR	LIB	SCO	CAP	AQU	10.25	TAU	26
27	08.35	19.38	04.57	16.27	05.58	VIR	LIB	00.15	CAP	21.36	ARI	21.58	27
28	PIS	TAU	TAU	CAN	LEO	07.41	03.38	SAG	06.03	PIS	11.49	GEM	28
29	10.44		05.13	21.25	13.22	LIB	SCO	11.57	AQU	PIS	TAU	22.07	29
30	ARI		GEM	LEO	VIR	19.48	16.08	CAP	11.46	00.40	11.14	CAN	30
31	12.55		08.14		VIR		SAG	20.37		ARI		23.09	31

sun

mth	day	sign
JAN	1	CAP
JAN	21	AQU
FEB	19	PIS
MAR	20	ARI
APR	20	TAU
MAY	21	GEM
JUN	21	CAN
JUL	22	LEO
AUG	23	VIR
SEP	23	LIB
OCT	23	SCO
NOV	22	SAG
DEC	21	CAP

mercury

mth	day	sign
JAN	1	CAP
FEB	10	AQU
FEB	29	PIS
MAR	16	ARI
APR	2	TAU
JUN	9	GEM
JUN	24	CAN
JUL	9	LEO
JUL	27	VIR
OCT	3	LIB
OCT	20	SCO
NOV	8	SAG
NOV	30	CAP
DEC	16	SAG

venus

mth	day	sign
JAN	1	AQU
JAN	17	PIS
FEB	10	ARI
MAR	7	TAU
APR	4	GEM
MAY	9	CAN
JUN	17	GEM
AUG	5	CAN
SEP	8	LEO
OCT	5	VIR
OCT	31	LIB
NOV	25	SCO
DEC	19	SAG

mars

mth	day	sign
JAN	1	CAP
JAN	13	AQU
FEB	20	PIS
MAR	29	ARI
MAY	7	TAU
JUN	17	GEM
JUL	30	CAN
SEP	15	LEO
NOV	6	VIR

saturn

mth	day	sign
JAN	1	AQU
MAR	24	PIS
SEP	16	AQU
DEC	16	PIS

jupiter

mth	day	sign
JAN	1	ARI
APR	12	TAU

moon

DAY	JAN	FEB	MAR	APR	MAY	JUN	JUL	AUG	SEP	OCT	NOV	DEC	DAY
1	LEO	19.25	LIB	09.41	05.42	AQU	PIS	TAU	00.13	LEO	00.24	SCO	1
2	LEO	LIB	13.54	SAG	CAP	11.01	00.52	15.28	CAN	12.42	LIB	SCO	2
3	02.48	LIB	SCO	22.36	18.06	PIS	ARI	GEM	02.36	VIR	08.25	01.24	3
4	VIR	05.12	SCO	CAP	AQU	18.03	05.42	17.13	LEO	17.44	SCO	SAG	4
5	10.10	SCO	01.47	CAP	AQU	ARI	TAU	CAN	05.12	LIB	18.43	13.53	5
6	LIB	17.35	SAG	10.24	03.43	21.20	07.43	18.11	VIR	LIB	SAG	CAP	6
7	21.04	SAG	14.35	AQU	PIS	TAU	GEM	LEO	09.19	00.57	SAG	CAP	7
8	SCO	SAG	CAP	18.47	09.15	21.50	07.57	19.50	LIB	SCO	07.06	02.57	8
9	SCO	06.11	CAP	PIS	ARI	GEM	CAN	VIR	16.20	11.02	CAP	AQU	9
10	09.49	CAP	01.35	23.08	11.09	21.16	08.01	23.51	SCO	SAG	20.08	15.00	10
11	SAG	16.39	AQU	ARI	TAU	CAN	LEO	LIB	SCO	23.32	AQU	PIS	11
12	22.14	AQU	09.05	ARI	11.01	21.35	09.44	LIB	02.47	CAP	AQU	PIS	12
13	CAP	AQU	PIS	00.37	GEM	LEO	VIR	07.31	SAG	CAP	07.28	00.12	13
14	CAP	00.09	13.15	TAU	10.53	LEO	14.41	SCO	15.30	12.15	PIS	ARI	14
15	08.48	PIS	ARI	01.06	CAN	00.27	LIB	18.44	CAP	AQU	15.10	05.32	15
16	AQU	05.10	15.30	GEM	12.31	VIR	23.32	SAG	CAP	22.33	ARI	TAU	16
17	17.04	ARI	TAU	02.23	LEO	06.54	SCO	SAG	03.47	PIS	18.47	07.21	17
18	PIS	08.45	17.26	CAN	17.02	LIB	SCO	07.38	AQU	PIS	TAU	GEM	18
19	23.10	TAU	GEM	05.40	VIR	16.49	11.28	CAP	13.22	05.05	19.58	07.02	19
20	ARI	11.48	20.11	LEO	VIR	SCO	SAG	19.39	PIS	ARI	GEM	CAN	20
21	ARI	GEM	CAN	11.17	00.41	SCO	SAG	AQU	19.44	08.24	20.04	06.31	21
22	03.23	14.49	CAN	VIR	LIB	05.03	00.27	AQU	ARI	TAU	CAN	LEO	22
23	TAU	CAN	00.15	19.08	10.58	SAG	CAP	05.13	23.46	10.03	20.59	07.41	23
24	06.05	18.11	LEO	LIB	SCO	18.02	12.30	PIS	TAU	GEM	LEO	VIR	24
25	GEM	LEO	05.42	LIB	23.03	CAP	AQU	12.15	TAU	11.37	LEO	12.04	25
26	07.51	22.30	VIR	05.01	SAG	CAP	22.36	ARI	02.46	CAN	00.02	LIB	26
27	CAN	VIR	12.48	SCO	SAG	06.22	PIS	17.24	GEM	14.14	LEO	20.11	27
28	09.45	VIR	LIB	16.46	12.00	AQU	PIS	TAU	05.39	LEO	05.54	SCO	28
29	LEO	04.46	22.03	SAG	CAP	16.56	06.25	21.16	CAN	18.25	LIB	SCO	29
30	13.09		SCO	SAG	CAP	PIS	ARI	GEM	08.52	VIR	14.31	07.20	30
31	VIR		SCO		00.32		12.00	GEM		VIR		SAG	31

sun

mth	day	sign
JAN	1	CAP
JAN	20	AQU
FEB	18	PIS
MAR	20	ARI
APR	20	TAU
MAY	21	GEM
JUN	21	CAN
JUL	23	LEO
AUG	23	VIR
SEP	23	LIB
OCT	23	SCO
NOV	22	SAG
DEC	22	CAP

mercury

mth	day	sign
JAN	1	SAG
JAN	13	CAP
FEB	3	AQU
FEB	21	PIS
MAR	9	ARI
MAY	15	TAU
JUN	2	GEM
JUN	16	CAN
JUL	1	LEO
JUL	31	VIR
AUG	3	LEO
SEP	8	VIR
SEP	25	LIB
OCT	12	SCO
NOV	2	SAG

venus

mth	day	sign
JAN	1	SAG
JAN	12	CAP
FEB	5	AQU
MAR	1	PIS
MAR	25	ARI
APR	18	TAU
MAY	12	GEM
JUN	6	CAN
JUN	30	LEO
JUL	25	VIR
AUG	19	LIB
SEP	13	SCO
OCT	9	SAG
NOV	5	CAP
DEC	7	AQU

mars

mth	day	sign
JAN	1	VIR
JUN	29	LIB
AUG	20	SCO
OCT	4	SAG
NOV	14	CAP
DEC	23	AQU

saturn

mth	day	sign
JAN	1	PIS

jupiter

mth	day	sign
JAN	1	TAU
APR	22	GEM
SEP	21	CAN
NOV	17	GEM

moon

DAY	JAN	FEB	MAR	APR	MAY	JUN	JUL	AUG	SEP	OCT	NOV	DEC	DAY
1	20.06	AQU	AQU	02.19	TAU	07.05	LEO	03.54	SCO	18.29	AQU	PIS	1
2	CAP	AQU	09.38	ARI	20.26	CAN	17.11	LIB	00.00	CAP	AQU	23.22	2
3	CAP	02.56	PIS	08.29	GEM	07.47	VIR	08.20	SAG	CAP	03.23	ARI	3
4	09.04	PIS	18.45	TAU	22.39	LEO	19.43	SCO	10.51	06.48	PIS	ARI	4
5	AQU	12.43	ARI	12.55	CAN	09.33	LIB	16.49	CAP	AQU	14.21	08.11	5
6	21.06	ARI	ARI	GEM	CAN	VIR	LIB	SAG	23.34	19.14	ARI	TAU	6
7	PIS	20.24	01.49	16.24	00.50	13.29	01.38	SAG	AQU	PIS	22.29	13.27	7
8	PIS	TAU	TAU	CAN	LEO	LIB	SCO	04.22	AQU	PIS	TAU	GEM	8
9	07.08	TAU	07.14	19.23	03.47	20.04	10.53	CAP	11.56	05.54	TAU	15.57	9
10	ARI	01.36	GEM	LEO	VIR	SCO	SAG	17.09	PIS	AQU	03.54	CAN	10
11	14.10	GEM	11.03	22.14	08.04	SCO	22.29	AQU	22.50	14.16	GEM	17.08	11
12	TAU	04.14	CAN	VIR	LIB	05.10	CAP	AQU	ARI	TAU	07.29	LEO	12
13	17.48	CAN	13.23	VIR	14.10	SAG	CAP	05.37	ARI	20.40	CAN	18.35	13
14	GEM	04.54	LEO	01.38	SCO	16.20	11.08	PIS	07.56	GEM	10.13	VIR	14
15	18.35	LEO	14.55	LIB	22.32	CAP	AQU	16.57	TAU	GEM	LEO	21.33	15
16	CAN	05.05	VIR	06.42	SAG	CAP	23.45	ARI	15.06	01.27	12.54	LIB	16
17	17.57	VIR	17.04	SCO	SAG	04.51	PIS	ARI	GEM	CAN	VIR	LIB	17
18	LEO	06.45	LIB	14.31	09.20	AQU	PIS	02.27	20.01	04.51	16.10	02.40	18
19	17.55	LIB	21.32	SAG	CAP	17.29	11.13	TAU	CAN	LIB	LIB	SCO	19
20	VIR	11.45	SCO	SAG	21.50	PIS	ARI	09.20	22.35	07.13	20.37	10.01	20
21	20.28	SCO	SCO	01.24	AQU	PIS	20.14	GEM	LEO	VIR	SCO	SAG	21
22	LIB	20.57	05.37	CAP	AQU	04.29	TAU	13.04	23.30	09.21	SCO	19.27	22
23	LIB	SAG	SAG	14.04	10.14	ARI	TAU	CAN	VIR	LIB	02.56	CAP	23
24	03.01	09.17	17.07	AQU	PIS	12.16	01.48	14.01	VIR	12.31	SAG	CAP	24
25	SCO	CAP	CAP	AQU	20.19	TAU	GEM	LEO	00.15	SCO	11.45	06.44	25
26	13.32	CAP	CAP	02.02	ARI	16.18	03.53	13.36	LIB	18.09	CAP	AQU	26
27	SAG	22.14	05.59	PIS	ARI	GEM	CAN	VIR	02.47	SAG	23.03	19.17	27
28	SAG	AQU	AQU	11.12	02.48	17.20	03.37	13.52	SCO	SAG	AQU	PIS	28
29	02.21		17.32	ARI	TAU	CAN	LEO	LIB	08.42	03.05	AQU	PIS	29
30	CAP		PIS	17.03	05.58	16.59	02.55	16.54	SAG	CAP	11.40	07.40	30
31	15.17		PIS		GEM		VIR	SCO		14.49		ARI	31

sun

mth	day	sign
JAN	1	CAP
JAN	20	AQU
FEB	19	PIS
MAR	21	ARI
APR	20	TAU
MAY	21	GEM
JUN	21	CAN
JUL	23	LEO
AUG	23	VIR
SEP	23	LIB
OCT	23	SCO
NOV	22	SAG
DEC	22	CAP

mercury

mth	day	sign
JAN	1	SAG
JAN	7	CAP
JAN	27	AQU
FEB	13	PIS
MAR	3	ARI
MAR	22	PIS
APR	17	ARI
MAY	9	TAU
MAY	24	GEM
JUN	7	CAN
JUN	26	LEO
SEP	1	VIR
SEP	17	LIB
OCT	5	SCO
OCT	30	SAG
NOV	13	SCO
DEC	11	SAG

venus

mth	day	sign
JAN	1	AQU
FEB	6	CAP
FEB	25	AQU
APR	6	PIS
MAY	5	ARI
MAY	31	TAU
JUN	26	GEM
JUL	21	CAN
AUG	15	LEO
SEP	8	VIR
OCT	3	LIB
OCT	27	SCO
NOV	20	SAG
DEC	13	CAP

mars

mth	day	sign
JAN	1	AQU
JAN	30	PIS
MAR	9	ARI
APR	17	TAU
MAY	28	GEM
JUL	11	CAN
AUG	25	LEO
OCT	12	VIR
DEC	4	LIB

saturn

mth	day	sign
JAN	1	PIS

jupiter

mth	day	sign
JAN	1	GEM
MAY	5	CAN
SEP	27	LEO

moon

DAY	JAN	FEB	MAR	APR	MAY	JUN	JUL	AUG	SEP	OCT	NOV	DEC	DAY
1	17.46	GEM	22.48	LEO	19.31	SCO	23.51	AQU	22.27	16.47	GEM	CAN	1
2	TAU	13.41	CAN	10.31	LIB	CAP	AQU	AQU	ARI	TAU	17.43	05.02	2
3	TAU	CAN	CAN	VIR	21.23	SAG	CAP	03.36	ARI	TAU	CAN	LEO	3
4	00.06	14.14	00.57	10.40	SCO	16.10	09.14	PIS	10.59	03.43	23.36	08.48	4
5	GEM	LEO	LEO	LIB	SCO	CAP	AQU	16.15	TAU	GEM	LEO	VIR	5
6	02.40	13.11	00.36>VIR	11.30	00.52	CAP	20.39	ARI	21.52	12.12	LEO	11.43	6
7	CAN	VIR	23.48	SCO	SAG	01.21	PIS	ARI	GEM	CAN	03.10	LIB	7
8	02.50	12.50	LIB	14.54	07.12	AQU	PIS	04.38	GEM	17.25	VIR	14.18	8
9	LEO	LIB	LIB	SAG	CAP	12.57	09.16	TAU	05.26	LEO	04.54	SCO	9
10	02.34	15.15	00.47	22.02	16.52	PIS	ARI	14.38	CAN	19.27	LIB	17.13	10
11	VIR	SCO	SCO	CAP	AQU	PIS	21.03	GEM	09.01	VIR	05.53	SAG	11
12	03.53	21.33	05.18	CAP	AQU	01.26	TAU	20.41	LEO	19.29	SCO	21.30	12
13	LIB	SAG	SAG	08.42	04.55	ARI	TAU	CAN	09.25	LIB	07.37	CAP	13
14	08.08	SAG	13.55	AQU	PIS	12.29	05.51	22.50	VIR	19.21	SAG	CAP	14
15	SCO	07.26	CAP	21.13	17.15	TAU	GEM	LEO	08.33	SCO	11.37	04.19	15
16	15.39	CAP	CAP	PIS	ARI	20.26	10.44	22.35	LIB	20.59	CAP	AQU	16
17	SAG	19.25	01.35	PIS	ARI	GEM	CAN	08.34	SAG	19.03	19.03	14.17	17
18	SAG	AQU	AQU	09.27	03.49	GEM	12.27	22.05	SCO	SAG	AQU	PIS	18
19	01.45	AQU	14.18	ARI	TAU	01.05	LEO	LIB	11.21	01.55	AQU	PIS	19
20	CAP	08.05	PIS	20.00	11.40	CAN	12.47	23.24	SAG	CAP	05.53	02.39	20
21	13.26	PIS	PIS	TAU	GEM	03.29	VIR	SCO	17.53	10.41	PIS	ARI	21
22	AQU	20.30	02.33	TAU	17.00	LEO	13.38	SCO	CAP	AQU	18.31	15.07	22
23	AQU	ARI	ARI	04.27	CAN	05.08	LIB	03.51	CAP	22.20	ARI	TAU	23
24	01.58	ARI	13.32	GEM	20.37	VIR	16.32	SAG	03.48	PIS	ARI	TAU	24
25	PIS	07.53	TAU	10.48	LEO	07.23	SCO	11.37	AQU	PIS	06.37	01.13	25
26	14.33	TAU	22.41	CAN	23.22	LIB	22.04	CAP	15.48	11.03	TAU	GEM	26
27	ARI	17.03	GEM	15.09	VIR	11.04	SAG	21.56	PIS	ARI	16.31	07.58	27
28	ARI	GEM	GEM	LEO	VIR	SCO	SAG	AQU	PIS	23.05	GEM	CAN	28
29	01.43		05.23	17.50	02.00	16.31	06.04	AQU	04.29	TAU	23.50	11.57	29
30	TAU		CAN	VIR	LIB	SAG	CAP	09.48	ARI	TAU	CAN	LEO	30
31	09.43		09.12		05.11		16.02	PIS		09.28		14.33	31

sun

mth	day	sign
JAN	1	CAP
JAN	20	AQU
FEB	19	PIS
MAR	21	ARI
APR	20	TAU
MAY	21	GEM
JUN	22	CAN
JUL	23	LEO
AUG	23	VIR
SEP	23	LIB
OCT	24	SCO
NOV	23	SAG
DEC	22	CAP

mercury

mth	day	sign
JAN	1	CAP
JAN	19	AQU
FEB	6	PIS
APR	14	ARI
MAY	1	TAU
MAY	16	GEM
MAY	31	CAN
AUG	8	LEO
AUG	24	VIR
SEP	9	LIB
SEP	30	SCO
DEC	5	SAG
DEC	24	CAP

venus

mth	day	sign
JAN	1	CAP
JAN	6	AQU
JAN	30	PIS
FEB	23	ARI
MAR	20	TAU
APR	14	GEM
MAY	10	CAN
JUN	6	LEO
JUL	8	VIR
SEP	9	LEO
OCT	1	VIR
NOV	9	LIB
DEC	7	SCO

mars

mth	day	sign
JAN	1	LIB
FEB	12	SCO
MAR	31	LIB
JUL	19	SCO
SEP	10	SAG
OCT	23	CAP
DEC	1	AQU

saturn

mth	day	sign
JAN	1	PIS
MAR	3	ARI

jupiter

mth	day	sign
JAN	1	LEO
JAN	16	CAN
MAY	23	LEO
OCT	19	VIR

moon

DAY	JAN	FEB	MAR	APR	MAY	JUN	JUL	AUG	SEP	OCT	NOV	DEC	DAY
1	VIR	01.44	SCO	00.11	AQU	20.07	16.43	GEM	14.08	03.38	15.26	02.10	1
2	17.04	SCO	11.53	CAP	AQU	ARI	TAU	22.32	LEO	VIR	SCO	SAG	2
3	LIB	05.55	SAG	07.49	00.47	ARI	TAU	CAN	17.07	04.34	14.51	02.25	3
4	20.16	SAG	17.35	AQU	PIS	09.04	04.39	CAN	VIR	LIB	SAG	CAP	4
5	SCO	12.10	CAP	18.29	13.10	TAU	GEM	04.26	18.03	04.14	15.44	04.57	5
6	SCO	CAP	CAP	PIS	ARI	20.52	13.47	LEO	LIB	SCO	CAP	AQU	6
7	00.28	20.17	02.03	PIS	ARI	GEM	CAN	07.36	18.44	04.32	19.45	11.19	7
8	SAG	AQU	AQU	06.57	02.09	GEM	19.58	VIR	SCO	SAG	AQU	PIS	8
9	05.53	AQU	12.41	ARI	TAU	06.18	LEO	09.34	20.40	07.04	AQU	21.43	9
10	CAP	06.19	PIS	19.56	14.08	CAN	LEO	LIB	SAG	CAP	03.42	ARI	10
11	13.05	PIS	PIS	TAU	GEM	13.19	00.07	11.44	SAG	12.45	PIS	ARI	11
12	AQU	18.17	00.53	08.15	GEM	LEO	VIR	SCO	00.43	AQU	14.58	10.32	12
13	22.45	ARI	ARI	GEM	00.11	18.24	03.20	14.52	CAP	21.38	ARI	TAU	13
14	PIS	ARI	13.54	GEM	CAN	VIR	LIB	SAG	07.08	PIS	ARI	23.18	14
15	PIS	07.19	TAU	18.37	07.49	21.58	06.17	19.18	AQU	PIS	03.52	GEM	15
16	10.48	TAU	TAU	CAN	LEO	LIB	SCO	CAP	15.53	08.58	TAU	GEM	16
17	ARI	19.16	02.19	CAN	12.52	LIB	09.22	CAP	PIS	ARI	16.40	10.23	17
18	23.39	GEM	GEM	01.54	VIR	00.25	SAG	01.17	PIS	21.41	GEM	CAN	18
19	TAU	GEM	12.10	LEO	15.31	SCO	12.59	AQU	02.46	TAU	GEM	19.21	19
20	TAU	03.48	CAN	05.42	LIB	02.20	CAP	09.18	ARI	TAU	04.13	LEO	20
21	10.38	CAN	18.04	VIR	16.30	SAG	17.59	PIS	15.20	10.38	CAN	LEO	21
22	GEM	08.04	LEO	06.41	SCO	04.46	AQU	19.47	TAU	GEM	13.47	02.21	22
23	17.51	LEO	20.08	LIB	17.06	CAP	AQU	ARI	TAU	22.27	LEO	VIR	23
24	CAN	09.04	VIR	06.19	SAG	09.11	01.28	ARI	04.21	CAN	20.46	07.27	24
25	21.20	VIR	19.50	SCO	18.58	AQU	PIS	08.21	GEM	CAN	VIR	LIB	25
26	LEO	08.44	LIB	06.27	CAP	16.49	12.00	TAU	15.45	07.40	VIR	10.36	26
27	22.36	LIB	19.10	SAG	23.44	PIS	ARI	21.08	CAN	LEO	00.48	SCO	27
28	VIR	09.09	SCO	08.54	AQU	PIS	ARI	GEM	23.41	13.19	LIB	12.09	28
29	23.33		20.08	CAP	AQU	03.52	00.40	GEM	LEO	VIR	02.13	SAG	29
30	LIB		SAG	14.57	08.18	ARI	TAU	07.34	LEO	15.31	SCO	13.11	30
31	LIB		SAG		PIS		13.00	CAN		LIB		CAP	31

sun

mth	day	sign
JAN	1	CAP
JAN	20	AQU
FEB	19	PIS
MAR	20	ARI
APR	20	TAU
MAY	21	GEM
JUN	21	CAN
JUL	22	LEO
AUG	23	VIR
SEP	22	LIB
OCT	23	SCO
NOV	22	SAG
DEC	21	CAP

mercury

mth	day	sign
JAN	1	CAP
JAN	12	AQU
FEB	1	PIS
FEB	11	AQU
MAR	17	PIS
APR	7	ARI
APR	22	TAU
MAY	6	GEM
MAY	29	CAN
JUN	13	GEM
JUL	13	CAN
JUL	31	LEO
AUG	15	VIR
SEP	1	LIB
SEP	28	SCO
OCT	7	LIB
NOV	8	SCO
NOV	27	SAG
DEC	16	CAP

venus

mth	day	sign
JAN	1	SAG
JAN	26	CAP
FEB	20	AQU
MAR	15	PIS
APR	8	ARI
MAY	3	TAU
MAY	27	GEM
JUN	21	CAN
JUL	15	LEO
AUG	8	VIR
SEP	2	LIB
SEP	26	SCO
OCT	21	SAG
NOV	14	CAP
DEC	9	AQU

mars

mth	day	sign
JAN	1	AQU
JAN	9	PIS
FEB	17	ARI
MAR	27	TAU
MAY	8	GEM
JUN	21	CAN
AUG	5	LEO
SEP	21	VIR
NOV	9	LIB
DEC	29	SCO

saturn

mth	day	sign
JAN	1	ARI

jupiter

mth	day	sign
JAN	1	VIR
FEB	27	LEO
JUN	15	VIR
NOV	15	LIB

moon

DAY	JAN	FEB	MAR	APR	MAY	JUN	JUL	AUG	SEP	OCT	NOV	DEC	DAY
1	15.24	PIS	ARI	TAU	GEM	LEO	VIR	02.11	13.22	AQU	16.51	08.58	1
2	AQU	14.39	ARI	01.50	LEO	16.10	SCO	CAP	AQU	ARI	TAU		2
3	20.35	ARI	10.27	GEM	03.52	LIB	05.11	15.19	03.21	ARI	21.06		3
4	PIS	ARI	TAU	19.13	12.54	VIR	20.20	SAG	AQU	PIS	03.01	GEM	4
5	PIS	02.15	23.17	CAN	LEO	09.49	SCO	06.57	20.27	10.35	TAU	GEM	5
6	05.45	TAU	GEM	CAN	20.58	LIB	22.05	CAP	PIS	ARI	14.48	09.43	6
7	ARI	15.09	GEM	05.28	VIR	12.30	SAG	08.37	PIS	20.07	GEM	CAN	7
8	18.02	GEM	11.21	LEO	VIR	SCO	22.24	AQU	02.49	TAU	GEM	22.02	8
9	TAU	GEM	CAN	12.04	01.21	12.42	CAP	11.45	ARI	TAU	03.26	LEO	9
10	TAU	02.34	20.27	VIR	LIB	SAG	23.03	PIS	12.06	07.43	CAN	LEO	10
11	06.54	CAN	LEO	15.01	02.30	12.05	AQU	17.53	TAU	GEM	15.45	08.59	11
12	GEM	10.50	LEO	LIB	SCO	CAP	AQU	ARI	23.54	20.23	LEO	VIR	12
13	17.54	LEO	01.51	15.32	01.53	12.46	02.03	ARI	GEM	CAN	LEO	17.08	13
14	CAN	16.02	VIR	SCO	SAG	AQU	PIS	03.36	GEM	CAN	01.55	LIB	14
15	CAN	VIR	04.23	15.23	01.30	16.42	08.51	TAU	12.28	08.08	VIR	21.31	15
16	02.09	19.21	LIB	SAG	CAP	PIS	ARI	15.51	CAN	LEO	08.26	SCO	16
17	LEO	LIB	05.33	16.23	03.22	PIS	19.30	GEM	23.25	16.58	LIB	22.27	17
18	08.11	22.00	SCO	CAP	AQU	TAU	GEM	LEO	VIR	11.06	SAG	SAG	18
19	VIR	SCO	06.54	19.57	08.53	ARI	TAU	04.15	LEO	22.05	SCO	21.32	19
20	12.47	SCO	SAG	AQU	PIS	12.25	08.13	CAN	07.15	LIB	11.04	CAP	20
21	LIB	00.48	09.34	AQU	18.14	TAU	GEM	14.40	VIR	LIB	SAG	20.59	21
22	16.28	SAG	CAP	02.45	ARI	TAU	20.31	LEO	12.00	00.05	10.20	AQU	22
23	SCO	04.12	14.16	PIS	ARI	01.22	CAN	22.21	LIB	SCO	CAP	23.01	23
24	19.23	CAP	AQU	12.32	06.15	GEM	CAN	VIR	14.39	00.32	11.02	PIS	24
25	SAG	08.37	21.15	ARI	TAU	13.43	06.55	VIR	SCO	SAG	AQU	PIS	25
26	21.57	AQU	PIS	ARI	19.12	CAN	LEO	03.45	16.30	01.13	14.52	05.02	26
27	CAP	14.42	PIS	00.22	GEM	15.10	LIB	SAG	CAP	PIS	ARI		27
28	CAP	PIS	06.32	TAU	GEM	00.30	VIR	07.38	18.44	03.43	22.26	14.57	28
29	01.06	23.14	ARI	13.11	07.43	LEO	21.32	SCO	CAP	AQU	ARI	TAU	29
30	AQU		17.55	GEM	CAN	09.26	LIB	10.40	22.11	08.54	ARI	TAU	30
31	06.16		TAU		18.53		LIB	SAG		PIS		03.11	31

sun

mth	day	sign
JAN	1	CAP
JAN	20	AQU
FEB	18	PIS
MAR	20	ARI
APR	20	TAU
MAY	21	GEM
JUN	21	CAN
JUL	23	LEO
AUG	23	VIR
SEP	23	LIB
OCT	23	SCO
NOV	22	SAG
DEC	22	CAP

mercury

mth	day	sign
JAN	1	CAP
JAN	4	AQU
MAR	12	PIS
MAR	30	ARI
APR	14	TAU
APR	30	GEM
JUL	8	CAN
JUL	22	LEO
AUG	7	VIR
AUG	27	LIB
OCT	7	VIR
OCT	9	LIB
NOV	1	SCO
NOV	20	SAG
DEC	9	CAP

venus

mth	day	sign
JAN	1	AQU
JAN	4	PIS
FEB	2	ARI
JUN	6	TAU
JUL	6	GEM
AUG	3	CAN
AUG	29	LEO
SEP	23	VIR
OCT	17	LIB
NOV	10	SCO
DEC	4	SAG
DEC	28	CAP

mars

mth	day	sign
JAN	1	SCO
FEB	25	SAG
SEP	21	CAP
NOV	4	AQU
DEC	15	PIS

saturn

mth	day	sign
JAN	1	ARI
APR	29	TAU

jupiter

mth	day	sign
JAN	1	LIB
MAR	30	VIR
JUL	15	LIB
DEC	16	SCO

moon

DAY	JAN	FEB	MAR	APR	MAY	JUN	JUL	AUG	SEP	OCT	NOV	DEC	DAY
1	GEM	10.29	LEO	20.03	09.49	21.07	06.49	19.55	TAU	GEM	11.35	08.14	1
2	15.53	LEO	LEO	LIB	SCO	CAP	AQU	ARI	19.23	14.52	LEO	VIR	2
3	CAN	20.40	04.07	LIB	11.19	21.03	07.26	ARI	GEM	CAN	LEO	19.17	3
4	CAN	VIR	VIR	00.22	SAG	AQU	PIS	02.02	GEM	CAN	00.00	LIB	4
5	03.54	VIR	11.34	SCO	11.57	23.13	11.16	TAU	06.57	03.25	VIR	LIB	5
6	LEO	05.00	LIB	02.57	CAP	PIS	ARI	11.49	CAN	LEO	09.59	02.30	6
7	14.42	LIB	16.56	SAG	13.28	PIS	18.53	GEM	19.36	15.21	LIB	SCO	7
8	VIR	11.18	SCO	05.04	AQU	04.36	TAU	23.57	LEO	VIR	16.18	05.42	8
9	23.32	SCO	20.48	CAP	17.04	ARI	TAU	CAN	LEO	VIR	SCO	SAG	9
10	LIB	15.23	SAG	07.46	PIS	13.06	05.31	CAN	07.20	00.48	19.30	06.20	10
11	LIB	SAG	23.40	AQU	23.09	TAU	GEM	12.38	VIR	LIB	SAG	CAP	11
12	05.32	17.28	CAP	11.41	ARI	23.48	17.47	LEO	17.01	07.19	21.08	06.27	12
13	SCO	CAP	CAP	PIS	ARI	GEM	CAN	LEO	LIB	SCO	CAP	AQU	13
14	08.19	18.30	02.09	17.13	07.28	GEM	CAN	00.32	LIB	11.33	22.53	07.56	14
15	SAG	AQU	AQU	ARI	TAU	11.52	06.29	VIR	00.25	SAG	AQU	PIS	15
16	08.39	20.03	05.04	ARI	17.41	CAN	LEO	10.51	SCO	14.35	AQU	11.56	16
17	CAP	PIS	09.27	00.43	GEM	CAN	18.42	LIB	05.42	CAP	01.52	ARI	17
18	08.17	23.48	09.27	TAU	GEM	00.35	VIR	18.54	SAG	17.21	PIS	18.35	18
19	AQU	ARI	ARI	10.28	05.30	LEO	VIR	SCO	09.14	AQU	06.32	TAU	19
20	09.21	ARI	16.20	GEM	CAN	12.53	05.20	SCO	CAP	20.26	ARI	TAU	20
21	PIS	07.02	TAU	22.17	18.12	VIR	LIB	00.12	11.31	PIS	12.52	03.28	21
22	13.43	TAU	TAU	CAN	LEO	23.03	13.04	SAG	AQU	PIS	TAU	GEM	22
23	ARI	17.41	02.12	CAN	LEO	LIB	SCO	02.49	13.22	00.17	20.59	14.08	23
24	22.13	GEM	GEM	10.51	06.07	LIB	17.10	CAP	PIS	ARI	GEM	CAN	24
25	TAU	GEM	14.18	LEO	VIR	05.31	SAG	03.36	15.55	05.32	GEM	CAN	25
26	TAU	06.11	CAN	21.57	15.07	SCO	18.09	AQU	ARI	TAU	07.10	02.21	26
27	09.53	CAN	CAN	VIR	LIB	08.00	CAP	04.03	20.29	13.00	CAN	LEO	27
28	GEM	18.12	02.37	VIR	20.05	SAG	17.35	PIS	TAU	GEM	19.22	15.20	28
29	22.36		LEO	05.43	SCO	07.44	AQU	05.57	TAU	23.13	LEO	VIR	29
30	CAN		12.54	LIB	21.30	CAP	17.30	ARI	04.05	CAN	LEO	VIR	30
31	CAN		VIR		SAG		PIS	10.50		CAN		03.18	31

sun

mth	day	sign
JAN	1	CAP
JAN	20	AQU
FEB	19	PIS
MAR	21	ARI
APR	20	TAU
MAY	21	GEM
JUN	21	CAN
JUL	23	LEO
AUG	23	VIR
SEP	23	LIB
OCT	23	SCO
NOV	22	SAG
DEC	22	CAP

mercury

mth	day	sign
JAN	1	CAP
JAN	4	AQU
JAN	4	CAP
FEB	13	AQU
MAR	5	PIS
MAR	22	ARI
APR	6	TAU
JUN	13	GEM
JUN	30	CAN
JUL	14	LEO
JUL	31	VIR
OCT	7	LIB
OCT	25	SCO
NOV	13	SAG
DEC	3	CAP

venus

mth	day	sign
JAN	1	CAP
JAN	21	AQU
FEB	14	PIS
MAR	10	ARI
APR	3	TAU
APR	27	GEM
MAY	22	CAN
JUN	16	LEO
JUL	12	VIR
AUG	8	LIB
SEP	7	SCO

mars

mth	day	sign
JAN	1	PIS
JAN	24	ARI
MAR	7	TAU
APR	18	GEM
JUN	2	CAN
JUL	18	LEO
SEP	3	VIR
OCT	20	LIB
DEC	6	SCO

saturn

mth	day	sign
JAN	1	TAU

jupiter

mth	day	sign
JAN	1	SCO
APR	30	LIB
AUG	15	SCO

moon

DAY	JAN	FEB	MAR	APR	MAY	JUN	JUL	AUG	SEP	OCT	NOV	DEC	DAY
1	LIB	01.50	SAG	AQU	PIS	TAU	GEM	10.44	VIR	LIB	02.24	CAP	1
2	12.03	SAG	12.54	AQU	09.32	TAU	17.21	LEO	18.25	SAG	18.45		2
3	SCO	04.21	CAP	00.01	ARI	02.10	CAN	23.34	LIB	SCO	08.32	AQU	3
4	16.33	CAP	14.34	PIS	13.05	GEM	CAN	VIR	LIB	20.31	CAP	21.55	4
5	SAG	04.19	AQU	01.32	TAU	10.25	04.26	VIR	05.54	SAG	13.11	PIS	5
6	17.30	AQU	14.49	ARI	18.17	CAN	LEO	12.32	SCO	SAG	AQU	PIS	6
7	CAP	03.37	PIS	04.02	GEM	21.17	17.11	LIB	14.58	03.10	16.33	01.03	7
8	16.47	PIS	15.16	TAU	GEM	LEO	VIR	23.57	SCO	CAP	PIS	ARI	8
9	AQU	04.17	ARI	09.02	02.17	LEO	VIR	SCO	20.51	07.26	18.52	04.24	9
10	16.37	ARI	17.43	GEM	CAN	10.02	06.02	SCO	CAP	AQU	ARI	TAU	10
11	PIS	07.59	TAU	17.33	13.22	VIR	LIB	08.07	23.34	09.30	20.50	08.33	11
12	18.48	TAU	23.37	CAN	LEO	22.28	16.41	SAG	AQU	PIS	TAU	GEM	12
13	ARI	15.29	GEM	CAN	02.10	LIB	SCO	12.25	23.57	10.12	23.48	14.32	13
14	ARI	GEM	GEM	05.15	VIR	LIB	23.26	CAP	PIS	ARI	GEM	CAN	14
15	00.20	GEM	09.18	LEO	VIR	08.01	SAG	13.31	23.35	11.00	GEM	23.21	15
16	TAU	02.17	CAN	18.07	14.02	SCO	SAG	AQU	ARI	TAU	05.23	LEO	16
17	09.07	CAN	21.39	VIR	LIB	13.39	02.19	13.01	ARI	13.43	CAN	LEO	17
18	GEM	14.53	LEO	VIR	22.49	SAG	CAP	PIS	00.21	GEM	14.36	11.04	18
19	20.13	LEO	LEO	05.35	SCO	16.04	02.44	12.50	TAU	19.59	LEO	VIR	19
20	CAN	LEO	10.30	LIB	SCO	CAP	AQU	ARI	04.02	CAN	LEO	VIR	20
21	CAN	03.42	VIR	14.15	04.11	17.00	02.36	14.46	GEM	CAN	02.50	00.01	21
22	08.40	VIR	21.56	SCO	SAG	AQU	PIS	TAU	11.41	06.12	VIR	LIB	22
23	LEO	15.30	LIB	20.15	07.13	18.11	03.42	20.03	CAN	LEO	15.39	11.27	23
24	21.33	LIB	LIB	SAG	CAP	PIS	ARI	GEM	22.54	18.57	LIB	SCO	24
25	VIR	LIB	07.10	SAG	09.26	20.52	07.18	GEM	LEO	VIR	LIB	19.27	25
26	VIR	01.23	SCO	00.26	AQU	ARI	TAU	04.58	LEO	VIR	02.25	SAG	26
27	09.42	SCO	14.07	CAP	11.59	ARI	13.53	CAN	11.53	07.37	SCO	SAG	27
28	LIB	08.38	SAG	03.43	PIS	01.35	GEM	16.38	VIR	LIB	10.02	00.01	28
29	19.34		19.00	AQU	15.27	TAU	23.14	LEO	VIR	18.15	SAG	CAP	29
30	SCO		CAP	06.37	ARI	08.24	CAN	LEO	00.33	SCO	15.05	02.24	30
31	SCO		22.08		20.03		CAN	05.36		SCO		AQU	31

sun

mth	day	sign
JAN	1	CAP
JAN	20	AQU
FEB	19	PIS
MAR	21	ARI
APR	20	TAU
MAY	21	GEM
JUN	22	CAN
JUL	23	LEO
AUG	23	VIR
SEP	23	LIB
OCT	24	SCO
NOV	22	SAG
DEC	22	CAP

mercury

mth	day	sign
JAN	1	CAP
JAN	2	SAG
JAN	14	CAP
FEB	7	AQU
FEB	26	PIS
MAR	14	ARI
APR	1	TAU
APR	18	ARI
MAY	17	TAU
JUN	7	GEM
JUN	21	CAN
JUL	6	LEO
JUL	26	VIR
AUG	29	LEO
SEP	11	VIR
SEP	30	LIB
OCT	17	SCO
NOV	6	SAG

venus

mth	day	sign
JAN	1	SCO
JAN	7	SAG
FEB	5	CAP
MAR	4	AQU
MAR	29	PIS
APR	23	ARI
MAY	18	TAU
JUN	12	GEM
JUL	6	CAN
JUL	31	LEO
AUG	24	VIR
SEP	17	LIB
OCT	11	SCO
NOV	5	SAG
NOV	29	CAP
DEC	23	AQU

mars

mth	day	sign
JAN	1	SCO
JAN	23	SAG
MAR	12	CAP
MAY	3	AQU
NOV	6	PIS
DEC	26	ARI

saturn

mth	day	sign
JAN	1	TAU
JUN	18	GEM

jupiter

mth	day	sign
JAN	1	SCO
JAN	14	SAG
JUN	5	SCO
SEP	11	SAG

moon

DAY	JAN	FEB	MAR	APR	MAY	JUN	JUL	AUG	SEP	OCT	NOV	DEC	DY
1	04.08	15.49	TAU	16.51	09.34	VIR	LIB	08.49	SCO	19.36	ARI	16.25	1
2	PIS	TAU	TAU	CAN	LEO	17.26	13.46	SAG	07.04	PISI	05.55	GEM	2
3	06.26	20.34	03.01	CAN	21.03	LIB	SCO	16.32	AQU	19.40	TAU	17.51	3
4	ARI	GEM	GEM	02.05	VIR	LIB	23.59	CAP	08.51	ARI	05.27	CAN	4
5	10.00	GEM	09.47	LEO	VIR	05.36	SAG	20.47	PIS	18.42	GEM	22.17	5
6	TAU	04.07	CAN	14.16	09.59	SCO	SAG	AQU	08.43	TAU	07.15	LEO	6
7	15.08	CAN	19.55	VIR	LIB	15.28	07.03	22.34	ARI	18.53	CAN	LEO	7
8	GEM	14.06	LEO	VIR	22.03	SAG	CAP	PIS	08.37	GEM	12.56	06.40	8
9	22.09	LEO	LEO	03.17	SCO	22.45	11.26	23.27	TAU	22.10	LEO	VIR	9
10	CAN	LEO	08.10	LIB	SCO	CAP	AQU	ARI	10.25	CAN	22.44	18.19	10
11	CAN	01.58	VIR	15.28	08.08	CAP	14.14	ARI	GEM	CAN	VIR	LIB	11
12	07.24	VIR	21.06	SCO	SAG	04.03	PIS	00.55	15.21	05.30	VIR	LIB	12
13	LEO	14.50	LIB	SCO	16.09	AQU	16.32	TAU	CAN	LEO	11.05	07.01	13
14	18.57	LIB	LIB	02.03	CAP	08.01	ARI	04.10	23.38	16.16	LIB	SCO	14
15	VIR	LIB	09.31	SAG	22.19	PIS	19.10	GEM	LEO	VIR	23.49	18.37	15
16	VIR	03.22	SCO	10.38	AQU	11.06	TAU	09.50	LEO	VIR	SCO	SAG	16
17	07.53	SCO	20.23	CAP	AQU	ARI	22.47	CAN	10.29	LIB	SCO	SAG	17
18	LIB	13.45	SAG	16.46	02.39	13.39	GEM	17.57	VIR	LIB	11.30	04.07	18
19	20.04	SAG	SAG	AQU	PIS	TAU	GEM	LEO	22.47	17.31	SAG	CAP	19
20	SCO	20.37	04.37	20.07	05.11	16.24	03.56	LEO	LIB	SCO	21.36	11.32	20
21	SCO	CAP	CAP	PIS	ARI	GEM	CAN	04.19	LIB	SCO	CAP	AQU	21
22	05.15	23.43	09.28	21.08	06.31	20.30	11.16	VIR	11.33	05.31	CAP	17.10	22
23	SAG	AQU	AQU	ARI	TAU	CAN	LEO	16.22	SCO	SAG	05.52	PIS	23
24	10.32	AQU	11.07	21.06	08.01	CAN	21.09	LIB	23.43	16.05	AQU	21.09	24
25	CAP	00.05>PIS	PIS	TAU	GEM	03.12	VIR	LIB	SAG	CAP	11.48	ARI	25
26	12.36	23.30	10.45	21.58	11.26	LEO	VIR	05.09	SAG	CAP	PIS	23.45	26
27	AQU	ARI	ARI	GEM	CAN	13.06	09.12	SCO	09.53	00.11	15.03	TAU	27
28	13.02	23.54	10.16	GEM	18.16	VIR	LIB	16.56	CAP	AQU	ARI	TAU	28
29	PIS		TAU	01.43	LEO	VIR	21.50	SAG	16.39	04.56	16.08	01.38	29
30	13.36		11.43	CAN	LEO	01.22	SCO	SAG	AQU	PIS	TAU	GEM	30
31	ARI		GEM		04.48		SCO	01.54		06.26		04.01	31

1972

sun

mth	day	sign
JAN	1	CAP
JAN	20	AQU
FEB	19	PIS
MAR	20	ARI
APR	19	TAU
MAY	20	GEM
JUN	21	CAN
JUL	22	LEO
AUG	23	VIR
SEP	22	LIB
OCT	23	SCO
NOV	22	SAG
DEC	21	CAP

mercury

mth	day	sign
JAN	1	SAG
JAN	11	CAP
JAN	31	AQU
FEB	18	PIS
MAR	5	ARI
MAY	12	TAU
MAY	29	GEM
JUN	12	CAN
JUN	28	LEO
SEP	5	VIR
SEP	21	LIB
OCT	9	SCO
OCT	30	SAG
NOV	29	SCO
DEC	12	SAG

venus

mth	day	sign
JAN	1	AQU
JAN	16	PIS
FEB	10	ARI
MAR	7	TAU
APR	3	GEM
MAY	10	CAN
JUN	11	GEM
AUG	6	CAN
SEP	7	LEO
OCT	5	VIR
OCT	30	LIB
NOV	24	SCO
DEC	18	SAG

mars

mth	day	sign
JAN	1	ARI
FEB	10	TAU
MAR	27	GEM
MAY	12	CAN
JUN	28	LEO
AUG	15	VIR
SEP	30	LIB
NOV	15	SCO
DEC	30	SAG

saturn

mth	day	sign
JAN	1	GEM
JAN	10	TAU
FEB	21	GEM

jupiter

mth	day	sign
JAN	1	SAG
FEB	6	CAP
JUL	24	SAG
SEP	25	CAP

moon

DAY	JAN	FEB	MAR	APR	MAY	JUN	JUL	AUG	SEP	OCT	NOV	DEC	DAY
1	CAN	00.56	19.00	SCO	SAG	12.15	01.18	14.57	GEM	12.25	VIR	LIB	1
2	08.22	VIR	LIB	SCO	20.29	AQU	PIS	TAU	02.11	LEO	10.27	03.42	2
3	LEO	11.06	LIB	02.27	CP	19.52	06.22	17.33	CAN	19.31	LIB	SCO	3
4	15.50	LIB	07.00	SAG	CAP	PIS	ARI	GEM	06.54	VIR	21.46	16.22	4
5	VIR	23.18	SCO	14.20	06.35	PIS	09.25	20.18	LEO	VIR	SCO	SAG	5
6	VIR	SCO	19.36	CAP	AQU	00.27	TAU	CAN	13.15	04.35	SCO	SAG	6
7	02.33	SCO	SAG	23.37	13.28	ARI	11.05	23.56	VIR	LIB	10.16	05.06	7
8	LIB	11.38	SAG	AQU	PIS	02.14	GEM	LEO	21.36	15.27	SAG	CAP	8
9	15.03	SAG	06.49	AQU	16.35	TAU	12.29	LEO	LIB	SCO	23.11	16.53	9
10	SCO	21.50	CAP	04.58	ARI	02.24	CAN	05.23	LIB	SCO	CAP	AQU	10
11	SCO	CAP	14.42	PIS	16.47	GEM	15.05	VIR	08.15	03.52	CAP	AQU	11
12	02.57	CAP	AQU	06.32	TAU	02.45	LEO	13.27	SCO	SAG	11.02	02.32	12
13	SAG	04.36	18.39	ARI	15.57	CAN	20.16	LIB	20.42	16.44	AQU	PIS	13
14	12.26	AQU	PIS	05.54	GEM	05.10	VIR	LIB	SAG	CAP	19.56	08.59	14
15	CAP	08.11	19.57	TAU	16.16	LEO	VIR	00.19	SAG	CAP	PIS	ARI	15
16	19.04	PIS	ARI	05.16	CAN	11.03	04.49	SCO	09.07	03.51	PIS	11.59	16
17	AQU	09.51	19.27	GEM	19.38	VIR	LIB	12.49	CAP	AQU	00.44	TAU	17
18	23.28	ARI	TAU	06.46	LEO	20.39	16.15	SAG	19.04	11.12	ARI	12.24	18
19	PIS	11.11	20.12	CAN	LEO	LIB	SCO	SAG	AQU	PIS	01.53	GEM	19
20	PIS	TAU	GEM	11.47	02.56	LIB	SCO	00.38	AQU	14.22	TAU	11.57	20
21	02.35	13.35	23.26	LEO	VIR	08.43	04.46	CAP	01.09	ARI	01.05	CAN	21
22	ARI	GEM	CAN	20.24	13.36	SCO	SAG	09.43	PIS	14.37	GEM	12.34	22
23	05.17	17.52	CAN	VIR	LIB	21.14	16.10	AQU	03.44	TAU	00.31	LEO	23
24	TAU	CAN	05.46	VIR	LIB	SAG	CAP	15.28	ARI	14.02	CAN	16.03	24
25	08.14	CAN	LEO	07.34	02.01	SAG	CAP	PIS	04.27	GEM	02.12	VIR	25
26	GEM	00.15	14.47	LIB	SCO	08.36	01.07	18.40	TAU	14.44	LEO	23.21	26
27	12.01	LEO	VIR	19.56	14.33	CAP	AQU	ARI	05.14	CAN	07.24	LIB	27
28	CAN	08.39	VIR	SCO	SAG	18.02	07.29	20.43	GEM	18.14	VIR	LIB	28
29	17.21	VIR	01.42	SCO	SAG	AQU	PIS	TAU	07.39	LEO	16.15	10.10	29
30	LEO		LIB	08.31	02.13	AQU	11.50	22.56	CAN	LEO	LIB	SCO	30
31	LEO		13.48		CAP		ARI	GEM		00.59		22.51	31

338

sun

mth	day	sign
JAN	1	CAP
JAN	20	AQU
FEB	18	PIS
MAR	20	ARI
APR	20	TAU
MAY	21	GEM
JUN	21	CAN
JUL	22	LEO
AUG	23	VIR
SEP	23	LIB
OCT	23	SCO
NOV	22	SAG
DEC	22	CAP

mercury

mth	day	sign
JAN	1	SAG
JAN	4	CAP
JAN	23	AQU
FEB	9	PIS
APR	16	ARI
MAY	6	TAU
MAY	20	GEM
JUN	4	CAN
JUN	27	LEO
JUL	16	CAN
AUG	11	LEO
AUG	28	VIR
SEP	13	LIB
OCT	2	SCO
DEC	8	SAG
DEC	28	CAP

venus

mth	day	sign
JAN	1	SAG
JAN	11	CAP
FEB	4	AQU
FEB	28	PIS
MAR	24	ARI
APR	18	TAU
MAY	12	GEM
JUN	5	CAN
JUN	30	LEO
JUL	25	VIR
AUG	19	LIB
SEP	13	SCO
OCT	9	SAG
NOV	5	CAP
DEC	7	AQU

mars

mth	day	sign
JAN	1	SAG
FEB	12	CAP
MAR	26	AQU
MAY	8	PIS
JUN	20	ARI
AUG	12	TAU
OCT	29	ARI
DEC	24	TAU

saturn

mth	day	sign
JAN	1	GEM
AUG	1	CAN

jupiter

mth	day	sign
JAN	1	CAP
FEB	23	AQU

moon

DAY	JAN	FEB	MAR	APR	MAY	JUN	JUL	AUG	SEP	OCT	NOV	DEC	DAY
1	SAG	CAP	14.22	PIS	ARI		21.55		05.17	SAG	CAP	AQU	1
2	SAG	05.55	AQU	12.48	01.01	11.21	LEO	13.12	SCO	SAG	08.58	04.32	2
3	11.30	AQU	22.31	ARI	TAU	CAN	23.31	LIB	15.24	12.02	AQU	PIS	3
4	CAP	14.22	PIS	14.58	01.16	11.49	VIR	20.35	SAG	CAP	20.26	13.50	4
5	22.47	PIS	PIS	TAU	GEM	LEO	VIR	SCO	SAG	CAP	PIS	ARI	5
6	AQU	20.29	03.37	16.12	01.35	14.51	04.23	SCO	04.01	00.48	PIS	19.08	6
7	AQU	ARI	ARI	GEM	CAN	VIR	LIB	07.37	CAP	AQU	04.19	TAU	7
8	08.03	ARI	06.51	18.04	03.36	21.16	13.05	SAG	16.30	11.23	ARI	20.58	8
9	PIS	00.53	TAU	CAN	LEO	LIB	SCO	20.30	AQU	PIS	08.25	GEM	9
10	14.57	TAU	09.31	21.31	08.13	LIB	SCO	CAP	AQU	18.29	TAU	20.52	10
11	ARI	04.10	GEM	LEO	VIR	06.52	00.48	CAP	02.40	ARI	09.59	CAN	11
12	19.24	GEM	12.29	LEO	15.31	SCO	SAG	08.52	PIS	22.36	GEM	20.44	12
13	TAU	06.44	CAN	02.46	LIB	18.43	13.45	AQU	09.56	TAU	10.46	LEO	13
14	21.41	CAN	16.07	VIR	LIB	SAG	CAP	19.14	ARI	TAU	CAN	22.20	14
15	GEM	09.12	LEO	09.50	01.09	SAG	CAP	PIS	14.59	01.09	12.20	VIR	15
16	22.39	LEO	20.42	LIB	SCO	07.37	02.15	PIS	TAU	GEM	LEO	VIR	16
17	CAN	12.31	VIR	18.51	12.41	CAP	AQU	03.15	18.48	03.28	15.41	02.53	17
18	23.40	VIR	VIR	SCO	SAG	20.19	13.07	ARI	GEM	CAN	VIR	LIB	18
19	LEO	17.58	02.48	SCO	SAG	AQU	PIS	09.14	22.01	06.25	21.15	10.44	19
20	LEO	LIB	LIB	06.02	01.30	AQU	21.43	TAU	CAN	LEO	LIB	SCO	20
21	02.23	LIB	11.15	SAG	CAP	07.29	ARI	13.26	CAN	10.19	LIB	21.20	21
22	VIR	02.35	SCO	18.49	14.17	PIS	ARI	GEM	00.56	VIR	05.06	SAG	22
23	08.16	SCO	22.26	CAP	AQU	15.48	03.41	16.08	LEO	15.28	SCO	SAG	23
24	LIB	14.14	SAG	CAP	AQU	ARI	TAU	CAN	03.58	LIB	15.11	09.41	24
25	17.52	SAG	SAG	07.21	01.05	20.37	06.58	17.49	VIR	22.28	SAG	CAP	25
26	SCO	SAG	11.16	AQU	PIS	TAU	GEM	LEO	08.00	SCO	SAG	22.43	26
27	SCO	03.04	CAP	17.09	08.14	22.18	08.10	19.33	LIB	SCO	03.13	AQU	27
28	06.10	CAP	23.12	PIS	ARI	GEM	CAN	VIR	14.18	07.57	CAP	AQU	28
29	SAG		AQU	22.53	11.28	22.08	08.29	22.52	SCO	SAG	16.17	11.10	29
30	18.54		AQU	ARI	TAU	CAN	LEO	LIB	23.47	19.57	AQU	PIS	30
31	CAP		07.55		11.53		09.34	LIB		CAP		21.34	31

1974

sun

mth	day	sign
JAN	1	CAP
JAN	20	AQU
FEB	19	PIS
MAR	21	ARI
APR	20	TAU
MAY	21	GEM
JUN	21	CAN
JUL	23	LEO
AUG	23	VIR
SEP	23	LIB
OCT	23	SCO
NOV	22	SAG
DEC	22	CAP

mercury

mth	day	sign
JAN	1	CAP
JAN	16	AQU
FEB	2	PIS
MAR	2	AQU
MAR	17	PIS
APR	11	ARI
APR	28	TAU
MAY	12	GEM
MAY	29	CAN
AUG	5	LEO
AUG	20	VIR
SEP	6	LIB
SEP	28	SCO
OCT	26	LIB
NOV	11	SCO
DEC	2	SAG
DEC	21	CAP

venus

mth	day	sign
JAN	1	AQU
JAN	29	CAP
FEB	28	AQU
APR	6	PIS
MAY	4	ARI
MAY	31	TAU
JUN	25	GEM
JUL	21	CAN
AUG	14	LEO
SEP	8	VIR
OCT	2	LIB
OCT	26	SCO
NOV	19	SAG
DEC	13	CAP

mars

mth	day	sign
JAN	1	TAU
FEB	27	GEM
APR	20	CAN
JUN	9	LEO
JUL	27	VIR
SEP	12	LIB
OCT	28	SCO
DEC	10	SAG

saturn

mth	day	sign
JAN	1	CAN
JAN	7	GEM
APR	18	CAN

jupiter

mth	day	sign
JAN	1	AQU
MAR	8	PIS

moon

DAY	JAN	FEB	MAR	APR	MAY	JUN	JUL	AUG	SEP	OCT	NOV	DEC	DAY
1	ARI	16.53	GEM	11.40	VIR	11.10	01.20	CAP	01.29	ARI	18.23	06.22	1
2	ARI	GEM	GEM	LEO	23.39	SCO	SAG	06.46	PIS	ARI	GEM	CAN	2
3	04.38	19.05	02.59	13.56	LIB	19.21	12.19	AQU	12.58	04.39	23.01	08.31	3
4	TAU	CAN	CAN	VIR	LIB	SAG	CAP	19.26	ARI	TAU	CAN	LEO	4
5	08.00	19.11	04.49	16.22	04.43	SAG	CAP	PIS	22.50	12.00	CAN	10.40	5
6	GEM	LEO	LEO	LIB	SCO	05.48	00.41	PIS	TAU	GEM	02.30	VIR	6
7	08.28	18.52	05.33	20.25	12.05	CAP	AQU	07.15	TAU	17.30	LEO	13.42	7
8	CAN	VIR	VIR	SCO	SAG	18.02	13.25	ARI	06.36	CAN	05.18	LIB	8
9	07.42	20.10	06.52	SCO	22.15	AQU	PIS	17.13	GEM	21.03	VIR	18.13	9
10	LEO	LIB	LIB	03.27	CAP	AQU	PIS	TAU	11.39	LEO	07.58	SCO	10
11	07.41	LIB	10.40	SAG	CAP	06.43	01.10	TAU	CAN	22.56	LIB	SCO	11
12	VIR	00.58	SCO	13.56	10.34	PIS	ARI	00.15	13.54	VIR	11.23	00.34	12
13	10.21	SCO	18.20	CAP	AQU	17.52	10.21	GEM	LEO	VIR	SCO	SAG	13
14	LIB	10.01	SAG	CAP	23.33	ARI	TAU	03.49	14.12	00.11	16.39	09.04	14
15	16.54	SAG	SAG	02.34	ARI	15.54		CAN	VIR	LIB	SAG	CAP	15
16	SCO	22.16	05.41	AQU	PIS	01.46	GEM	04.26	14.17	02.23	SAG	19.48	16
17	SCO	CAP	CAP	14.44	09.19	TAU	17.56	LEO	LIB	SCO	00.42	AQU	17
18	03.12	CAP	18.38	PIS	ARI	05.59	CAN	03.42	16.14	07.14	CAP	AQU	18
19	SAG	11.21	AQU	PIS	16.10	GEM	17.43	VIR	SCO	SAG	11.39	08.12	19
20	15.47	AQU	AQU	00.20	TAU	07.21	LEO	03.45	21.46	15.44	AQU	PIS	20
21	CAP	23.15	06.33	ARI	19.54	CAN	17.10	LIB	SAG	CAP	AQU	20.35	21
22	CAP	PIS	PIS	06.53	GEM	07.30	VIR	06.37	SAG	CAP	00.11	ARI	22
23	04.50	PIS	16.02	TAU	21.46	LEO	18.19	SCO	07.22	03.20	PIS	ARI	23
24	AQU	09.12	ARI	11.11	CAN	08.11	LIB	13.34	CAP	AQU	11.59	06.44	24
25	17.00	ARI	23.09	GEM	23.12	VIR	22.45	SAG	19.38	15.57	ARI	TAU	25
26	PIS	17.11	TAU	14.17	LEO	10.57	SCO	SAG	AQU	PIS	21.05	13.15	26
27	PIS	TAU	TAU	CAN	VIR	LIB	SCO	00.15	AQU	PIS	TAU	GEM	27
28	03.32	23.10	04.33	17.03	01.25	16.40	07.00	CAP	08.14	03.13	TAU	16.15	28
29	ARI		GEM	LEO	VIR	SCO	SAG	12.52	PIS	ARI	02.58	CAN	29
30	11.41		08.40	20.00	05.16	SCO	18.11	AQU	19.25	12.00	GEM	17.05	30
31	TAU		CAN		LIB		CAP	AQU		TAU		LEO	31

sun

mth	day	sign
JAN	1	CAP
JAN	20	AQU
FEB	19	PIS
MAR	21	ARI
APR	20	TAU
MAY	21	GEM
JUN	22	CAN
JUL	23	LEO
AUG	23	VIR
SEP	23	LIB
OCT	24	SCO
NOV	22	SAG
DEC	22	CAP

mercury

mth	day	sign
JAN	1	CAP
JAN	8	AQU
MAR	16	PIS
APR	4	ARI
APR	19	TAU
MAY	4	GEM
JUL	12	CAN
JUL	28	LEO
AUG	12	VIR
AUG	30	LIB
NOV	6	SCO
NOV	25	SAG
DEC	14	CAP

venus

mth	day	sign
JAN	1	CAP
JAN	6	AQU
JAN	30	PIS
FEB	23	ARI
MAR	19	TAU
APR	13	GEM
MAY	9	CAN
JUN	6	LEO
JUL	9	VIR
SEP	2	LEO
OCT	4	VIR
NOV	9	LIB
DEC	7	SCO

mars

mth	day	sign
JAN	1	SAG
JAN	21	CAP
MAR	3	AQU
APR	11	PIS
MAY	21	ARI
JUL	1	TAU
AUG	14	GEM
OCT	17	CAN
NOV	25	GEM

saturn

mth	day	sign
JAN	1	CAN
SEP	17	LEO

jupiter

mth	day	sign
JAN	1	PIS
MAR	18	ARI

moon

DAY	JAN	FEB	MAR	APR	MAY	JUN	JUL	AUG	SEP	OCT	NOV	DEC	DAY
1	17.32	LIB	14.33	SAG	01.32	ARI	TAU	CAN	LEO	LIB	SCO		1
2	VIR	05.53	SCO	11.08	05.34	PIS	ARI	04.02	23.08	10.03	20.07	07.33	2
3	19.21	SCO	19.05	CAP	AQU	14.01	09.54	GEM	LEO	VIR	SCO	SAG	3
4	LIB	12.10	SAG	21.45	17.34	ARI	TAU	10.17	23.29	09.39	21.10	10.58	4
5	23.39	SAG	SAG	AQU	PIS	ARI	18.58	CAN	VIR	LIB	SAG	CAP	5
6	SCO	21.42	03.39	AQU	PIS	01.19	GEM	12.44	22.38	09.09	SAG	17.12	6
7	SCO	CAP	CAP	10.17	06.03	TAU	GEM	LEO	LIB	SCO	00.45	AQU	7
8	06.39	CAP	15.09	PIS	ARI	09.49	00.23	12.53	22.46	10.35	CAP	AQU	8
9	SAG	09.16	AQU	22.44	17.03	GEM	CAN	VIR	SCO	SAG	07.59	02.52	9
10	15.58	AQU	AQU	ARI	TAU	15.21	02.50	12.51	SCO	15.29	AQU	PIS	10
11	CAP	21.45	03.49	ARI	TAU	CAN	LEO	LIB	01.41	CAP	18.42	15.06	11
12	CAP	PIS	PIS	09.53	01.44	18.45	03.55	14.30	SAG	CAP	PIS	ARI	12
13	03.03	PIS	16.18	TAU	GEM	LEO	VIR	SCO	08.11	00.10	PIS	ARI	13
14	AQU	10.22	ARI	19.14	08.08	21.11	05.21	18.59	CAP	AQU	07.17	03.39	14
15	15.23	ARI	ARI	GEM	CAN	VIR	LIB	SAG	17.51	11.40	ARI	TAU	15
16	PIS	22.09	03.52	GEM	12.38	23.41	08.23	SAG	AQU	PIS	19.38	14.12	16
17	PIS	TAU	TAU	02.27	LEO	LIB	SCO	02.25	AQU	PIS	TAU	GEM	17
18	04.03	TAU	13.43	CAN	15.45	LIB	13.32	CAP	05.32	00.20	TAU	21.49	18
19	ARI	07.35	GEM	07.14	VIR	02.59	SAG	12.09	PIS	ARI	06.14	CAN	19
20	15.21	GEM	20.48	LEO	18.05	SCO	20.46	AQU	18.07	12.43	GEM	CAN	20
21	TAU	13.18	CAN	09.42	LIB	07.34	CAP	23.32	ARI	TAU	14.36	02.54	21
22	23.23	CAN	CAN	VIR	20.25	SAG	CAP	PIS	ARI	23.51	CAN	LEO	22
23	GEM	15.13	00.31	10.41	SCO	13.56	05.56	PIS	06.43	GEM	20.48	06.28	23
24	GEM	LEO	LEO	LIB	23.51	CAP	AQU	12.02	TAU	GEM	LEO	VIR	24
25	03.20	14.37	01.21	11.39	SAG	22.33	16.58	ARI	18.13	08.57	LEO	09.27	25
26	CAN	VIR	VIR	SCO	SAG	AQU	PIS	ARI	GEM	CAN	01.04	LIB	26
27	04.00	13.38	00.51	14.20	05.31	AQU	PIS	00.45	GEM	15.20	VIR	12.28	27
28	LEO	LIB	LIB	SAG	CAP	09.33	05.27	TAU	03.07	LEO	03.48	SCO	28
29	03.14		01.08	20.08	14.09	PIS	ARI	11.53	CAN	18.47	LIB	15.53	29
30	VIR		SCO	CAP	AQU	22.02	17.53	GEM	08.20	VIR	05.36	SAG	30
31	03.13		04.09		AQU		TAU	19.35		19.55		20.16	31

341

sun

mth	day	sign
JAN	1	CAP
JAN	20	AQU
FEB	19	PIS
MAR	20	ARI
APR	19	TAU
MAY	20	GEM
JUN	21	CAN
JUL	22	LEO
AUG	23	VIR
SEP	22	LIB
OCT	23	SCO
NOV	22	SAG
DEC	21	CAP

mercury

mth	day	sign
JAN	1	CAP
JAN	2	AQU
JAN	25	CAP
FEB	15	AQU
MAR	9	PIS
MAR	26	ARI
APR	10	TAU
APR	29	GEM
MAY	19	TAU
JUN	13	GEM
JUL	4	CAN
JUL	18	LEO
AUG	3	VIR
AUG	25	LIB
SEP	21	VIR
OCT	10	LIB
OCT	29	SCO
NOV	16	SAG
DEC	6	CAP

venus

mth	day	sign
JAN	1	SAG
JAN	26	CAP
FEB	19	AQU
MAR	15	PIS
APR	8	ARI
MAY	2	TAU
MAY	27	GEM
JUN	20	CAN
JUL	14	LEO
AUG	8	VIR
SEP	1	LIB
SEP	26	SCO
OCT	20	SAG
NOV	14	CAP
DEC	9	AQU

mars

mth	day	sign
JAN	1	GEM
MAR	18	CAN
MAY	16	LEO
JUL	6	VIR
AUG	24	LIB
OCT	8	SCO
NOV	20	SAG

saturn

mth	day	sign
JAN	1	LEO
JAN	14	CAN
JUN	5	LEO

jupiter

mth	day	sign
JAN	1	ARI
MAR	26	TAU
AUG	23	GEM
OCT	16	TAU

moon

DAY	JAN	FEB	MAR	APR	MAY	JUN	JUL	AUG	SEP	OCT	NOV	DEC	DAY
1	CAP	19.47	PIS	09.34	04.05	CAN	15.46	LIB	SAG	CAP	PIS	ARI	1
2	CAP	PIS	14.22	TAU	GEM	04.37	VIR	03.55	16.29	03.49	PIS	23.41	2
3	02.33	PIS	ARI	22.15	14.53	LEO	19.34	SCO	CAP	AQU	04.46	TAU	3
4	AQU	07.17	ARI	GEM	CAN	10.21	LIB	07.03	22.20	12.10	ARI	TAU	4
5	11.35	ARI	03.18	GEM	23.09	VIR	22.33	SAG	AQU	PIS	17.23	12.38	5
6	PIS	20.13	TAU	09.06	LEO	14.00	SCO	10.54	AQU	22.50	TAU	GEM	6
7	23.21	TAU	15.56	CAN	LEO	LIB	SCO	CAP	06.11	ARI	TAU	GEM	7
8	ARI	TAU	GEM	16.36	04.21	15.58	01.05	15.57	PIS	ARI	06.21	00.21	8
9	ARI	08.16	GEM	LEO	VIR	06.39	SAG	AQU	16.18	11.11	GEM	10.12	9
10	12.10	GEM	01.59	LEO	20.16	17.06	03.49	23.00	ARI	TAU	18.28	10.12	10
11	TAU	16.59	CAN	VIR	LIB	SAG	CAP	PIS	ARI	TAU	CAN	LEO	11
12	23.19	CAN	07.55	20.54	07.03	18.45	07.53	PIS	04.30	00.14	CAN	17.55	12
13	GEM	21.32	LEO	LIB	SCO	CAP	AQU	08.49	TAU	GEM	04.36	VIR	13
14	GEM	LEO	09.59	20.14	07.04	22.31	14.36	ARI	17.32	12.24	LEO	23.13	14
15	07.00	22.59	VIR	SCO	SAG	AQU	PIS	21.05	GEM	CAN	11.46	LIB	15
16	CAN	VIR	09.44	20.15	08.31	AQU	PIS	TAU	GEM	21.49	VIR	LIB	16
17	11.15	23.14	LIB	SAG	CAP	05.43	00.40	TAU	05.07	LEO	15.34	02.01	17
18	LEO	LIB	09.18	22.43	13.02	PIS	ARI	09.54	CAN	LEO	LIB	SCO	18
19	13.25	LIB	SCO	CAP	AQU	16.32	13.11	GEM	13.10	03.25	16.31	02.54	19
20	VIR	00.14	10.34	CAP	21.27	ARI	TAU	20.34	LEO	VIR	SCO	SAG	20
21	15.10	SCO	SAG	04.47	PIS	ARI	TAU	CAN	17.16	05.26	16.03	03.12	21
22	LIB	03.18	14.48	AQU	PIS	05.21	01.40	CAN	VIR	LIB	SAG	CAP	22
23	17.48	SAG	CAP	14.28	09.07	TAU	GEM	03.30	18.28	05.17	16.03	04.48	23
24	SCO	08.54	22.19	PIS	ARI	17.37	11.39	LEO	LIB	SCO	CAP	AQU	24
25	21.51	CAP	AQU	PIS	22.07	GEM	CAN	07.03	18.34	04.49	18.30	09.36	25
26	SAG	16.48	AQU	02.37	TAU	GEM	18.19	VIR	SCO	SAG	AQU	PIS	26
27	SAG	AQU	08.34	ARI	03.29	CAN	08.42	19.21	05.55		AQU	18.32	27
28	03.24	AQU	PIS	15.37	10.22	CAN	22.23	LIB	SAG	CAP	00.47	ARI	28
29	CAP	02.42	20.37	TAU	GEM	10.39	VIR	10.05	22.13	10.05	PIS	ARI	29
30	10.34		ARI	TAU	20.39	LEO	VIR	SCO	CAP	AQU	11.01	06.43	30
31	AQU		ARI		CAN		01.13	12.28		17.53		TAU	31

sun

mth	day	sign
JAN	1	CAP
JAN	20	AQU
FEB	18	PIS
MAR	20	ARI
APR	20	TAU
MAY	21	GEM
JUN	21	CAN
JUL	22	LEO
AUG	23	VIR
SEP	23	LIB
OCT	23	SCO
NOV	22	SAG
DEC	21	CAP

mercury

mth	day	sign
JAN	1	CAP
FEB	10	AQU
MAR	2	PIS
MAR	18	ARI
APR	3	TAU
JUN	10	GEM
JUN	26	CAN
JUL	10	LEO
JUL	28	VIR
OCT	4	LIB
OCT	21	SCO
NOV	9	SAG
DEC	1	CAP
DEC	21	SAG

venus

mth	day	sign
JAN	1	AQU
JAN	4	PIS
FEB	2	ARI
JUN	6	TAU
JUL	6	GEM
AUG	2	CAN
AUG	28	LEO
SEP	22	VIR
OCT	17	LIB
NOV	10	SCO
DEC	4	SAG
DEC	27	CAP

mars

mth	day	sign
JAN	1	CAP
FEB	9	AQU
MAR	20	PIS
APR	27	ARI
JUN	6	TAU
JUL	17	GEM
SEP	1	CAN
OCT	26	LEO

saturn

mth	day	sign
JAN	1	LEO
NOV	17	VIR

jupiter

mth	day	sign
JAN	1	TAU
APR	3	GEM
AUG	20	CAN
DEC	30	GEM

moon

DAY	JAN	FEB	MAR	APR	MAY	JUN	JUL	AUG	SEP	OCT	NOV	DEC	DAY
1	19.43	CAN	CAN	01.25	LIB	02.54	CAP	01.23	ARI	20.33	CAN	LEO	1
2	GEM	CAN	09.25	VIR	12.56	SAG	06.54	TAU	00.52	GEM	CAN	23.05	2
3	GEM	00.11	LEO	04.39	SCO	02.07	AQU	06.54	TAU	GEM	05.03	VIR	3
4	07.12	LEO	15.19	LIB	15.59	CAP	15.31	ARI	12.27	09.09	LEO	VIR	4
5	CAN	06.17	VIR	05.40	SAG	02.44	PIS	16.18	GEM	CAN	15.16	07.17	5
6	16.20	VIR	18.34	SCO	15.54	AQU	22.03	TAU	GEM	20.58	VIR	LIB	6
7	LEO	10.36	LIB	06.09	CAP	06.35	ARI	TAU	01.03	LEO	21.51	11.33	7
8	23.23	LIB	20.37	SAG	18.00	PIS	ARI	04.29	CAN	LEO	LIB	SCO	8
9	VIR	14.04	SCO	07.40	AQU	14.34	GEM	08.33	GEM	12.14	LIB	12.22	9
10	VIR	SCO	22.42	CAP	23.29	ARI	TAU	17.04	LEO	VIR	00.42	SAG	10
11	04.48	17.11	SAG	11.24	PIS	ARI	21.15	CAN	20.34	11.29	SCO	11.26	11
12	LIB	SAG	SAG	AQU	PIS	01.56	GEM	CAN	VIR	LIB	01.03	CAP	12
13	08.44	20.14	01.40	17.49	08.29	TAU	GEM	03.57	VIR	14.11	SAG	10.59	13
14	SCO	CAP	CAP	PIS	ARI	14.50	09.50	LEO	02.07	SCO	00.50	AQU	14
15	11.18	23.45	06.00	PIS	20.04	GEM	CAN	12.26	LIB	15.27	CAP	13.09	15
16	SAG	AQU	AQU	02.52	TAU	GEM	20.51	VIR	05.45	SAG	02.00	PIS	16
17	13.02	AQU	12.06	ARI	TAU	03.28	LEO	18.49	SCO	16.51	AQU	19.11	17
18	CAP	04.45	PIS	14.02	08.50	CAN	LEO	LIB	08.28	CAP	05.58	ARI	18
19	15.12	PIS	20.23	TAU	GEM	14.53	05.58	23.35	SAG	18.36	PIS	ARI	19
20	AQU	12.22	ARI	TAU	21.35	LEO	VIR	SCO	11.04	AQU	13.13	04.54	20
21	19.30	ARI	ARI	02.37	CAN	LEO	13.09	SCO	CAP	AQU	ARI	TAU	21
22	PISA	23.06	07.05	GEM	CAN	00.29	LIB	03.03	14.12	00.26	23.09	16.51	22
23	PIS	TAU	TAU	15.25	09.13	VIR	18.13	SAG	AQU	PIS	TAU	GEM	23
24	03.19	TAU	19.39	CAN	LEO	07.35	SCO	05.30	18.30	TAU	TAU	GEM	24
25	ARI	11.50	GEM	CAN	18.31	LIB	21.04	CAP	PIS	ARI	10.48	05.30	25
26	14.41	GEM	GEM	02.43	VIR	11.42	SAG	07.41	IS	16.53	GEM	CAN	26
27	TAU	GEM	08.16	LEO	VIR	SCO	22.15	AQU	00.40	TAU	23.20	17.52	27
28	TAU	00.02	CAN	10.52	00.28	13.02	CAP	10.46	ARI	TAU	CAN	LEO	28
29	03.37		18.40	VIR	LIB	SAG	23.04	PIS	09.21	CAN	CAN	LEO	29
30	GEM		LEO	15.13	02.56	12.48	AQU	16.11	TAU	GEM	11.53	05.13	30
31	15.20		LEO		SCO		AQU	ARI		16.40		VIR	31

sun

mth	day	sign
JAN	1	CAP
JAN	20	AQU
FEB	19	PIS
MAR	20	ARI
APR	20	TAU
MAY	21	GEM
JUN	21	CAN
JUL	23	LEO
AUG	23	VIR
SEP	23	LIB
OCT	23	SCO
NOV	22	SAG
DEC	22	CAP

mercury

mth	day	sign
JAN	1	SAG
JAN	13	CAP
FEB	4	AQU
FEB	22	PIS
MAR	10	ARI
MAY	16	TAU
JUN	3	GEM
JUN	17	CAN
JUL	2	LEO
JUL	27	VIR
AUG	13	LEO
SEP	9	VIR
SEP	26	LIB
OCT	14	SCO
NOV	3	SAG

venus

mth	day	sign
JAN	1	CAP
JAN	20	AQU
FEB	13	PIS
MAR	9	ARI
APR	2	TAU
APR	27	GEM
MAY	22	CAN
JUN	16	LEO
JUL	12	VIR
AUG	8	LIB
SEP	7	SCO

mars

mth	day	sign
JAN	1	LEO
JAN	26	CAN
APR	10	LEO
JUN	14	VIR
AUG	4	LIB
SEP	19	SCO
NOV	2	SAG
DEC	12	CAP

saturn

mth	day	sign
JAN	1	VIR
JAN	5	LEO
JUL	26	VIR

jupiter

mth	day	sign
JAN	1	GEM
APR	12	CAN
SEP	5	LEO

moon

DAY	JAN	FEB	MAR	APR	MAY	JUN	JUL	AUG	SEP	OCT	NOV	DEC	DAY
1	14.31	SCO	13.02	CAP	09.00	ARI	19.37	CAN	20.46	14.17	SCO	20.44	1
2	LIB	07.13	SAG	00.05	PIS	03.05	GEM	CAN	VIR	LIB	10.03	CAP	2
3	20.35	SAG	15.58	AQU	14.27	TAU	GEM	02.10	VIR	21.48	SAG	21.35	3
4	SCO	08.50	CAP	03.20	ARI	13.53	LEO	07.15	SCO	12.40		AQU	4
5	22.03	CAP	17.50	PIS	21.52	GEM	CAN	14.29	GEM	SCO	CAP	23.36	5
6	SAG	09.04	AQU	07.51	TAU	GEM	20.13	VIR	15.38	03.06	15.04	PIS	6
7	22.55	AQU	19.45	ARI	TAU	01.30	LEO	VIR	SCO	SAG	AQU	PIS	7
8	CAP	09.47	PIS	14.21	07.18	CAN	01.30	LIB	21.39	06.52	18.06	03.39	8
9	22.05	PIS	23.08	TAU	GEM	14.07	08.44	LIB	SAG	CAP	PIS	ARI	9
10	AQU	12.56	ARI	23.27	18.41	LEO	VIR	10.11	SAG	09.42	22.11	09.50	10
11	22.50	ARI	ARI	GEM	CAN	LEO	19.48	SCO	01.20	AQU	ARI	TAU	11
12	PIS	19.50	05.18	GEM	CAN	02.35	LIB	15.43	CAP	12.12	ARI	17.54	12
13	PIS	TAU	TAU	10.59	07.17	VIR	LIB	SAG	03.08	PIS	03.35	GEM	13
14	03.05	TAU	14.48	CAN	LEO	12.55	03.47	18.03	AQU	15.06	TAU	GEM	14
15	ARI	06.24	GEM	23.30	19.15	LIB	SCO	CAP	04.09	ARI	10.45	03.50	15
16	11.30	GEM	GEM	LEO	VIR	19.28	07.50	18.15	PIS	19.22	GEM	CAN	16
17	TAU	18.56	02.49	LEO	VIR	SCO	SAG	AQU	05.50	TAU	20.16	15.37	17
18	23.06	CAN	CAN	10.44	04.24	22.01	08.33	18.04	ARI	TAU	CAN	LEO	18
19	GEM	CAN	15.12	VIR	LIB	SAG	CAP	PIS	09.43	02.05	CAN	LEO	19
20	GEM	07.09	LEO	18.53	09.39	21.52	07.41	19.29	TAU	GEM	08.09	04.34	20
21	11.50	LEO	LEO	LIB	SCO	CAP	AQU	ARI	16.56	11.52	LEO	VIR	21
22	CAN	17.39	01.49	23.39	11.31	21.07	07.26	ARI	GEM	CAN	20.57	16.40	22
23	CAN	VIR	VIR	SCO	SAG	AQU	PIS	00.06	GEM	CAN	VIR	LIB	23
24	00.02	VIR	09.41	SCO	11.41	21.57	09.46	TAU	08.31	00.04	08.07	01.32	24
25	LEO	02.03	LIB	02.00	CAP	PIS	ARI	08.31	CAN	LEO	LIB	SCO	25
26	10.56	LIB	15.01	SAG	12.10	PIS	15.50	GEM	16.01	12.32	LIB	SCO	26
27	VIR	08.28	SCO	03.27	AQU	01.53	TAU	19.59	LEO	VIR	15.38	06.07	27
28	20.08	SCO	18.37	CAP	14.37	ARI	TAU	CAN	LEO	22.51	SCO	SAG	28
29	LIB		SAG	05.28	PIS	09.21	01.31	CAN	04.11	LIB	19.23	07.15	29
30	LIB		21.23	AQU	19.52	TAU	GEM	08.40	VIR	LIB	SAG	CAP	30
31	03.03		CAP		ARI		13.28	LEO		05.52		06.53	31

sun

mth	day	sign
JAN	1	CAP
JAN	20	AQU
FEB	19	PIS
MAR	21	ARI
APR	20	TAU
MAY	21	GEM
JUN	21	CAN
JUL	23	LEO
AUG	23	VIR
SEP	23	LIB
OCT	24	SCO
NOV	22	SAG
DEC	22	CAP

mercury

mth	day	sign
JAN	1	SAG
JAN	8	CAP
JAN	28	AQU
FEB	14	PIS
MAR	3	ARI
MAR	28	PIS
APR	17	ARI
MAY	10	TAU
MAY	26	GEM
JUN	9	CAN
JUN	27	LEO
SEP	2	VIR
SEP	18	LIB
OCT	7	SCO
OCT	30	SAG
NOV	18	SCO
DEC	12	SAG

venus

mth	day	sign
JAN	1	SCO
JAN	7	SAG
FEB	5	CAP
MAR	3	AQU
MAR	29	PIS
APR	23	ARI
MAY	18	TAU
JUN	11	GEM
JUL	6	CAN
JUL	30	LEO
AUG	24	VIR
SEP	17	LIB
OCT	11	SCO
NOV	4	SAG
NOV	28	CAP
DEC	22	AQU

mars

mth	day	sign
JAN	1	CAP
JAN	20	AQU
FEB	27	PIS
APR	7	ARI
MAY	16	TAU
JUN	26	GEM
AUG	8	CAN
SEP	24	LEO
NOV	19	VIR

saturn

mth	day	sign
JAN	1	VIR

jupiter

mth	day	sign
JAN	1	LEO
FEB	28	CAN
APR	20	LEO
SEP	29	VIR

moon

DAY	JAN	FEB	MAR	APR	MAY	JUN	JUL	AUG	SEP	OCT	NOV	DEC	DAY
1	AQU	ARI	ARI	GEM	CAN	22.41	19.08	SCO	11.33	AQU	10.09	TAU	1
2	07.08	22.03	07.09	GEM	CAN	LIB	22.05	CAP	AQU	ARI	23.02	GEM	2
3	PIS	TAU	TAU	06.24	01.56	VIR	LIB	SAG	13.59	00.23	11.16	GEM	3
4	09.41	TAU	12.58	CAN	LEO	11.12	05.57	SAG	AQU	PIS	TAU	GEM	4
5	ARI	05.33	GEM	17.58	14.41	LIB	SCO	02.23	14.03	00.28	13.26	04.01	5
6	15.17	GEM	22.34	LEO	VIR	21.05	12.55	CAP	PIS	ARI	GEM	CAN	6
7	TAU	16.06	CAN	LEO	VIR	SCO	SAG	03.28	13.29	00.45	18.24	12.09	7
8	23.42	CAN	CAN	06.52	02.47	SCO	16.07	AQU	ARI	TAU	CAN	LEO	8
9	GEM	CAN	10.47	VIR	LIB	03.14	CAP	03.05	14.12	03.07	23.33	9	
10	GEM	04.25	LEO	18.45	12.10	SAG	16.59	PIS	TAU	GEM	03.14	VIR	10
11	10.14	LEO	23.42	LIB	SCO	06.23	AQU	03.10	17.54	09.09	LEO	VIR	11
12	CAN	17.18	VIR	LIB	CAP	17.23	ARI	GEM	CAN	15.20	12.29	12	
13	22.16	VIR	VIR	04.16	SAG	08.06	PIS	05.21	GEM	19.12	VIR	LIB	13
14	LEO	VIR	11.41	SCO	22.25	AQU	18.57	TAU	01.27	LEO	VIR	LIB	14
15	LEO	05.37	LIB	11.18	CAP	09.56	ARI	10.41	CAN	LEO	04.16	00.08	15
16	11.10	LIB	21.49	SAG	CAP	PIS	22.43	GEM	12.25	07.51	LIB	SCO	16
17	VIR	16.12	SCO	16.23	01.26	12.52	TAU	19.17	LEO	VIR	15.29	08.36	17
18	23.40	SCO	SCO	CAP	AQU	ARI	TAU	CAN	LEO	20.44	SCO	SAG	18
19	LIB	23.51	05.38	22.02	04.18	17.18	04.59	CAN	01.15	LIB	23.56	13.54	19
20	LIB	SAG	SAG	AQU	PIS	TAU	GEM	06.28	VIR	LIB	SAG	CAP	20
21	09.51	SAG	10.56	22.41	07.30	23.23	13.40	LEO	14.11	08.02	SAG	17.13	21
22	SCO	04.00	CAP	PIS	ARI	GEM	CAN	19.11	LIB	SCO	06.01	AQU	22
23	16.08	CAP	13.52	PIS	11.20	GEM	CAN	VIR	LIB	17.09	CAP	19.50	23
24	SAG	05.12	AQU	00.51	TAU	07.24	00.30	VIR	01.54	SAG	10.37	PIS	24
25	18.27	AQU	15.04	ARI	16.28	CAN	LEO	08.13	SCO	SAG	AQU	22.40	25
26	CAP	04.52	PIS	03.27	GEM	17.47	13.01	LIB	11.36	00.11	14.17	ARI	26
27	18.12	PIS	15.47	TAU	23.51	LEO	VIR	20.12	SAG	CAP	PIS	ARI	27
28	AQU	04.54	ARI	07.49	CAN	VIR	VIR	SCO	18.40	05.16	17.17	02.08	28
29	17.25		17.36	GEM	CAN	06.14	02.06	SCO	CAP	AQU	ARI	TAU	29
30	PIS		TAU	15.11	10.08	VIR	LIB	05.39	22.49	08.29	19.54	06.32	30
31	18.11		22.08		LEO		13.46	SAG		PIS		GEM	31

345

1980

sun

mth	day	sign
JAN	1	CAP
JAN	20	AQU
FEB	19	PIS
MAR	20	ARI
APR	19	TAU
MAY	20	GEM
JUN	21	CAN
JUL	22	LEO
AUG	22	VIR
SEP	22	LIB
OCT	23	SCO
NOV	22	SAG
DEC	21	CAP

mercury

mth	day	sign
JAN	1	SAG
JAN	2	CAP
JAN	21	AQU
FEB	7	PIS
APR	14	ARI
MAY	2	TAU
MAY	16	GEM
MAY	31	CAN
AUG	9	LEO
AUG	24	VIR
SEP	10	LIB
SEP	30	SCO
DEC	5	SAG
DEC	25	CAP

venus

mth	day	sign
JAN	1	AQU
JAN	16	PIS
FEB	9	ARI
MAR	6	TAU
APR	3	GEM
MAY	12	CAN
JUN	5	GEM
AUG	6	CAN
SEP	7	LEO
OCT	4	VIR
OCT	30	LIB
NOV	24	SCO
DEC	18	SAG

mars

mth	day	sign
JAN	1	VIR
MAR	11	LEO
MAY	4	VIR
JUL	10	LIB
AUG	29	SCO
OCT	12	SAG
NOV	22	CAP
DEC	30	AQU

saturn

mth	day	sign
JAN	1	VIR
SEP	21	LIB

jupiter

mth	day	sign
JAN	1	VIR
OCT	27	LIB

moon

DAY	JAN	FEB	MAR	APR	MAY	JUN	JUL	AUG	SEP	OCT	NOV	DEC	DAY
1	12.29	LEO	VIR	LIB	22.22	CAP	AQU	ARI	01.50	CAN	12.18	07.13	1
2	CAN	15.21	VIR	05.21	SAG	19.29	05.48	16.55	GEM	19.57	VIR	LIB	2
3	20.47	VIR	10.40	SCO	SAG	AQU	PIS	TAU	06.39	LEO	VIR	20.00	3
4	LEO	VIR	LIB	16.35	07.14	AQU	08.46	20.10	CAN	LEO	00.31	SCO	4
5	LEO	04.04	23.22	SAG	CAP	00.10	ARI	GEM	14.22	06.19	LIB	SCO	5
6	07.48	LIB	SCO	SAG	14.03	PIS	11.30	GEM	LEO	VIR	13.19	07.57	6
7	VIR	16.46	SCO	01.43	AQU	03.23	TAU	01.12	LEO	18.30	SCO	SAG	7
8	20.38	SCO	10.38	CAP	18.33	ARI	14.33	CAN	00.31	LIB	SCO	18.12	8
9	LIB	SCO	SAG	08.00	PIS	05.29	GEM	08.23	VIR	LIB	01.25	CAP	9
10	LIB	03.19	19.02	AQU	20.44	TAU	18.33	LEO	12.22	07.15	SAG	CAP	10
11	08.55	SAG	CAP	11.07	ARI	07.22	CAN	17.54	LIB	SCO	12.15	02.36	11
12	SCO	10.12	23.45	PIS	21.24	GEM	CAN	VIR	LIB	19.37	CAP	AQU	12
13	18.17	CAP	AQU	11.40	TAU	10.29	01.03	VIR	01.06	SAG	21.10	09.03	13
14	SAG	13.19	AQU	ARI	22.07	CAN	LEO	05.32	SCO	SAG	AQU	PIS	14
15	23.51	AQU	01.10	11.11	GEM	16.22	10.11	LIB	13.28	06.37	AQU	13.21	15
16	CAP	13.54	PIS	TAU	GEM	LEO	VIR	18.15	SAG	CAP	03.21	ARI	16
17	CAP	PIS	00.41	11.41	00.52	LEO	21.55	SCO	23.45	14.53	PIS	15.36	17
18	02.25	13.43	ARI	GEM	CAN	01.47	LIB	SCO	CAP	AQU	06.21	TAU	18
19	AQU	ARI	00.13	15.11	07.14	VIR	LIB	06.07	CAP	19.31	ARI	16.39	19
20	03.33	14.35	TAU	CAN	LEO	13.55	10.33	SAG	06.30	PIS	06.51	GEM	20
21	PIS	TAU	01.47	22.52	17.32	LIB	SCO	15.11	AQU	20.43	TAU	18.03	21
22	04.52	17.58	GEM	LEO	VIR	LIB	21.42	CAP	09.27	ARI	06.27	CAN	22
23	ARI	GEM	06.55	LEO	VIR	02.26	SAG	20.32	PIS	19.55	GEM	21.34	23
24	07.31	GEM	CAN	10.12	06.11	SCO	SAG	AQU	09.37	TAU	07.18	LEO	24
25	TAU	00.34	15.58	VIR	LIB	13.02	05.45	22.43	ARI	19.17	CAN	LEO	25
26	12.11	CAN	LEO	23.09	18.37	SAG	CAP	PIS	08.53	GEM	11.23	04.32	26
27	GEM	10.10	LEO	LIB	SCO	20.46	10.34	23.11	TAU	21.00	LEO	VIR	27
28	19.02	LEO	03.52	LIB	SCO	CAP	AQU	ARI	09.21	CAN	19.37	15.05	28
29	CAN	21.53	VIR	11.35	05.05	CAP	13.11	23.41	GEM	CAN	VIR	LIB	29
30	CAN		16.49	SCO	SAG	02.04	PIS	TAU	12.46	02.38	VIR	LIB	30
31	04.08		LIB		13.14		14.53	TAU		LEO		03.36	31

sun

mth	day	sign
JAN	1	CAP
JAN	20	AQU
FEB	18	PIS
MAR	20	ARI
APR	20	TAU
MAY	21	GEM
JUN	21	CAN
JUL	22	LEO
AUG	23	VIR
SEP	23	LIB
OCT	23	SCO
NOV	22	SAG
DEC	21	CAP

mercury

mth	day	sign
JAN	1	CAP
JAN	12	AQU
JAN	31	PIS
FEB	16	AQU
MAR	18	PIS
APR	8	ARI
APR	24	TAU
MAY	8	GEM
MAY	28	CAN
JUN	22	GEM
JUL	12	CAN
AUG	1	LEO
AUG	16	VIR
SEP	2	LIB
SEP	27	SCO
OCT	14	LIB
NOV	9	SCO
NOV	28	SAG
DEC	17	CAP

venus

mth	day	sign
JAN	1	SAG
JAN	11	CAP
FEB	4	AQU
FEB	28	PIS
MAR	24	ARI
APR	17	TAU
MAY	11	GEM
JUN	5	CAN
JUN	29	LEO
JUL	24	VIR
AUG	18	LIB
SEP	12	SCO
OCT	9	SAG
NOV	5	CAP
DEC	8	AQU

mars

mth	day	sign
JAN	1	AQU
FEB	6	PIS
MAR	17	ARI
APR	25	TAU
JUN	5	GEM
JUL	18	CAN
SEP	2	LEO
OCT	21	VIR
DEC	16	LIB

saturn

mth	day	sign
JAN	1	LIB

jupiter

mth	day	sign
JAN	1	LIB
NOV	27	SCO

moon

DAY	JAN	FEB	MAR	APR	MAY	JUN	JUL	AUG	SEP	OCT	NOV	DEC	DAY
1	SCO	10.37	CAP	18.41	06.57	16.48	02.57	18.54	LIB	SCO	12.46	07.09	1
2	15.42	CAP	CAP	PIS	ARI	GEM	CAN	VIR	21.10	16.59	CAP	AQU	2
3	SAG	17.55	03.51	20.25	06.59	16.38	04.47	VIR	SCO	SAG	CAP	17.16	3
4	SAG	AQU	AQU	ARI	TAU	CAN	LEO	02.24	SCO	SAG	00.51	PIS	4
5	01.41	22.21	08.12	20.04	06.01	18.43	09.26	LIB	09.24	05.49	AQU	23.49	5
6	CAP	PIS	PIS	TAU	GEM	LEO	VIR	12.58	SAG	CAP	09.52	ARI	6
7	09.12	PIS	09.48	19.47	06.18	LEO	17.42	SCO	21.48	17.01	PIS	ARI	7
8	AQU	01.01	ARI	GEM	CAN	00.25	LIB	SCO	CAP	AQU	14.38	02.31	8
9	14.42	ARI	10.22	21.34	09.40	VIR		01.22	CAP	AQU	ARI	TAU	9
10	PIS	03.11	TAU	CAN	LEO	09.55	05.02	SAG	07.58	00.32	15.44	02.30	10
11	18.43	TAU	11.42	CAN	16.55	LIB	SCO	13.20	AQU	PIS	TAU	GEM	11
12	ARI	05.51	GEM	02.36	VIR	21.54	17.35	CAP	14.34	04.01	14.59	01.40	12
13	21.45	GEM	15.06	LEO	VIR	SCO	SAG	22.56	PIS	ARI	GEM	CAN	13
14	TAU	09.43	CAN	10.56	03.24	SCO	SAG	05.19	ARI	04.43	14.37	02.08	14
15	TAU	CAN	21.02	VIR	LIB	10.31	05.19	AQU	ARI	TAU	CAN	LEO	15
16	00.17	15.10	LEO	21.38	15.37	SAG	CAP	05.34	19.30	04.41	16.33	05.38	16
17	GEM	LEO	LEO	LIB	SCO	22.21	15.02	PIS	TAU	GEM	LEO	VIR	17
18	03.08	22.34	05.20	LIB	SCO	CAP	AQU	09.49	20.59	05.52	21.53	12.58	18
19	CAN	VIR	VIR	09.39	04.14	CAP	22.26	ARI	GEM	CAN	VIR	LIB	19
20	07.21	VIR	15.31	SCO	SAG	08.36	PIS	12.43	23.39	09.34	VIR	23.39	20
21	LEO	08.12	LIB	22.50	16.20	AQU	PIS	TAU	CAN	LEO	06.33	SCO	21
22	14.02	LIB	LIB	SAG	CAP	16.44	03.43	15.18	CAN	16.05	LIB	SCO	22
23	VIR	19.54	03.14	SAG	CAP	PIS	ARI	GEM	04.08	VIR	17.36	12.11	23
24	23.45	SCO	10.31	03.00	22.18	07.18	18.17		LEO	VIR	SCO	SAG	24
25	LIB	SCO	15.51	CAP	AQU	ARI	TAU	CAN	10.29	00.56	SCO	SAG	25
26	LIB	08.29	SAG	20.57	11.05	ARI	09.42	22.10	VIR	LIB	06.00	00.59	26
27	11.49	SAG	SAG	AQU	PIS	01.16	GEM	LEO	18.40	11.38	SAG	CAP	27
28	SCO	19.46	03.52	AQU	15.44	TAU	11.41	LEO	LIB	SCO	18.53	12.53	28
29	SCO		03.56	ARI	02.21	CAN	03.31	LIB	23.48	CAP	AQU	29	
30	00.11		13.15	PIS	17.10	GEM	14.20	VIR	04.53	SAG	CAP	23.01	30
31	SAG		AQU		TAU		LEO	11.02		SAG		PIS	31

sun

mth	day	sign
JAN	1	CAP
JAN	20	AQU
FEB	18	PIS
MAR	20	ARI
APR	20	TAU
MAY	21	GEM
JUN	21	CAN
JUL	23	LEO
AUG	23	VIR
SEP	23	LIB
OCT	23	SCO
NOV	22	SAG
DEC	22	CAP

mercury

mth	day	sign
JAN	1	CAP
JAN	5	AQU
MAR	13	PIS
MAR	31	ARI
APR	15	TAU
MAY	1	GEM
JUL	9	CAN
JUL	24	LEO
AUG	8	VIR
AUG	28	LIB
NOV	3	SCO
NOV	21	SAG
DEC	10	CAP

venus

mth	day	sign
JAN	1	AQU
JAN	23	CAP
MAR	2	AQU
APR	6	PIS
MAY	4	ARI
MAY	30	TAU
JUN	25	GEM
JUL	20	CAN
AUG	14	LEO
SEP	7	VIR
OCT	2	LIB
OCT	26	SCO
NOV	18	SAG
DEC	12	CAP

mars

mth	day	sign
JAN	1	LIB
AUG	3	SCO
SEP	20	SAG
OCT	31	CAP
DEC	10	AQU

saturn

mth	day	sign
JAN	1	LIB
NOV	29	SCO

jupiter

mth	day	sign
JAN	1	SCO
DEC	26	SAG

moon

DAY	JAN	FEB	MAR	APR	MAY	JUN	JUL	AUG	SEP	OCT	NOV	DEC	DAY
1	PIS	TAU	TAU	CAN	23.45	LIB	SCO	09.36	AQU	PIS	TAU	GEM	1
2	06.33	20.20	01.50	13.36	VIR	21.12	14.25	CAP	16.11	08.06	TAU	10.58	2
3	ARI	GEM	GEM	LEO	VIR	SCO	SAG	22.17	PIS	ARI	00.23	CAN	3
4	11.02	22.28	04.48	18.18	06.32	SCO	SAG	AQU	PIS	13.09	GEM	11.26	4
5	TAU	CAN	CAN	VIR	LIB	08.31	03.15	AQU	00.24	TAU	01.59	LEO	5
6	12.48	23.50	07.50	VIR	15.24	SAG	CAP	09.23	ARI	16.39	CAN	13.32	6
7	GEM	LEO	LEO	00.26	SCO	21.12	16.03	PIS	06.27	GEM	04.10	VIR	7
8	13.01	LEO	11.27	LIB	SCO	CAP	AQU	18.21	TAU	19.39	LEO	18.11	8
9	CAN	02.15	VIR	08.33	02.17	CAP	AQU	ARI	10.57	CAN	07.40	LIB	9
10	13.21	VIR	16.34	SCO	SAG	10.08	03.35	ARI	GEM	22.44	VIR	LIB	10
11	LEO	07.02	LIB	19.07	14.50	AQU	PIS	01.00	14.18	LEO	12.46	01.34	11
12	15.37	LIB	LIB	SAG	CAP	21.44	12.49	TAU	CAN	LEO	LIB	SCO	12
13	VIR	15.16	00.17	SAG	CAP	PIS	ARI	05.22	16.46	02.09	19.42	11.27	13
14	21.17	SCO	SCO	07.41	03.44	PIS	19.00	GEM	LEO	VIR	SCO	SAG	14
15	LIB	SCO	11.03	CAP	AQU	06.20	07.40	18.57	06.23	SCO		23.15	15
16	LIB	02.45	SAG	20.18	14.46	ARI	22.03	CAN	VIR	LIB	04.52	CAP	16
17	06.46	SAG	23.47	AQU	PIS	11.07	GEM	08.40	22.02	12.21	SAG	CAP	17
18	SCO	15.36	CAP	AQU	22.04	TAU	22.46	LEO	LIB	SCO	16.21	12.12	18
19	19.00	CAP	CAP	06.19	ARI	12.34	CAN	09.40	LIB	21.02	CAP	AQU	19
20	SAG	CAP	11.53	PIS	ARI	GEM	22.35	VIR	03.32	SAG	CAP	AQU	20
21	SAG	03.15	AQU	12.23	01.22	12.13	LEO	12.22	SCO	SAG	05.20	00.56	21
22	07.51	AQU	21.01	ARI	TAU	CAN	23.20	LIB	12.30	08.38	AQU	PIS	22
23	CAP	12.09	PIS	14.59	01.54	11.57	VIR	18.21	SAG	CAP	17.43	11.34	23
24	19.25	PIS	PIS	TAU	GEM	LEO	VIR	SCO	SAG	21.36	PIS	ARI	24
25	AQU	ARI	02.37	15.48	01.38	13.36	02.45	SCO	00.31	AQU	PIS	18.37	25
26	AQU	ARI	ARI	GEM	CAN	VIR	LIB	04.11	CAP	AQU	03.07	TAU	26
27	04.49	22.32	05.39	16.43	02.27	18.30	09.58	SAG	13.21	09.12	ARI	21.49	27
28	PIS	TAU	TAU	CAN	LEO	LIB	SCO	16.42	AQU	PIS	08.31	GEM	28
29	11.58		07.44	19.09	05.43	LIB	20.48	CAP	AQU	17.25	TAU	22.12	29
30	ARI		GEM	LEO	VIR	03.02	SAG	CAP	00.18	ARI	10.36	CAN	30
31	17.03		10.09		12.02		SAG	05.23		22.04		21.33	31

sun

mth	day	sign
JAN	1	CAP
JAN	20	AQU
FEB	19	PIS
MAR	21	ARI
APR	20	TAU
MAY	21	GEM
JUN	21	CAN
JUL	23	LEO
AUG	23	VIR
SEP	23	LIB
OCT	23	SCO
NOV	22	SAG
DEC	22	CAP

mercury

mth	day	sign
JAN	1	AQU
JAN	12	CAP
FEB	14	AQU
MAR	7	PIS
MAR	23	ARI
APR	7	TAU
JUN	14	GEM
JUL	1	CAN
JUL	15	LEO
AUG	1	VIR
AUG	29	LIB
SEP	6	VIR
OCT	8	LIB
OCT	26	SCO
NOV	14	SAG
DEC	4	CAP

venus

mth	day	sign
JAN	1	CAP
JAN	5	AQU
JAN	29	PIS
FEB	22	ARI
MAR	19	TAU
APR	13	GEM
MAY	9	CAN
JUN	6	LEO
JUL	10	VIR
AUG	27	LEO
OCT	5	VIR
NOV	9	LIB
DEC	6	SCO

mars

mth	day	sign
JAN	1	AQU
JAN	17	PIS
FEB	25	ARI
APR	5	TAU
MAY	16	GEM
JUN	29	CAN
AUG	13	LEO
SEP	30	VIR
NOV	18	LIB

saturn

mth	day	sign
JAN	1	SCO
MAY	6	LIB
AUG	24	SCO

jupiter

mth	day	sign
JAN	1	SAG

moon

DAY	JAN	FEB	MAR	APR	MAY	JUN	JUL	AUG	SEP	OCT	NOV	DEC	DAY
1	LEO	09.47	LIB	16.20	11.01	AQU	PIS		GEM	12.54	23.31	09.41	1
2	21.49	LIB	23.51	SAG	CAP	19.42	14.47	TAU	02.53	LEO	LIB	SCO	2
3	VIR	14.32	SCO	SAG	23.09	PIS	ARI	14.43	CAN	14.15	LIB	14.56	3
4	VIR	SCO	SCO	02.30	AQU	PIS	ARI	GEM	04.47	VIR	01.53	SAG	4
5	00.44	23.28	07.15	CAP	AQU	06.59	00.05	18.09	LEO	14.42	SCO	22.28	5
6	LIB	SAG	SAG	15.06	11.44	ARI	TAU	CAN	04.36	LIB	06.09	CAP	6
7	07.16	SAG	18.29	AQU	PIS	15.05	05.41	18.37	VIR	16.06	SAG	CAP	7
8	SCO	11.33	CAP	AQU	22.16	TAU	07.50	17.49	LIB	04.13	SCO	13.31	8
9	17.14	CAP	CAP	03.30	ARI	19.37	CAN	VIR	LIB	20.21	CAP	AQU	9
10	SAG	CAP	07.30	PIS	ARI	GEM	CAN	VIR	05.49	SAG	CAP	20.53	10
11	SAG	00.40	AQU	13.37	05.36	21.32	07.54	17.51	SCO	SAG	00.10	PIS	11
12	05.26	AQU	19.47	ARI	TAU	CAN	LEO	LIB	11.08	04.30	AQU	PIS	12
13	CAP	13.02	PIS	20.59	10.03	22.21	07.43	20.44	SAG	CAP	12.41	09.17	13
14	18.26	PIS	PIS	TAU	GEM	LEO	VIR	SCO	20.34	16.00	PIS	ARI	14
15	AQU	23.46	06.00	TAU	12.48	23.38	09.10	SCO	CAP	AQU	PIS	19.33	15
16	AQU	ARI	ARI	02.15	CAN	VIR	LIB	03.33	CAP	AQU	00.36	TAU	16
17	07.02	ARI	14.04	GEM	15.01	VIR	13.38	SAG	08.45	04.41	ARI	TAU	17
18	PIS	08.30	TAU	06.14	LEO	02.36	SCO	13.59	AQU	PIS	10.06	02.23	18
19	18.08	TAU	20.20	CAN	17.37	LIB	21.31	CAP	21.30	16.18	TAU	GEM	19
20	ARI	14.52	GEM	09.26	VIR	07.59	SAG	CAP	PIS	ARI	16.45	06.02	20
21	ARI	GEM	GEM	LEO	21.11	SCO	SAG	02.25	PIS	ARI	GEM	CAN	21
22	02.36	18.31	00.52	12.12	LIB	15.55	08.11	AQU	09.10	01.47	21.10	07.44	22
23	TAU	CAN	CAN	VIR	LIB	SAG	CAP	15.10	ARI	TAU	CAN	LEO	23
24	07.40	19.46	03.43	14.04	02.17	SAG	20.26	PIS	19.12	CAN	09.01	VIR	24
25	GEM	LEO	LEO	LIB	SCO	02.08	AQU	PIS	TAU	GEM	00.19	VIR	25
26	09.28	19.49	05.18	19.04	09.27	CAP	AQU	03.08	TAU	14.47	LEO	11.18	26
27	CAN	VIR	VIR	SCO	SAG	14.07	09.11	ARI	03.24	CAN	03.02	LIB	27
28	09.10	20.30	06.48	SCO	19.07	AQU	PIS	13.38	GEM	18.50	VIR	15.27	28
29	LEO		LIB	01.28	CAP	AQU	21.21	TAU	09.24	LEO	05.57	SCO	29
30	08.35		09.57	SAG	CAP	02.52	ARI	21.49	CAN	21.33	LIB	21.44	30
31	VIR		SCO		07.00		ARI	GEM		VIR		SAG	31

1984

sun

mth	day	sign
JAN	1	CAP
JAN	20	AQU
FEB	19	PIS
MAR	20	ARI
APR	19	TAU
MAY	20	GEM
JUN	21	CAN
JUL	22	LEO
AUG	22	VIR
SEP	22	LIB
OCT	23	SCO
NOV	22	SAG
DEC	21	CAP

mercury

mth	day	sign
JAN	1	CAP
FEB	9	AQU
FEB	27	PIS
MAR	14	ARI
MAR	31	TAU
APR	25	ARI
MAY	15	TAU
JUN	7	GEM
JUN	22	CAN
JUL	6	LEO
JUL	26	VIR
SEP	30	LIB
OCT	18	SCO
NOV	6	SAG
DEC	1	CAP
DEC	7	SAG

venus

mth	day	sign
JAN	1	SAG
JAN	25	CAP
FEB	19	AQU
MAR	14	PIS
APR	7	ARI
MAY	2	TAU
MAY	26	GEM
JUN	20	CAN
JUL	14	LEO
AUG	7	VIR
SEP	1	LIB
SEP	25	SCO
OCT	20	SAG
NOV	13	CAP
DEC	9	AQU

mars

mth	day	sign
JAN	1	LIB
JAN	11	SCO
AUG	17	SAG
OCT	5	CAP
NOV	15	AQU
DEC	25	PIS

saturn

mth	day	sign
JAN	1	SCO

jupiter

mth	day	sign
JAN	1	SAG
JAN	19	CAP

moon

DAY	JAN	FEB	MAR	APR	MAY	JUN	JUL	AUG	SEP	OCT	NOV	DEC	DAY
1	SAG	AQU	17.29	ARI	TAU	05.53	LEO	04.03	16.30	05.28	AQU	PIS	1
2	06.07	AQU	PIS	23.55	16.02	CAN	19.28	LIB	SAG	CAP	07.50	03.42	2
3	CAP	11.22	PIS	TAU	GEM	10.19	VIR	06.04	22.55	14.03	PIS	ARI	3
4	16.31	PIS	06.07	TAU	23.26	LEO	21.27	SCO	CAP	AQU	20.20	16.20	4
5	AQU	PIS	ARI	10.04	CAN	13.27	LIB	10.30	CAP	AQU	ARI	TAU	5
6	AQU	00.04	18.09	GEM	CAN	VIR	LIB	SAG	08.11	01.19	ARI	TAU	6
7	04.34	ARI	TAU	17.59	04.43	16.03	00.28	17.24	AQU	PIS	08.53	03.24	7
8	PIS	1205	TAU	CAN	LEO	LIB	SCO	CAP	19.26	13.51	TAU	GEM	8
9	17.15	TAU	04.30	23.01	08.02	18.48	05.03	CAP	PIS	ARI	20.10	11.56	9
10	ARI	21.39	GEM	LEO	VIR	SCO	SAG	02.25	PIS	ARI	GEM	CAN	10
11	ARI	GEM	11.48	LEO	09.54	22.26	11.23	AQU	07.47	02.28	GEM	18.08	11
12	04.36	GEM	CAN	01.11	LIB	SAG	CAP	13.13	ARI	TAU	05.31	LEO	12
13	TAU	03.20	15.21	VIR	11.22	SAG	19.41	PIS	20.33	14.14	CAN	22.35	13
14	12.40	CAN	LEO	01.29	SCO	03.48	AQU	PIS	TAU	GEM	12.34	VIR	14
15	GEM	05.09	15.47	LIB	13.50	CAP	AQU	01.28	TAU	GEM	LEO	VIR	15
16	16.47	LEO	VIR	01.41	SAG	11.41	06.10	ARI	08.26	00.00	17.08	01.52	16
17	CAN	04.32	14.51	SCO	18.43	AQU	PIS	14.13	GEM	CAN	VIR	LIB	17
18	17.49	VIR	LIB	03.44	CAP	22.18	18.26	TAU	17.36	06.41	19.29	04.27	18
19	LEO	03.39	14.49	SAG	CAP	PIS	ARI	TAU	CAN	LEO	LIB	SCO	19
20	17.35	LIB	SCO	09.10	02.55	PIS	ARI	01.31	22.49	09.56	20.30	06.58	20
21	VIR	04.44	17.41	CAP	AQU	10.40	06.52	GEM	LEO	VIR	SCO	SAG	21
22	18.07	SCO	SAG	18.27	14.09	ARI	TAU	09.20	LEO	10.31	21.34	10.21	22
23	LIB	09.22	SAG	AQU	PIS	22.38	17.10	CAN	00.19>VIR	LIB	SAG	CAP	23
24	21.04	SAG	00.36	AQU	PIS	TAU	GEM	13.00	23.41	10.08	SAG	15.47	24
25	SCO	17.49	CAP	06.26	02.39	TAU	23.44	LEO	LIB	SCO	00.17	AQU	25
26	SCO	CAP	11.09	PIS	ARI	08.04	CAN	13.32	23.04	10.43	CAP	AQU	26
27	03.12	CAP	AQU	19.02	14.13	GEM	CAN	VIR	SCO	SAG	06.06	00.18	27
28	SAG	05.02	23.37	ARI	TAU	14.09	02.41	12.57	SCO	14.05	AQU	PIS	28
29	12.12	AQU	PIS	ARI	23.23	CAN	LEO	LIB	00.32	CAP	15.33	11.49	29
30	CAP		PIS	06.30	GEM	17.30	03.29	13.23	SAG	21.13	PIS	ARI	30
31	23.11		12.14		GEM		VIR	SCO		AQU		ARI	31

350

1985

sun

mth	day	sign
JAN	1	CAP
JAN	20	AQU
FEB	18	PIS
MAR	20	ARI
APR	20	TAU
MAY	21	GEM
JUN	21	CAN
JUL	22	LEO
AUG	23	VIR
SEP	23	LIB
OCT	23	SCO
NOV	22	SAG
DEC	21	CAP

mercury

mth	day	sign
JAN	1	SAG
JAN	11	CAP
FEB	1	AQU
FEB	18	PIS
MAR	7	ARI
MAY	14	TAU
MAY	30	GEM
JUN	13	CAN
JUN	29	LEO
SEP	6	VIR
SEP	22	LIB
OCT	10	SCO
OCT	31	SAG
DEC	4	SCO
DEC	12	SAG

venus

mth	day	sign
JAN	1	AQU
JAN	4	PIS
FEB	2	ARI
JUN	6	TAU
JUL	6	GEM
AUG	2	CAN
AUG	28	LEO
SEP	22	VIR
OCT	16	LIB
NOV	9	SCO
DEC	3	SAG
DEC	27	CAP

mars

mth	day	sign
JAN	1	PIS
FEB	2	ARI
MAR	15	TAU
APR	26	GEM
JUN	9	CAN
JUL	25	LEO
SEP	10	VIR
OCT	27	LIB
DEC	14	SCO

saturn

mth	day	sign
JAN	1	SCO
NOV	17	SAG

jupiter

mth	day	sign
JAN	1	CAP
FEB	6	AQU

moon

DAY	JAN	FEB	MAR	APR	MAY	JUN	JUL	AUG	SEP	OCT	NOV	DEC	DAY
1	00.36	GEM	15.23	LEO	21.21	SCO	18.22	AQU	05.42	00.35	GEM	CAN	1
2	TAU	05.59	CAN	10.25	LIB	07.33	CAP	12.33	ARI	TAU	08.31	00.59	2
3	12.00	CAN	21.28	VIR	21.17	SAG	21.36	PIS	17.28	13.36	CAN	LEO	3
4	GEM	11.02	LEO	10.54	SCO	08.34	AQU	21.43	TAU	GEM	19.04	09.14	4
5	20.18	LEO	23.43	LIB	20.56	CAP	AQU	ARI	TAU	GEM	LEO	VIR	5
6	CAN	13.09	VIR	10.10	SAG	11.52	03.40	ARI	06.27	01.59	LEO	14.33	6
7	CAN	VIR	23.47	SCO	22.11	AQU	PIS	09.41	GEM	CAN	02.18	LIB	7
8	01.28	14.10	LIB	10.18	CAP	PIS	18.47	13.21	18.10	11.33	VIR	16.56	8
9	LEO	LIB	23.47	SAG	CAP	PIS	ARI	22.31	CAN	LEO	05.52	SCO	9
10	04.40	15.49	SCO	12.57	02.38	PIS	ARI	GEM	CAN	17.09	LIB	17.13	10
11	VIR	SCO	SCO	CAP	AQU	05.24	01.44	GEM	02.27	VIR	06.31	SAG	11
12	07.13	19.09	01.29	19.04	10.56	ARI	TAU	09.28	LEO	19.12	SCO	16.59	12
13	LIB	SAG	SAG	AQU	PIS	18.11	14.23	CAN	06.52	LIB	05.52	CAP	13
14	10.07	SAG	05.55	22.25	TAU	GEM	16.57	VIR	19.13	SCO	18.15	AQU	14
15	SCO	00.27	CAP	04.30	ARI	TAU	GEM	LEO	08.34	SCO	05.53	AQU	15
16	13.48	CAP	13.11	PIS	ARI	06.45	00.54	21.15	LIB	19.06	CAP	22.50	16
17	SAG	07.36	AQU	16.18	11.23	GEM	CAN	VIR	09.17	SAG	08.25	PIS	17
18	18.29	AQU	22.50	ARI	TAU	17.22	08.25	23.44	SCO	20.35	AQU	PIS	18
19	CAP	16.38	PIS	ARI	TAU	CAN	LEO	LIB	10.40	CAP	14.42	07.36	19
20	CAP	PIS	PIS	05.12	00.01	CAN	13.29	LIB	SAG	CAP	PIS	ARI	20
21	00.38	PIS	10.20	TAU	GEM	01.32	VIR	01.51	13.49	00.54	PIS	19.41	21
22	AQU	03.43	ARI	18.01	11.05	LEO	17.10	SCO	CAP	AQU	00.42	TAU	22
23	09.02	ARI	23.06	GEM	CAN	07.32	LIB	04.36	19.11	08.27	ARI	TAU	23
24	PIS	16.27	TAU	GEM	19.54	VIR	20.16	SAG	AQU	PIS	13.07	08.45	24
25	20.05	TAU	TAU	05.26	LEO	11.48	SCO	08.24	AQU	18.47	TAU	GEM	25
26	ARI	TAU	12.02	CAN	LEO	LIB	23.12	CAP	02.50	ARI	TAU	20.44	26
27	ARI	05.11	GEM	14.10	02.06	14.37	SAG	13.31	PIS	ARI	02.08	CAN	27
28	08.53	GEM	23.13	LEO	VIR	SCO	SAG	AQU	12.43	06.59	GEM	CAN	28
29	TAU		CAN	19.24	05.40	16.30	02.21	20.25	ARI	TAU	14.23	06.44	29
30	21.01		CAN	VIR	LIB	SAG	CAP	PIS	ARI	19.59	CAN	LEO	30
31	GEM		06.51		07.07		06.25	PIS		GEM		14.43	31

sun

mth	day	sign
JAN	1	CAP
JAN	20	AQU
FEB	18	PIS
MAR	20	ARI
APR	20	TAU
MAY	21	GEM
JUN	21	CAN
JUL	23	LEO
AUG	23	VIR
SEP	23	LIB
OCT	23	SCO
NOV	22	SAG
DEC	22	CAP

mercury

mth	day	sign
JAN	1	SAG
JAN	5	CAP
JAN	25	AQU
FEB	11	PIS
MAR	3	ARI
MAR	11	PIS
APR	17	ARI
MAY	7	TAU
MAY	22	GEM
JUN	5	CAN
JUN	26	LEO
JUL	23	CAN
AUG	11	LEO
AUG	30	VIR
SEP	15	LIB
OCT	4	SCO
DEC	10	SAG
DEC	29	CAP

venus

mth	day	sign
JAN	1	CAP
JAN	20	AQU
FEB	13	PIS
MAR	9	ARI
APR	2	TAU
APR	26	GEM
MAY	21	CAN
JUN	15	LEO
JUL	11	VIR
AUG	7	LIB
SEP	7	SCO

mars

mth	day	sign
JAN	1	SCO
FEB	2	SAG
MAR	28	CAP
OCT	9	AQU
NOV	26	PIS

saturn

mth	day	sign
JAN	1	SAG

jupiter

mth	day	sign
JAN	1	AQU
FEB	20	PIS

moon

DAY	JAN	FEB	MAR	APR	MAY	JUN	JUL	AUG	SEP	OCT	NOV	DEC	DAY
1	VIR	06.19	SCO	CAP	AQU	04.43	TAU	GEM	01.08	VIR	14.19	02.08	1
2	20.45	SCO	14.51	CAP	14.30	ARI	TAU	06.04	LEO	VIR	SCO	SAG	2
3	LIB	09.31	SAG	03.11	PIS	15.45	10.32	CAN	10.06	01.03	15.19	01.28	3
4	LIB	SAG	17.56	AQU	23.01	TAU	GEM	17.26	VIR	LIB	SAG	CAP	4
5	00.44	12.02	CAP	09.03	ARI	TAU	23.19	LEO	16.33	04.35	15.49	01.23	5
6	SCO	CAP	21.42	PIS	ARI	04.26	CAN	LEO	LIB	SCO	CAP	AQU	6
7	02.47	14.35	AQU	17.12	09.59	GEM	CAN	02.44	21.12	06.48	17.29	03.48	7
8	SAG	AQU	AQU	ARI	TAU	17.16	10.56	VIR	SCO	SAG	AQU	PIS	8
9	03.42	18.32	02.48	ARI	22.26	CAN	LEO	10.05	SCO	08.52	21.30	09.49	9
10	CAP	PIS	PIS	03.36	GEM	CAN	20.50	LIB	00.40	CAP	PIS	ARI	10
11	05.01	PIS	10.03	TAU	GEM	05.11	VIR	15.36	SAG	11.45	PIS	19.10	11
12	AQU	01.21	ARI	15.51	11.18	LEO	VIR	SCO	03.28	AQU	04.14	TAU	12
13	08.39	ARI	20.04	GEM	GEM	15.18	04.40	19.17	CAP	16.03	ARI	TAU	13
14	PIS	11.38	TAU	GEM	23.15	VIR	LIB	SAG	06.07	PIS	13.24	06.41	14
15	16.03	TAU	TAU	04.42	LEO	22.38	09.58	21.22	AQU	22.13	TAU	GEM	15
16	ARI	TAU	08.23	CAN	LEO	LIB	SCO	CAP	09.27	ARI	TAU	19.09	16
17	ARI	00.17	GEM	16.10	08.45	LIB	12.34	22.44	PIS	ARI	00.26	CAN	17
18	03.14	GEM	21.04	LEO	VIR	02.36	SAG	AQU	14.33	06.35	GEM	CAN	18
19	TAU	12.39	CAN	LEO	14.41	SCO	13.10	AQU	ARI	TAU	12.46	07.44	19
20	16.12	CAN	CAN	00.24	LIB	03.36	CAP	00.52	22.25	17.15	CAN	LEO	20
21	GEM	22.25	07.38	VIR	17.02	SAG	13.17	PIS	TAU	GEM	CAN	19.30	21
22	GEM	LEO	LEO	04.50	SCO	03.00	AQU	05.27	TAU	GEM	01.25	VIR	22
23	04.14	LEO	14.39	LIB	16.57	CAP	14.59	ARI	09.13	05.37	LEO	VIR	23
24	CAN	04.58	VIR	06.15	SAG	02.50	PIS	13.36	GEM	CAN	12.46	05.05	24
25	13.47	VIR	18.22	SCO	16.15	AQU	20.02	TAU	21.44	18.02	VIR	LIB	25
26	LEO	09.07	LIB	06.16	CAP	05.12	ARI	TAU	CAN	LEO	20.59	11.06	26
27	20.51	LIB	20.05	SAG	17.00	PIS	ARI	01.00	CAN	LEO	LIB	SCO	27
28	VIR	12.06	SCO	06.41	AQU	11.35	05.11	GEM	09.39	04.20	LIB	13.20	28
29	VIR		21.20	CAP	20.54	ARI	TAU	13.40	LEO	VIR	01.13	SAG	29
30	02.10		SAG	09.06	PIS	21.54	17.19	CAN	18.57	11.04	SCO	12.54	30
31	LIB		23.25		PIS		GEM	CAN		LIB		CAP	31

sun

mth	day	sign
JAN	1	CAP
JAN	20	AQU
FEB	19	PIS
MAR	21	ARI
APR	20	TAU
MAY	21	GEM
JUN	21	CAN
JUL	23	LEO
AUG	23	VIR
SEP	23	LIB
OCT	23	SCO
NOV	22	SAG
DEC	22	CAP

mercury

mth	day	sign
JAN	1	CAP
JAN	17	AQU
FEB	4	PIS
MAR	11	AQU
MAR	13	PIS
APR	12	ARI
APR	29	TAU
MAY	13	GEM
MAY	30	CAN
AUG	6	LEO
AUG	21	VIR
SEP	7	LIB
SEP	28	SCO
NOV	1	LIB
NOV	11	SCO
DEC	3	SAG
DEC	22	CAP

venus

mth	day	sign
JAN	1	SCO
JAN	7	SAG
FEB	5	CAP
MAR	3	AQU
MAR	28	PIS
APR	22	ARI
MAY	17	TAU
JUN	11	GEM
JUL	5	CAN
JUL	30	LEO
AUG	23	VIR
SEP	16	LIB
OCT	10	SCO
NOV	3	SAG
NOV	28	CAP
DEC	22	AQU

mars

mth	day	sign
JAN	1	PIS
JAN	8	ARI
FEB	20	TAU
APR	5	GEM
MAY	21	CAN
JUL	6	LEO
AUG	22	VIR
OCT	8	LIB
NOV	24	SCO

saturn

mth	day	sign
JAN	1	SAG

jupiter

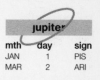

mth	day	sign
JAN	1	PIS
MAR	2	ARI

moon

DAY	JAN	FEB	MAR	APR	MAY	JUN	JUL	AUG	SEP	OCT	NOV	DEC	DAY
1	11.54	PIS	12.37	TAU	GEM	03.25	VIR	LIB	SAG	CAP	PIS	ARI	1
2	AQU	02.09	ARI	12.16	07.39	LEO	VIR	01.09	17.04	01.51	13.40	01.06	2
3	12.36	ARI	18.11	GEM	CAN	15.56	09.55	SCO	CAP	AQU	ARI	TAU	3
4	PIS	08.53	TAU	23.33	20.06	VIR	LIB	06.47	18.22	03.39	18.02	08.13	4
5	16.51	TAU	TAU	CAN	LEO	VIR	18.03	SAG	AQU	PIS	TAU	GEM	5
6	ARI	19.23	03.26	CAN	LEO	02.24	SCO	08.51	18.37	05.35	TAU	17.20	6
7	ARI	GEM	GEM	12.04	08.07	LIB	22.05	CAP	PIS	ARI	00.16	CAN	7
8	01.13	GEM	15.24	LEO	VIR	09.06	SAG	08.37	19.34	08.57	GEM	CAN	8
9	TAU	07.55	CAN	23.28	17.29	SCO	22.43	AQU	ARI	TAU	09.10	04.40	9
10	12.39	CAN	CAN	VIR	LIB	11.53	CAP	08.01	22.57	15.04	CAN	LEO	10
11	GEM	20.21	03.54	VIR	23.09	SAG	21.49	PIS	TAU	GEM	20.45	17.30	11
12	GEM	LEO	LEO	08.06	SCO	12.05	AQU	09.09	TAU	GEM	LEO	VIR	12
13	01.18	LEO	14.55	LIB	SCO	CAP	21.36	ARI	05.54	00.31	LEO	VIR	13
14	CAN	07.26	VIR	13.41	01.41	11.45	PIS	13.38	GEM	CAN	09.29	05.40	14
15	13.45	VIR	23.34	SCO	SAG	AQU	PIS	TAU	16.22	12.34	VIR	LIB	15
16	LEO	16.44	LIB	17.01	02.37	12.54	00.00	21.59	CAN	LEO	20.48	14.41	16
17	LEO	LIB	LIB	SAG	CAP	PIS	ARI	GEM	CAN	LEO	LIB	SCO	17
18	01.15	LIB	05.57	19.21	03.42	16.56	06.04	GEM	04.50	01.06	LIB	19.33	18
19	VIR	00.04	SCO	CAP	AQU	ARI	TAU	09.19	LEO	VIR	04.47	SAG	19
20	11.09	SCO	10.32	21.45	06.24	ARI	15.33	CAN	17.13	11.50	SCO	21.08	20
21	LIB	05.09	SAG	AQU	PIS	00.09	GEM	21.58	VIR	LIB	09.16	CAP	21
22	18.30	SAG	13.48	AQU	11.23	TAU	GEM	LEO	VIR	19.41	SAG	21.20	22
23	SCO	07.57	CAP	01.02	ARI	09.54	03.13	LEO	03.58	SCO	11.32	AQU	23
24	22.35	CAP	16.18	PIS	18.39	GEM	CAN	10.23	LIB	SCO	CAP	22.10	24
25	SAG	09.08	AQU	05.41	TAU	21.22	15.50	VIR	12.30	00.57	13.13	PIS	25
26	23.42	AQU	18.46	ARI	TAU	CAN	LEO	21.35	SCO	SAG	AQU	PIS	26
27	CAP	10.07	PIS	12.06	03.55	CAN	LEO	LIB	18.49	04.33	15.41	01.05	27
28	23.17	PIS	22.12	TAU	GEM	09.52	04.26	LIB	SAG	CAP	PIS	ARI	28
29	AQU		ARI	20.43	14.59	LEO	VIR	06.49	23.08	07.27	19.36	06.37	29
30	23.24		ARI	GEM	CAN	22.34	15.59	SCO	CAP	AQU	ARI	TAU	30
31	PIS		03.46		CAN		LIB	13.24		10.19		14.29	31

sun

mth	day	sign
JAN	1	CAP
JAN	20	AQU
FEB	19	PIS
MAR	20	ARI
APR	19	TAU
MAY	20	GEM
JUN	21	CAN
JUL	22	LEO
AUG	22	VIR
SEP	22	LIB
OCT	23	SCO
NOV	22	SAG
DEC	21	CAP

mercury

mth	day	sign
JAN	1	CAP
JAN	10	AQU
MAR	16	PIS
APR	4	ARI
APR	20	TAU
MAY	4	GEM
JUL	12	CAN
JUL	28	LEO
AUG	12	VIR
AUG	30	LIB
NOV	6	SCO
NOV	25	SAG
DEC	14	CAP

venus

mth	day	sign
JAN	1	AQU
JAN	15	PIS
FEB	9	ARI
MAR	6	TAU
APR	3	GEM
MAY	17	CAN
MAY	27	GEM
AUG	6	CAN
SEP	7	LEO
OCT	4	VIR
OCT	29	LIB
NOV	23	SCO
DEC	17	SAG

mars

mth	day	sign
JAN	1	SCO
JAN	8	SAG
FEB	22	CAP
APR	6	AQU
MAY	22	PIS
JUL	13	ARI
OCT	23	PIS
NOV	1	ARI

saturn

mth	day	sign
JAN	1	SAG
FEB	13	CAP
JUN	10	SAG
NOV	12	CAP

jupiter

mth	day	sign
JAN	1	ARI
MAR	8	TAU
JUL	21	GEM
NOV	30	TAU

moon

DAY	JAN	FEB	MAR	APR	MAY	JUN	JUL	AUG	SEP	OCT	NOV	DEC	DAY
1	GEM	18.06	LEO	08.05	01.39	20.58	07.30	17.53	TAU	22.39	LEO	VIR	1
2	GEM	LEO	13.06	LIB	SCO	CAP	AQU	ARI	08.11	CAN	LEO	VIR	2
3	00.17	LEO	VIR	18.26	08.52	23.34	08.33	20.24	GEM	CAN	04.02	00.56	3
4	CAN	06.54	VIR	SCO	SAG	AQU	PIS	TAU	15.37	08.31	VIR	LIB	4
5	11.47	VIR	01.32	SCO	13.54	AQU	10.37	TAU	CAN	LEO	17.04	12.51	5
6	LEO	19.36	LIB	02.29	CAP	02.00	ARI	01.43	CAN	21.01	LIB	SCO	6
7	LEO	LIB	12.27	SAG	17.37	PIS	14.27	GEM	02.14	VIR	LIB	21.55	7
8	00.35	LIB	SCO	08.19	AQU	05.04	TAU	09.52	LEO	04.46	SCO	SAG	8
9	VIR	06.42	20.59	CAP	20.39	ARI	20.16	CAN	14.48	10.03	SCO	SAG	9
10	13.17	SCO	SAG	12.10	PIS	09.02	GEM	20.26	VIR	LIB	14.06	04.07	10
11	LIB	14.36	SAG	AQU	23.23	TAU	GEM	LEO	VIR	21.58	SAG	CAP	11
12	23.39	SAG	02.31	14.24	ARI	14.14	04.08	LEO	03.51	SCO	21.12	08.25	12
13	SCO	18.36	CAP	PIS	ARI	GEM	CAN	08.46	LIB	SCO	CAP	AQU	13
14	SCO	CAP	05.08	15.47	02.22	21.19	14.11	VIR	16.07	07.58	CAP	11.53	14
15	05.58	19.25	AQU	ARI	TAU	CAN	LEO	21.52	SCO	SAG	02.36	PIS	15
16	SAG	AQU	05.42	17.31	06.31	CAN	LEO	LIB	SCO	15.44	AQU	15.03	16
17	18.15	18.44	AQU	GEM	06.57	02.17	LIB	02.25	CAP	06.34	PIS	ARI	17
18	CAP	PIS	05.45	21.10	13.05	LEO	VIR	10.12	SAG	21.05	PIS	18.11	18
19	08.02	18.35	ARI	GEM	CAN	19.03	15.22	SCO	09.45	AQU	09.12	TAU	19
20	AQU	ARI	07.05	GEM	22.51	VIR	LIB	19.55	CAP	23.58	ARI	21.43	20
21	07.27	20.51	TAU	04.04	LEO	VIR	LIB	SAG	13.43	PIS	11.02	GEM	21
22	PIS	TAU	11.21	CAN	LEO	07.57	03.13	SAG	AQU	PIS	TAU	GEM	22
23	08.31	TAU	GEM	14.34	11.12	LIB	SCO	01.49	14.51	00.59	13.12	02.35	23
24	ARI	02.42	GEM	LEO	VIR	18.58	11.42	CAP	PIS	ARI	GEM	CAN	24
25	12.36	GEM	CAN	LEO	23.49	SCO	SAG	04.05	14.29	01.22	17.20	09.57	25
26	TAU	12.12	CAN	03.16	LIB	SCO	16.07	AQU	ARI	TAU	CAN	LEO	26
27	20.02	CAN	06.54	VIR	LIB	02.18	CAP	04.01	14.29	02.55	CAN	20.27	27
28	GEM	CAN	LEO	15.37	10.06	SAG	17.25	PIS	TAU	GEM	00.52	VIR	28
29	GEM	00.12	19.49	LIB	SCO	06.00	AQU	03.29	16.43	07.28	LEO	VIR	29
30	06.11		VIR	LIB	16.57	CAP	17.23	ARI	GEM	CAN	12.00	09.09	30
31	CAN		VIR		SAG		PIS	04.22		16.03		LIB	31

sun

mth	day	sign
JAN	1	CAP
JAN	20	AQU
FEB	18	PIS
MAR	20	ARI
APR	20	TAU
MAY	21	GEM
JUN	21	CAN
JUL	22	LEO
AUG	23	VIR
SEP	23	LIB
OCT	23	SCO
NOV	22	SAG
DEC	21	CAP

mercury

mth	day	sign
JAN	1	CAP
JAN	2	AQU
JAN	29	CAP
FEB	14	AQU
MAR	10	PIS
MAR	28	ARI
APR	11	TAU
APR	29	GEM
MAY	28	TAU
JUN	12	GEM
JUL	6	CAN
JUL	20	LEO
AUG	5	VIR
AUG	26	LIB
SEP	26	VIR
OCT	11	LIB
OCT	30	SCO
NOV	18	SAG
DEC	7	CAP

venus

mth	day	sign
JAN	1	SAG
JAN	10	CAP
FEB	3	AQU
FEB	27	PIS
MAR	23	ARI
APR	16	TAU
MAY	11	GEM
JUN	4	CAN
JUN	29	LEO
JUL	24	VIR
AUG	18	LIB
SEP	12	SCO
OCT	8	SAG
NOV	5	CAP
DEC	10	AQU

mars

mth	day	sign
JAN	1	ARI
JAN	19	TAU
MAR	11	GEM
APR	29	CAN
JUN	16	LEO
AUG	3	VIR
SEP	19	LIB
NOV	4	SCO
DEC	18	SAG

saturn

mth	day	sign
JAN	1	CAP

jupiter

mth	day	sign
JAN	1	TAU
MAR	11	GEM
JUL	30	CAN

moon

DAY	JAN	FEB	MAR	APR	MAY	JUN	JUL	AUG	SEP	OCT	NOV	DEC	DAY
1	21.34	SAG	SAG	AQU	PIS	TAU	GEM	LEO	VIR	20.53	SAG	CAP	1
2	SCO	23.30	08.58	AQU	11.50	22.02	09.19	LEO	01.47	SCO	SAG	17.42	2
3	SCO	CAP	CAP	01.37	ARI	GEM	CAN	07.19	LIB	SCO	02.47	AQU	3
4	07.11	CAP	13.36	PIS	11.55	GEM	14.37	VIR	14.23	09.29	CAP	AQU	4
5	SAG	02.51	AQU	01.51	TAU	00.17	LEO	18.28	SCO	SAG	12.09	00.48	5
6	13.14	AQU	14.59	ARI	12.03	CAN	23.04	LIB	SCO	20.45	AQU	PIS	6
7	CAP	03.52	PIS	01.07	GEM	05.28	VIR	LIB	02.51	CAP	18.25	05.11	7
8	16.31	PIS	14.36	TAU	14.19	LEO	07.05	SCO	13.13	CAP	21.08	ARI	8
9	AQU	04.18	ARI	01.31	CAN	14.29	10.30	SCO	CAP	05.06	PIS	06.59	9
10	18.31	ARI	14.25	GEM	20.23	VIR	LIB	19.02	CAP	AQU	ARI	TAU	10
11	PIS	05.45	TAU	04.58	LEO	VIR	23.09	SAG	20.02	09.37	21.09	07.15	11
12	20.36	TAU	16.16	CAN	LEO	02.31	SCO	SAG	AQU	PIS	TAU	GEM	12
13	ARI	09.22	GEM	12.31	06.30	LIB	SCO	04.16	23.08	10.41	20.19	07.49	13
14	23.36	GEM	21.27	LEO	VIR	15.11	10.31	CAP	PIS	ARI	GEM	CAN	14
15	TAU	15.40	CAN	23.39	19.07	SCO	SAG	09.59	23.38	09.52	20.51	10.41	15
16	TAU	CAN	CAN	VIR	LIB	SCO	19.01	AQU	ARI	TAU	CAN	LEO	16
17	03.57	CAN	06.13	VIR	02.12	CAP	12.46	23.22	ARI	LEO	17.19	VIR	17
18	GEM	00.33	LEO	12.31	07.48	SAG	CAP	PIS	TAU	GEM	00.45	VIR	18
19	09.57	LEO	17.39	LIB	SCO	10.41	00.35	13.59	TAU	11.09	LEO	VIR	19
20	CAN	11.34	VIR	LIB	18.52	CAP	AQU	ARI	00.16	CAN	08.54	03.45	20
21	18.02	VIR	VIR	01.13	SAG	16.57	04.07	15.10	GEM	16.47	VIR	LIB	21
22	LEO	VIR	06.24	SCO	SAG	AQU	PIS	TAU	03.50	LEO	20.25	16.18	22
23	LEO	00.05	LIB	12.38	03.54	21.36	06.41	17.39	CAN	LEO	LIB	SCO	23
24	04.32	LIB	19.10	SAG	CAP	PIS	ARI	GEM	10.44	02.15	LIB	SCO	24
25	VIR	12.57	SCO	12.15	11.01	PIS	09.10	22.13	LEO	VIR	09.13	04.37	25
26	17.02	SCO	SCO	CAP	AQU	01.06	TAU	CAN	20.32	14.11	SCO	SAG	26
27	LIB	SCO	06.54	CAP	16.13	ARI	12.15	CAN	VIR	LIB	21.30	15.10	27
28	LIB	00.29	SAG	05.33	PIS	03.45	GEM	05.12	VIR	LIB	SAG	CAP	28
29	05.49		16.26	AQU	19.25	TAU	16.32	LEO	08.15	02.56	SAG	23.38	29
30	SCO		CAP	10.03	ARI	06.08	CAN	14.29	LIB	SCO	08.26	AQU	30
31	16.30		22.45		20.59		22.41	VIR		15.23		AQU	31

sun

mth	day	sign
JAN	1	CAP
JAN	20	AQU
FEB	18	PIS
MAR	20	ARI
APR	20	TAU
MAY	21	GEM
JUN	21	CAN
JUL	23	LEO
AUG	23	VIR
SEP	23	LIB
OCT	23	SCO
NOV	22	SAG
DEC	22	CAP

mercury

mth	day	sign
JAN	1	CAP
FEB	12	AQU
MAR	3	PIS
MAR	20	ARI
APR	4	TAU
JUN	12	GEM
JUN	27	CAN
JUL	11	LEO
JUL	29	VIR
OCT	5	LIB
OCT	23	SCO
NOV	11	SAG
DEC	2	CAP
DEC	25	SAG

venus

mth	day	sign
JAN	1	AQU
JAN	16	CAP
MAR	3	AQU
APR	6	PIS
MAY	4	ARI
MAY	30	TAU
JUN	25	GEM
JUL	20	CAN
AUG	13	LEO
SEP	7	VIR
OCT	1	LIB
OCT	25	SCO
NOV	18	SAG
DEC	12	CAP

mars

mth	day	sign
JAN	1	SAG
JAN	29	CAP
MAR	11	AQU
APR	20	PIS
MAY	31	ARI
JUL	12	TAU
AUG	31	GEM
DEC	14	TAU

saturn

mth	day	sign
JAN	1	CAP

jupiter

mth	day	sign
JAN	1	CAN
AUG	18	LEO

moon

DY	JAN	FEB	MAR	APR	MAY	JUN	JUL	AUG	SEP	OCT	NOV	DEC	DY
1	06.12	19.27	01.43	12.50	00.08	23.31	18.01	SAG	20.51	13.42	ARI	16.23	1
2	PIS	TAU	TAU	CAN	LEO	LIB	SCO	SAG	AQU	PIS	05.31	GEM	2
3	10.58	22.12	03.37	17.50	07.18	LIB	SCO	02.09	AQU	17.42	TAU	15.27	3
4	ARI	GEM	GEM	LEO	VIR	11.21	06.35	CAP	04.06	ARI	05.06	CAN	4
5	14.04	GEM	07.04	LEO	17.28	SCO	SAG	12.21	PIS	19.06	GEM	16.00	5
6	TAU	01.27	CAN	01.42	LIB	23.59	18.39	AQU	08.23	TAU	05.07	LEO	6
7	16.02	CAN	12.24	VIR	LIB	SAG	CAP	19.54	ARI	19.47	CAN	19.39	7
8	GEM	05.51	LEO	11.44	05.23	SAG	CAP	PIS	10.55	GEM	07.24	VIR	8
9	17.52	LEO	19.47	LIB	SCO	12.12	05.07	PIS	TAU	21.29	LEO	VIR	9
10	CAN	12.13	VIR	23.18	17.56	CAP	AQU	01.13	13.05	CAN	12.48	03.00	10
11	21.02	VIR	VIR	SCO	SAG	23.09	13.29	ARI	GEM	CAN	VIR	LIB	11
12	LEO	21.09	05.09	SCO	SAG	AQU	PIS	04.55	15.53	01.16	21.08	13.26	12
13	LEO	LIB	LIB	11.48	06.21	AQU	19.36	TAU	CAN	LEO	LIB	SCO	13
14	02.57	LIB	16.25	SAG	CAP	08.00	ARI	07.41	19.52	07.21	LIB	SCO	14
15	VIR	08.34	SCO	SAG	17.30	PIS	23.29	GEM	LEO	VIR	07.39	01.44	15
16	12.18	SCO	SCO	00.15	AQU	13.55	TAU	10.12	LEO	15.26	SCO	SAG	16
17	LIB	21.07	04.58	CAP	AQU	ARI	TAU	CAN	01.15	LIB	19.37	14.35	17
18	LIB	SAG	SAG	10.53	01.54	16.43	01.32	13.11	VIR	LIB	SAG	CAP	18
19	00.16	SAG	17.01	ARI	PIS	TAU	GEM	LEO	08.34	01.24	SAG	CAP	19
20	SCO	08.30	CAP	17.57	06.31	17.14	02.44	17.33	LIB	SCO	08.32	02.55	20
21	12.44	CAP	CAP	PIS	ARI	GEM	CAN	VIR	18.08	13.09	CAP	AQU	21
22	SAG	16.52	02.32	20.58	07.44	17.10	04.32	VIR	SCO	SAG	21.07	13.42	22
23	23.27	AQU	AQU	ARI	TAU	CAN	LEO		SCO	SAG	AQU	PIS	23
24	CAP	21.49	08.08	21.03	07.00	18.25	08.17	LIB	05.52	02.03	AQU	21.45	24
25	CAP	PIS	PIS	TAU	GEM	LEO	VIR	09.56	SAG	CAP	07.32	ARI	25
26	07.25	PIS	10.15	20.12	06.34	22.42	15.19	SCO	18.36	14.14	PIS	ARI	26
27	AQU	00.16	ARI	GEM	CAN	VIR	LIB	21.57	CAP	AQU	14.06	02.08	27
28	12.51	ARI	10.28	20.40	08.29	VIR	LIB	SAG	CAP	23.22	ARI	TAU	28
29	PIS		TAU	CAN	LEO	06.47	01.43	SAG	05.57	PIS	16.37	03.26	29
30	16.34		10.42	CAN	14.08	LIB	SCO	10.23	AQU	PIS	TAU	GEM	30
31	ARI		GEM		VIR		14.00	CAP		04.14		03.02	31

rising signs table

Birthdate		Aries	Taurus	Gemini
ARIES	21 to 31 Mar.	5.30am to 6.29am	6.30am to 7.44am	7.45am to 9.29am
	1 to 10 Apr.	5am to 5.59am	6am to 7.14am	7.15am to 8.59am
	11 to 20 Apr.	4.15am to 5.14am	5.15am to 6.29am	6.30am to 8.14am
TAURUS	21 to 30 Apr.	3.30am to 4.29am	4.30am to 5.44am	5.45am to 7.29am
	1 to 10 May	3am to 3.59am	4am to 5.14am	5.15am to 6.59am
	11 to 21 May	2.30am to 3.29am	3.30am to 4.44am	4.45am to 6.29am
GEMINI	22 to 31 May	2am to 2.59am	3am to 4.14am	4.15am to 5.59am
	1 to 10 Jun.	1.30am to 2.29am	2.30am to 3.44am	3.45am to 5.29am
	11 to 21 Jun.	12.45am to 1.44am	1.45am to 2.59am	3am to 4.44am
CANCER	22 to 30 Jun.	12am to 12.59am	1am to 2.14am	2.15am to 3.59am
	1 to 11 Jul.	11.30pm to 12.29am	12.30am to 1.44am	1.45am to 3.29am
	12 to 22 Jul.	11pm to 11.59pm	12am to 1.14am	1.15am to 2.59am
LEO	23 to 31 Jul.	9.45pm to 10.44pm	10.45pm to 11.59pm	12am to 1.44am
	1 to 11 Aug.	9.15pm to 10.14pm	10.15pm to 11.29pm	11.30pm to 1.14am
	12 to 23 Aug.	8.30pm to 9.29pm	9.30pm to 10.44pm	10.45pm to 12.29pm
VIRGO	24 to 31 Aug.	7.30pm to 8.29pm	8.30pm to 9.44pm	9.45pm to 11.29pm
	1 to 11 Sep.	7pm to 7.59pm	8pm to 9.14pm	9.15pm to 10.59pm
	12 to 22 Sep.	6.15pm to 7.14pm	7.15pm to 8.29pm	8.30pm to 10.14pm
LIBRA	23 to 30 Sep.	5.30pm to 6.29pm	6.30pm to 9.44pm	9.45pm to 11.29pm
	1 to 11 Oct.	5pm to 5.59pm	6pm to 7.14pm	7.15pm to 8.59pm
	12 to 23 Oct.	4.15pm to 5.14pm	5.15pm to 6.29pm	6.30pm to 8.14pm
SCORPIO	24 to 31 Oct.	3.30pm to 4.29pm	4.30pm to 5.44pm	5.45pm to 7.29pm
	1 to 11 Nov.	2.45pm to 3.44pm	3.45pm to 4.59pm	5pm to 6.44pm
	12 to 22 Nov.	2.15pm to 3.14pm	3.15pm to 4.29pm	4.30pm to 6.14pm
SAGITTARIUS	23 to 30 Nov.	1.30pm to 2.29pm	2.30pm to 3.44pm	3.45pm to 5.29pm
	1 to 11 Dec.	12.45pm to 1.44pm	1.45pm to 2.59pm	3pm to 4.44pm
	12 to 21 Dec.	12.15pm to 1.14pm	1.15pm to 2.29pm	2.30pm to 4.14pm
CAPRICORN	22 to 31 Dec.	11.15am to 12.14pm	12.15pm to 1.29pm	1.30pm to 3.14pm
	1 to 11 Jan.	10.45am to 11.44am	11.45am to 12.59pm	1pm to 2.44pm
	12 to 20 Jan.	10.15am to 11.14am	11.15am to 12.29pm	12.30pm to 2.14pm
AQUARIUS	21 to 31 Jan.	9.30am to 10.29am	10.30am to 11.44am	11.45am to 1.29pm
	1 to 10 Feb.	9am to 9.59am	10am to 11.14am	11.15am to 12.59pm
	11 to 18 Feb.	8.15am to 9.15am	9.15am to 10.29am	10.30am to 12.14pm
PISCES	19 to end Feb.	7.30am to 8.29am	8.30am to 9.44am	9.45am to 11.29am
	1 to 10 Mar.	7.15am to 8.14am	8.15am to 9.29am	9.30am to 11.14am
	11 to 20 Mar.	6.30am to 7.29am	7.30am to 8.44am	8.45am to 10.29am

Birthdate		Cancer	Leo	Virgo
ARIES	21 to 31 Mar.	9.30am to 11.59am	12pm to 2.44pm	2.45pm to 5.29pm
	1 to 10 Apr.	9am to 11.29am	11.30am to 2.14pm	2.15pm to 4.59pm
	11 to 20 Apr.	8.15am to 10.44am	10.45am to 1.29pm	1.30pm to 4.14pm
TAURUS	21 to 30 Apr.	7.30am to 9.59am	10am to 12.44pm	12.45pm to 3.29pm
	1 to 10 May	7am to 9.29am	9.30am to 12.14pm	12.15pm to 2.59pm
	11 to 21 May	6.30am to 8.59am	9am to 11.44am	11.45am to 2.29pm
GEMINI	22 to 31 May	6am to 8.29am	8.30am to 11.14am	11.15am to 1.59pm
	1 to 10 Jun.	5.30am to 7.59am	8am to 10.44am	10.45am to 1.29pm
	11 to 21 Jun.	4.45am to 7.14am	7.15am to 9.59am	10am to 12.44pm
CANCER	22 to 30 Jun.	4am to 6.29am	6.30am to 9.14am	9.15am to 1.59am
	1 to 11 Jul.	3.30am to 5.59am	6am to 8.44am	8.45am to 11.59pm
	12 to 22 Jul.	3am to 5.29am	5.30am to 8.14am	8.15am to 10.59am
LEO	23 to 31 Jul.	1.45am to 4.14am	4.15am to 6.59am	7am to 9.44am
	1 to 11 Aug.	1.15am to 3.44am	3.45am to 6.29am	6.30am to 9.14am
	12 to 23 Aug.	12.30am to 2.59am	3am to 5.44am	5.45am to 8.29am
VIRGO	24 to 31 Aug.	11.30pm to 1.59pm	2am to 4.44am	4.45am to 7.29am
	1 to 11 Sep.	11pm to 1.29am	1.30am to 4.14am	4.15am to 6.59am
	12 to 22 Sep.	10.15pm to 12.44am	12.45am to 3.29am	3.30am to 6.14am
LIBRA	23 to 30 Sep.	9.30pm to 11.59pm	12am to 2.44am	2.45am to 5.29am
	1 to 11 Oct.	9pm to 11.29pm	11.30pm to 2.14am	2.15am to 4.59am
	12 to 23 Oct.	8.15pm to 10.44pm	10.45pm to 1.29am	1.30am to 4.14am
SCORPIO	24 to 31 Oct.	7.30pm to 9.59pm	10pm to 12.44am	12.45am to 3.29am
	1 to 11 Nov.	6.45pm to 9.14pm	9.15pm to 11.59pm	12am to 2.44am
	12 to 22 Nov.	6.15pm to 8.44pm	8.45pm to 11.29pm	11.30pm to 2.14am
SAGITTARIUS	23 to 30 Nov.	5.30pm to 7.59pm	8pm to 10.44pm	10.45pm to 1.29am
	1 to 11 Dec.	4.45pm to 7.14pm	7.15pm to 9.59pm	10pm to 12.44am
	12 to 21 Dec.	4.15pm to 6.44pm	6.45pm to 9.29pm	9.30pm to 12.14am
CAPRICORN	22 to 31 Dec.	3.15pm to 5.44pm	5.45pm to 8.29pm	8.30pm to 11.14pm
	1 to 11 Jan.	2.45pm to 5.14pm	5.15pm to 7.59pm	8pm to 10.44pm
	12 to 20 Jan.	2.15pm to 4.44pm	4.45pm to 7.29pm	7.30pm to 10.14pm
AQUARIUS	21 to 31 Jan.	1.30pm to 3.59pm	4pm to 6.44pm	6.45pm to 9.29pm
	1 to 10 Feb.	1pm to 3.29pm	3.30pm to 6.14pm	6.15pm to 8.59pm
	11 to 18 Feb.	12.15pm to 3.44pm	2.45pm to 5.29pm	5.30pm to 8.14pm
PISCES	19 to end Feb.	11.30am to 1.59pm	2pm to 4.44pm	4.45pm to 7.29pm
	1 to 10 Mar.	11.15am to 1.44pm	1.45pm to 4.29pm	4.30pm to 7.14pm
	11 to 20 Mar.	10.30am to 12.59pm	1pm to 3.44pm	3.45pm to 6.29pm